D0717378

nsho

ﾓﾔｰ
ﾌﾅ

THE HISTORY OF THE US AIR FORCE

PILOT CAPT C KIRKEY
CAC 75th F/S SUNNYDALE

THE HISTORY OF THE US AIR FORCE

BILL YENNE

Bison Books

Published by
Bison Books Ltd.
176 Old Brompton Road,
London, SW 5
England.

Copyright © 1984 Bison Books Ltd.

All rights reserved. No part of this publication may be reproduced, stored in a retrieval system or transmitted in any form by any means electronic, mechanical, photocopying or otherwise, without first obtaining written permission of the copyright owner.

ISBN 0 86124 161 4

Printed in Hong Kong

Reprinted 1986

Page 1: An F-86 Sabre-jet unleashes a salvo of 5-inch High Velocity Aerial Rockets (HVAR) over the test range at Nellis AFB. During the early 1950s the HVAR was one of the US Air Force's principal air-to-air weapons.

Page 2-3: As the sun sets over the Nevada hills, ground crews rest near a line of TAC A-10 'Warthogs' on the ramp at Nellis AFB during a *Red Flag* exercise.

Below: SAC B-52Ds (left and background) and B-52G (right) photographed from the top of a C-5A in the huge hangar at AFLC's San Antonio Air Logistics Center at Kelly AFB.

Picture Credits

Unless otherwise specified all illustrations are Official US Air Force photographs.

American Graphic Systems Archives 18

Boeing Airplane Company 28-29, 31 (both), 35, 39, 42-43, 145 (bottom right), 159 (bottom right), 168, 169, 218-19

© **George Hall** 2-3, 103, 110-11, 112, 138-39, 139, 146-47, 186 (top), 188

National Aeronautics and Space Administration 215

National Air and Space Museum, Smithsonian Institution 19, 20 (both), 23 (bottom)

USAF via Bausch 86 (bottom right, both)

US Department of Defense 191

© **Bill Yenne** 7, 9 (all 3), 10 (all 3), 11, 14 (all 3), 15 (both), 27 (all 3), 34 (bottom), 36 (top), 40 (top), 41, 47 (bottom), 48-49 (bottom 6), 52, 78 (above), 81 (top), 82, 105, 109, 113, 116 (both), 117, 119 (top), 120, 130(both), 131 (both), 151, 153, 154, 162 (both), 163 (both), 166-67, 167 (top), 170 (both), 171, 175, 183, 184, 186-87, 187 (top), 191 (bottom), 195, 196, 203 (bottom), 205, 209, 212, 213, 216 (top), 222

All charts, graphs and maps were compiled, designed and drawn by the author.

Edited by Robin Sommer and Susan Garratt.

Acknowledgments

The author would like to thank First Lieutenant Peter Meltzer, Deputy Chief of the Air Force Office of Public Affairs (Magazines and Books); George Hall for the use of his pictures; and Carol Yenne for typing the manuscript.

CONTENTS

A Portrait of the US Air Force	6
American Air Power before the US Air Force	18
A Separate US Air Force	38
The US Air Force in Korea	46
The US Air Force in Southeast Asia	48
Tactical Air Power in the US Air Force	102
Strategic Air Power in the US Air Force	150
Military Airlift in the US Air Force	174
US Air Force Training	192
Reserve Power for the US Air Force	198
Logistics and Research in the US Air Force	202
Communication and Electronic Warfare in the US Air Force	210
The US Air Force in Space	214
Index	222
Aircraft and Missile Designations	224

PROFILES OF THE MAJOR COMMANDS

Tactical Air Command (TAC)	104
US Air Forces in Europe (USAFE)	114
Pacific Air Forces (PACAF)	117
Alaskan Air Command (AAC)	120
Strategic Air Command (SAC)	150
Military Airlift Command (MAC)	174
Air Training Command (ATC)	192
Air Force Systems Command (AFSC)	203
Air Force Logistics Command (AFLC)	207
Air Force Communications Command (AFCC)	210
Electronic Security Command (ESC)	211
Space Command (SPACECOM)	214

Biographies of US Air Force Chiefs of Staff 30, 33, 45, 56-57, 223

A PORTRAIT OF THE US AIR FORCE

A PORTRAIT OF THE US AIR FORCE

The United States Air Force was officially created on 18 September 1947 but had existed as an air arm of the US Army since 1 August 1907, when the Aeronautical Division of the US Army Signal Corps was established. The independent US Air Force is the successor of the US Army Air Forces, an autonomous air arm that became the largest air force in history during World War II with 2,373,292 personnel and 787,757 aircraft (1944). Today the US Air Force has about 600,000 personnel, making it still the world's largest air force in terms of manpower. The USSR is next, with about 550,000 in its Air Defense Forces, Long Range Aviation and Frontal Aviation. The Peoples' Republic of China is third with 500,000; India, France, Great Britain and the Federal Republic of Germany each have around 100,000. In terms of aircraft, the US Air Force is in third place worldwide with about 3700 combat aircraft (out of a total inventory of 7300), against 7500 combat aircraft for the USSR (excluding 755 in naval aviation). China has nearly 5500 combat aircraft (excluding about 800 in naval aviation). In fourth place is the US Navy (including US Marine Corps Aviation) with about 1800 combat aircraft. The air forces of India, France, Great Britain, Germany, Poland and Israel form a second tier of strength – between 500 and 700 combat aircraft each. While the Soviet Union and China have enhanced their statistics by retaining many planes built in the fifties, half the US Air Force inventory consists of aircraft built since 1970.

Of the roughly 7300 aircraft in the US Air Force inventory, 42% are tactical (interceptors, fighters, attack planes), 23% trainers, 12% transports, 8% aerial refueling tankers, 5% strategic bombers, 3% helicopters, and the remainder range from reconnaissance and electronic warfare to utility and observation.

This active inventory is complemented by an additional 450 aircraft flown in the Air Force Reserve (AFRES) and another 1600 assigned to the Air National Guard (ANG). Of these 2050 additional aircraft, 70% are tactical, 19% transports, 7% aerial refueling tankers, with the rest including trainers, observation planes and helicopters. The US Air Force and its reserve forces maintain only a small number of helicopters for utility and search-and-rescue purposes. The bulk of America's military helicopters are assigned to the US Army. Under the 1947 executive order that separated the US Air Force (formerly the US Army Air Forces) from the US Army, the latter retained only light observation and transport aircraft, but was permitted to build up its helicopter fleet for short-range transportation and attack functions. This fleet, presently numbering around 8000 helicopters, outnumbers the US Air Force helicopter fleet by a ratio of 34 to 1.

Of the nearly 600,000 uniformed personnel in the US Air Force, 82% are enlisted airmen and 18% are officers. Nearly three-quarters of US Air Force personnel are sergeants and 15% are officers under the rank of lieutenant colonel. The greatest number of officers in any career area are pilots and navigators,

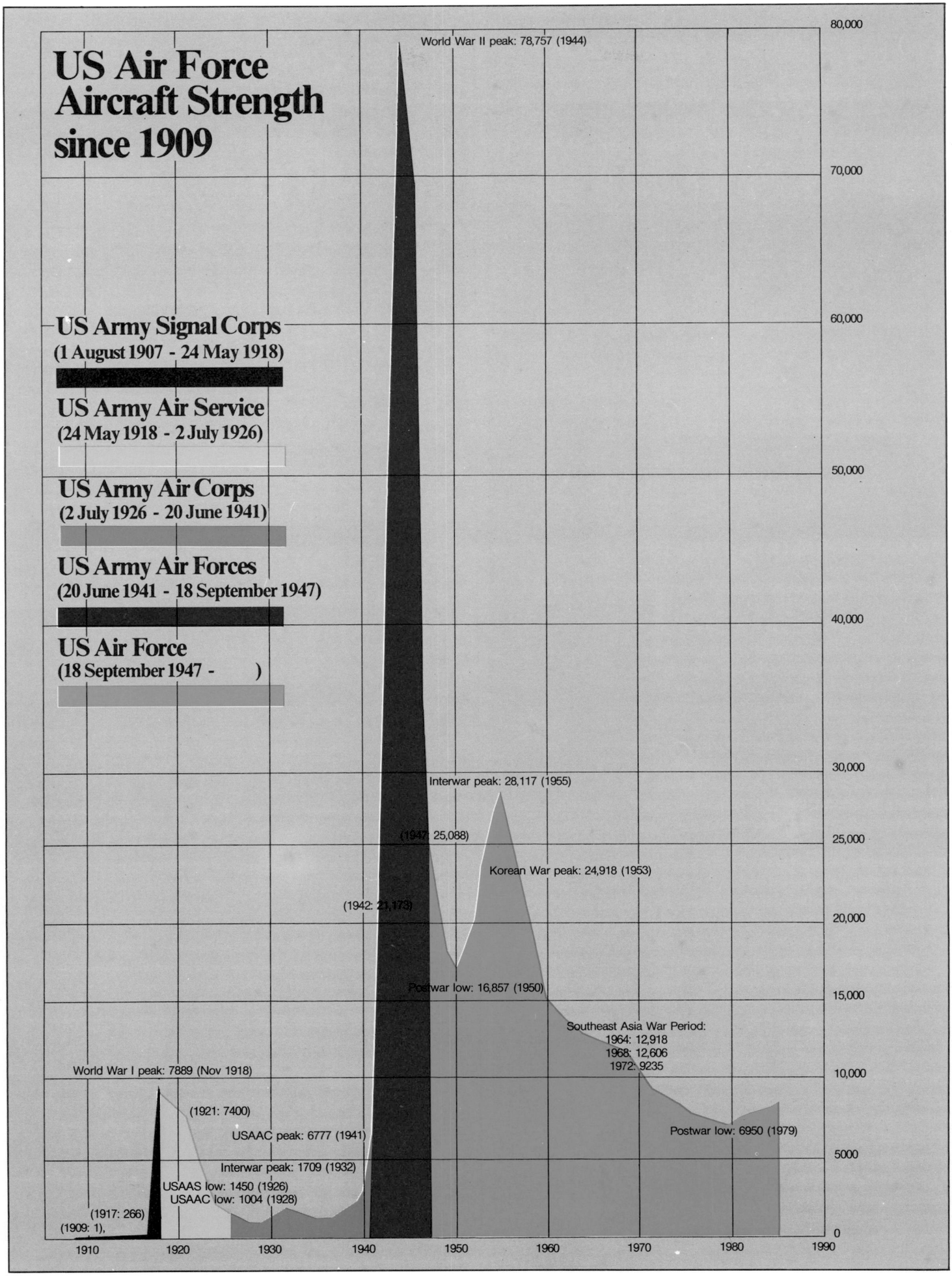
US Air Force Aircraft Strength since 1909
US Army Signal Corps
(1 August 1907 - 24 May 1918)
US Army Air Service
(24 May 1918 - 2 July 1926)
US Army Air Corps
(2 July 1926 - 20 June 1941)
US Army Air Forces
(20 June 1941 - 18 September 1947)
US Air Force
(18 September 1947 -)
World War II peak: 78,757 (1944)
Interwar peak: 28,117 (1955)
(1947: 25,088)
Korean War peak: 24,918 (1953)
(1942: 21,173)
Postwar low: 16,857 (1950)
Southeast Asia War Period:
1964: 12,918
1968: 12,606
1972: 9235
World War I peak: 7889 (Nov 1918)
(1921: 7400)
USAAC peak: 6777 (1941)
Postwar low: 6950 (1979)
Interwar peak: 1709 (1932)
USAAS low: 1450 (1926)
USAAC low: 1004 (1928)
(1917: 266)
(1909: 1),
80,000
70,000
60,000
50,000
40,000
30,000
25,000
20,000
15,000
10,000
5000
0
1910
1920
1930
1940
1950
1960
1970
1980
1990

The Commanders of the US Army Air Service

Maj Gen William Kenly (Chief, Div of Military Aeronautics) 20 May 1913–22 Dec 1918
Maj Gen Charles Menoher (Chief of the Air Service) 23 Dec 1918–4 Oct 1921
Maj Gen Mason Patrick (Chief of the Air Service) 5 Oct 1921–1 July 1926

Chiefs of the US Army Air Corps

Maj Gen Mason Patrick	2 July 1926–12 Dec 1927
Maj Gen James Fechet	14 Dec 1927–19 Dec 1931
Maj Gen Benjamin Foulois	19 Dec 1931–21 Dec 1935
Maj Gen Oscar Westover	22 Dec 1935–21 Sept 1938
Gen H H Arnold 29 Sept	1938–20 June 1941

The Commanders of the US Army Air Forces

Gen H H Arnold (Chief of the AAF)	20 June 1941–8 March 1942
Gen H H Arnold (Commanding General AAF)	9 Mar 1942–28 Feb 1946
Gen Carl Spaatz (Commanding General AAF)	1 Mar 1946–25 Sept 1947

Chiefs of Staff of the US Air Force

Gen Carl Spaatz	26 Sept 1947–29 Apr 1948
Gen Hoyt Vandenberg	30 Apr 1948–29 June 1953
Gen Nathan Twining	20 June 1953–30 June 1957
Gen Thomas White	1 July 1957–30 June 1961
Gen Curtis LeMay	30 June 1961–31 Jan 1965
Gen John McConnell	1 Feb 1965–31 July 1969
Gen John Ryan	1 Aug 1969–31 July 1973
Gen George Brown	1 Aug 1973–30 June 1974
Gen David Jones	1 July 1974–30 June 1978
Gen Lew Allen, Jr.	1 July 1978–30 June 1982
Gen Charles Gabriel	1 July 1982–

Secretaries of the Air Force

Stuart Symington	18 Sept 1947–24 Apr 1950
Thomas Finletter	24 Apr 1950–20 Jan 1953
Harold Talbott	4 Feb 1953–13 Aug 1955
Donald Quarles	15 Aug 1955–30 Apr 1957
James Dougles, Jr.	1 May 1957–10 Dec 1959
Dudley Sharp	11 Dec 1959–20 Jan 1961
Eugene Zuckert	24 Jan 1961–30 Sept 1965
Harold Brown	1 Oct 1965–15 Feb 1969
Robert Seamans, Jr.	15 Feb 1969–14 May 1973
John McLucas	18 July 1973–23 Nov 1975
James Plummer (Acting)	24 Nov 1975–1 Jan 1976
Thomas Reed	2 Jan 1976–6 Apr 1977
John Stetson	6 Apr 1977–18 May 1979
Hans Mark	26 July 1979–9 Feb 1981
Verne Orr	9 Feb 1981–

Chief Master Sergeants of the Air Force

CMSAF Paul Airey	3 Apr 1967–1 Aug 1969
CMSAF Donald Harlow	1 Aug 1969–1 Oct 1971
CMSAF Richard Kisling	1 Oct 1971–1 Oct 1973
CMSAF Thomas Barnes	1 Oct 1973–1 Aug 1977
CMSAF Robert Gaylor	1 Aug 1977–1 Aug 1979
CMSAF James McCoy	1 Aug 1979–1 July 1981
CMSAF Arthur Andrews	1 Aug 1981–

who number almost 30,000 or nearly a third of the total number of officers in the USAF.

Ten percent of US Air Force officers are women and five percent are black. Of the enlisted personnel, 12% are women and 17% are black. The average age of US Air Force personnel is 34 for officers and 26 for enlisted airmen. Sixty percent of the officers have college degrees, 39% have master's degrees and 2% have doctorates.

THE DEPARTMENT OF DEFENSE

The United States Air Force was established in 1947 by the National Defense Act of that year as one of the nation's three principal military forces within the Department of Defense. The Department of Defense (DoD) is headed by a civilian Secretary of Defense who has full cabinet rank. Under the Secretary of Defense are three civilian Executive Departments – Army, Navy and Air Force – each headed by a Secretary who does not have full cabinet rank. Within each Executive Department are the small Office of the Secretary and a vastly larger military service. Each of these three military services is commanded by a Chief of Staff (in the case of the US Navy, the Chief of Naval Operations). These three plus the Commandant of the US Marine Corps (which is contained within the Department of the Navy) form the five-man Joint Chiefs of Staff (JCS) with the JCS Chairman. These officers are drawn from the service they command, with the chairman's position rotating among the services, and are of four-star rank. At the end of World War II the equivalent JCS positions were held by officers of five-star rank, but no regular service officers have been promoted beyond four-star rank since that time.

THE OFFICE OF THE SECRETARY OF THE AIR FORCE

The Secretary is appointed by the President and has his office, like those of the other Secretaries, at the Pentagon, ten minutes drive from the White House and just across the Potomac River from Washington DC. Geographically it is in the state of Virginia, but its telephone and postal code system are those of the District of Columbia. The Secretary's staff includes an Under Secretary, Assistant Secretaries for (a) Manpower, Reserve Affairs and Installations; (b) Research, Development and Logistics; and (c) Financial Management. Also on the staff are General Counsel, the Auditor General and special assistants, administrative assistants and Deputy Under Secretaries as required. All of the above are civilian appointees, but the Secretary may have US Air Force officers on his staff in such roles as Director of Public Affairs and Director of the Office of Legislative Liaison. The staff is completed by the necessary clerical and administrative personnel.

THE US AIR FORCE AIR STAFF

The military Air Staff commands the US Air Force and is headed by the Chief of Staff, under whom are the Vice Chief of Staff, the Assistant Vice Chief and Assistant Chiefs for Information, Intelligence, and Studies and Analysis. Other Air Staff members are the Judge Advocate General, Surgeon General, Chief of Air Force Chaplains, Director of Administration, Chief of the Air Force Reserve and Director of the Air National Guard. All of the above are officers of General rank but the staff includes civilian scientists and one enlisted man, the Chief Master Sergeant of the Air Force.

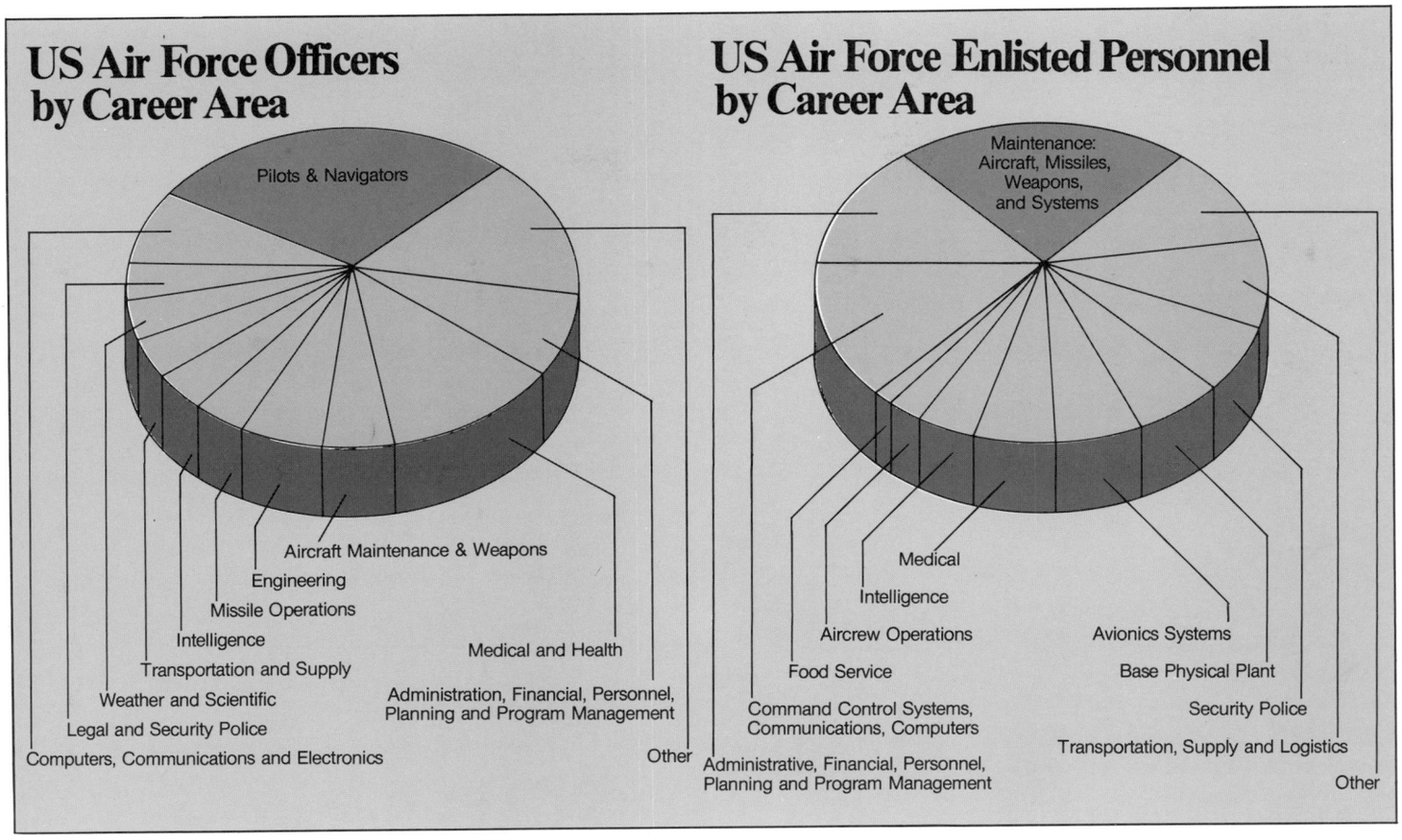

In addition to the Air Staff there are the Comptroller of the Air Force, the Inspector General of the Air Force, and Deputy Chiefs of Staff for (a) Programs and Resources; (b) Research Development and Acquisition; (c) Manpower and Personnel; (d) Plans and Operations; and (e) Logistics and Engineering.

Together, the Office of the Secretary, the Air Staff and the National Guard Bureau are staffed by about 2700 uniformed and 2000 civilian personnel.

The Air Staff, like the Office of the Secretary, is headquartered at the Pentagon, and is also supported by two Air Force Bases (AFB) in the Washington DC area: Bolling AFB in the District of Columbia and Andrews AFB 11 miles southeast of the capital near Suitland, Maryland. Both bases are assigned to the Military Airlift Command (MAC) but have been host to a number of other major commands over the years including the Strategic Air Command (SAC) and the now defunct Continental Air Command and Headquarters Command. Andrews AFB, though a MAC base, today houses the headquarters of the Air Force Systems Command (AFSC). Bolling AFB and the adjoining Anacostia Naval Air Station (NAS) were once the major landing fields in the District of Columbia, but the runways have long since been inoperative. Andrews AFB, on the other hand, serves as the major military airfield in the area with tenants including the Air Force Reserve, Air National Guard and Naval Air units, as well as MAC's 89th Military Airlift Wing (MAW) operating VC-137 (Boeing Model 707) VIP executive aircraft. These include *Air Force One*, the personal plane of the President of the United States.

BASIC ORGANIZATION

Within the Department of the Air Force and under the Air Staff there are three basic components to the full-time USAF: Major Commands, Direct Reporting Units (DRU) and Separate Operating Agencies (SOA) totalling nearly 600,000 uniformed and 250,000 civilian personnel. The largest number (91%) are assigned to twelve Major Commands. Of the 750,000 total personnel in the Major Commands, 26% are civilians compared to 69% in the DRUs and SOAs.

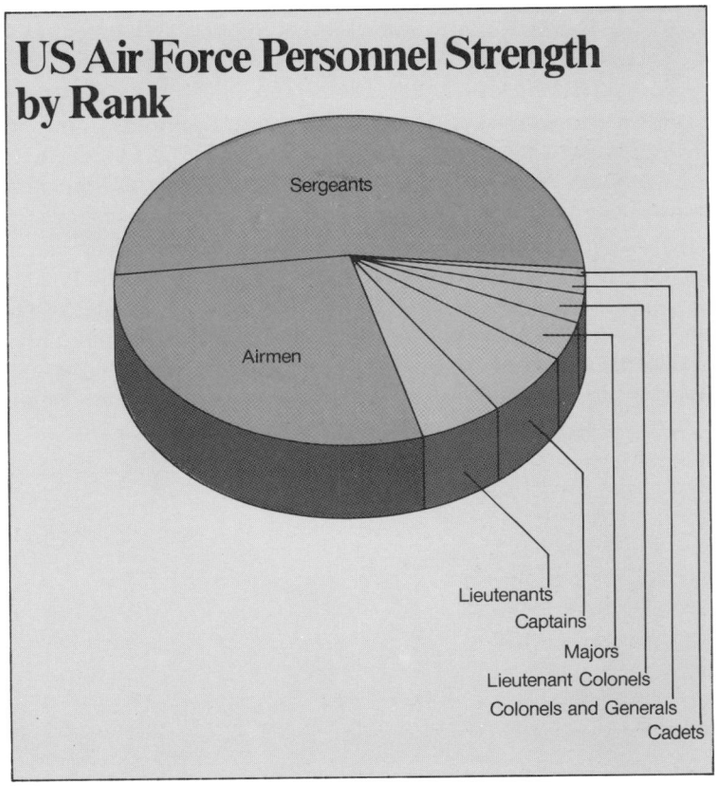

In addition to the three full-time components of the US Air Force there are just over 200,000 Reserve personnel in the Air National Guard and Air Force Reserve, which would bring the total personnel strength of the Air Force to slightly more than a million if all were called up at the same time.

THE DIRECT REPORTING UNITS

The Direct Reporting Units total about 40,000 personnel and include the Air Force Technical Application Center (AFTAC) which has DoD responsibility to maintain facilities and personnel for detecting and monitoring nuclear detonations in the atmosphere, underground and in outer space. AFTAC was established for this purpose in 1947 by JCS chairman General Dwight D Eisenhower and was responsible for discovering the first Soviet atomic test in September 1949, when an AFTAC sensor aboard an RB-29 over the North Pacific detected the Russian fallout. AFTAC is currently headquartered at Patrick AFB, Florida with squadrons at McClellan AFB, California, Wheeler AFB, Hawaii and Lindsey AS in Germany; there are 19 detachments and 50 equipment locations worldwide.

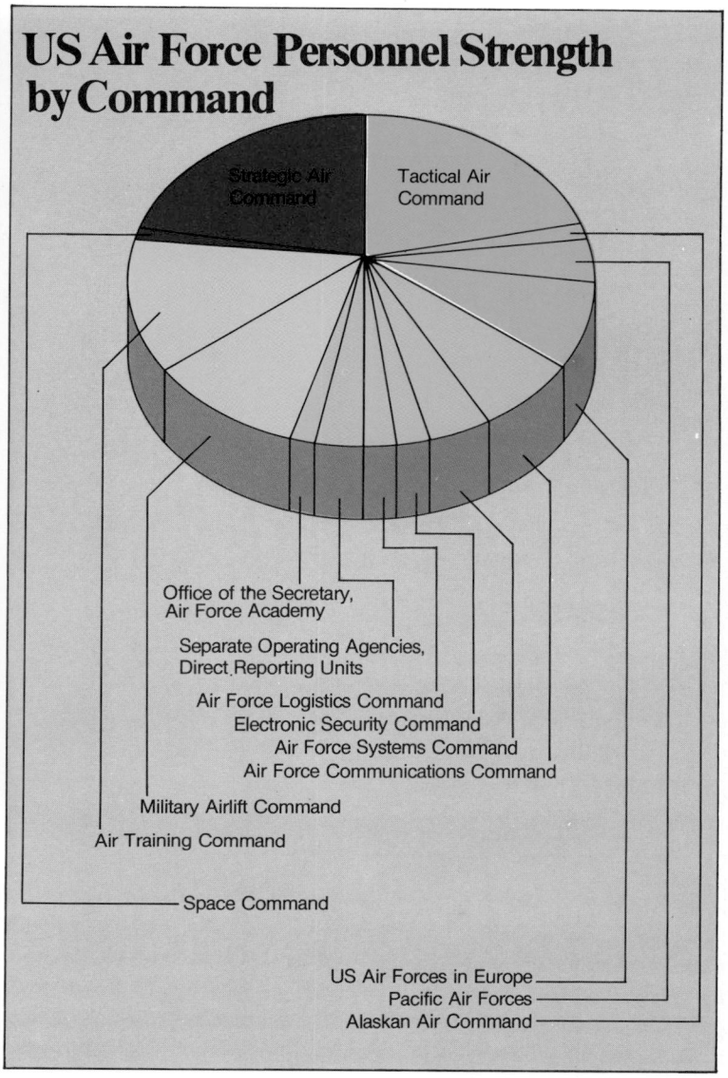

Above: **Most of the personnel in the US Air Force are assigned to the Major Commands, with over three quarters of them assigned to the flying commands, which are divided between training and transport (yellow), strategic (red), and tactical (blue).**

Above left: **There is probably no more familiar landmark at stateside Air Force bases than the ubiquitous checkered water tower.**

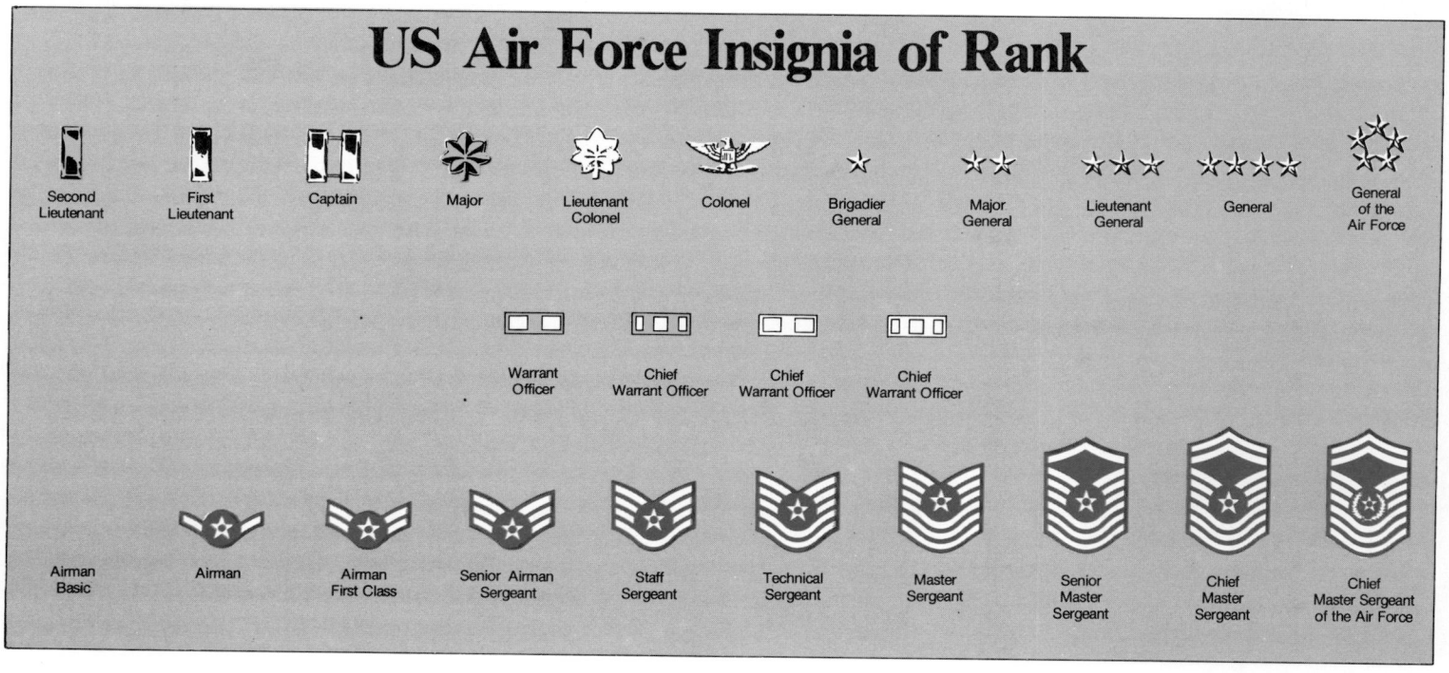

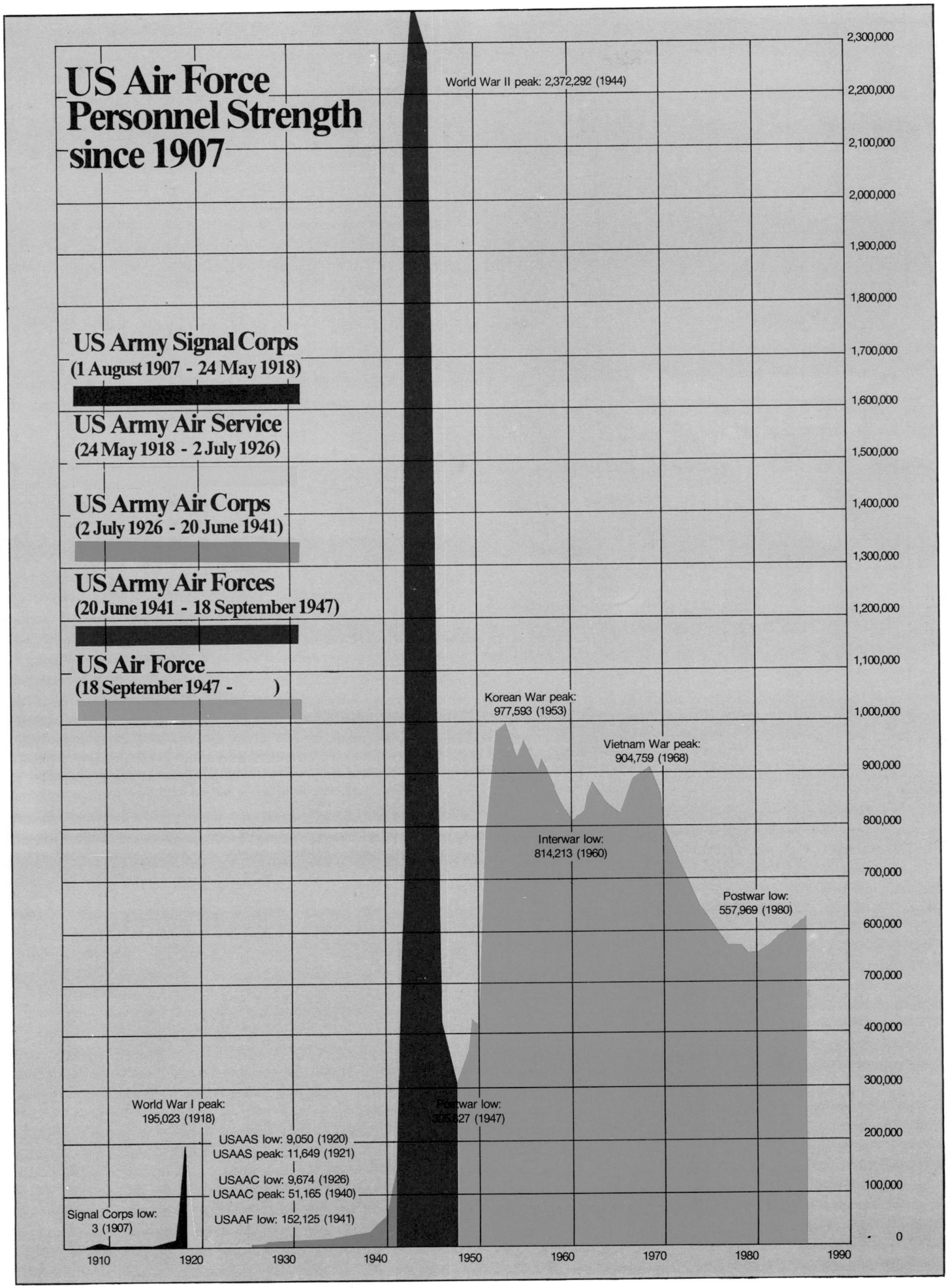
US Air Force Personnel Strength since 1907
US Army Signal Corps
(1 August 1907 - 24 May 1918)
US Army Air Service
(24 May 1918 - 2 July 1926)
US Army Air Corps
(2 July 1926 - 20 June 1941)
US Army Air Forces
(20 June 1941 - 18 September 1947)
US Air Force
(18 September 1947 -)
World War II peak: 2,372,292 (1944)
Korean War peak: 977,593 (1953)
Vietnam War peak: 904,759 (1968)
Interwar low: 814,213 (1960)
Postwar low: 557,969 (1980)
World War I peak: 195,023 (1918)
Postwar low: 305,027 (1947)
USAAS low: 9,050 (1920)
USAAS peak: 11,649 (1921)
USAAC low: 9,674 (1926)
USAAC peak: 51,165 (1940)
USAAF low: 152,125 (1941)
Signal Corps low: 3 (1907)
2,300,000
2,200,000
2,100,000
2,000,000
1,900,000
1,800,000
1,700,000
1,600,000
1,500,000
1,400,000
1,300,000
1,200,000
1,100,000
1,000,000
900,000
800,000
700,000
600,000
700,000
400,000
300,000
200,000
100,000
0
1910
1920
1930
1940
1950
1960
1970
1980
1990

Left: A cadet sailplane flies over the heart of the Academy campus at the foot of the Rampart range.

Right: The Eagle and Fledglings statue with the Academy's 17-spired chapel in the background.

The Air Force Academy is also a Direct Reporting Unit. With the creation of an independent US Air Force in 1947, its leaders, who had come up through the ranks of the US Army, many of them via its Military Academy at West Point, recognized the need for an Air Force Academy. Established by Act of Congress, signed into law by President Dwight D Eisenhower on 1 April 1954, the Air Force Academy joined West Point, Annapolis and the Coast Guard Academy as one of four service academies. Later, in 1954, Secretary of the Air Force Harold Talbott appointed a commission to help him select a permanent site. It considered 580 sites in 45 states, narrowing these prospective locations to three, from which Talbott selected one near Colorado Springs, Colorado.

The first Air Force Academy class began its academic career in temporary facilities at Lowry AFB in Denver in July 1958, as construction began on the Academy campus. The Cadet Wing made its move to the nearly complete campus in August 1958, and the first class of 207 graduates was commissioned as second lieutenants in June 1959 with the Academy's degree program accredited by the Commission of Colleges and Universities of the North Central Association of Colleges and Secondary Schools. In 1964 President Lyndon Johnson signed a bill authorizing the Cadet Wing to increase its students from 2529 to 4417. On 7 October 1975 President Gerald Ford signed legislation permitting women to enter the nation's military academies, and the first female cadets entered the Air Force Academy in June 1976, graduating in May 1980. The Academy has graduated over fifteen thousand officers including a future Medal of Honor winner, seventeen who would become generals, and two who would become combat aces. Among its graduates have been nearly ten thousand pilots, of whom several have been selected as astronauts for the space program.

Cadet training includes professional military studies and training, leadership, aviation science and flight training in gliders as well as T-43 and T-41 aircraft. The cadet honor code is 'We will not lie, steal, cheat, nor tolerate among us anyone who does.' The fourth part of the code is considered its backbone, but is also its most controversial provision. It has resulted in occasional scandals whereby cadets had to choose, in a damned-if-we-do-damned-if-we-don't way, whether or not to turn in cheating classmates. Cadets found guilty of violating the code are expected to resign from the Academy.

Parachuting or sky-diving is also part of the training program at the Academy. The school's parachute demonstration team, Wings of Blue, competes annually in intercollegiate competitions, winning first place in the 40-school national competition nearly every year since they became involved. In addition to the competitions, the Wings of Blue put on about 40 public demonstrations each year. The cadets compete in intercollegiate athletics through their teams, whose mascot is the 'Fighting Falcon.' More than a mascot, the birds are integral to the unusual extracurricular program in falconry. Under special permits issued by the US Fish and Wildlife Service and the Colorado Division of Wildlife, the Academy acquired and bred wild prairie falcons for use by cadets in demonstrations. Since 1974 the prairie falcons used have been bred in captivity, most of them at the Academy; no wild birds have been captured. In demonstrations the falconer whirls a rectangular leather lure, with meat attached, on a ten-foot cord. The bird has learned to strike the swiftly moving lure in mid-air, with the meat as its reward. The Academy usually has about ten Colorado prairie falcons and one or two white gyrfalcons. The most famous of these was Baffin, named for the bay in Canada where she was captured, with the permission of the Canadian Government, in 1965. She was an important part of campus life for 13 years until her death in 1978. In July 1980 a fourth white gyrfalcon succeeded Baffin as the school's official mascot. Named Glacier, he was captured on the Seward Peninsula in Alaska by an Academy search team and has since become a feature of many Air Force Academy functions.

SEPARATE OPERATING AGENCIES

While each of the Major Commands and DRUs occupies a specific niche, the SOAs, totaling about 20,000 military and civilian personnel, provide services to all the Commands across the full breadth of the service.

The Air Force Accounting and Finance Center (AFAFC), based at Lowry AFB, Colorado, is the centerpiece of a computerized global network of over a hundred Accounting and Finance Offices (AFO) that issue payrolls and conduct billings and collections. Over a million active-duty US Air Force personnel and retirees, plus 165,000 reservists, get their regular paychecks via the AFAFC with a better than 99% record for accuracy. The center handles all the monies appropriated to the USAF by Congress and maintains trust fund accounts for Department of Defense foreign military sales.

The Air Force Audit Agency (AFAA) operating out of Norton AFB, California, under direction of the Auditor General in the Secretary's office, evaluates the economy and effectiveness of

The Superintendents of the Air Force Academy

Lt Gen Hubert Harmon	27 July 1954–27 July 1956
Maj Gen James Briggs	28 July 1956–16 Aug 1959
Maj Gen William Stone	17 Aug 1959–30 June 1962
Maj Gen Robert Warren	1 July 1962–30 June 1965
Lt Gen Thomas Moorman	1 July 1965–31 July 1970
Lt Gen Albert Clark	1 Aug 1970–31 July 1974
Lt Gen James Allen	1 Aug 1974–31 July 1977
Lt Gen Kenneth Tallman	1 Aug 1977–16 June 1981
Maj Gen Robert Kelley	16 June 1981–

Air Force operations. The AFAA is composed of three Directorates – Aquisition and Logistics (based at Wright-Patterson AFB, Ohio), Forces and Support Management and Field Activities (both at Norton AFB).

The Air Force Commissary Service (AFCOMS) operates from a headquarters at Kelly AFB, Texas, and fifteen other sites in the US as well as two overseas regions (Europe and the Pacific). AFCOMS purchases and provides food for all authorized Air Force appropriated-fund dining facilities. Many commissaries feature delicatessans and on-site full-service bakeries with the latest in technology, including laser scanners to read universal product codes (bar coding) at the check-out counter. The commissaries offer their wares at the lowest possible prices consistent with covering their overhead and operating costs. AFCOM's motto is 'We serve where you serve.'

The Air Force Engineering and Services Center (AFESC) based at Tyndall AFB, Florida, provides the Air Force worldwide with a broad range of basic support services. These include readiness and contingency operations, facility energy, environmental planning, fire protection, installation operation and maintenance, food service, billeting and civil engineering. AFESC has Regional Civil Engineers based in Atlanta, San Francisco, Dallas and at Norton AFB to provide support for construction projects ranging from housing and dining halls to runways and missile support facilities. Among AFESC's recent activities have been a two-year study of USAF engineering requirements in wartime, developing rapid runway repair procedures utilizing crushed stone and fiberglass-reinforced polyester covers, and development of a system to remove trichloroethylene and other volatile organic chemical wastes from contaminated groundwater.

The mission of **the Air Force Inspection and Safety Center (AFISC)** at Norton AFB is to assess USAF fighting capability and resource management for the Commands. AFISC divisions include the Directorates of Aerospace Safety, Inspection, Nuclear Surety (at Kirtland AFB, New Mexico), and Medical Inspection, plus the Offices of Management Support and Data Automation. AFISC supports the Air Force Inspector General through the Office of the Assistant for Inquiries and Complaints operating their Computerized Complaints Data Collection System.

The Air Force Intelligence System (AFIS) based in Washington DC gathers, evaluates and disburses intelligence information for Air Force Headquarters and USAF field commanders worldwide and supplies intelligence for the Defense Department. While the USAF has been involved in such activities since its inception in 1947, the AFIS was not established as an SOA until 27 June 1972. Among its Directorates are Operational Intelligence, Target Intelligence, Security and Communications

Above: The 65-ton Oshkosh P-15, developed by AFESC, is the flagship of the USAF fire-protection fleet. It is powered by two 430 hp diesel engines.

Below: The Air Force in the railroad business. Fuel and supplies arrive by rail and are often shuttled around larger bases by switch engines. Some cars also carry training and technical facilities between bases.

Management, Intelligence Data Management, Attaché Affairs, Intelligence Reserve Forces, Soviet Affairs and Evasion and Escape/Prisoner of War Matters. The AFIS Special Studies Division gathers and analyzes data about foreign camouflage concealment and deception techniques.

The Air Force Legal Services Center (AFLSC), also in Washington DC, is under the Judge Advocate General. AFLSC functions as the Air Force's in-house law firm, handling claims for and against the Air Force, legal aid, labor law, and other matters. AFLSC provides legal services for the USAF ranging from patent and copyright protection to court-martial. Within AFLSC are the Divisions of Military Justice, Defense Services, Trial Judiciary, Government Trial and Appellate Counsel, Claims and Tort Litigation and General Litigation. AFLSC also includes the Court of Military Review and a Special Assistant for Clemency and Rehabilitation Matters.

The Air Force Manpower and Personnel Center (AFMPC) is headquartered at Randolph AFB, Texas; its commander also serves as the Assistant Deputy Chief of Staff for Manpower and Personnel on the Air Staff. AFMPC administers Air Force programs covering the lives and careers of USAF personnel and their families. Its objective, summed up in the AFMPC motto 'Responsive to the Mission – Sensitive to the People,' is to see that the right people are in the right places at the right time, with optimum attitude and morale. AFMPC's areas of activity include libraries, sports, child care, recreation, re-enlishment, retirement, voting assistance and awards and decorations, to name a few.

The Air Force Medical Service Center (AFMSC), headquartered at Brooks AFB, Texas, was established in July 1978 under the Deputy Surgeon General of the Air Force for Operations. The AFMSC oversees health-care policy and practice and USAF medical research. There are two AFMSC Directorates: Health Care Support and Professional Services.

The Air Force Office of Security Police (AFOSP) was estab-

lished as SOA in September 1979 at Kirtland AFB in New Mexico, under the command of the already existing office of Air Force Chief of Security Police who is answerable in both roles to the Inspector General of the Air Force. The AFOSP operates theAir Force Security Clearance Office in Washington and is concerned with all issues relating to the security of Air Force bases, personnel, systems and aircraft. While AFOSP has only about a hundred people, the worldwide Security Police Force that they support totals nearly 39,000. In peacetime the Security Police Force (known as Air Police until 1967) functions much like a civilian police force. In wartime, with much tighter security imposed and enemy attack on USAF facilities possible, it would function more like an Army or Marine combat unit, with Air Base Ground Defense its primary mission. The tools of the Security Policeman's trade range from civilian-type police cars to armored vehicles, from a wide variety of small arms to K-9 working dog teams.

The Air Force Office of Special Investigations (AFOSI), headquartered at Bolling AFB, DC, provides the Air Force and its Commands with investigative services including antiterrorist operations, counterintelligence, forensics, personnel protection and polygraph. More than half of AFOSI's activities deal with criminal investigations; about a third deal with fraud in contracts, computer systems, property disposition etc. AFOSI antiterrorist activities are credited for a decline in terrorist attacks against USAF personnel in recent years.

The Air Force Operational Test and Evaluation Center (AFOTEC) at Kirtland AFB, New Mexico, is charged with testing Air Force procedures, systems, and hardware under operational conditions. The center has four detachments based at Edwards AFB, California; Eglin AFB, Florida; Nellis AFB, Nevada; and Kapuan AS in Germany. The headquarters structure co-ordinates and supports the test teams, operating at about two dozen field sites around the world, with the test team personnel generally drawn from the Major Commands.

Above: An assortment of Security Police vehicles in familiar Air Force blue, including both pickups and vans.

Below: The AFOSI headquarters at Bolling AFB in the District of Columbia.

The Air Force Service Information and News Center (AFSINC) headquartered at Kelly AFB, Texas, is the in-house communications department, providing information for Air Force as well as Army personnel through both print and broadcast media. Answerable to the Director of Public Affairs in the Office of the Secretary of the Air Force, AFSINC was founded in June 1978 and merged with the Air Force Hometown News Center one year later. The Army Hometown News Center became part of AFSINC in October 1980. AFSINC is composed of four Directorates: Administration & Resources, Internal Information, Armed Forces Radio & TV and Army & Air Force Hometown News. The Radio and TV Directorate manages all Air Force broadcasting throughout the Pacific, in Alaska, Europe, Greenland and the Middle East.

Left: Colonel Arnold Gabriel, Commander and Conductor of the US Air Force Band, directs the band in a concert at the Jefferson Memorial in Washington, DC. Colonel Gabriel is one of the world's most widely traveled directors, having conducted in all 50 states and 45 foreign countries since he assumed his command in 1964.

Below: An Army Air Forces band in concert at Colfax Army Air Field during World War II. North American T-6 trainers and Douglas C-47 transports are visible in the background.

Right: The Airmen of Note pose in a hangar with a World War II era P-38. Organized to perpetuate the 1940s Big Band sound, the Airmen of Note are the only organization in the USAF to wear USAAF uniforms.

THE US AIR FORCE BAND

The Air Force Band has individual ensembles servicewide that provide entertainment at Air Force functions, air shows and off-base concerts. The ensembles range from the 702nd Air Force Band (the Strategic Air Command Band) at Offutt AFB, a full 60-piece band, to small ensembles like the Strolling Strings and the Singing Sergeants, who are based near Air Force Headquarters. Musical styles represented range from the traditional marching bands and drum and bugle corps to rock and soul groups.

Like many Air Force traditions, the Band had its roots in the Army. The US Army Band was officially formed in 1921 from remnants of the American Expeditionary Force Headquarters Band that had been formed at Chaumont, France, during World War I. By World War II, the USAAF had its own bands, from which the USAF Band would be derived. There is probably no wartime Air Force Band more famous than the USAAF Band, Europe, under the direction of Major Glenn Miller.

Before the war, Glenn Miller was one of the top Big Band leaders in the country: in 1939 he had had two enormous hits with *Tuxedo Junction* and *In the Mood*. By 1940 one of every three nickels shoveled into an American jukebox went to play a Glenn Miller song. In 1942, with the United States at war, Miller joined the USAAF and was sent to England where he took charge of the USAAF Band, Europe. It was Major Miller's idea to give the troops the kind of music they wanted to hear, and his group was immensely popular. On 16 December 1944, he set out by air from a USAAF base in the South of England en route to a show in Paris. He was never seen again. His plane was presumed lost in the English Channel.

The USAAF band broke up a year later, but in 1950 the US Air Force formed a new band, called the Airmen of Note, dedicated to perpetuating the Glenn Miller/Big Band sound. In 1953 the Airmen portrayed the Miller Band in the movie *The Glenn Miller Story*. For over thirty years, the Airmen of Note have been one of the most popular units in the US Air Force Band, playing Big Band concerts in 25 countries on four continents and around the United States. Based at Bolling AFB, the Airmen were described by *Downbeat* Magazine as 'One of the best bands anyone interested in big band jazz or good dance music can hope to hear today.'

FIRE STATION #3

AMERICAN AIR POWER BEFORE THE US AIR FORCE

EARLY AERONAUTICS

The first commentary on air power by an American was written by the preeminent stateman Benjamin Franklin less than a year after the United States had won its war of independence. Franklin, serving as American envoy to France, had been on hand when Jean de Rozier made the first manned ascent in a balloon in Paris on 15 October 1783, and had made his first reference to the military potential of balloons in a letter dated 21 November 1783. Franklin observed that an army could employ balloons for functions 'Such as elevating an engineer to take a view of an enemy's army, works, etc, conveying intelligence into or out of a beseiged town, giving signals to distant places, or the like.'

Much more than a politician, Franklin was also a journalist, an inventor and a man of great foresight. In January 1783 he wrote that the balloon's potential in warfare was 'of great importance, and what may possibly give a new turn to human affairs. . . . Five thousand balloons, capable of raising two men each, could not cost more than five ships of the line; and where is the prince who can afford to so cover his country with troops for its defense as that ten thousand men descending from the clouds might not in many places do an infinite deal of mischief before a force could be brought together to repel them?'

Daring aeronauts had been experimenting with balloons in Europe for a number of years when the Frenchman Jean Pierre Blanchard made the first ascent in the United States in Philadelphia on 9 January 1793. In attendance were not only President George Washington, but four future presidents: John Adams, Thomas Jefferson, James Madison and James Monroe. Blanchard was aloft for almost an hour and rose to an altitude of nearly a mile.

While the balloon was still regarded as a curiosity in America, the French had already made note of the military potential observed by Franklin a decade earlier. In 1794 the first military air service, the French Aerostatic Corps, was born. Staffed by energetic and imaginative men a hundred years ahead of their time, the corps first saw action on 26 June 1794 in the Battle of Fleurus, Belgium, directing artillery and generally overseeing the defeat of the Austrian forces under the Prince of Saxe-Coburg. The world's first air force went on to serve with some success until it was disbanded by Napoleon in 1799.

It was not until the Civil War that the United States would officially take up the notion of an aerial corps, but it was not for want of an occasional proposal. During the Seminole War in 1841, when the US Army was engaged in a protracted fight with the Seminole Indians in the Florida Everglades, Army Colonel John Sherburne suggested to Secretary of War Joel Poinsett that balloons could help infantry columns locate Indian camps: they could be sent aloft at night to spot the Seminole campfires, without the Indians' awareness. Poinsett complimented Sherburne for his idea but placed approval of the scheme with General W K Armistead, the Army Commander in Florida, who rejected it out of hand. The war was soon over and Sherburne's

Far left: Benjamin Franklin was the first American statesman to see a future in air power.

Above: The French Aerostatic Corps in action at Fleurus, Belgium in 1794. It was air power's first application in warfare.

'commendable idea' remained just that.

The first documented instance of a proposal to use a balloon as an American combat weapon came in the course of the assault on Veracruz in 1846 during the Mexican War. General Winfield Scott's invasion troops were pinned down by the fort of San Juan de Ulloa at Veracruz and needed a way out to punch through to Mexico City. The troops had been bottled up for several months, with both the Army and the Navy making unsuccessful attempts to secure the fort. Then a Pennsylvania balloonist named John Wise (who would later attempt to secure money from Congress for a transatlantic balloon voyage) came forward. Wise suggested that he could float a balloon over the forests out of range of enemy artillery and drop 'a thousand percussion bombshells' on the castle of Veracruz. In retrospect, the tactic might have worked, but in fact the War Department, in typical bureaucratic style, chose to ignore Wise. Ultimately the issue became moot when Scott's ground forces succeeded in taking the citadel.

The point worth making in these two anecdotes goes beyond the ingenuity and foresight of Sherburne and Wise. At the heart of both is the beginning of a pattern of official opposition to air power that stymied its advocates right up to the eve of the creation of the Air Force in 1947.

It was not until 1861, in the first months of the Civil War, that the US Army first enlisted the services of aeronauts and their 'bags of air.' Among them were John Wise, who volunteered his services again: this time his offer was accepted. Another balloonist, James Allen, was also enlisted and both were placed at the disposal of General Irvin McDowell. Mishaps plagued their first operations, but Wise succeeded in observing Confederate lines and obtained useful reconnaissance information on 24 July in the wake of the first Battle of Bull Run. McDowell was pleased and sent him on another scouting mission a few days later, only have the balloon break free of its moorings; it had to be shot down. Wise had now lost favor with the top brass and he threw up his hands in disgust, abandoning the balloon for a cavalry mount.

Meanwhile the flamboyant Thaddeus S C Lowe, the 29-year-old Ohio aeronaut, had made the first aerial reconnaissance behind enemy lines on 20 April, purely by accident. He was preparing for a transatlantic flight and had taken off that morning on a practice flight from Cincinnatti that took him to Unionville, South Carolina. Lowe was taken prisoner by Confederate civilians and held until someone recognized him as being *the* Thaddeus Lowe, a famous aeronaut and not a Yankee spy. He was released with a safe-conduct pass and allowed to return home across Confederate lines. Lowe decided to forgo the adventure of crossing the great water for that of serving in the great war. He offered his services and those of his balloon, *Enterprise*, to President Lincoln. Lowe was Lincoln's guest at the White House and on 18 June, in a demonstration in Washington,

Above: A Balloon Corps balloon observing Confederate lines from its station a thousand feet above the James and York Rivers, looking upriver toward Rebel gun batteries.

Left: Thaddeus Lowe, Chief Aeronaut of America's first air force, with map case and telescope.

Lincoln received the first telegraph message from an airship. Lowe had achieved a great milestone in the history of air power by taking his case directly to the President. Coming down strongly in favor of developing balloons for military service, Lincoln personally asked crusty General Winfield ('Old Fuss and Feathers') Scott, now commander of the Union Army, to 'See Professor Lowe . . . about his balloon.'

Scott refused Lowe's repeated attempts to see him, and it took the President's personal intervention to bring the general around. Under duress, Scott finally ordered that Lowe be given 'everything he needs to set up an aeronautical service on land and sea.' As of 19 June 1861, with James Allen's first flight, the Balloon Corps of the Army of the Potomac was a reality, and the United States had its first air service.

On 2 August 1861, after the failed attempts of Wise and the others, Lowe and his corps were given their initial task to build the Army's first balloon, the *Union*. By 24 September Lowe was aloft with his aerial telegraph and was directing artillery fire. By the end of the year the Balloon Corps had expanded dramatically, with numerous aeronauts signed up and seven balloons – *Union, Intrepid, Eagle, Constitution, Excelsior, United States* and *Washington* – completed or on order.

Over the next two years, the aeronauts proved the practical worth of the corps, making thousands of flights (Chief Aeronaut Lowe himself made more than 3000) observing Confederate lines and directing artillery. Though successful in the field, the Balloon Corps was doomed to logistical and administrative failure. There had never been a coherent plan for its placement in the command structure. In the beginning it was attached to the Topographic Engineers, but on 31 March 1862 control was transferred to the Quartermaster Corps and a year later to the Corps of Engineers. Meanwhile there had never been a decision on the rank of the aeronauts, numerous paydays were missed, expense money became snarled in red tape and the Quartermaster Corps was prone to commandeering the Balloon Corps' horses and wagons. Because they had no specified place in the command structure, the corps always found themselves in last place in the supply line, and without any specified rank, Lowe had to scrounge supplies or dip into his own pocket. The transfer of Lowe's air service to the Engineers was really its death knell. A 40% salary cut was imposed – despite the fact that the paychecks often didn't arrive at all. On 7 May 1863 Lowe resigned and the corps was disbanded. The war would last another two years, but the great promise shown by the nation's first air corps had receded into history.

By the mid-1880s balloon corps had found their way into the military services of all the major European Powers, but for the US Army it was officially a dead issue. It was not until General Adolphus Greely became commander of the Army Signal Corps in 1891 that things began to change. Greely, who had taken an interest in balloons, methodically researched their potential and ultimately hired carnival aeronaut William Ivy. Ivy became a sergeant and his balloon became the *General Myer*. The *General Myer* burst and was replaced with a new balloon, which was on hand when the Spanish American War broke out in 1898. Signal Corps Lieutenant-Colonel Joseph Maxfield and Sergeant Ivy were ordered to sail for Cuba with two 'Balloon Companies,' which at that time consisted of themselves and the single balloon. They arrived in Cuba with 27 men, a damaged balloon and no hydrogen generator.

Ivy repaired the balloon and it was filled with bottled hydrogen. After several tentative flights it was in position to help direct artillery fire and observe the Spanish positions during the 1st July assault on San Juan Hill. The battle was a turning point in the war, and some say that the balloon played a decisive part in the American victory by helping to direct fire and locating an alternate route of attack. There are others who claim the balloon was actually a hindrance, helping to draw fire to American positions. In any event, it was severely punctured and could not be used again.

Even as balloon flights were becoming common-place, men around the world were tinkering with the notion of powered, manned, heavier-than-air flight. Samuel Pierpont Langley of the Smithsonian Institution had been working on the problem for some years before he was able to get a steam-powered model to fly in 1896. With the moral support of both General Greely and inventor Alexander Graham Bell, Langley obtained a grant of $50,000 from the War Department in 1898 to build a full-scale, powered and manned flying machine. Charles Manly, a promising engineering student from Cornell, was commissioned to build a gasoline engine. By October 1903 the craft was ready to fly, but its first attempt, on 7 October, was unsuccessful. On 8 December they tried again, and again the vehicle crashed before it was airborne. This second failure was the end of the government's attempt to achieve heavier-than-air flight. Many who had long thought it impossible now felt vindicated.

Ironically, even as the War Department was closing its ledger book on Langley's costly mishap, the private sector was flourishing amid the icy gales that buffeted a small nowhere on the North Carolina coast called Kill Devil Hill. On 17 December 1903 a pair of bicycle shop owners from Ohio climbed that uncelebrated knoll outside the town of Kitty Hawk to try their hands at conquering the obstacles to powered flight. By the middle of that cold December day, Wilbur and Orville Wright had accomplished powered flight not once but four times, with the last trial covering 852 feet and lasting 59 seconds. For the first time in history, a manned machine had risen from the ground, traveled under its own power and landed successfully.

The British Government took an immediate interest in the experiments of the Wright brothers, to the extent of offering to buy their machine in 1904. The Wrights declined, hoping instead to elicit some interest among officials in their own capital. The War Department, perhaps still smarting from the Langley affair, took a decidedly arm's-length approach to the Wrights, despite their now having made over a hundred successful flights in several machines. It was not until the Aero Club of America went directly to President Theodore Roosevelt that the Board of Ordnance and Fortification issued a Signal Corps Specification for a heavier-than-air machine on 27 December 1907.

Above: General James Allen, the Signal Corps' first Air Chief (1907-13).

Even as the War Department was finally negotiating with the Wrights, the long years of air-power advocacy by General Greely and his successor, Brigadier General James Allen, were coming to fruition. On 1 August 1907, Chief Signal Officer Allen signed the confidential War Department directive establishing the Aeronautical Division of the Signal Corps to oversee matters pertaining to military application of 'ballooning, air machines and all kindred subjects.' That day marked the establishment of the first permanent air service in American military history, which would evolve and change for forty years until it became, on 18 September 1947, the United States Air Force.

A PERMANENT AIR SERVICE

For several years during the Civil War, the United States had its first officially sanctioned, though short-lived, aviation service in the US Balloon Corps; it was half a century before the Aeronautical Division of the Signal Corps took its place in the roster of America's military forces. The

Left: Benny Foulois as an Air Service Captain in France, 1918. He was the Signal Corps' first pilot, learning to fly from the Wright Brothers, and later went on to serve as Chief of the US Army Air Corps between 1931 and 1935.

Right: Early air chiefs: General George Scriven, Signal Corps Air Chief from 1913 to 1917: the highly decorated General George Squier, last Signal Corps Air Chief who served between February 1917 and May 1918; General William Kenl ey, the first USAAS Chief who served through the peak of World War I and until 22 December 1918; and General Mason Patrick, who oversaw the transition of the US Army Air Service into the US Army Air Corps in July of 1926 (*see chart on page 8*).

Aeronautical Division would grow and change, but there was now a permanent air service. Speaking in 1982 on the 75th anniversary of the establishment of the Aeronautical Division and the 35th anniversary of the US Air Force, chief of Staff General Charles Gabriel recalled that:

In August 1907 the Army Signal Corps assigned an officer, two enlisted men, and a civilian clerk to its new Aeronautical Division. In the summers of 1908 and 1909, the Wright Flyer thrilled thousands of spectators who watched at Fort Myer as Wilbur and Orville Wright flight-tested improved versions of their 1905 model. It was not until August 1909 that the Army finally accepted "Aeroplane Number 1.' Three months later, the nation temporarily lost its total air strength when the plane crashed.

As the only officer on flying duty in early 1910 [Lieutenant Benjamin Foulois] taught himself how to fly in the only plane the Army had. Foulois received instruction from the Wrights by mail, becoming the first correspondence-school pilot in history. The Wrights later sent him an instructor to help with the hardest part . . . landing. Over the next months and years, the young air pioneers trained hard and developed tactics to turn the airplane into an effective military weapon. They did the best they could with what they had, and worked hard to show the Army and Navy how air power could contribute to joint operations.

Lieutenant Foulois, whose career grew with the new Army air arm, and who as a Major General was Chief of the Air Corps for four years in the mid-thirties, did not remain the only pilot for long. Though the Aeronautical Division started with three uniformed personnel in 1907, there was an average of 25 people in the division between 1908 and 1912; in 1913 that number was up to 114. Nevertheless, despite its invention in the United States, heavier-than-air aviation was growing much faster in Europe than in America. In England the Royal Flying Corps had already been established, and there were many more pilots on the Continent than in the US. The fledgling birdmen in the US Army petitioned hard for an expanded service and were rewarded by an Act of Congress (2 March 1913) that authorized the Signal Corps to add pilots and to pay them at a higher scale for their time aloft. A year later the number of authorized pilots was increased again, and on 18 July 1914 the Aeronautical Division officially became the Aviation Section of the Signal Corps.

On 5 March 1913, three days after it had been authorized to expand, the Aeronautical Division had issued Field Order Number 1, establishing what was to be the First Provisional Aero Squadron. But due to a typographical error on the part of an anonymous but perhaps foresighted clerk, the word 'provisional' was not inserted. The First Aero Squadron was established at the air field near Texas City, Texas, on Galveston Bay under Captain Charles Chandler. The early Wright Pusher was soon joined in the First's inventory by the Curtiss D, the Burgess H and the Martin TT seaplane. In search of good weather in which to learn the art of flying their fragile craft, the First moved in early 1914 from the Texas Gulf Coast to San Diego, California, where the Signal Corps Aviation School was established.

Meanwhile, the Imperial Powers of nineteenth-century Europe had blustered their way to the brink of war. As these great nations dropped over the edge into the seething cauldron of 20th-century warfare, their forces included pilots and their flying machines for the first time. While there were more aeroplanes per se in France, the Germans had a larger air force – 500 aircraft, more than double the number available to the Royal Flying Corps. The Aviation Section had fewer than 20.

As millions of men went to war under the withering firepower of enormous fighting machines on Europe's center stage, the United States was being drawn into a brushfire war in its own backyard, reminiscent of the Indian wars of fifty years before. A Mexican bandit turned revolutionary and folk hero, Francisco 'Pancho' Villa, had recently been ousted after two years as dictator of Mexico and was riding with his outlaw gang in Northern Mexico. Since the United States had recognized the new government formed by his former cohort Carranza, Pancho Villa had no qualms about occasionally crossing the border on one of his raids. On 8 March 1916 he came north on a raid against the town of Columbus, New Mexico, in which 17 Americans were killed. The War Department promptly ordered General John J 'Blackjack' Pershing, commanding the Presidio of San Francisco, to proceed south and form a military expedition to capture the legendary *bandito*. Among the forces placed at Pershing's disposal was the First Aero Squadron, back in Texas at Fort Sam Houston and commanded by Major Benny Foulois. America's first air squadron was going into its first conflict, albeit in an observatory role. The eight Curtiss JN-2s and JN-3s of the First arrived in Columbus three days after the Villa raid and were ordered south into Mexico. On the flight to Casas Grandes,

about a hundred miles south of the border, two of the 'Jennys' crashed and the others, already the worse for wear, ran afoul of sandstorms that seriously jeopardized their airworthiness. Moreover, the Villa gang was holed up in the 12,000-foot mountains of the high Sonora desert plateau country, an altitude at which the JN-3s could not function. When the Pershing expedition ended five months later, the results of America's first 'air war' were disappointing. Pancho Villa was still at large, and the only two JN-3s to come out of Mexico were written off as no longer safe. Nevertheless, the First Aero Squadron had logged 346 hours on 540 courier and reconnaissance missions.

Less than a year later the United States was pulled into the Great War in Europe – World War I. While air combat over the Continental trenches and steppes had developed into something of an art, the Aviation Section was scarcely better equipped than it had been a year earlier for the foray into Mexico. Of more than 1100 men in the section, only 35 were pilots. The inventory of fewer than 300 planes did not include a single combat aircraft. The United States faced the reality of going to war with an enemy far superior in aviation technology, and changes would have to be made quickly. From the creation of the Aeronautical Division in 1907 through the time of the Mexican incursion, the US Army had spent a little more than half a million dollars on aviation. On 24 July 1917, three and a half months after the declaration of war, President Woodrow Wilson signed the Aviation Act of 1917, which budgeted over six hundred million dollars for military aviation. This huge increase in spending bolstered not only the Aviation Section, but the American aircraft industry as well. While manufacturers geared up, the Army sent Colonel Raynal Bolling to Europe for a first-hand look at what would be required of the air units joining the American forces. What he saw was American pilots flying French and British planes of a type superior to what American industry could design and produce in the limited time available. Thus it was decided that the United States would not build pursuit aircraft, but would concentrate on trainers and reconnaissance planes while American fighter pilots flew SPADs and Nieuports. The principal aircraft produced in the US during this period were the Curtiss JN-4, a descendant of the planes Foulois had flown into the Sonora Desert, and the British-designed de Havilland DH-4, built in America by license.

On 24 May 1918, six weeks after American pilots shot down ther first enemy aircraft in combat, the Army decided to take its air arm out from under the wing of the Signal Corps and make it a new unit equal in importance in the military organization. The

Below: The Curtiss JN series 'Jennys' were the first aircraft to be built in large numbers for the Signal Corps.

Left: Flying French-built SPADs, Captain Eddie Rickenbacker of the 94th Aero Squadron was the top-scoring ace in the USAAS during World War I with 26 victories. When the war ended in November 1918, 3800 of the 7889 USAAS aircraft were from foreign manufacturers.

Right: **A formation of Keystone bombers over the Golden Gate, 25 April 1930, seven years before the bridge was built. The Crissy Field landing strip at the Presidio of San Francisco can be seen in the lower left. In the dozen years since the end of the war the USAAC was building a sturdy fleet of American-made aircraft, which, thanks to Billy Mitchell, included bombers.**

US Army Air Service was born. The first Commander of the USAAS, Major General William Kenley, himself a pilot, now held a rank equivalent to that of his old boss, Chief Signal Corps Officer Major General George Squier.

While Kenley was attending to his new duties in Washington, the star of his field commanders was on the rise. When General John Pershing of Pancho Villa campaign fame, now commander of the American Expeditionary Forces, arrived in France, he had on his advisory board as air officer a young major named Billy Mitchell, who was to become one of the most outspoken advocates of the air-power doctrine in the postwar years. Mitchell soon became Air Commander for the Zone of Advance, and by October 1918 was a Brigadier General and Chief of the Air Service for the entire Army Group. Throughout the period, as American air power grew steadily, Mitchell continued to press for a more vigorous use of that power in an offensive or strategic way. Pershing steadfastly continued to think of air power (beyond the dog-fighting air-superiority role) as supportive of ground offensives, rather than as an offensive force in itself.

In the air-superiority role, American pilots were riding the crest of the battle tide now running in favor of the Allies. In all, American aviators shot down only 781 enemy aircraft and 73 balloons, but among them were some standouts. Twenty-two of the 71 American aces had more than ten victories, and Captain Eddie Rickenbacker of the famous 94th ('Hat in the Ring') Aero Squadron scored 26. By the end of the war, 11 November 1918, the personnel strength of America's air arm had increased from 311 two years before to 195, 023 – an increase of over 6000%!

The halcyon days of 1918 were not to last. America was determined that the Great War was indeed to be the 'war to end all wars' and disarmed accordingly. The isolationists prevailed. The League of Nations, an idea carefully conceived and nurtured by President Wilson, was embraced by the world but rejected by Congress at home. The domestic aircraft industry went into a tail-spin, as vast quantities of surplus Army Jennies were dumped on the civilian market. The Air Service remained intact, but its strength in 1919 had fallen to only 13% of its wartime peak, though it was still considerably ahead of prewar levels.

On the other hand, among those 9050 men who remained in 1920 were a hard core of young officers who had come out of the war convinced that air power represented the future of American military might. The staunchest advocate was Billy Mitchell. Mitchell and like-minded airmen had some important allies in the Secretary of War's Cromwell Commission, which proposed, after a careful study of the recent air war, that a separate air force on a par with the Army and Navy should be created, as Britain had done in June 1918 when the Royal Flying Corps became the Royal Air Force. But opposition was enormous. The Navy saw its battleships as the nation's first line of defense, and would

tolerate no competition for that role from bombers. General Pershing's own commission on the question agreed with the general that air power should stay under Army control. Secretary of War Baker concurred, but authorized an expansion of the Air Service and better flight pay. He also ordered that Air Service squadron commanders, some of whom were still cavalry officers, must all be pilots.

Mitchell, now Assistant Chief of the Air Service, wanted more. Air Service units were still subordinate to Army field commanders, and he wanted them independent. While the War and Navy Departments were intransigent, public attention was attracted to the flamboyant Mitchell, who had become something of a celebrity. Congress was also intrigued and compelled the reluctant Navy to allow Mitchell a chance to prove his claim – which the Navy disputed – that Air Service bombers could sink a battleship. The Navy organized tests in which Mitchell's bombers attacked some captured German ships, including the battleship *Ostfriesland*, off the mouth of Chesapeake Bay. Mitchell's bombers sank the ship, but the War and Navy De-

partments were unmoved. Additional experiments two years later were also successful, and Mitchell became more and more outspoken, while the military establishment grew increasingly irritated with him. In September 1925, in the wake of the tragic crash of the airship *Shenandoah*, Mitchell accused the authorities of 'criminal negligence.' This was about all they could take from the plucky Mitchell. He was promptly court-martialed, convicted and suspended from duty for five years. Air power's foremost prophet became its foremost martyr. Mitchell resigned his commission and devoted himself, until his death in February 1936, to the crusade for air power through the public press.

While Mitchell was in the headlines, others were at work behind the scenes, refining air tactics and building a professional service within a service. In December 1925, the same month that Mitchell was convicted by court-martial, the Lambert Congressional Committee called for the establishment of a single Defense Department combining the US Army, Navy and Air Force as coequals. At the same time the Morrow Board, appointed by President Calvin Coolidge, also turned in its report, which rejected the notion of a separate air force, but did advocate that the Air Service be upgraded to Corps status, with the appointment of an Assistant Secretary of War for Air. On 2 July 1926 Congress passed the Air Corps Act creating the US Army Air Corps, with General Staff representation and an increased budget designed to bring USAAC strength to 1800 aircraft and 20,000 men in five years. Since the demobilization peak of 1919, the Air Service had never had more than 11,649 men in uniform (1921); the new Air Corps began with only 9674. Personnel strength would increase steadily, but it would be twelve years before it topped 20,000.

In December 1931 Major General Benjamin Foulois, the Army's first pilot and a long-time advocate of air power, became Chief of the Air Corps. Soft-spoken where Billy Mitchell had been outspoken, he began to lobby for more Air Corps autonomy. In 1934 the Baker Board joined a long line of commissions to take up the question of a separate air force and report in favor of the status quo. A notable voice of dissent on the Baker Board was that of Shell Oil Company executive and pilot James Doolittle, whose air-power stance would be confined eight years later in the skies over Tokyo. The Baker Board did, however, support the notion of establishing a General Headquarters Air Force to centralize command of the Air Corps, rather than having its command structure entangled with that of ground forces. The GHQ Air Force was established at Langley Field, Virginia, under command of Brigadier General Frank Andrews, in charge of all tactical Air Corps units; authority for training and logistics remained under control of General Foulois as Chief of USAAC. This arrangement was not without a potential for interservice conflict, since the GHQ commander did not have direct control of his training and supply services. The situation would not be resolved for another four years, by which time the Air Corps and the nation were facing a far more serious threat from without.

With the Czechoslovakian crisis of mid-1938, the eyes of the world were focused on Germany and her military might. In a few short years Germany had gone from a defeated and demoralized empire, beset by anarchy and hyperinflation, to a prosperous and highly ordered society with a military force that seemed second to none. Special attention was focused on the German Air Force, the Luftwaffe, with its modern aircraft and prestigious position within the German command structure. In his January 1939 message to Congress, President Franklin D Roosevelt, the former Navy Secretary, remarked on this and cited the need to expand the capabilities of America's Air Corps, which now ranked sixth in strength among the world's air forces. Eight months later the Germans put their Luftwaffe to the practical test in Poland, and the world teetered into the abyss of the 20th century's second world war.

The Luftwaffe was instrumental in the attack against Poland and, half a year later, on Scandinavia and Benelux. When France fell on 22 June 1940, and Germany squared off against England in the Battle of Britain, the role of air power in modern warfare was no longer theoretical: official attitudes toward it changed overnight. Though there was still some isolationist opposition, the prevailing mood favored a rapid expansion of American air power. All Europe seemed doomed to fall under the shadow of the swastika, and there was a strong sense of urgency. General Henry H 'Hap' Arnold, now Chief of the Air Corps, found himself in the position not of having to beg for men and planes, but rather of being begged to demand more of them. In 1938, when Arnold took command of the Air Corps, personnel strength stood at 21,089. Two years later it had more than doubled, and by December 1941 it had increased nearly seventeenfold to 354,000. During the same period the number of bases more than quintupled and training facilities proliferated, as did (with generous new tax advantages) aircraft factories in the private sector. At the time France fell in June 1940, military aircraft production in the United States stood at a little more than 400 units per month. By the end of 1941 the figure was up to 2464 and rising. Of the 22,077 planes produced during the period, 6756 went to Britain, 4034 to the US Navy and 9932 to the Air Corps. It was just the beginning, however belated.

AN AUTONOMOUS AIR SERVICE

In early 1941, with the frenetic growth in size and activities of the Air Corps, there was a clear need for organizational changes. General Arnold found in Army Chief of Staff General George Marshall a leader more willing than his predecessors to allow a measure of independence. On 20 June 1941, under the War Powers Act of 1941, President Roosevelt signed the executive order permitting Marshall to create the US Army Air Forces – an autonomous, if not independent, air arm, with Arnold as chief. Six months later Arnold's position was changed to Commanding General, USAAF, and he gained a seat on the Joint Chiefs of Staff and the Allied Combined Chiefs of Staff. Meanwhile, Secretary of War Henry Stimson appointed Robert Lovett to the long-vacant post of Assistant Secretary of War for Air. By executive order, the new autonomy was designed to last only until six months after cessation of hostilities, but neither Marshall nor Arnold saw it as anything but permanent. Hap Arnold now commanded an organization still closer to the kind of air force envisioned by the earlier air-power pioneers.

General Headquarters Air Force came back under direct control of the Air Corps Chief. Tactical and Air Defense units in the continental United States were divided geographically into four numbered Air Forces, with the First and Second in the northeast and northwest quadrants of the country and the Third and Fourth in the southwest and southeast. Separate Commands similar to the Commands of today's US Air Force were established to oversee such duties as training and maintenance, while the Ferry Command supervised delivery of lend-lease aircraft to Britain.

Among the other subsidiary commands of the USAAF were regional commands in US possessions in the Pacific. The Hawaiian Air Force was established in November 1940, and a year later the Far East Air Force was set up in the Commonwealth of the Philippines. When the Japanese launched the surprise air attacks against Hawaii and the Philippines on 7 and 8 December 1941 that brought the United States into World War II, these Commands bore the brunt of the initial attack. While the US Naval base at Pearl Harbor was the primary target in the attack on Hawaii, Hickam, Bellows and Wheeler Army Air Fields were also high on the list. Across the Pacific in the Philippines, Clark Field was a primary objective of Japanese raiders.

Throughout the 18 months prior to December 1941, the USAAC/USAAF had grown and expanded at a far greater rate than could have been imagined just a few years earlier, but faced with a global war, the pressure was on to grow even faster. As operations spread around the world, the idea of numbered air forces, previously used only in the continental United States, was extended to USAAF tactical forces worldwide. The Far East Air Force, which had relocated to Australia when the Japanese captured the Philippines, was redesignated the Fifth Air Force and the Hawaiian Air Force became the Seventh. When USAAF strength increased in the Western Pacific in 1944, the Thirteenth, born in the jungles of the Solomon Islands and nicknamed the Jungle Air Force, combined with the Fifth under the Far East Air Forces, into which the Seventh would also be incorporated. Within the Far East Command, the Thirteenth was assigned to Guadalcanal and the Solomons; the Fifth directed its attention westward toward New Guinea and the Philippines, with the objective of recapturing Clark Field north of Manila, its former home base and now the major Japanese air base for the entire region.

For the Hawaii-based Seventh, it was the island-hopping campaign in the vastness of the Central and Western Pacific. Picking themselves up from the humiliation of Pearl Harbor, the Seventh took part in the victory at Midway and helped spearhead the drive up through the Marshall Islands, the Carolines, the Marianas, Iwo Jima and ultimately Japan itself.

A month after the United States entered the war, the USAAF began to establish units in Europe for conduct of the war against Germany. The Eighth Air Force was established in England, where it merged with the RAF Bomber Command to form the Allied Strategic Air Forces that conducted the strategic air offensive against Germany and Occupied Europe. The Ninth Air

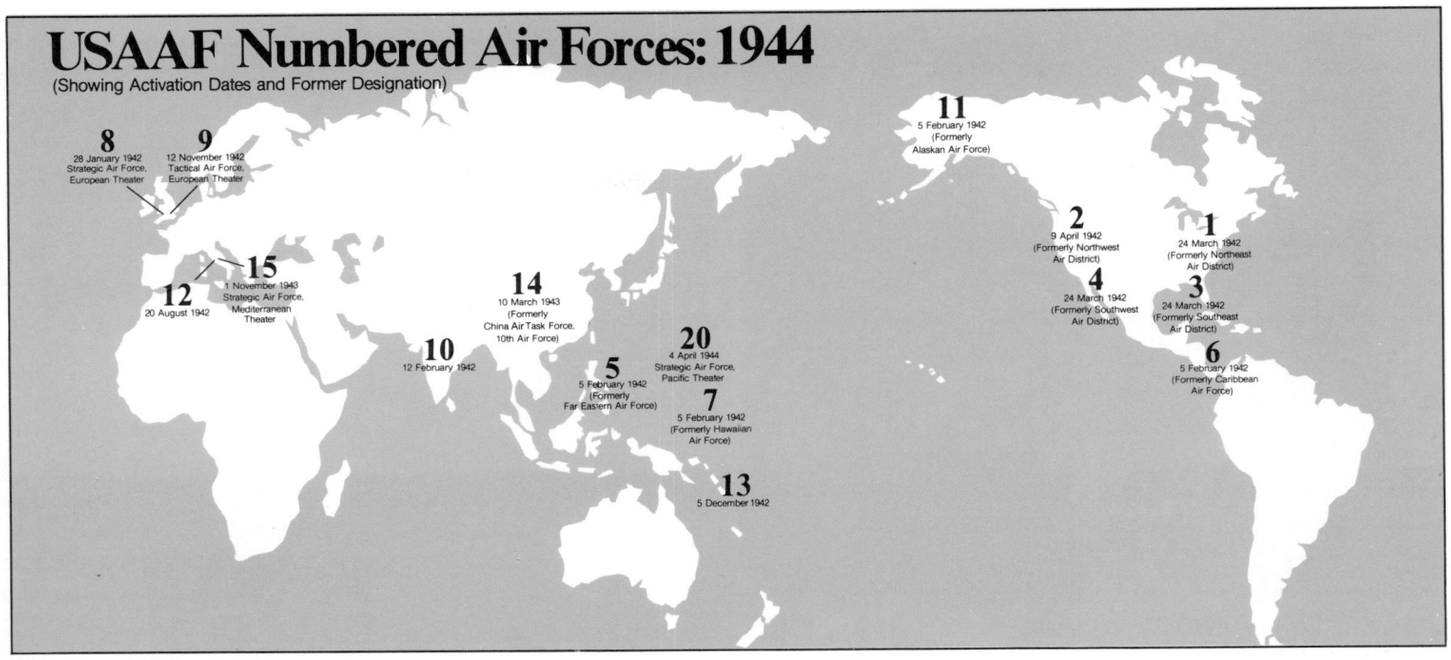
USAAF Numbered Air Forces: 1944
(Showing Activation Dates and Former Designation)
8
28 January 1942
Strategic Air Force,
European Theater
9
12 November 1942
Tactical Air Force,
European Theater
12
20 August 1942
15
1 November 1943
Strategic Air Force,
Mediterranean
Theater
10
12 February 1942
14
10 March 1943
(Formerly
China Air Task Force,
10th Air Force)
5
5 February 1942
(Formerly
Far Eastern Air Force)
20
4 April 1944
Strategic Air Force,
Pacific Theater
7
5 February 1942
(Formerly Hawaiian
Air Force)
13
5 December 1942
11
5 February 1942
(Formerly
Alaskan Air Force)
2
9 April 1942
(Formerly Northwest
Air District)
4
24 March 1942
(Formerly Southwest
Air District)
1
24 March 1942
(Formerly Northeast
Air District)
3
24 March 1942
(Formerly Southeast
Air District)
6
5 February 1942
(Formerly Caribbean
Air Force)

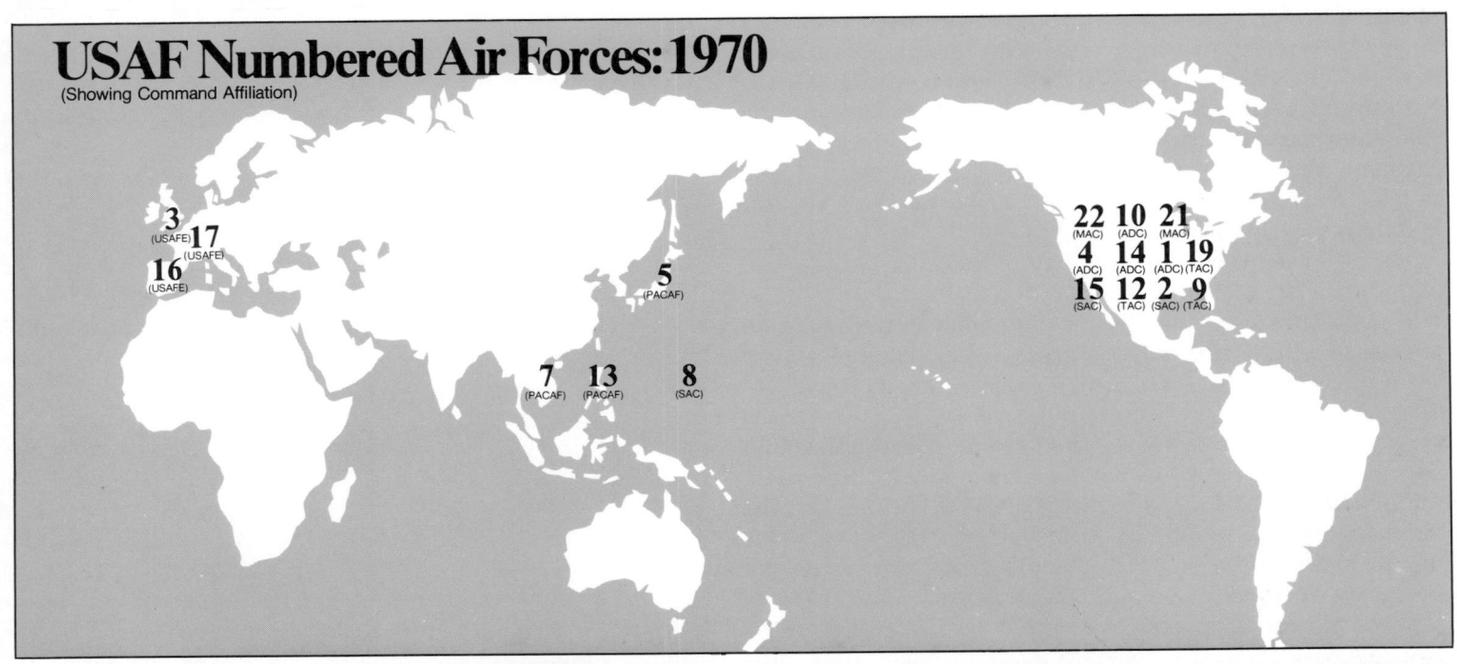
USAF Numbered Air Forces: 1970
(Showing Command Affiliation)
3
(USAFE)
17
(USAFE)
16
(USAFE)
5
(PACAF)
7
(PACAF)
13
(PACAF)
8
(SAC)
22
(MAC)
10
(ADC)
21
(MAC)
4
(ADC)
14
(ADC)
1
(ADC)
19
(TAC)
15
(SAC)
12
(TAC)
2
(SAC)
9
(TAC)

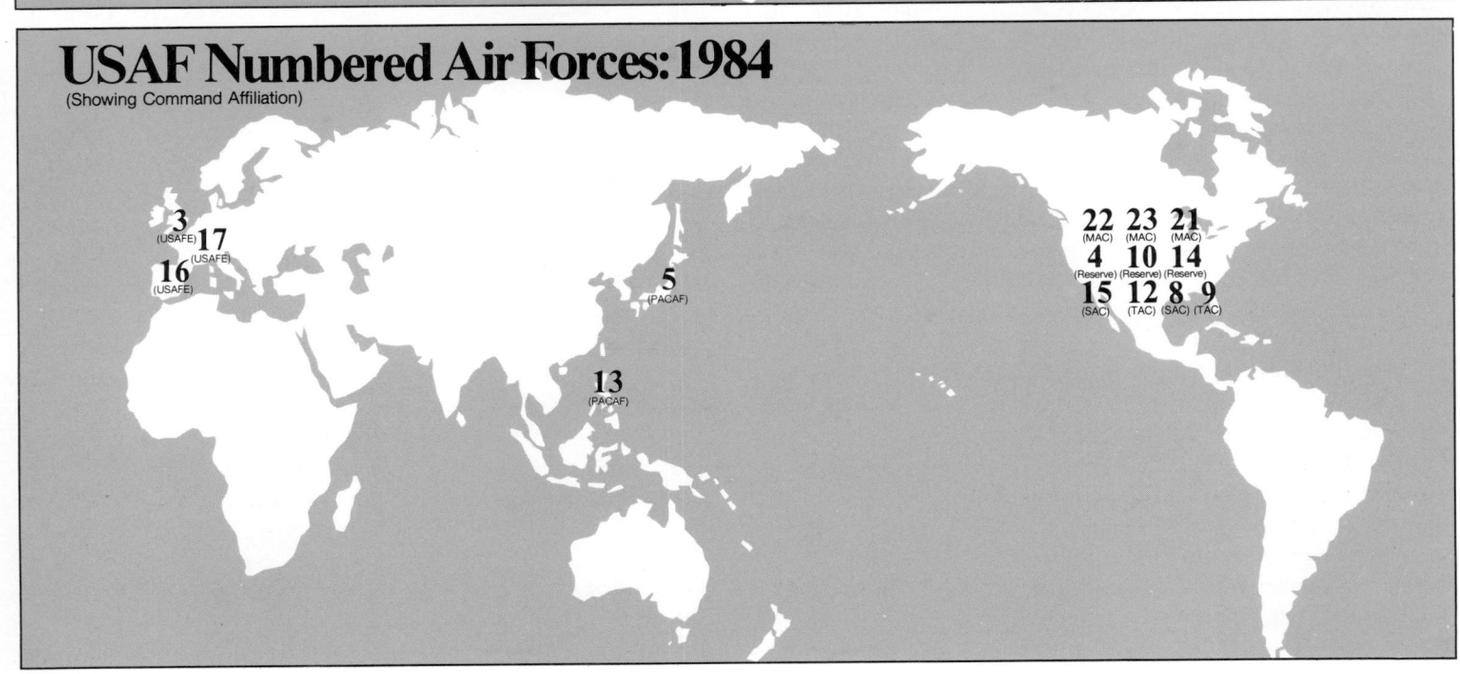
USAF Numbered Air Forces: 1984
(Showing Command Affiliation)
3
(USAFE)
17
(USAFE)
16
(USAFE)
5
(PACAF)
13
(PACAF)
22
(MAC)
23
(MAC)
21
(MAC)
4
(Reserve)
10
(Reserve)
14
(Reserve)
15
(SAC)
12
(TAC)
8
(SAC)
9
(TAC)

Left: A Martin B-26 Marauder medium bomber of the Twelfth Air Force over St Tropez, France during Operation *Anvil* in August 1944. The Twelfth was born in the North African desert and went on to serve in Italy and France.

Below: General Arnold and General Chennault inspect some of the latter's shark-faced Curtiss P-40s in China during General Arnold's round-the-world inspection tour in 1943. Chennault's China Air Task Force was first attached to the Tenth Air Force, but became the Fourteenth Air Force in March 1943.

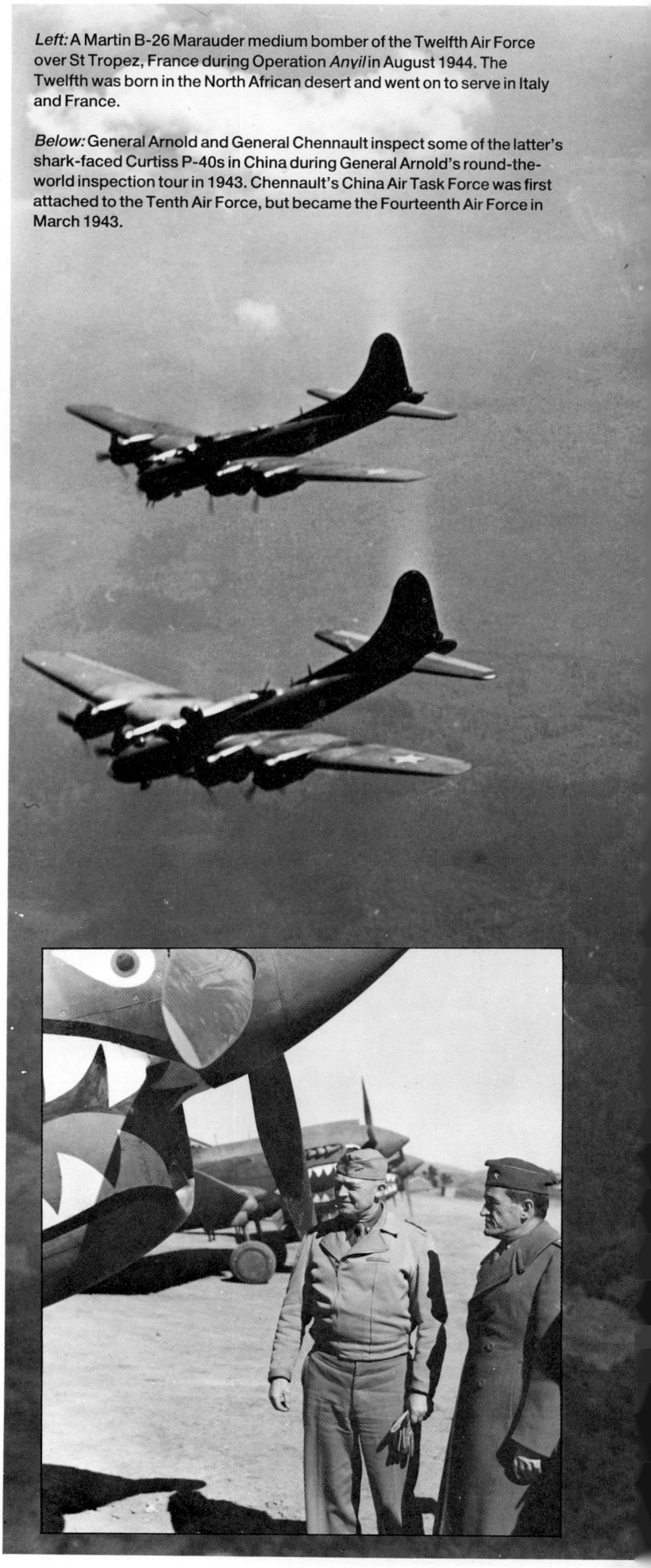

Force joined the RAF Middle East in Egypt to form the Allied Middle East Air Forces. Across North Africa the Twelfth Air Force was formed from components of the Eighth when it joined the RAF to form the Northwest Africa Air Forces. While the Twelfth remained in the Mediterranean Theater, following the Allied advance to Sicily and then Italy, the Ninth moved to England where it became the tactical complement to the strategic Eighth Air Force. The Ninth went on to play a key role in the Normandy invasion in June 1944 and in maintaining air supremacy over the battlefields of Western Europe until the end of the war.

With the strategic bombing campaign underway from England involving the RAF Bomber Command and the USAAF Eighth Air Force, a new Strategic Air Force, the Fifteenth, was established in Italy. Its role was to conduct a campaign against targets in Italy, Southern Germany, Southern France, Austria and other targets like the huge petroleum complex at Ploesti, Rumania.

On the far side of the world in the Asian subcontinent, the Tenth Air Force was being formed. Major General Lewis Brereton, late of the retreating Far East Air Force, arrived in Ceylon in February 1942 with six planes and some currency wrapped in an army blanket, to establish the Tenth Air Force as the USAAF operating Command for the China/Burma/India Theater. In the least publicized theater of the war, the Tenth attacked Japanese positions in the jungles and rivers of Southeast Asia, frequently striking targets in and around Rangoon and Bangkok. As the Allied advance into Burma began in 1943, the Tenth was overhead providing cover. Through it all one of the most difficult ongoing air operations in the theater, and perhaps in the entire war, was the Air Transport Command airlift of supplies supported by the Tenth from India over the Himalayas to China. The 'Hump,' as it came to be known, was one of the most treacherous air routes in the world and a supply link vital to maintaining operations in China.

Across the Hump in China, American pilots had been fighting the Japanese since before Pearl Harbor as members of the American Volunteer Group under Brigadier General Claire Chennault. The AVG, better known as the 'Flying Tigers' because of their shark's-mouth-decorated P-40s, had been the first real threat to the Japanese since they invaded China in the thirties. Though overwhelmingly outnumbered, the Flying Tigers exacted a severe toll in men and planes from the frustrated Japanese by flying hit-and-run, guerrilla-style missions, catching the enemy off guard.

Below: A playful P-38 Lightning flirts with a formation of B-17 Flying Fortress heavy bombers.

Right: 'Finito Benito, Next Hirohito' reads the slogan painted on the back of this Fifteenth Air Force B-25 Mitchell medium bomber seen over the Gulf of Naples in 1944. The reference is to Italian dictator Benito Mussolini, whose demise was imminent, and Japanese emperor Hirohito, whose empire would be gone the following year but who would survive another four decades.

Bottom: One of General Hoyt Vandenberg's Ninth Air Force P-47 Thunderbolts on a snow-covered runway in France during the winter of 1944-45. A top fighter-bomber, the P-47 dropped 113,963 tons of bombs as against 20,139 dropped by the second-place P-38.

GENERAL HENRY HARLEY ARNOLD
USAAF Commanding General during World War II

'Hap' Arnold was born on 25 June 1886 in Gladwyn, Pennsylvania, and served as Commander of the US Army Air Corps and the US Army Air Forces between 29 September 1938 and 28 February 1946. During his tenure, Arnold saw the USAAF through all of World War II and ended it presiding over the largest air force in history.

Graduating from the US Military Academy at West Point on 14 June 1907, Arnold's first assignment was with the 29th Infantry in the Philippine Islands. He returned to the United States in October 1909 and served at Governor's Island, New York, until April 1911, when he was assigned to the Aeronautical Division of the Signal Corps and sent to Dayton, Ohio, for flight training in the Wright Flyer. Upon completing his training, he became a flight instructor at the Signal Corps Aviation School at College Park Maryland. On 1 June 1912 he established a new altitude record of 6540 feet in a Burgess-Wright aircraft. After another tour in the Philippines (1913-16) he was sent to the Panama Canal Zone in February 1917 to help organize a pursuit squadron for the defense of the Canal. When World War I broke out in Europe, he was brought to Washington and placed in charge of the Information Service of the Signal Corps Aviation Division. In February 1918, with the temporary rank of Colonel, he became Executive Officer and later Assistant to the Director of Military Aeronautics. After the war he became Supervisor of the US Army Air Service Western District at Coronado, California.

On 30 May 1919 Arnold became Air Officer of the Ninth Corps Area based at the Presidio of San Francisco; on 30 June 1920 he was promoted to a permanent rank of Captain. In 1925 he became Chief of the Information Division of the Office of the Chief of the Air Service in Washington. The creation of the US Army Air Corps on 2 July 1926 found Captain Arnold in command of the Air Corps detachment at Marshall Field, Fort Riley, Kansas; on 1 February 1931 he was promoted to Lieutenant Colonel and became Commanding Officer of March Field near Riverside, California. Between 19 July and 20 August 1934, he led a ten-plane bomber squadron from Washington, DC, to Fairbanks, Alaska, a difficult feat for that era and one for which Arnold was awarded the Distinguished Flying Cross.

On 11 January 1936 he left March Field to become Assistant Chief of the USAAC in Washington, and two months later was promoted to the permanent rank of Colonel. Two years later (29 September 1938) he became Chief of the USAAC and Deputy Chief of Staff for Air, with the temporary rank of Major General. With creation of the US Army Air Forces on 20 June 1941, he became Chief of the USAAF with permanent rank of Major General. On 9 March 1942 his title was changed to Commanding General, USAAF. He was promoted to the temporary rank of General (four star) on 19 March 1943 and to General of the Army (five stars) on 21 December 1944. The four-star rank was made permenant on 23 March 1946, and on 7 May 1949, by Act of Congress, he became the first and only permanent General of the Air Force.

During World War II General Arnold sat on the Joint Chiefs of Staff as commander of the nearly two-and-a-half-million-man USAAF. In 1942 he received the Distinguished Service Medal for his command of a 77-hour flight from Bolling Field, DC, through the war-torn South Pacific to Brisbane, Australia. In early 1943 he made a 35,000-mile, globe-circling inspection tour of the world's battlefronts, from North Africa through the Middle East to India, China and the Pacific. During this tour he joined President Roosevelt in attending the unconditional surrender conference at Casablanca, where he also received the decoration *Ouissam Alaovite* from the Sultan of Morocco. After World War II he turned command of the USAAF over to his deputy, General Carl Spaatz, on 28 February 1946. He returned from the service on 30 June 1946 and moved to Sonoma County, California, where he died on 15 January 1950.

During his career, Hap Arnold was awarded the MacKay Trophy for outstanding achievements in aviation in 1912 and again in 1934. He received the Distinguished Flying Cross in 1936 and the Distinguished Service Medal in 1942. Two Oak Leaf Clusters were added to the latter in 1945, in recognition of his wartime leadership and contribution to the war effort. In addition to these decorations, he received the World War II Victory Medal, three theater ribbons and foreign decorations and awards from Brazil, England, France, Mexico, Morocco, Peru, and Yugoslavia. General Arnold was also the author of a number of books on aviation, including *The Bill Bruce Series* (1928), *Air Men and Aircraft* (1929), *This Flying Game* (with General Ira Eaker, 1936), *Winged Warfare* (1941), *Army Flyer* (1942) and *Global Mission* (1949).

Because they were initially cut off from the outside world, the AVG continued to operate independently of the USAAF for over six months after the United States entered the war. On 4 July 1942 the AVG was incorporated into the slightly larger China Air Task Force, part of the Tenth Air Force. With American markings instead of Chinese, and with a more regular flow of supplies, Chennault's Flying Tigers continued to pick away at the Japanese. Finally, in March 1943, the CATF was sufficiently supplied and equipped to be upgraded to numbered status; it was redesignated the Fourteenth Air Force. For the duration, when other commands were achieving numerical superiority in their theaters, the Fourteenth fought as an underdog. While the Japanese were losing in the Pacific, the Fourteenth tenaciously harassed them in China. Often fighting from improvised bases spread across a rugged 5000-mile front, the Fourteenth constantly disrupted rail and boat traffic along the coasts of Japanese-occupied China. In the skies over the vast Asian mainland, the Fourteenth shot down nearly eight enemy aircraft for every one they lost.

While the United States was bent on taking the war to the enemy, concern grew about possible enemy action against the US and its possessions. With German U-Boats active in the Caribbean, and the probability of another air attack like that on Pearl Harbor, the Panama Canal was particularly vulnerable. Air units had been based in the Canal Zone since 1917. In fact, young Hap Arnold, then a captain, had commanded a pursuit squadron at the Atlantic entrance in 1917. Because of the canal's strategic importance, the Air Corps had created the Panama Canal Air Force in October 1940 (changed to the Caribbean Air Force in August 1941); in February 1942 it became the Sixth Air Force. The Sixth became active not only in defense of the canal but in antisubmarine warfare. Later in the war, it conducted tactical training in the Canal Zone for the USAAF as well as various Latin American air forces, particularly that of Brazil.

In Alaska the new Alaskan Air Force became the Eleventh Air Force, joining land and naval forces of both the United States and Canada in defense of Alaska and in retaking the Aleutian Islands that had been occupied by the Japanese. In July 1943 Eleventh Air Force bombers based in the liberated Aleutians launched the first land-based air attacks on Japanese territory with raids on the northern Kurile Islands. Plans to use the Alaska-based Eleventh for the strategic air offensive against Japan were shelved in favor of using the newly formed Twentieth Air Force operating from the Marianas Islands in the Pacific, where the weather was far more conducive to air operations.

The Twentieth Air Force was activated on 4 April 1944 for the sole purpose of conducting the strategic air offensive against Japan. The Twentieth was the only USAAF component to receive the giant Boeing B-29 Very Heavy Bomber. The B-29 Stratofortress was the largest strategic bomber ever built, with a far greater range than any other. It had been one of Hap Arnold's pet projects since the late thirties when earlier, smaller heavy bombers were barely off the drawing boards; now it was a reality. Arnold's objective was to use the B-29 to demonstrate that a major world power, Japan, could be defeated by air power. Arnold felt that a strategic offensive using B-29s would negate the need for the planned invasion of Japan. The Twentieth Air Force was unlike the other fifteen in that it reported directly (via Arnold) to the Joint Chiefs of Staff, rather than being under the operational control of a theater commander. This was by design: Arnold intended the organization to be prototypical for the postwar Air Force he envisioned. By the early months of 1945, the Twentieth had inflicted severe damage on the Japanese home islands and on the nation's war economy. In August the Twentieth made history as the only unit ever to use nuclear weapons in wartime.

Above: The crew of the Eighth Air Force B-17 Flying Fortress 'Hell's Angels' after the plane's 31st mission over Europe.

Below: After 48 missions, 'Hell's Angels' had downed 18 German fighters.

Top: General Spaatz (seated, center) at his headquarters with Generals Ralph Royce (note his RAF wings), Hoyt Vandenberg and Hugh Knerr.

Above: Ninth Air Force Commander Vandenberg during a press conference at his field headquarters in northern France, 1944.

AIR-POWER COMMAND AND THE USAAF

In 1942, despite the reorganization that accompanied creation of the USAAF, the Army Field Manual still called for air units under operational control of the ground-force commander. The inherent fallacy in this directive, which would not be fully recognized until the USAAF got into combat, was that it disallowed the need to gain air superiority over the theater of operations. It can be said, as indeed it has, that the fundamental basis for the organization of air power in a theater came out of the first American experiences over the sands of North Africa in the fall of 1942. At that time the Twelfth Air Force, organized as an Air Support Command, was assigned to the Second American Corps to cover the invasion of Northwest Africa. The British had assigned RAF 242 Group to support their First Army. At the same time, Egypt-based units of the RAF and the USAAF were not co-ordinated with those in Northwest Africa. The Luftwaffe on the other hand, despite serious supply problems, was well organized and a serious adversary. Because they were attempting to provide ground support before gaining air superiority, Allied planes were easy pickings for the Germans and consequently failed in their ground-support mission as well.

Losses both on the ground and in the air were severe, and Allied air commanders went to work formalizing a new command structure. It was presented at the Casablanca Conference in January 1942 and approved by President Roosevelt and Prime Minister Churchill. The cornerstone of the new structure was creation of a single unified air command for the entire Mediterranean Theater. The air commander would be RAF Air Marshal Arthur Tedder; under him the newly unified Northwest African

GENERAL CARL ARTHUR SPAATZ
Second USAAF Commanding General, First USAF Chief of Staff

Carl 'Tooey' Spaatz was born on 28 June 1891 in Boyertown, Pennsylvania, and served as Commanding General of the US Army Air Forces and as the first Chief of Staff of the US Air Force between 1 March 1946 and 29 April 1948. He graduated from the US Military Academy at West Point in June 1914 and was assigned to the 25th Infantry at Schofield Barracks, Hawaii, until 13 October 1915 when he was transferred to the Signal Corps Aviation School at San Diego. In June 1916, just after completing his flight training, Spaatz was assigned to the First Aero Squadron which was being sent into Mexico under General John J Pershing to track down the Mexican bandit Pancho Villa. In May 1917 he was promoted to Captain and assigned to the Third Aero Squadron in San Antonio, Texas. With the active entry of the United States into World War I, Spaatz went to France as Commander of the 31st Aero Squadron. On 15 November he was assigned to the American Aviation School at Issoudin where he served continuously, except for a month on the British Front, until 30 August 1918. In September he joined the Second Pursuit Squadron as a pursuit pilot and flight leader; serving in combat for barely two months he managed to shoot down three German Fokkers and was awarded the Distinguished Service Cross.

After the war Captain Spaatz served in California and Texas, becoming Assistant Air Service Officer for the Western Department in July 1919. On 1 July 1920 he was promoted to Major and placed in command of Kelly Field, Texas, on 5 October of the same year; he served there until February 1921. Then he became commander of the First Pursuit Group at Ellington Field, Texas, and later at Selfridge Field, Michigan, until 24 September 1924. In June 1925, after graduating from the Air Corps Tactical School, Langley Field, Virginia, he was assigned to the Office of the Chief of the Air Corps in Washington. In January 1929 Spaatz commanded the aircraft *Question Mark*, which set an endurance record of 150 hours 50 minutes by means of aerial refuelling, for which he was awarded the Distinguished Service Cross.

Between May 1929 and June 1933, in a transition from fighters to bombers, Spaatz served as commander of the Seventh Bombardment Group and later the First Bombardment Wing at Rockwell and March Field in California. On 10 June 1933, he became Chief of the Air Corps Training and Operations Division. He enrolled in the Command and General Staff School at Fort Leavenworth, Kansas, in August 1935 and emerged the following June as a Lieutenant Colonel. In November 1939, with the temporary rank of Colonel, he was sent to Britain as a special military observer.

In January 1942 with the temporary rank of Major General he was assigned as Chief of the USAAF Combat Command in Washington. In May 1942 he became commander of the Eighth Air Force and was transferred to England to prepare for the American strategic bombing of Germany. On 1 December 1942, with the permanent rank of Colonel, Spaatz took command of the Twelfth Air Force in North Africa. Three months later, with the temporary rank of Lieutenant General, he assumed command of the Northwest African Air Force, which incorporated the Twelfth. After the Germans had been driven out of North Africa and the invasion of Italy was launched, General Spaatz became deputy commander of the Mediterranean Allied Air Forces, incorporating both the Twelfth and Fifteenth Air Forces.

In January 1944 he returned to England as Commander of the US Strategic Air Forces in Europe, presiding over the strategic air offensive against Germany until that country's defeat. After a brief assignment in Washington, Spaatz was, in June 1945, named commander of the US Strategic Air Forces in the Pacific, where he served during the final two months of the strategic air offensive against Japan. He received the temporary rank of four-star General on 11 March 1945, and was one of few officers present at all three signings of unconditional surrender documents by the enemy – at Rheims, Berlin and Tokyo. In October 1945, with the permanent rank of Major General, he returned to USAAF Headquarters. On 1 March 1946 he became Commanding General of the USAAF, and with the creation of the independent US Air Force, he became its first Chief of Staff on 26 September 1947, serving until 29 April 1948. He retired from the service on 30 June 1948 as a four-star General and became a contributing editor at *Newsweek* Magazine. He died on 14 July 1974.

During his career, General Spaatz was awarded the Distinguished Flying Cross, the Distinguished Service Cross, the Distinguished Service Medal, the Mexican Interior Campaign Ribbon, the World War I ribbon with three bronze battle stars, the European, Pacific and American theater ribbons and the World War II Victory ribbon. His foreign decorations included the French Croix de Guerre, Grand Commander of the British Empire, Russia's Second Order of Suvorov and Poland's *Polonia Restituta* Commander's Cross with Star.

Air Force would be commanded by USAAF General Carl 'Tooey' Spaatz, then commander of the US Twelfth Air Force. Units could now be distributed and deployed where they were most needed.

The first order of business for the new Northwest Africa Air Forces was air superiority. No longer shackled by the old command structure, the NAAF was able to exploit enemy weaknesses. With control of all air units, Spaatz could shift them in any level of concentration to wherever they were most needed. Ultimately, unified command of air power proved decisive in the battle over North Africa. It was the Germans' turn to feel the brunt of well-organized air power.

If North Africa was the proving ground for the practical application of tactical air power, Operation *Overlord*, 18 months later, would provide an opportunity for integrating tactical and strategic air power against a single enemy. Germany had designed and built what it called *Festung Europa*, Fortress Europe, a theoretically impregnable wall of defenses that had kept Allied armies from setting foot on the Continent. Operation *Overlord*, the Allied attempt to breach those defenses with an invasion of northern France, would be the biggest operation of its type ever undertaken, calling for precise integration of vast land, sea and air forces.

The outline for *Overlord* was drawn up at the Quebec Conference by President Roosevelt and Prime Minister Churchill in August 1943. The plan called for direction by a single Supreme Commander of the Allied Expeditionary Force who would be, despite some reservations on the part of the British, an American. General Marshall, the American Chief of Staff, was the first choice, but Roosevelt felt that he was indispensable in his current post. General Dwight D Eisenhower, who had been supreme commander for the Operation *Torch* landings in North Africa, was named Commander in Chief of Supreme Headquarters, Allied Expeditionary Force (SHAEF). With an American in the top job, the British wanted one of their officers as deputy commander. Eisenhower, to his credit, recognized the importance of air power's role in the operation and selected Air Marshal Arthur Tedder.

Until the spring of 1944 the Allied Strategic Air Forces based in England (RAF Bomber Command and USAAF Eighth Air Force) had conducted an intensifying strategic offensive against targets in the German heartland. The nature of strategic opera-

Above: Smoke billows up from an enemy railyard struck by Fifteenth Air Force B-24s in September 1945. These aircraft dropped 452,508 tons of bombs during the war, 29 percent of the total USAAF tonnage.

Right: An Eighth Air Force, First Bombardment Wing, 351st Bombardment Group B-17 during a mission over Germany. The B-17s dropped 640,036 tons of bombs during the war, 41 percent of the total USAAF tonnage.

Allied Chain of Command, Europe 6 June 1944

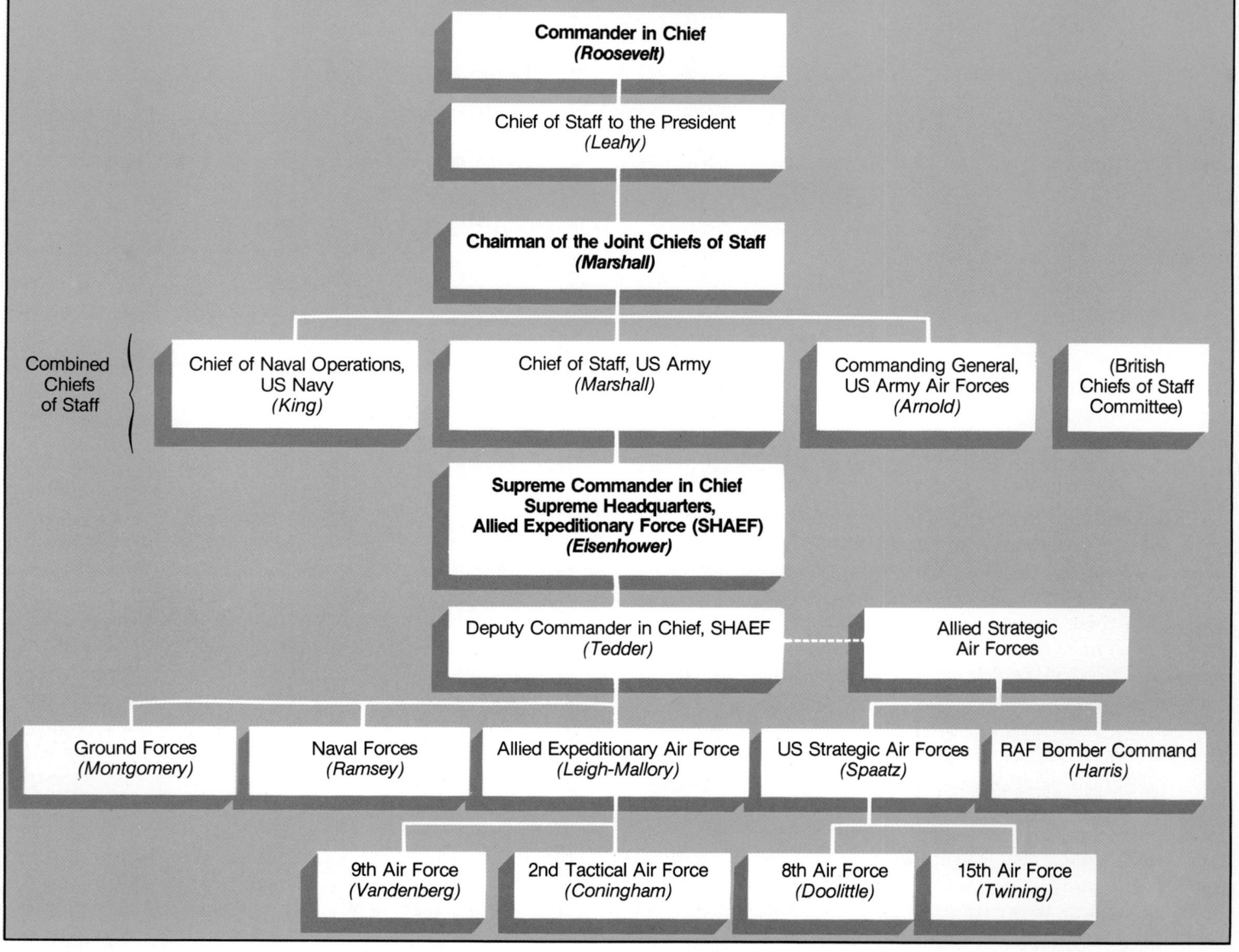

J

Chain of Command, Pacific Theater 1945

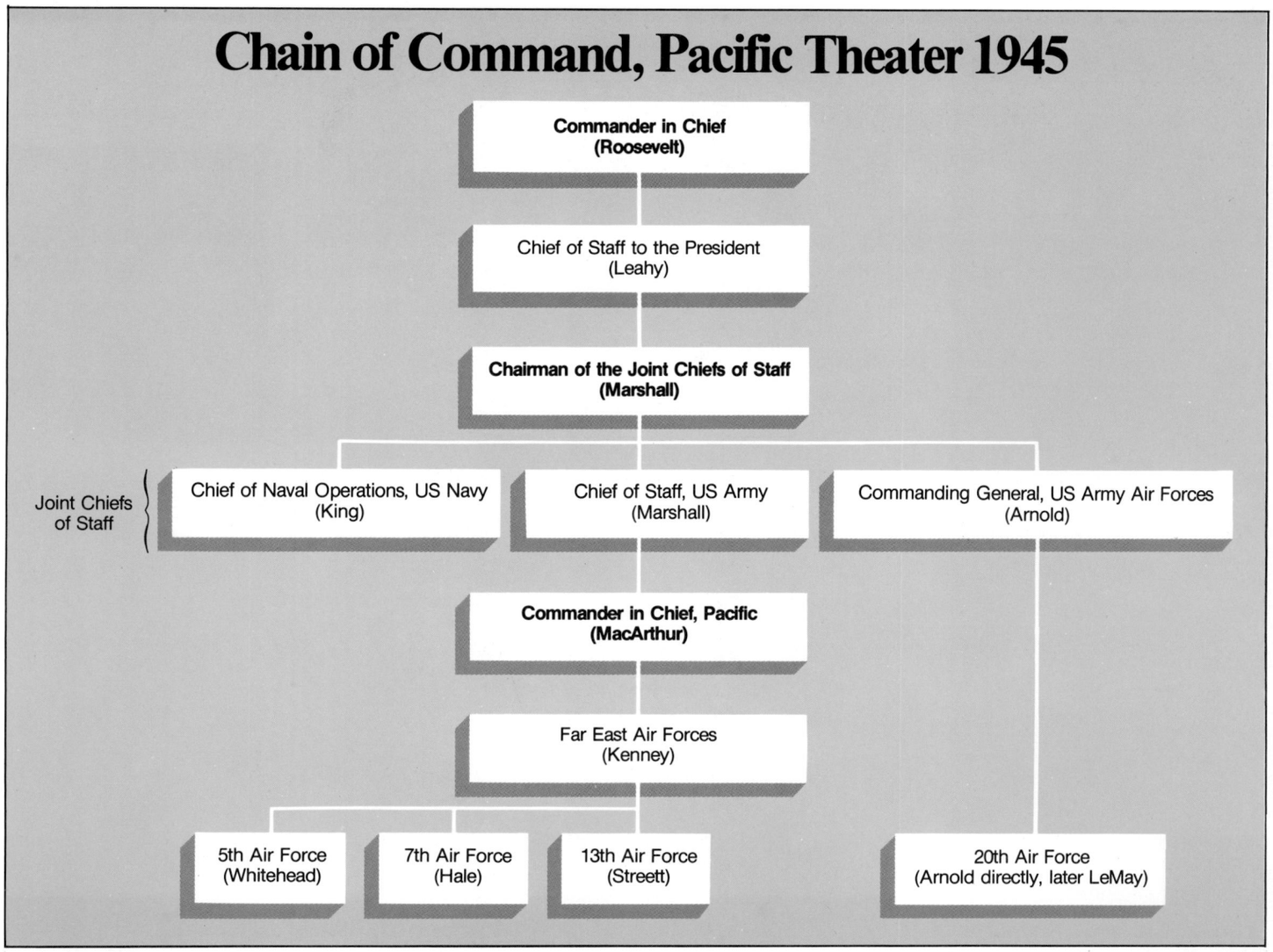

Above: General Spaatz (left) confers with Far East air chief General George Kenney at the New Grand Hotel in Yokohama shortly after VJ Day.

tions is such that their effects are not seen immediately at the front – strategic targeting involves hitting an enemy's warmaking power at the source. Destruction of a tank factory does not immediately reduce the number of tanks at the front, but its effects will be felt when disabled vehicles cannot be replaced. In spring 1944 this factor was not fully understood, and the fact that bomber forces were only then getting up to strength also led observers to criticize the lack of perceptible results. Therefore, plans were laid to divert the strategic bomber force, placing it under SHAEF (Eisenhower's) control. General Spaatz, now overall commander of the US Strategic Air Forces (including both the Eighth and the Fifteenth), and Arthur Harris of RAF Bomber Command, were strongly opposed to the idea. *Overlord* would require several months of tactical bombing over northern France to pave the way for the invasion; strategic-bomber commanders did not want their planes turned into tactical weapons when they felt close to a decisive moment in the strategic offensive.

Despite objections, both Eisenhower and Arnold felt it was important for all forces to be under operational control of the Supreme Allied Commander. The plan for *Overlord* called for three tactical commanders under Eisenhower, responsible for ground, sea and air operations. The air commander would be RAF Air Marshal Leigh-Mallory, who would direct all units now designated Allied Expeditionary Air Forces (AEAF). After much consideration, with Eisenhower's favorable attitude toward independent air power and the objections of Harris and Spaatz factored in, a compromise was reached. Under the

Above: A formation of B-29 Stratofortresses over a Japanese airfield.

revised plan, Leigh-Mallory would command only tactical air forces, while Eisenhower would have direct operational control over strategic air forces through his deputy, Air Marshal Tedder. When the invasion came on 6 June 1944, Tedder and Leigh-Mallory co-ordinated their efforts, with Leigh-Mallory managing all activities in the Normandy battle zone but not strategic operations removed from the immediate engagement area. In October 1944, after the Allies had established themselves in France, the AEAF was disbanded with the two tactical air forces and individual army groups placed under SHAEF command (Tedder, via Eisenhower). With SHAEF now devoting its time to control of tactical air power in support of the three Army Groups, Spaatz and Harris could devote their full resources to the strategic air offensive against the heart of the Reich.

In the Pacific the situation was similar, with General Douglas MacArthur as Supreme Commander; he had control of General George Kenney's Far East Air Force – the Fifth, Seventh and Thirteenth. When the Twentieth Air Force was introduced, however, it was not under MacArthur's tactical control, but directly under the joint Chiefs of Staff. Thus the Twentieth was the most independent US Army Air Force and a forerunner of the autonomous postwar USAF.

When World War II began the USAAC had 23,455 men and a few hundred planes and ranked sixth in size among the air forces of the world. Five years later the USAAF had 2,372,292 men and nearly 80,000 planes; it was not only the largest air force in the world, but the largest air force the world has seen to this date.

World War II had been a war of air power. Hitler's first lightning jabs into Poland in 1939 had shown the brutal precision and effectiveness of ably wielded tactical aircraft. The USAAF Air Transport Command had demonstrated that vast quantities of material could be airlifted more quickly than transported by land or sea, to locations often inaccessible by other means, as in the case of crossing the Hump into China. Finally, the Twentieth Air Force proved, as airmen from Billy Mitchell to Hap Arnold had known, that air power could be a decisive factor in the defeat of an enemy, saving countless American lives that would otherwise have been lost.

Air power affected the tactics, strategy and logistics of World War II, and altered forever the way in which wars would be fought. The war began and ended in the skies, and ultimately the strongest air force was the USAAF.

A Separate US Air Force

EMERGENT US AIR FORCE INDEPENDENCE

When the Japanese delegation came aboard the battleship USS *Missouri* in Tokyo Bay on 2 September 1945 to sign the instruments of unconditional surrender, it was fitting that the sky should be filled with 435 B-29s, the planes that represented the triumph of American air power. The USAAF had proved it could play a decisive role in modern warfare. Hap Arnold could see in his mind's eye a completely independent postwar US Air Force; he had been working toward that goal since he became Chief of the US Army Air Corps in 1938, even more so since the creation of the USAAF in 1941. Throughout the war he had built up the structure and promoted the careers of those men whom he thought could perpetuate the vision.

In 1944, the same year that they had created the autonomous all-B-29 Twentieth Air Force under their own control, the Joint Chiefs of Staff had appointed a Special Committee for Reorganization of National Defense to look into the question of overall postwar command structure. In April 1945, after a year of extensive investigation, the committee recommended – as had many others over the years – that an Air Force be established on a coequal basis with the Army and Navy under a single Department of National Defense. The Navy, in the person of Committee Chairman Admiral James Richardson, dissented. The Navy sensed that as a result of long-range bombers and nuclear weapons, it was losing its former position as America's first line of defense, and feared it would lose its own air fleet as well. The loss of their cabinet-level secretary when the Navy and War Departments merged could also put them at a disadvantage in lobbying for appropriations.

Displeased with the JCS Committee report, the Navy appointed its own commission: much to the chagrin of Navy Secretary Forrestal, it returned with the same conclusion as the JCS. Beginning with the bill introduced in January by Senator Lister Hill of Alabama, Congress considered in 1945 no fewer than eight bills calling for a single department, including one introduced in October by Senator Edwin Johnson of Colorado, which called for a single Department of Military Security with six branches.

By the end of the year the tide was running in favor of change. In November Eisenhower returned from his triumph in Europe to take the place of George Marshall, who was retiring as Army Chief of Staff. Eisenhower was a firm believer in air power and wasted no time in presenting his view that a separate and independent US Air Force should be created. By now, General Arnold's health was beginning to fail. He had suffered several heart attacks during the war and realized he would be unable to continue for long as Commanding General of the USAAF. By October General Spaatz had returned from overseas to become a Major General. He was assigned to AAF headquarters, where Arnold put him in charge of efforts to bring about the creation of a separate Air Force. Spaatz would succeed Arnold five months later as Commanding General of the USAAF, but he began taking on some of the workload immediately. He devoted his time not only to promoting an independent air force but to planning its internal structure. In the case of the latter, the

Left: General Hap Arnold was the father of the modern USAF and was the only airman to eventually wear five stars.

Above: In the wake of World War II, the B-29 was symbolic of America's unrivaled air power.

groundwork had already been laid. A year earlier Arnold had assigned Brigadier General Laurence Kuter, who had been a member of the team that designed the USAAF before the war, to set up a planning group for a unit that could succeed the USAAF as a US Air Force. Early in 1945, General Ira Eaker, who had commanded the Eighth Air Force and later the Allied Mediterranean Air Forces, joined Kuter in the planning.

General Arnold retired on 28 February 1946 and Spaatz was sworn in as the USAAF's Commanding General the following day. When Spaatz had arrived in Washington the preceding fall the entity that he wanted to mold into a separate air force was very different from the one he now commanded. From a 1945 peak of 2,282,259 men, the USAAF had diminished to 890,000 by the end of the year and was now down to 450,000. The tens of thousands of aircraft spread across the globe were being sold for scrap. C-47 Skytrains were being sold off for 500 dollars each, to be snapped up by small airlines and ex-USAAF pilots turned entrepreneur. Brand new P-51 Mustangs, the top USAAF fighter during the war, were sold for a few thousand dollars, cheaper (though ironically more plentiful) than some postwar automobile models. The aircraft sell-off would cut too deeply into the muscle, but the demobilization was part of the larger picture of postwar military reorganization into which the airmen were penciling their independent force.

Not the least of the reorganizers was President Harry S Truman who had submitted to Congress (over the grumbling of Navy Secretary James Forrestal) a plan for the now-familiar tripartite Defense Department (December 1945). The Senate Military Affairs Committee took up the matter early in 1946, resulting in Senate Bill 2044 which began its odyssey through both Houses of Congress in April. In May Truman told the War and Navy Departments to prepare for the inevitable.

Over the summer the Joint Chiefs assigned USAAF Major General Lauris Norstad, who had acted as an adviser to the Senate Military Affairs Committee earlier in the year, and Navy Vice Admiral Forrest Sherman, to design a system wherein the Navy air elements could work with a US Air Force toward a common goal within a combat scenario. The result was a quasi-unified command plan, approved by the War and Navy Departments and by the President at the end of the year. The Sherman-Norstad Report was the backbone of the unification bill taken up by the Eightieth Congress in February 1947.

The unification bill was finally passed by Congress and taken by courier to National Airport, where President Truman was boarding his presidential aircraft, the C-54 called *Sacred Cow*, en route to Missouri and the bedside of his dying mother. At a few minutes past noon on 26 July 1947 the President signed into law the National Security Act of 1947, appropriately aboard a USAAF plane. Simultaneously he signed Executive Order 9877, which defined the roles and missions of the three new branches, as well as the nomination of Navy Secretary Forrestal to be the nation's first Secretary of Defense.

The Act provided for three 'executive departments' under the new Department of Defense. These subdepartments, Army, Navy and Air Force (the Marine Corps remained in the Navy Department) would each be presided over by a civilian Secretary

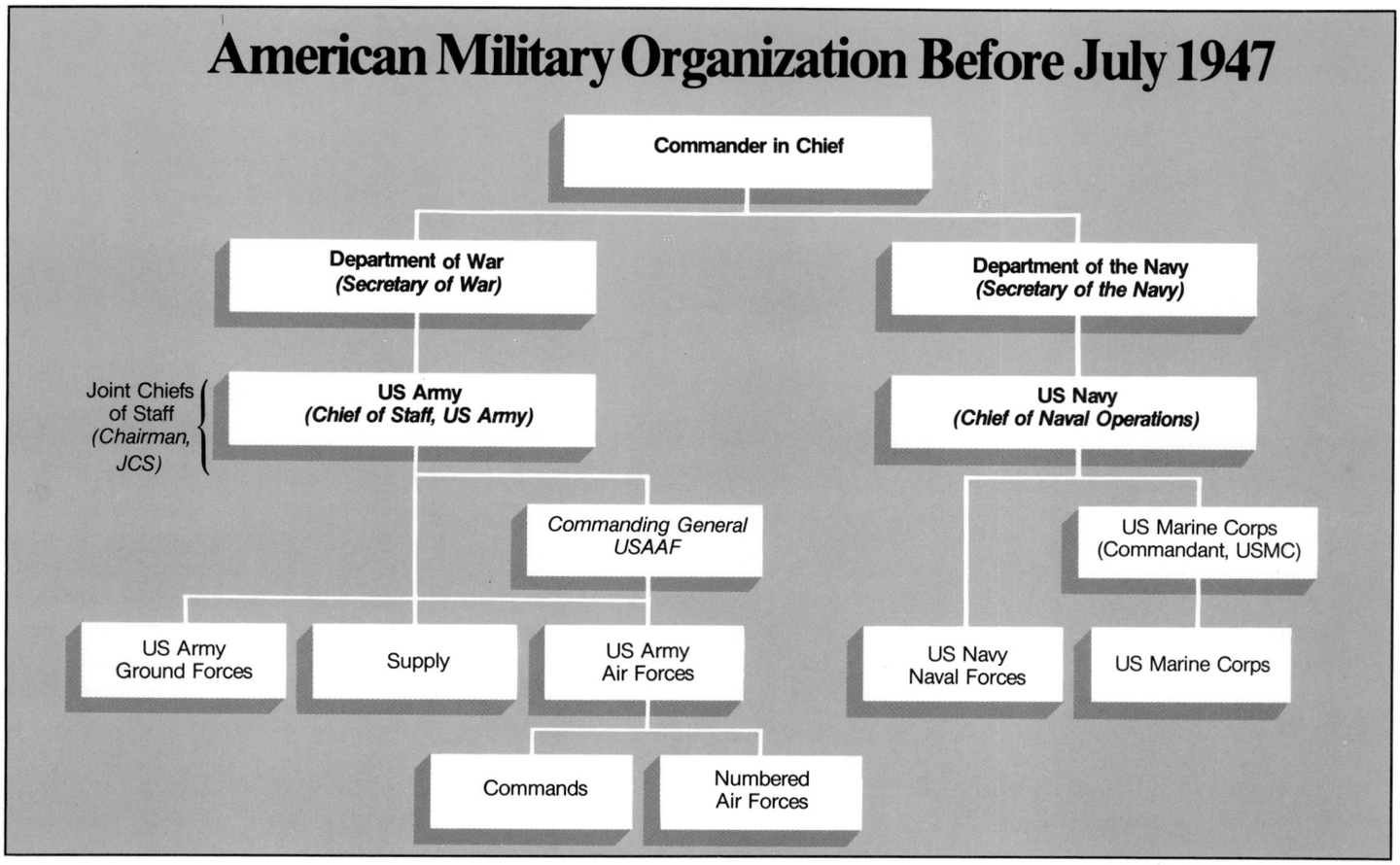

Above: General Arnold presenting the Legion of Merit to Brigadier General Laurence Kuter. General Kuter was involved in the analysis of Billy Mitchell's early air attacks on warships in the 1920s and of Allied and Axis strategic bombing during World War II. After his important work in the creation of the USAF, he went on to command MATS (1948-51), the Air University (1953-55), FEAF (1955-57) and NORAD (1959-62) before his retirement from the Air Force.

and comprise a branch of the Military commanded by a Chief of Staff. The three Secretaries would be members of the new National Security Council, while the Chiefs of Staff would be members of the now-institutionalized Joint Chiefs of Staff. The first Secretary of the Air Force was Stuart Symington, who was the current Under Secretary of War for Air and had himself been among those working toward the goal of an independent Air Force. General Spaatz changed hats and was sworn in as the first Chief of Staff of the US Air Force on 26 September 1947. General Hoyt Vandenberg, Deputy Commander and Chief of the Air Staff, who had served as Commander of the Ninth Air Force during the war, became Vice Chief of Staff on 1 October 1947.

As the sign painters were busy at the Pentagon changing the designations on office doors, the ownership papers of America's military aircraft were also changing hands. The Navy Department retained its carrier-based air fleet, antisubmarine aircraft and Marine Corps Aviation. Across the hall, however, the scene at the Army was reminiscent of a contemporary news photo of a staffer at the national library in British India. British India was about to become independent as two separate countries, India and Pakistan, and the photo's subject was part of a team that had to divide the library's vast collection into two piles, one for India, one for Pakistan. Now everything the Army owned pertaining to aviation had to be evaluated and in most cases turned over to the new Air Force. The list began with aircraft and personnel but also included other items from research and development reports to those paintings in the Official US Army Collection with aircraft and aviation themes. The Air Force would now be responsible for the transport aircraft that would airlift Army personnel over long distances, but the Army would, by compromise, retain a few light aircraft for forward observation and courier work and be permitted to develop its fleet of helicopters for short-distance transportation.

The mission assigned to the Air Force in Executive Order 9877 was largely a product of the planning teams that Hap Arnold had put together during the war and had a firm basis in the kind of Air Force the airmen envisioned. The Air Force was directed to (A) Organize, train and equip air forces for general global and specific theater air superiority, strategic combat, reconnaissance, and airlift and support of Army and Navy forces except in those instances specifically assigned to the Navy air arm; (B) Develop weapons, organization and tactics of an air force, co-ordinating them with those of the other services; (C) Provide planning and execution of missions throughout the world as required by national interests and policies; (D) Co-ordinate Air Defense among the services (the Army would control antiaircraft missiles, the Air Force the interceptors); (E) The Air Force would assist the Army and Navy when necessary by providing supplies and common services.

THE MAJOR COMMANDS

The USAF now had its independence, but it had been no overnight affair. The reorganization efforts that Arnold and Spaatz had presided over just after the war had played a part. Even before the war was over, the organizational entity known as the Major Command had begun to supersede the numbered air forces as the basic building block of the Air Force. A good example was the Far East Air Forces that began as an umbrella for the Fifth and Thirteenth Air Forces, and to which the Seventh was later assigned and, after the war, the Twentieth.

The first important step in the reorganization had come on 21 March 1946, when the Continental Air Forces were divided and redesignated by function. The result was the Strategic, Tactical and Air Defense Commands. The Strategic Air Command began with the Second Air Force but soon gained the famous strategic air forces from the European Theater, the Eighth and Fifteenth. The Tactical Air Command was assigned the tactical Ninth Air Force. On 1 October the Eleventh Air Force became the Alaskan Air Command; the following summer air units assigned to the occupation forces in Europe became the US Air Forces in Europe, another Major Command. The first Major Command established by the new USAF was the Air Materiel Command, created 14 October 1947 to take over the supply and logistics function lost when the service separated from the Army. The Air Transport Command, which had been a separate unit from the numbered air forces, became a Major Command – the Military Air Transport Service – on 1 June 1948. Its mission was to supply transport services to the Air Force and other branches of the military, notably the Army.

Though it was not unique to the Air Force, research and development or R&D became symbolic of the new Air Force, presiding over development of new aircraft and systems in the technology boom that followed the war. To oversee its multiplying facets, the Air Force created the Air Research and Development Command in February 1950.

RESEARCH AND DEVELOPMENT

Even before the end of World War II, it was clear that the immediate postwar period would see an unprecedented explosion in technical fields. During the war aircraft technology advanced at a rate many times faster than had been dreamed of before the war. When the war began, open-cockpit biplanes of a 25-year-old design were common in the world's major air forces. When the war ended, these services were flying jet-propelled aircraft, which Germany had used in combat throughout the last year of the war. This technology explosion was erupting in fields beyond aeronautics: radar had evolved dramatically during the war and guided-missile technology had emerged.

General Hap Arnold once said that World War I had been a war of brawn, World War II a war of logistics and World War III would be a war of brains. He knew at the time – as the world didn't – that nuclear weapons were in the offing, and probably recognized, as Einstein observed, that World War IV would be a war of sticks and clubs if World War III took place. With this in mind, and the shock of Pearl Harbor fresh in his memory, he was bent on making his service a world leader in aviation and defense technology. Arnold was determined not only to end the present war, but to prevent another.

In 1944 he had contacted the Hungarian-born Caltech (California Institute of Technology) scientist Dr Theodore von Karman and asked him to set up a Scientific Advisory Group (SAG), which would bring together scientists and researchers nationwide, from many high-technology fields. One of the first and most important tasks undertaken by von Karman and SAG was a trip to Germany in the wake of the Allied victory to study the breakthrough technology developed by the Germans during the war, including jet propulsion. The Germans had several jet-propelled combat aircraft in service during the war: the Arado Ar-234 bomber, the Messerschmitt Me-262 and Heinkel He-162 fighters and the Messerschmitt's Me-163 rocket-powered interceptor. Of these, the Me-262 was produced in greater numbers, saw more service and was the most advanced. A crucial factor in its success was the swept-wing design. The aerodynamics of swept wings were not fully understood in Britain and the US, and consequently their first operational jet fighters had the traditional straight wings.

George Schairer, an engineer with the Boeing Company, was among the SAG group investigating German facilities. At that same time Boeing was at work on the successor to the famous B-17 and B-29 strategic bombers it had produced for the USAAF during the war; the configuration of a new bomber was not yet decided. After evaluating what he saw in Germany, Schairer decided that Boeing's next bomber would be solely jet-propelled, with swept wings. The result was the sleek B-47 Stratojet.

The Scientific Advisory Group was also looking into the status of German rocket research, where they found two sobering items. The first was development of a successor to the V-2 (technical designation A-4) guided missile that Germany had used against Britain. This new missile, designated A-10, was a two-stage rocket with sufficient range to strike the United States from a launch site in Europe. SAG's second sobering find was that the Russians had not only appropriated vast quantities of rocket data, but had removed scientists and personnel from the principal German rocket test center at Peenemünde on the Baltic coast. The arms race with the Soviets had started even before the Germans had been defeated. At the end of 1945 Dr von Karman and SAG presented their findings to Arnold in a report titled *Science, the Key to Air Supremacy*. Arnold was delighted with the report and made the Scientific Advisory Group a permanent Scientific Advisory Board.

The first obstacle encountered by the new SAB was the familiar one of funding. Postwar demobilization meant that the operational commands were fighting for money, for planes and for the fuel to fly them; it was hard to justify appropriations for research and development when the results would not be visible for many fiscal years. There was, of course, strong Air Force support for R&D. Von Karman remained as a principal scientific

adviser and one of his former Caltech pupils, Brigadier General Donald Putt, was made Director of Research and Development by the Chief of Staff in October 1948. A little over a year later (1 February 1950) the Air Research and Development Command became a Major Command. Two years later the Arnold Engineering Development Center, near Manchester, Tennessee, was dedicated. Named for General Hap Arnold, the man whose foresight had led not only to the independence of the US Air Force, but to its emphasis on R&D, the center is the largest site of its kind in the Western world, supporting all phases of aviation and aerospace research.

AIR FORCE BLUE

Less than a year after he became the first Air Force Chief of Staff, General Spaatz turned over the reins to his Vice-Chief, General Hoyt Vandenberg, who became the US Air Force's first full-time Chief of Staff on 30 April 1948. He would oversee many growing pains. Vandenberg was part of the generation of USAAF officers who came to the forefront during World War II. He had commanded both the Twelfth and Ninth Air Forces and had worked his way through the upper ranks after the war.

While the Air Force had anticipated its independence and had designed a command structure, the new service was still Army-oriented. Most of its commanders had spent their adult lives in the Army. Spaatz had flown in its first air war in Mexico in 1916; Vandenberg himself had joined the Army in the 1920s. When the Air Force inherited the components of the Army Air Force, it was marked by nearly two centuries of tradition. Even the uniform worn by Air Force personnel was an Army uniform, one

Above: Stuart Symington was Undersecretary of War for Air when the US Air Force was created and thus became the first Secretary of the Air Force. Symington later went on to serve as a US Senator from Missouri and in 1960 he made an unsuccessful bid for the Democratic presidential nomination.

Below: With postwar demobilization, much of the USAF's aircraft strength was scrapped or put into storage. These B-29s were mothballed at the Air Materiel Command's Military Aircraft Storage and Disposition Center at Davis Monthan AFB near Tucson. *See page 208 for a discussion of MASDC.*

of Vandenberg's priorities for change. The new blue uniform leaned more toward that of Britain's Royal Air Force than toward the US Army garb. While officers would still be captains, colonels and generals, enlisted men below the grade of sergeant would no longer be corporals and privates, but would be called airmen instead.

The national insignia on aircraft changed also, albeit subtly, with the addition of a red bar in the white fields flanking a white star in a blue circle. This change would be adopted by the Navy, Marines and Army ground forces (for their light planes and helicopters) as well. Pursuit planes had been known as fighters since well before the war; effective 11 June 1948 the prefix *P* was changed to *F*. The P-51 became the F-51, the P-80 the F-80. Photo reconnaissance aircraft formerly designated by the prefix *F* assumed the prefix *R*. The F-13 for example, the reconnaissance version of the B-29, was now the RB-29.

In the post-war years Air Force strength diminished even as reorganization was accomplished. Demobilization was partly to blame; so too was over-reliance on nuclear weapons as a deterrent. Beyond the small number of aircraft that supported occupation forces in Germany and Japan, the Air Force was badly depleted. As of the end of 1947 the Strategic Air Command, the strongest Command, had only 319 B-29s (the only plane capable of dropping nuclear weapons) and 350 fighters, of which only 180 were F-80 jet fighters.

Vandenberg and Secretary Symington began to lobby for increased funding to supply aircraft to the wings and squadrons, many of which existed only on paper. The personnel strength of the Air Force at the time of its creation stood at 305,827, less than that of the USAAF at the time of Pearl Harbor. The prevailing school of thought called on the threat of nuclear war to prevent war. After all, Truman had used it to get the Russians out of Iran. The theory was valid only so long as the United States had a monopoly on nuclear weapons. While men like Major General John Samford, Chief of Air Force Intelligence, predicted that the Russians could produce atomic weapons by the early fifties, others went along with Dr Vannevar Bush of MIT who doubted a Soviet nuclear capability before the late 1960s or early 1970s. The controversy ended with detonation of the first Russian atomic bomb in 1949.

Symington and Vandenberg consistently held that the US needed an adequate conventional military force to prevent a choice between losing a conflict and resorting to nuclear weapons. The debate would live on past their terms in office.

Though Congress was beginning to authorize more money for defense, the rebuilding process was slow. Development of a new generation of aircraft was underway; leap-frogging technology meant that the new generation must be revolutionary. Lockheed, which had produced the famous P-38 Lightning fighter during the war, was responsible for the first operational jet fighter, the P-80 (F-80 as of 1948). Republic, which had given the USAAF the P-47, was developing the F-84 series, a straight-winged fighter that would evolve into a swept-wing aircraft with the F-84F. North American Aviation, which produced the P-51 Mustang, the top USAAF fighter of the war years, was at work on its F-86 Sabre Jet, which would be the first swept-wing fighter for the USAF. With the funding battle and development costs, the personnel strength of the Air Force edged slowly higher. From 305,827 it was up to 419,347 by 1949; in 1950 it had fallen back to 411,277 when there came the surprise many had feared and few had prepared for.

Below: Three US Air Force aircraft built by Republic Aircraft are seen at the company's plant in March 1949. From the left are the F-47 (formerly P-47) Thunderbolt of World War II fame, the then-new but ultimately unsuccessful XF-91 Thunderceptor, and the F-84 Thunderjet that would soon be going to war in the skies over Korea.

GENERAL HOYT SANFORD VANDENBERG
Second USAF Chief of Staff

Hoyt Vandenberg was born in Milwaukee, Wisconsin, on 24 January 1899 and served as the first full-term Chief of Staff of the US Air Force from 30 April 1948 to 29 June 1953. Vandenberg graduated from the US Military Academy in June 1923, whereupon he attended the Air Service Flying School and Advanced Flying School at Brooks and Kelly Fields in Texas, graduating in September 1924. His first assignment was with the Third Attack Group, whose 90th Attack Squadron he commanded until 1927 when he became a flying instructor at March Field, California. Between May 1929 and September 1931 he served in Hawaii, commanding the Sixth Pursuit Squadron at Schofield Barracks. From Hawaii, Vandenberg returned to the mainland, attending the Air Corps Tactical School (where he later taught), the Command and General Staff School and the Army War College, from which he graduated as a Captain in June 1939. Prior to the US entry into World War II, he served with the Air Corps Plans Division and as Operations and Training Officer to the Air Staff.

In June 1942, with the temporary rank of Lieutenant Colonel, Vandenberg went to England to help plan and organize air operations in North Africa. On 18 February 1943, with the temporary rank of Brigadier General, he became Chief of Staff of the Northwest African Strategic Air Force, with which he flew numerous missions over Tunisia, Sicily, Italy and Sardinia. He was awarded the Silver Star, the Distinguished Flying Cross and the Legion of Merit for his service with the NASAF. In September 1943, after a month at headquarters in Washington, he was assigned to head the Air Mission in Moscow under Ambassador Averell Harriman: he served there until January 1944. Three months later he was designated Deputy Commander-in-Chief of the Allied Expeditionary Air Forces for the Invasion of Europe and assumed command of the Ninth Air Force. For his part in the planning of Operation *Overlord*, the invasion of Europe, he was awarded the Distinguished Service Medal. General Vandenberg, now with the temporary rank of Major General, returned to Headquarters in June 1945, where he served as Assistant Chief of the Air Staff, and later as Director of Intelligence on the War Department General Staff. In June 1946 he was appointed director of the Central Intelligence Agency (CIA), returning to the USAAF a year later as Deputy Commander-in-Chief of the Air Staff. With the creation of the US Air Force, he became Vice-Chief of Staff on 1 October 1947, with the permanent rank of Brigadier General retroactive to 12 December 1942. On 30 April 1948 General Vandenberg succeeded General Spaatz as US Air Force Chief of Staff. In that position he presided over the rebuilding of the postwar Air Force and its activities during the Korean War. He made several trips to Korea and flew over much of Chinese occupied territory in an observation plane to get a first-hand look at the situation.

When the Eisenhower Administration took office in January 1953, the new Secretary of Defense, Charles Wilson, stated his intention to reduce the size of the Air Force. During subsequent Congressional hearings, Vandenberg, now stricken with terminal cancer, did an admirable job of testifying against Wilson. He under-scored the need to maintain a strong conventional Air Force to avoid being painted into the corner of choosing between defeat and recourse to nuclear war in a future conflict.

Vandenberg retired a few months later (30 June 1953) at the end of his second term as Chief of Staff. On 2 April 1954 he died after the painful final bout with his disease. In addition to his American decorations, Vandenberg was honored by Argentina, Belgium, Chile, China, Egypt, Great Britain, Italy, Luxembourg, the Netherlands, Poland and Portugal.

THE US AIR FORCE IN KOREA

THE US AIR FORCE GOES TO WAR

When World War II ended Korea was still part of the Japanese Empire. As with Germany and Austria in Europe, Korea was divided into occupation zones, the north being occupied by Russian forces, the south by the Americans, who also occupied the Japanese home islands. As they did in their zone of Germany and in parts of Eastern Europe, the Russians established a communist government in North Korea, while a Western-style government took over in South Korea. It was soon clear that the two Koreas could not be reunited by political means and North Korea, with the urging of its sponsors in Soviet Russia and Communist China, decided to take another course.

On the morning of 25 June 1950, 135,000 North Korean troops supported by armor crossed the 38th parallel, the demarcation line between the two Koreas. Late on the 25th, with the South Korean capital of Seoul at risk, US Air Force transports were dispatched from Japan to evacuate Americans. The South Korean units, more of a constabulary than a military force, were badly outnumbered and had none of the heavy weapons available to the invaders. On 27 June the United Nations Security Council passed a resolution calling for 'urgent military measures . . . to restore international peace and security' and asked member nations to 'furnish such assistance to the Republic of Korea as may be necessary to repel armed attack.'

General Douglas MacArthur, Commander of US Forces in the Far East, had already ordered the Fifth Air Force to cover the American evacuation and support the South Koreans. On the morning of the 27th a group of Russian-built Yakovlev fighter bombers attacked Kimpo Airfield, where they were intercepted by F-82s of the 68th All Weather Fighter Squadron of the Fifth Air Force based at Itazuke, Japan. The results were unfortunate for the Yaks and the first American air-to-air kill of the Korean War was chalked up by Lieutenant William Hudson. Later that day four Fifth Air Force F-80s shot down a like number of North Korean Il-10 attack bombers, bringing the toll for the first day of the air war over Korea to seven.

On the ground there was no comparable success. The South Korean defenses crumbled and Seoul fell. The Security Council voted on 7 July to establish a unified military command with the United States functioning as operative agent. General MacArthur was named Commander in Chief of the UN Command and the US Eighth Army was introduced into combat to block the North Korean drive to capture the entire Korean Peninsula. Under MacArthur, Air Force General George Stratemeyer was in command of the Far East Air Forces composed of the Fifth in Japan, the Twentieth on Okinawa, the Thirteenth in the Philippines and the Far East Air Materiel Command. The Far East Bomber Command was soon established, largely from SAC B-29s sent out from US bases. Initial targets for all bombers, B-29s and fighters alike, were tactical

Above: A flight of F-86 Sabre Jets of the US Air Force 51st Fighter Interceptor Wing streak toward 'MiG Alley' in Northwest Korea in search of enemy MiG-15s. During the preceding month of September 1952, Fifth Air Force Sabres had downed a record 61 MiGs while losing only four of their own number.

Left: This monsoon-formed lake was not the most ideal taxi-way, but neither was it a sufficient hazard to stop operations of 18th Fighter Bomber Wing F-51s at this Korean air base in September 1951.

Chain of Command, Korean War

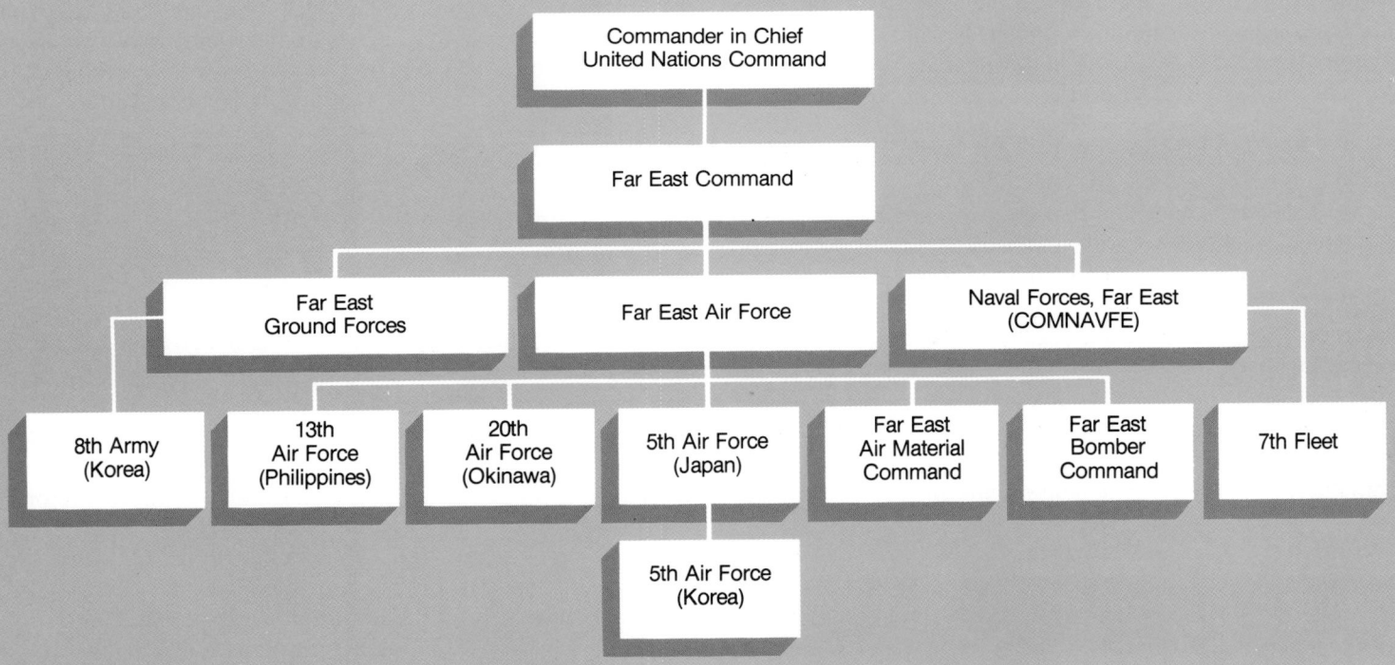

Below: 'Heavenly Laden,' a 98th Bomb Wing B-29 on the ground in Japan after her 60th mission in April 1951.

due to the pressing need to halt the North Korean advance. Tactical aircraft proved to be more effective against the targets, and by the end of July the B-29s were conducting strikes against strategic targets like railyards, hydroelectric plants and factory complexes in North Korea. By 15 September strategic targets in North Korea had been all but eliminated, and supply lines to North Korean forces in the south had been successfully interdicted by Fifth Air Force fighter bombers and occasional FEAF B-29s. Also on 15 September MacArthur successfully landed his X Corps at Inch'on near Seoul behind enemy lines. At the same time the Eighth Army under General Walker, which had been bottled up at Pusan, counterattacked.

By the first of October Seoul had been recaptured and UN forces had reached the 38th parallel. By 26 October some UN and South Korean units had reached the Yalu River, the North Korean border with Communist China. North Korea had been defeated, its air force destroyed, its warmaking power curtailed. Talk now turned to UN-sponsored elections to reunify the country. The following day, its job completed, the FEAF Bomber Command was deactivated; the B-29s borrowed from SAC were scheduled to return home.

In the midst of this silver lining was a cloud. There had been growing evidence of Chinese 'volunteers' with the North Korean Army, and on 1 November Chinese MiGs were first encountered by the Fifth Air Force. It was clear that the Chinese were rushing quantities of men and supplies into North Korea to stem the UN advance. The Chinese successfully counterattacked during the last week of November and by 15 December had pushed the UN forces south of the 38th parallel.

The FEAF bomber command was reactivated and sent north again, but now it was a different war in several important ways. First, the UN forces were outnumbered again, this time by the vast manpower reserves of China; second, the FEAF B-29s had not been effectively threatened by the tiny North Korean Air Force, but the Chinese MiG-15 jet fighters were a serious adversary; finally, the FEAF was forbidden, for political reasons to

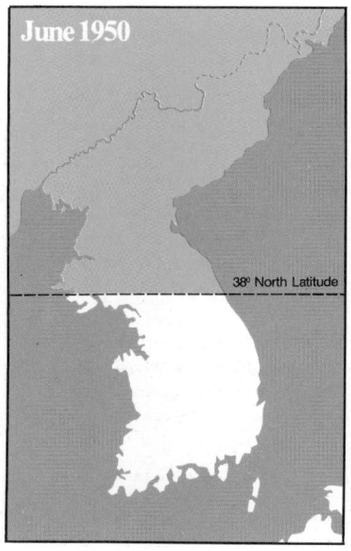

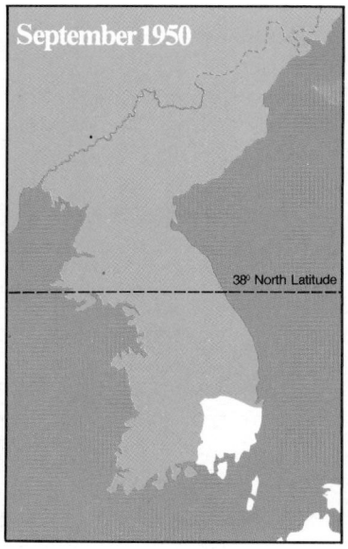

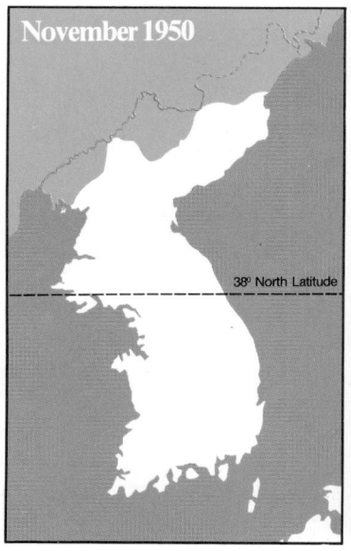

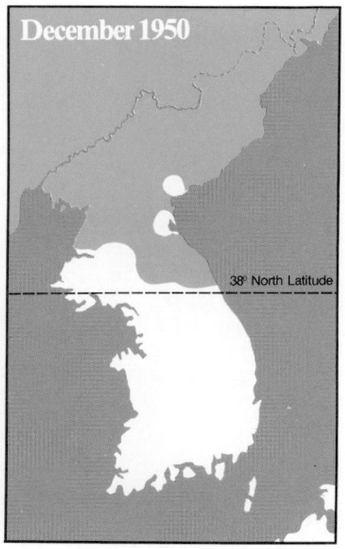

Below: Chief of Staff Vandenberg addresses airmen at a FEAF base in Japan from the wing of an F-80, 13 July 1950.

attack strategic targets north of the Yalu River in China. Both Stratemeyer and MacArthur wanted to use the B-29s to destroy the Yalu bridges, cutting Chinese supply lines. George Marshall, the World War II Chief of Staff, now Secretary of Defense, had ordered that targets within five miles of the Chinese border could not be bombed. This would permit the Chinese not only access across a formidable natural barrier, but a bridgehead and supply area on the Korean side as well. Under protest, Marshall compromised to permit bombing of the Korean end of the Yalu bridges. Bombing one end of a bridge across a twisting boundary river under prohibition of overflying any Chinese territory in the process was one of the most difficult tasks ever undertaken by the US Air Force. The Chinese MiGs could and did attack American bombers over Korea. MiGs and antiaircraft guns could fire on the B-29s from China without fear of retaliation. It was a grueling task, but the bombers did the job.

On the ground, Chinese forces under Lin Piao made a swift and dramatic advance. The last UN forces in North Korea had

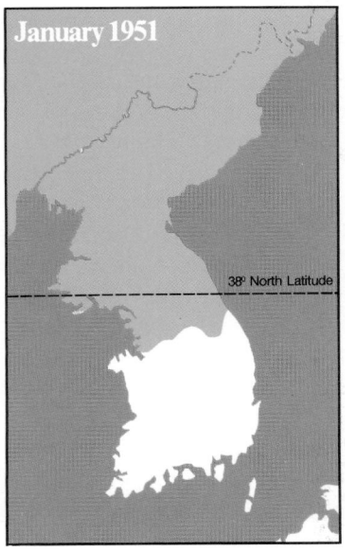

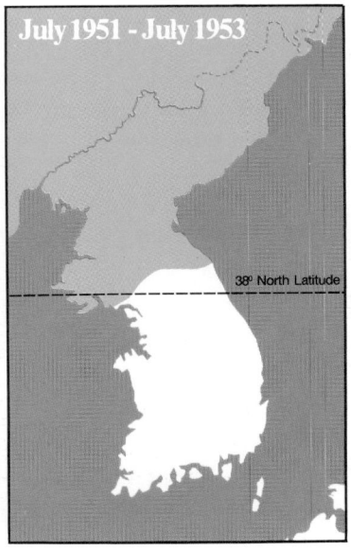

US Air Force Medal of Honor Winners of the Korean War

Maj George Davis, Jr (Dublin, Tex) 10 Feb 1952, Sinuiju-Yalu River, North Korea (KIA 10 Feb 1952)
Maj Charles Loring, Jr (Portland, Me) 22 Nov 1952, Sniper Ridge, North Korea (KIA 22 Nov 1952)
Maj Louis Sebille (Harbor Beach, Mich), 5 Aug 1950, Hamch'ang, South Korea (KIA 5 Aug 1950)
Capt John Walmsley, Jr (Baltimore, Md) 14 Sept 1951, Yangdok, North Korea (KIA 14 Sept 1951)

US Air Force Aces of the Korean War

Capt Joseph McConnell, Jr	16	Maj Donald Adams	6.5
Maj James Jabara	15*	Col Francis Gabreski	6.5*
Capt Manuel Fernandez	14.5	Lt Col George Jones	6.5
Maj George Davis, Jr	14*	Maj Winton Marshall	6.5
Col Royal Baker	13*	1st Lt James Kasler	6
Maj Frederick Blesse	10	Capt Robert Love	6
1st Lt Harold Fischer	10	Maj William Whisner, Jr	5.5*
Lt Col Vermont Garrison	10*	Col Robert Baldwin	5
Col James Johnson	10*	Capt Richard Becker	5
Capt Lonnie Moore	10	Maj Stephen Bettinger	5
Capt Ralph Parr, Jr	10	Maj Richard Creighton	5*
Capt Cecil Foster	9	Capt Clyde Curtin	5
1st Lt James Low	9	Capt Ralph Gibson	5
Maj James Hagerstrom	8.5*	Capt Iven Kincheloe, Jr	5
Capt Robinson Risner	8	Capt Robert Latshaw, Jr	5
Lt Col George Ruddell	8*	Capt Robert Moore	5
1st Lt Henry Buttlemann	7	Capt Dolphin Overton, III	5
Capt Clifford Jolley	7	Col Harrison Thyng	5*
Capt Leonard Lilley	7	Maj William Westcott	5

*Pilot also scored victories in World War II that are not included in this total.

Below: US Air Force aircraft of the Korean War, clockwise from top center: the F-80 Shooting Star, the USAF's first jet fighter; the F-82 Twin Mustang, the first USAF plane to down an enemy aircraft in Korea; the F-94 Starfire, an all-weather interceptor introduced late in the war; and in the rear, the superb F-86 Sabre Jet.

F-80C Shooting Star
Manufacturer: Lockheed Aircraft Corporation
First year of service: 1948
Aircraft type: Single-seat jet fighter
Wingspan: 39ft 11in
Length: 34ft 6in
Weight: 16,856lb (gross)
Range: 1380 miles
Service ceiling: 42,750 feet
Top speed: 580mph
Powerplant: (1) 5400lb thrust Allison J33-A-23 turbojet
Armament: Six .50 caliber machine guns

F-82E Twin Mustang
Manufacturer: North American Aviation
First year of service: 1948
Aircraft type: Long-range escort fighter/interceptor
Wingspan: 51ft 3in
Length: 39ft 1in
Weight: 24,813lb (gross)
Range: 2504 miles
Service ceiling: 40,000 feet
Top speed: 465mph
Powerplant: (2) 1600hp Allison V-1710-143/145
Armament/Capacity: Six .50 caliber machine guns, plus 4000lb of bombs or (25) HVAR rockets

F-86F Sabre Jet
Manufacturer: North American Aviation
First year of service: 1952 (F-86A, 1950)
Aircraft type: Single-seat fighter
Wingspan: 37ft 1in
Length: 37ft 6in
Weight: 16,357lb (gross)
Range: 1270 miles (with drop tanks)
Service ceiling: 50,000 feet
Top/Cruising speed: 690mph
Powerplant: (1) 5970lb thrust General Electric J47-GE-27 turbojet
Armament/Capacity: Six .50 caliber machine guns, plus 2000lbs of ordnance

been surrounded at Hungnam and evacuated by sea on Christmas Eve. Seoul fell to the communists for the second time on 4 January 1951 and UN troops were driven farther south.

By mid-February, however, Chinese supply lines through North Korea were stretched thin and under attack by American planes. The tide began to turn: UN forces spearheaded by the American Eighth Army under General Matthew Ridgway rolled back the communist offensive. Seoul was retaken by UN forces in mid-March, and the front returned to the area of the 38th parallel, after nine months of war that had extended it the length of the Korean Peninsula. UN strategy was redirected from unification of Korea toward preventing additional Chinese advances and negotiating a cease-fire in place. For the next two and a half years the front would move very little, as the two sides dug into static defensive positions maintained until the cease-fire was signed on 27 July 1953.

AIR COMBAT IN KOREA

The Chinese intervention in Korea produced a change in air strategy. The MiG-15 was a more potent adversary than anything the North Koreans had put up, one that drastically reduced the effectiveness of the B-29s. As the Air Force had learned in World War II, the priority was achievement of air superiority in the theater of operations. This had been relatively easy against the North Korean Air Force but was quickly lost to the Russian-built MiG-15, a top-of-the-line jet fighter superior to the Fifth Air Force's F-80s and piston-engine F-51s and F-82s. Nevertheless, in the first jet-to-jet air battle of the war, Lieutenant Russell Brown of the 51st Fighter Interceptor Wing, flying an F-80, shot down a Chinese MiG-15 on 8 November 1950. For the most part, though, the F-80s were outmatched. Because they were 100 mph faster than the F-80s, the MiGs could, for example, dive through a formation of bombers escorted by F-80s and escape without being engaged. In a dogfight, the F-80's .50 caliber machine guns were out-classed by the MiG's 37 mm and 23 mm cannons.

Below: 'Miss Jacque II,' a 136th Fighter Bomber Wing F-84, the first Thunderjet to fly 1000 hours, taxis across metal runway matting after having completed an incredible 363 missions against North Korean targets during the all-out interdiction effort codenamed Operation *Strangle*.

The Lockheed F-80 Shooting Star, a product of World War II technology, had been the first jet propelled combat aircraft in service with the USAAF, although the jet-propelled Bell P-59 Airacomet had preceded it experimentally. Designated P-80 (F-80 from 1948) the Shooting Star entered service in early 1945, but the war ended before it could be used in combat. When the Korean War broke out, the Fifth Air Force had 365 F-80Cs in its operational units. They were pressed into service as both interceptors and ground-attack aircraft and served well until the Chinese intervention. In the end, 277 F-80s were lost in Korea, most to ground fire, only 14 in aerial combat.

The North American F-82, the first American aircraft to score a combat victory in Korea, also originated in the previous war. North American's P-51 Mustang had been the top USAAF air-to-air fighter of World War II; when asked to come up with a bomber escort with extremely long range to escort B-29s, North American had the idea of combining two P-51 fuselages on a single wing. The resulting aircraft, the XP-82 Twin Mustang, first flew in mid-1945, too late to get into the war. The first Twin Mustang finally entered USAF Service under the designation F-82E in May 1948 with SAC. When the war in Korea broke out there were 40 F-82s in the Far East Air Forces, assigned to both the Fifth and the Twentieth. In service, though used sparingly, the F-82s performed well, destroying 20 enemy aircraft. Their downfall was to come from a lack of parts. The plane had been produced in fairly small numbers because production delays made it obsolescent when delivered; thus parts were inadequately stocked. As of December 1949 the USAF classified all its aircraft as either first-line or second-line. A new aircraft would be first-line for three years, then revert to second-line status. The F-82 was never classified first-line and was withdrawn from combat in February 1952.

It is ironic that there were more F-51s (former P-51s) in combat in Korea, and they served longer than the F-82s. The F-51s were common early in the war, as Air National Guard units equipped with them were activated. The last F-51 did not leave combat until 26 January 1953.

F-84E Thunderjet
Manufacturer: Republic Aviation
First year of service: 1949
Aircraft type: Single-seat jet fighter/fighter-bomber
Wingspan: 36ft 5in
Length: 38ft 6in
Weight: 22,463lb (gross)
Range: 1485 miles (1950 miles with drop tanks)
Service ceiling 43,220 feet
Top speed: 613mph
Powerplant: (1) 4900lb thrust Allison J35-A-17 turbojet
Armament/Capacity: Six .50 caliber machine guns, plus up to 4500lbs of ordnance

While the P-51 had been the top USAAF fighter during World War II, the Republic P-47 Thunderbolt was close, and was certainly the top fighter-bomber. With the dawn of the jet age, Republic, like other leading manufacturers, sought to retain its position by updating successful designs. The result was the jet-propelled P-84 Thunderjet, delivered to the USAAF in February 1947 and reaching operational units as the F-84 a year later. In combat over Korea the straight-winged F-84 was found inferior in speed and maneuverability to the swept-wing MiG-15 and a minor improvement over the F-80. Though the F-84 suffered heavy losses during the first year, it found a niche (not unlike that of the P-47) and by the end of 1951 was being called 'the best ground-support jet in the theater.'

While the F-80 and F-84 were clearly not state of the art jets when the Korean War began, the opposite was true of North American's F-86 Sabre Jet, the Air Force's first swept-wing fighter. It had been operational for only a year when the war broke out. When UN forces lost air superiority to the Chinese, F-86s were rushed to the Fifth Air Force, the first 19 arriving at Korean bases on 1 December 1950. They flew on 16 December and downed their first MiG the following day. There were more MiGs in the theater, and the Sabres had their Korean bases temporarily overrun by the Chinese but F-86s operating from bases in Japan soon regained the advantage for UN forces.

Having attained air superiority the FEAF, supported by F-86s, concentrated on destroying all bases in North Korea capable of supporting MiGs, forcing them to operate largely from bases in the area around Antung, China. To prevent the Russian-built fighters from harassing UN forces farther south, the Fifth Air Force set up combat air patrols and fighter sweeps in the sky south of Antung and the Yalu – it became known as 'MiG Alley.' In the first six months there the F-86s downed 44 MiG-15s and damaged 77, with combat losses of only six planes. The fact that 77 were damaged and not destroyed pointed up the persistent deficiency in American aircraft of the period. While the F-86 and its pilots were decidedly superior to the MiGs, their armament, consisting of six nose-mounted Colt Browning .50 caliber machine guns was less than ideal for the short target time of a high-speed jet dogfight.

By the fall of 1952, the F-86As were being replaced by F-86Es and F-86Fs with more provision for external fuel tanks, which increased their range. Also introduced on the later F-86s were extended, solid wing leading edges that increased operating altitude (by 4000 feet), speed and rate of climb. Though machine guns were still the basic armament, there was provision for eight High Velocity Aerial Rockets (HVAR). A 20 mm Cannon was tested in combat, though not placed widely into service.

The basic combat air patrol or fighter sweep involved 'gaggles' of F-86s in four-plane cells patroling MiG Alley to lure the enemy into combat or intercept MiGs trying to slip through to

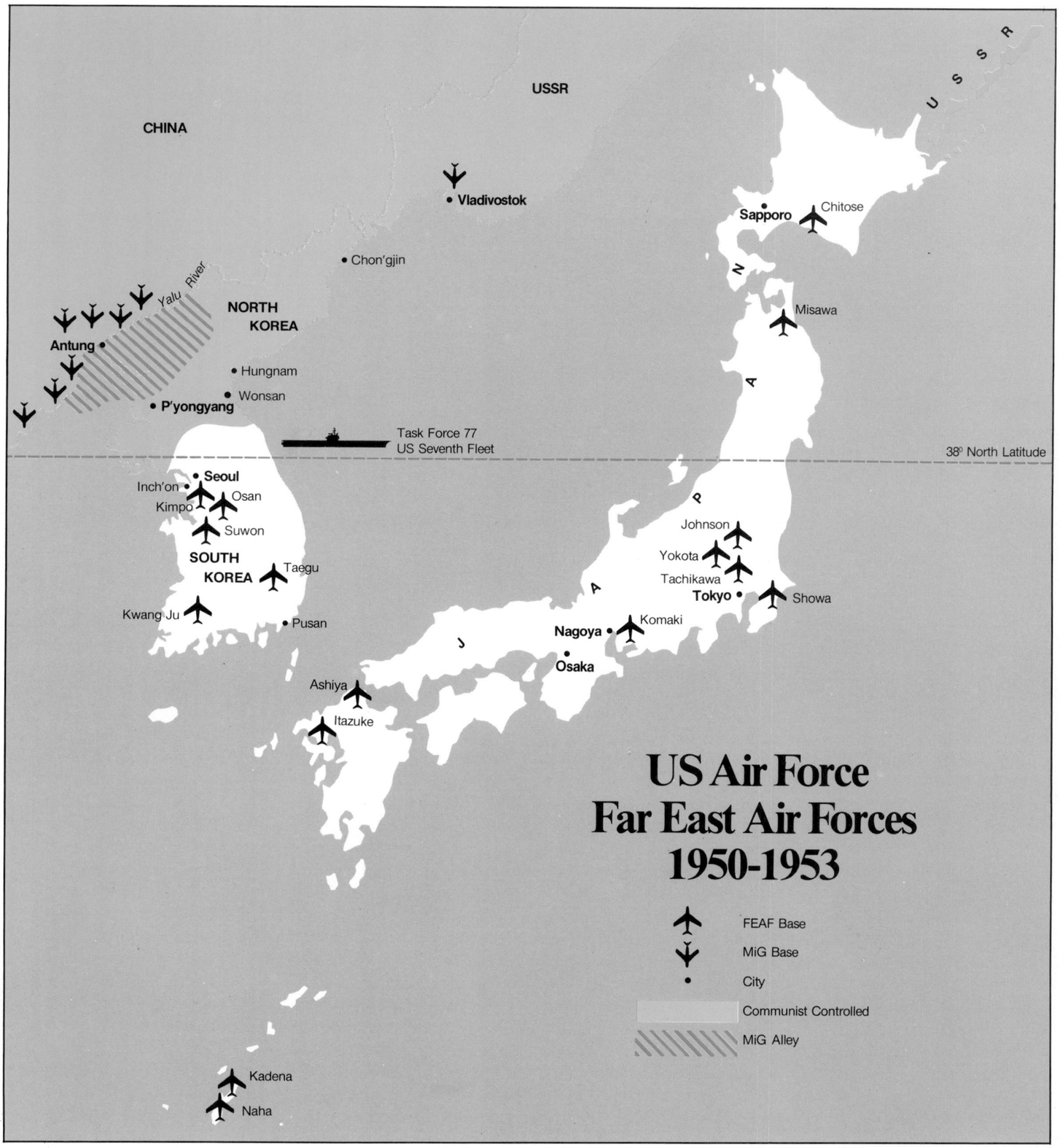

Below: A damaged F-80 was captured making a wheels-up 170 mph landing in this remarkable photo by FEAF planning engineer Frank Hopkins. Note the damage from an enemy shell just above the wing.

Below: The same F-80 seen at left, after a safe landing in a rice paddy. A wheels-up landing on the hard surface of the nearby runway could have been disastrous.

Above: Its hydraulic system shot out over North Korea, this B-26 comes in for a belly landing. No one was injured.

Below: Using the Y in the track as his aiming point, a B-26 bombardier napalms a group of North Korean rail cars south of Wonsan.

Below: MiG masters on patrol. US Air Force F-86s of the 51st Fighter Interceptor Wing prowl MiG Alley in search of the enemy. The 51st was led by Colonel Francis Gabreski, the third-highest-scoring ace of World War II (28 victories), who added six and a half kills to his score in Korea.

Below: A FEAF Fifth Air Force Sabre taxis past a pair of MATS transports (a C-47 and in the foreground a C-54) at a busy Korean airfield during March 1951.

Right: A US Air Force C-119 Flying Boxcar prepares to air-drop supplies to United Nations troops in the rugged mountains of Korea. In Korea transport aircraft turned days into hours in the delivery of essential supplies.

attack F-80 or F-84 fighter bombers. Once engaged, the classic maneuver was to get behind the enemy and attack from the six o'clock position. Most aerial victories in Korea, as in World War II, were from six o'clock and achieved with the forward-mounted machine guns.

The enemy aircraft was almost always the MiG-15, designed and produced in the Soviet Union by the Mikoyan-Gurevich design bureau (hence the initials). The swept-wing MiG-15 was the top Soviet fighter, originating in the same German technology that produced the American swept-wing aircraft. The MiG-15 entered Soviet service in August 1948, and was promptly supplied to Poland and to China before the latter's incursion into Korea. It is no secret that the planes encountered by American pilots in MiG Alley, officially Chinese and North Korean, were often flown by Russian and Polish pilots who were being rotated through the Chinese squadrons for six-week periods for practical combat experience. The Soviet involvement was discovered early in the war when Russian pilots were heard conversing on their radios, a fact that Chief of Staff Vandenberg hastened to point out. It was also reported that one of the Soviet pilots shot down by the Americans was the son of Josef Stalin.

In the final tally, the performance of the American pilots was excellent despite the handicap of restrictive rules of engagement. The F-86 pilots shot down 792 MiGs and lost only 78 Sabres. In all, 1020 enemy aircraft were shot down by the USAF in the Korean War, 839 of them MiG-15s.

The US Air Force flew 716,979 sorties in its first war, firing 183 million rounds of ammunition and 511,329 rockets, dropping 448,366 tons of bombs and nine million gallons of napalm. The sorties destroyed 9417 railroad cars, 869 locomotives and 75,749 vehicles, including 1160 enemy tanks. In addition to the 1020 enemy aircraft confirmed as destroyed, another 182 were probable kills and at least another 1010 were damaged. Against this, the US Air Force lost 104 aircraft of all types in aerial combat, 544 to ground fire and 153 to other causes. Away from the front, the Military Air Transport Service carried 670,000 tons of materiel and 2,700,000 passengers and evacuated 325,000 wounded to hospitals in the States aboard such aircraft as specially fitted Boeing C-97C Stratofreighters.

On the ground, the Korean War was a brutal, frustrating affair, especially from the fall of 1951 to the cease-fire in the summer of 1953, when the situation resembled the hellish trench warfare of World War I. In the air, however, the Korean War was a triumph for American air power and for the men and planes of the new US Air Force.

GENERAL NATHAN FARRAGUT TWINING
Third USAF Chief of Staff

Nathan Twining was born on 11 October 1897 in Monroe, Wisconsin. He began active service in June 1916 with the Third Oregon Infantry on Mexican border duty. In 1917 he entered the US Military Academy, graduating in November 1918. In July 1919 he was assigned to the American Forces in Germany as an observer. His aviation career began in August 1923, when he entered Primary Flying School at Brooks Field, Texas. He graduated from Advanced Flying School at nearby Kelly Field in September 1924 and served as an instructor at Brooks Field for two years until he was transferred to March Field, California. In February 1929 he joined the 18th Pursuit Group at Schofield Barracks, Hawaii.

During the early 1930s he served at several US posts, including duty as an engineering officer with the US Army Air Mail Service. In June 1937 he graduated from the Command General Staff College and was assigned to the San Antonio Air Depot as Technical Supervisor. In August 1940 he was assigned to Washington, where he served at US Air Corps (later USAAF) headquarters until July 1942, when he went to the South Pacific as Chief of Staff to General M F Harmon, Commanding General of Army Forces in the theater. In January 1943 he became Commander of the newly formed 13th Air Force, and on 25 July joint commander of all Allied Air Forces in the South Pacific. In November 1943 he assumed command of the 15th Air Force in Italy and two months later became Commander of the Allied Mediterranean Strategic Air Forces. On 2 August 1945 he succeeded Curtis LeMay as Commander of the Twentieth Air Force in the Pacific, which a few days later dropped the first atomic bomb.

After the war General Twining served as Commander of the Air Materiel Command and of the Unified Alaskan Command. He became USAF Vice-Chief of Staff in 1950 and Chief of Staff of the Air Force on 30 June 1953. On 15 August 1957 General Twining became the first USAF Officer to be named Chairman of the Joint Chiefs of Staff. He retired on 30 September 1960 and stayed on in Washington as Vice-Chairman of the Textbook Division of the Holt, Rinehart and Winston Publishing Company. General Twining died of cardio-pulmonary arrest at Wilford Hall USAF Medical Center, on 29 March 1982 and is buried at Arlington National Cemetery.

GENERAL THOMAS DRESSER WHITE
Fourth USAF Chief of Staff

Thomas D White was born on 6 August 1901 in Walker, Minnesota, and graduated from the US Military Academy on 2 July 1920. His first active duty was with the 14th Infantry at Fort Davis in the Canal Zone. In September 1924 he entered Primary Flying School at Brooks Field, Texas, graduating from Advanced Flying School one year later. After duty with the 99th Observation Squadron at Bolling Field, he was sent to Peking in 1927 where he spent four years learning the Chinese language. Upon his return to the US he was assigned to Air Corps Headquarters. In February 1934 he was named Assistant Military Attaché for Air to Russia and a year later took up the same post in Rome.

In April 1940, after graduating from the Command and General Staff School at Fort Leavenworth, he became Military Attaché (later Chief of the Military Air Mission) to Brazil. Returning to the United States in March 1942, he served as Chief of Staff of the Third Air Force, headquartered at Tampa, Florida, and in January 1944, he became Assistant Chief of the Air Staff for Intelligence. In September 1944 he went to the South Pacific as Deputy Commander of the Thirteenth Air Force and nine months later became Commander of the Seventh Air Force in Okinawa. In January 1946 he returned with the Seventh to Hawaii; in October 1947 he assumed Command of the Fifth Air Force in Japan.

In October 1948 General White was transferred to the Office of the Secretary of the Air Force in Washington, and in July 1951 he was named USAF Deputy Chief of Staff for Operations. On 30 June 1953 he was promoted to four-star General rank and appointed Vice-Chief of Staff. He became US Air Force Chief of Staff on 1 July 1957. During his tenure, the Air Force test-fired its first air-to-air nuclear rocket, the Genie, over Yucca Flat, Nevada, and became operational with its first Atlas ICBM. General White retired on 30 June 1961 and died on 22 December 1965.

GENERAL CURTIS EMERSON LeMAY
Fifth USAF Chief of Staff

Curtis LeMay was born on 15 November 1906 and graduated from Ohio State University. In 1928 he entered the Army as a flying cadet, completing his training in October 1929. His first tour of duty was with the 27th Pursuit Squadron at Selfridge Field in Michigan. After several tours with fighter squadrons, he transferred to bombers in 1937. LeMay participated in a number of long-range bomber exercises including the first mass deployment of B-17s to South America in 1938.

In 1942 he organized and trained the 305th Bomb Group and led it into combat against Germany. He developed the formation procedures and bombing techniques used by B-17 bomber units throughout the European theater. As Commanding General of the Third Bomb Division, he led the famous B-17 raid on Regensberg in 1943. In July 1944 he was transferred to the Pacific to direct strategic bombing efforts against Japan. After the war, LeMay returned to the US (piloting a B-29 nonstop from Hokkaido to Chicago) to become Deputy Chief of the Air Staff for Research and Development.

In October 1947 he went to Wiesbaden, Germany, to take up command of USAFE. In this position General LeMay organized the Berlin Airlift that supplied the city for a year while it was blockaded by Russian forces. On 16 October 1948 he became Commander of the Strategic Air Command, a post he held for nearly a decade. During this time he built up SAC from remnants of World War II that survived demobilization into an unprecedented all-jet bomber force.

In July 1957 General LeMay became Air Force Vice-Chief of Staff, and on 30 July 1961 Chief of Staff. During his tenure, the first Minuteman ICBM Wing became operational, as did the entire Titan II force. He oversaw the introduction of USAF combat forces in Southeast Asia and formulated the air-war plan that could have – had it been implemented – achieved decisive results against the enemy and ended the war much sooner, saving thousands of American lives.

General LeMay retired on 31 January 1965 but remained active in national defense matters. In 1968 he was selected as the vice-presidential candidate of the American Independent Party. In the election, he and the AIP presidential candidate, George Corley Wallace, gained more of the popular vote than any third-party candidacy in American history, winning five states and nearly ten million votes nationwide. In terms of electoral votes, the AIP earned more than any third-party bid since Theodore Roosevelt's Progressive (Bull Moose) Party came in second in the 1912 election.

GENERAL JOHN PAUL McCONNELL
Sixth USAF Chief of Staff

John McConnell was born in Booneville, Arkansas, on 7 February 1908, and graduated from the US Military Academy at West Point in 1932. He received his pilot's wings in 1933 and served in a variety of operational and administrative positions for the next decade. In November 1944 Colonel McConnell became Chief of Staff of the China/Burma/India (CBI) Air Force Training Command at Karachi, British India. He served for eight months with the Third Allied Tactical Air Force at Comilla, India, taking part in combat operations against the Japanese in Burma. He next became Senior Air Staff Officer in the Southeast Asia Air Command at Kandy, Ceylon, a post he held from September 1944 until June 1945.

After the war, General McConnell was named Senior Air Advisor to the Chinese Government. In 1947 he returned to the United States as Chief of the Reserve and National Guard Division, and in 1950 he went to England as Deputy Commander and later Commander of SAC's Third Air Division. He spent four years as Director of Plans for SAC at Offutt AFB before being named Commander of SAC's Second Air Force in 1957. In 1962, after a year as Vice-Commander-in-Chief of SAC, he was promoted to four-star rank and sent to Europe as Deputy Commander of the unified European Command. He was appointed USAF Vice-Chief of Staff in 1964 and became Chief of Staff on 1 February 1965. During his tenure, General McConnell presided over the buildup of USAF forces in Southeast Asia, to which he made several trips. He retired on 31 July 1969, the same month that the USAF supported the first manned lunar landing.

GENERAL JOHN DALE RYAN
Seventh USAF Chief of Staff

John Ryan was born on 10 December 1915 in Cherokee, Iowa, and graduated from the US Military Academy at West Point in 1938. He received his pilot's wings the following year and served as a flight instructor until January 1942. He went on to serve as Director of Training at Midland Field, Texas, where he was instrumental in establishing an advanced bombardier training school. He served with the Second Air Force at Colorado Springs before being transferred to the Fifteenth Air Force in Italy in February 1944.

He returned to Midland Field after the war and served briefly with the Air Training Command before being assigned to SAC in April 1946. He moved up the ladder in SAC as commander of the 58th Bomb Wing, 509th Bomb Wing, 97th Bomb Wing and the 810th Air Division before becoming Director of Materiel at SAC Headquarters in June 1956. In 1960 General Ryan assumed command of SAC's Sixteenth Air Force in Spain and a year later of SAC's Second Air Force at Barksdale AFB in Louisiana. After a year in Washington as USAF Inspector General, he was named Vice-Commander-in-Chief of SAC in August 1964.

In December 1964 General Ryan became Commander of SAC, and three years later Commander in Chief of PACAF, which he led through the peak of its war effort in Southeast Asia. He became USAF Vice-Chief of Staff in August 1968 and Chief of Staff a year later. During his tenure, the Air Force ended its inconclusive project *Blue Book* study of Unidentified Flying Objects (UFOs) (1969). Gen Ryan retired effective 31 July 1973.

GENERAL GEORGE SCRATCHLEY BROWN
Eighth USAF Chief of Staff

George S Brown was born in Montclair, New Jersey, on 17 August 1918 and graduated from the US Military Academy at West Point in 1941, earning his wings at Kelly Field the following year. That August his group, the 93rd Bomb Group, became the first B-24 wing to join the Eighth Air Force in its strategic offensive against Germany. He received the Distinguished Service Cross for his part in the daring low-level bombing raid on the German petroleum facilities at Ploesti, Rumania (1 August 1943).

In May 1945 Colonel Brown was assigned to ATC as Assistant Operations Officer; the following year he went to ADC to take up a similar role. In May 1952 he became Director of Operations with the Fifth Air Force in Korea. After the Korean War he attended the National War College and held several positions on the Air Staff and in the Office of the Secretary of the Air Force in Washington. In 1963 General Brown became Commander of the MATS Eastern Transport Air Force at McGuire AFB and a year later was selected to organize the JCS Joint Task Force II for weapons-systems testing.

After two years in Washington, DC, General Brown took command of the Seventh Air Force in Vietnam (August 1966). In September 1970 he was named Commander of the Air Force Systems Command at Andrews AFB. On 1 August 1973, the 40th anniversary of the famed Ploesti raid, General Brown became Chief of Staff of the US Air Force. Less than a year later, 1 July 1974, he became Chairman of the Joint Chiefs of Staff, the second USAF officer to hold the position. He retired as JCS Chairman on 21 June 1978.

GENERAL DAVID C JONES
Ninth USAF Chief of Staff

David C Jones was born on 9 July 1921 in Aberdeen, South Dakota, and earned his wings at Roswell Field, New Mexico, in 1943. He was the first USAF Chief of Staff not to have served in combat in World War II and one of two chiefs (the other was Curtis LeMay) who did not attend the US Military Academy at West Point. He did, however serve in combat in the Korean War, flying more than 300 hours of bombing missions over North Korea with the 19th Bomb Squadron out of March AFB. After the Korean War he served with SAC until August 1959, when he enrolled in the National War College in Washington.

Beginning in July 1960 Colonel Jones was assigned to the Pentagon for four years, after which he served for a year with TAC before being assigned to Plans and Operations with USAFE until January 1969. When he left USAFE, General Jones served for six months as Vice-Commander of the Seventh Air Force in Vietnam before taking command of SAC's Second Air Force.

In April 1971 General Jones returned to USAFE as Vice-Commander, being promoted to Commander in August of the same year. On 1 July 1974, he became USAF Chief of Staff, and on 1 July 1978 he succeeded Air Force General George Brown as Chairman of the Joint Chiefs of Staff, a position he held for the next four years.

THE US AIR FORCE IN SOUTHEAST ASIA

GOING TO WAR

In April 1961 the 4400th Combat Crew Training Squadron was activated at Eglin AFB in Florida: in October it was deployed to South Vietnam to train the ramshackle South Vietnam Air Force (RVNAF) in the rudiments of tactical air power as a tool of counterinsurgency. In this way the US Air Force made its unheralded entry into what began as a limited exercise in counterinsurgency, but would become the longest and costliest war in American history.

It began in the jungles and mountains of a remnant of the French Empire adjacent to the South China Sea, where the bulk of the Asian land mass meets the Malay Peninsula and the Indonesian archipelago. It was fought in those rugged backwoods where international boundaries exist only on maps read by the uninitiated, and in the blue tropical skies over those jungles where the cumulus clouds of the monsoon season can be as unmerciful to a million-dollar jet fighter as the most intense ground fire. It would be fought between a force with the best technology in the world but no sense of strategic purpose and a force of limited means but a firm idea of its objective.

That area of Southeast Asia which later became the nations of Vietnam, Cambodia and Laos had been ruled by France as French Indochina from the mid-19th century until World War II. When France was defeated by Germany in 1940, Japan occupied Indochina. When Indochina was liberated from Japanese control at the end of the war, France attempted to reinstate its rule over the lost colony. An eight-year war ensued between France and various nationalist guerrilla groups, notably the communist Viet Minh led by Ho Chi Minh. The climactic defeat for the French came in 1954 when the Viet Minh overran their garrison at Dien Bien Phu. The French withdrew from Indochina and as a result of accords signed in Geneva in 1954, Vietnam was partitioned at the 17th parallel, the northern part becoming the communist-controlled Democratic Republic of Vietnam under Ho Chi Minh, and the Southern part the Republic of Vietnam, whose first president was Ngo Dinh Diem.

North Vietnam, like North Korea a few years earlier, was bent on unifying the divided nation under a single communist government. Unlike the North Koreans, who used an overt conventional attack, Ho Chi Minh and his able military commander General Vo Nguyen Giap waged a protracted guerrilla war similar to that which had dislodged the French. The US, meanwhile, decided to support the noncommunist governments of Southeast Asia, including South Vietnam, to prevent them

Above: **Chief of Staff General John McConnell, Marine Corps General Lew Walt and Seventh Air Force commander Joseph Moore confer at Bien Hoa AB in 1965 during one of the Chief's visits to South Vietnam.**

Right; **US Air Force *Pack Train* C-123s drop South Vietnamese paratroops into Tay Ninh Province during Operation *Phi Hoa II* in March 1963. The C-123s were among the first USAF aircraft to serve in Vietnam.**

Above: A veteran of three wars, the B-26 attack bomber, seen here with a C-123 at Korat RTAFB in Thailand with its rocket racks and eight machine guns loaded, was the right plane at the right time for *Farm Gate.*

Below: A Gleaming U-10 observation plane parked on the steel-mesh flight line matting at Korat. Piston-engined aircraft like the U-10 and the T-28s seen behind it were typical of the aircraft committed by the USAF early in the war.

from being pulled into the communist orbit. For this purpose, the Eisenhower Administration sponsored in 1955 the establishment of the Southeast Asia Treaty Organization (SEATO) and began supplying military aid to South Vietnam, as well as neighboring Cambodia, Laos and Thailand. In 1960 North Vietnam established in the jungles and backwaters of South Vietnam that they had infiltrated an entity they called the National Liberation Front (NLF) or Viet Cong (VC). Because it was composed largely of native South Vietnamese and Vietnamese from the north who had come south when the country was partitioned, the NLF had the appearance of an indigenous guerrilla movement. North Vietnam could then conduct the war through the Viet Cong, establishing the fiction that the ensuing guerrilla war was a civil war within South Vietnam. When North Vietnamese regular forces were introduced later it could be said that they intervened in support of one side in this civil war. The fact that the NLF was not a completely independent liberation movement would not be clear until 1975, when the North Vietnamese promptly disbanded the NLF and dissolved South Vietnam after achieving victory through conventional warfare.

In 1961 Soviet Premier Nikita Khrushchev proclaimed that communist influence would be spread around the world by means of 'wars of liberation.' With the Viet Cong already active in South Vietnam, and Soviet aircraft dropping supplies to communist insurgents in Laos, Southeast Asia seemed ripe for picking by such a war. The Kennedy Administration responded by sending both Army Special Forces and Air Force Air Commandos to South Vietnam as 'advisors' to help build a South Vietnamese force to resist the NLF. The 4400th Combat Crew Training Squadron, known as *Jungle Jim*, was the first US Air Force unit to become involved. After its activation on 14 April, the President authorized deployment of Detachment 2A (11 October 1961) to Bien Hoa AB near Saigon under the designation First Air Commando Group, codenamed *Farm Gate*. The Group was composed of 151 men with eight North American T-28 Trainers refitted as attack aircraft, four World War II vintage Douglas B-26s (previously designated A-26) and four aging C-47 Skytrains, all marked as South Vietnamese aircraft. It was an unimpressive assortment, but *Farm Gate's* stated function was to train the South Vietnam Air Force (RVNAF). Because the training missions were flown de facto in actual combat, and because the US aircraft carried RVNAF markings, missions had to include at least one RVNAF crew member. By the fall of 1961 the Viet Cong controlled large portions of rural South Vietnam and there was a strong need for air support. Given the limited RVNAF capability to fly the missions, and the need to train under combat conditions, *Farm Gate* found itself at war.

The United States, as part of its SEATO commitment, had established in 1955 the Military Assistance Advisory Group, Vietnam (MAAG) to co-ordinate military assistance to South Vietnam. Now, with an active USAF role developing, the Thirteenth Air Force of the Pacific Air Forces (PACAF) set up an advance headquarters (ADVON) on 15 November for its Second Air Division at Tan Son Nhut Airport in Saigon to co-ordinate USAF activities in South Vietnam. Detachments were also established at Nha Trang and Danang Air Bases. Though technically part of the Thirteenth Air Force, based at Clark AB in the Philippines, the Second Air Division ADVON was under operational control of MAAG in Saigon. Also under Second Air Division control were four 15th Tactical Reconnais-

Below: Pilots and ground crews of the 64th Fighter Interceptor Squadron scramble for *Candy Machine* F-102s at Danang AB.

sance Squadron RF-101C Voodoo reconnaissance aircraft deployed to Tan Son Nhut AB between 20 October and 21 November from Kadena AB, Okinawa, under the code name *Pipe Stem*. The four Voodoos, and four that followed from the 45th TRS at Misawa AB, Japan (code name *Able Mabel*), flew 197 photo-reconnaissance missions over South Vietnam and Laos before the end of the year observing Viet Cong supply routes and hideouts.

The *Farm Gate* missions had been underway for a scant two months when it became clear that the need for air support in the field was beyond the capability of the RVNAF, even augmented by *Farm Gate* crews. Thus in December the Joint Chiefs of Staff (JCS), through PACAF, directed development of a tactical air-control system for combat introduction of US Air Force crews flying aircraft with American markings. The system would become effective on New Year's Day 1962 under the code name *Barn Door* and would co-ordinate RVNAF and USAF combat, recon and airlift activities. The US Air Force contingent would include units assigned to the Second Air Division ADVON and those on temporary duty (TDY) in Vietnam from other PACAF units and from Stateside TAC units. On 8 February 1962, MAAG was replaced by the Military Assistance Command, Vietnam (MACV) under US Army General Paul Harkins. MACV was to function as an umbrella group to co-ordinate the growing American military role in South Vietnam. With the situation in Laos also deteriorating, President Kennedy authorized deployment of forces to Thailand as well. This force would be composed of Air Force, Army and Marine units designated Joint Task Force 116. Proposals for a unified Southeast Asia (Thailand-Vietnam) Command directly under the JCS were vetoed by the Commander in Chief, Pacific (CINCPAC), Admiral Harry Felt, who wanted to keep Southeast Asia activities under the Pacific Theater Command rather than establish a new theater command. Thus a Military Assistance Command, Thailand (MACTHAI) absorbed Joint Task Force 116 and was established alongside MACV, both under CINCPAC control. MACTHAI was activated on 13 May 1962, but it was not until Air Force Chief of Staff General Curtis LeMay upgraded the Second Air Division ADVON to reinforced air-division status (8 October) that air units in both countries came under a single unified command.

By the end of 1962 the need for co-ordinated control of air power highlighted an evolving conflict between the Air Force and the US Army. Under Executive Order 9877 (1947) the Army had been permitted to retain light aircraft and helicopters. The Army was now operating its C-7A Caribou twin-engine STOL transports in Vietnam, but did not have the air operations and planning staff needed to control their operations effectively or to co-ordinate them with other – especially Air Force – operations in-country. When this was brought to the attention of CINCPAC, the Caribous were placed under operational control of the USAF Second Air Division Commander. The C-7s would remain US Army property until January 1967, when the 134 remaining Caribous were turned over to the Air Force.

One of the major problems encountered by crews flying the early *Farm Gate* missions was the difficulty or impossiblity of seeing enemy positions hidden in the dense jungle. Air Force planners tackled the problem, and late in 1961 came up with the idea of eliminating the jungle canopy that obscured the view of the ground. Because of moisture and frequent rain, it would be impossible to burn down all the trees (though it would be attempted in Operation *Sherwood Forest* four years later), so it was decided to spray the jungles with a powerful herbicide or weed killer. Six specially modified C-123 transports, equipped with spray bars and chemical tanks, were deployed to Vietnam by TAC via Clark AB. The operation was code named *Ranch Hand* and spraying began on 13 January 1962. The chemical defoliant used was manufactured by Dow Chemical and called *Agent Orange*. Though it was not known at the time, the active ingredient in *Agent Orange*, Dioxin, would ultimately be responsible for dangerous side effects. The legacy of *Agent Orange* was one of the most devastating to be brought home by returning Vietnam War veterans. Many *Ranch Hand* crewmen discovered years later that Dioxin was responsible for sterility in some of them and birth defects in the children of others. Ironically, the *Ranch Hand* operation was never very effective in its mission of destroying Viet Cong hideouts. When the health hazards related to *Agent Orange* were discovered, restrictions placed on its use by the Secretary of Defense resulted in its discontinuation after May 1970. However, the use of *Herbicide White* continued until 16 January 1971. It would be over twenty years before *Ranch* Hand crews would begin receiving govern-

Below: A U-10 of the Fifth Special Operations Squadron out of Nha Trang AB and Bien Thuy AB scatters psychological warfare leaflets over the highlands.

ment compensation for this insidious service-related disability. Coincidentally, the first USAF aircraft lost in Southeast Asia was a *Ranch Hand* C-123 that crashed, killing the three men on board, on 2 February 1962 while spraying defoliant on a Viet Cong ambush site.

Throughout 1961-63 US Air Force activities were geared primarily toward assisting the South Vietnamese Army (ARVN) and Air Force rather than taking a leading air-power role. The mission of *Farm Gate*, which was augmented by 10 B-26s, 5 T-28s and a pair of C-47s, was ground support and related training operations. Prop-driven aircraft were selected because their slower speed made them more suitable for ground support than jets, and because it was felt that the use of jets would give the USAF much too high a profile in the war. In addition to the *Ranch Hand* operations, the USAF C-123s were being used under the code names *Saw Buck* and *Mule Train* as assault transports, to augment RVNAF C-47s in paratroop drops. Two notable operations occurred on 29 June 1962 and 24 March 1963, when up to 16 *Mule Train* C-123s and 10 RVNAF C-47s dropped over a thousand (ARVN) paratroopers in offensive operations northwest of Saigon. Though no jet aircraft were authorized for combat in South Vietnam, the *Able Mable* RF-101C reconnaissance aircraft that had been deployed to Tan Son Nhut with their photo-processing unit continued their recon flights, completing a thousand sorties by December 1962. In addition to the RF-101s, PACAF F-102 all-weather interceptors were brought into Tan Son Nhut and other bases on a rotational TDY basis to safeguard the growing American air presence against the possibility of enemy air attack from North Vietnam. The first F-102s were brought in from Clark AB on 21 March 1962 under the code name *Water Glass* when unidentified radar tracks were detected over South Vietnam. The classified *Water Glass* deployments continued, as did the Operation *Bell Tone* deployments of F-100s and F-102s to Thailand (begun in 1961); when *Water Glass* was compromised in December of 1963, the code name was changed to *Candy Machine*. In June of the following year PACAF *Candy Machine* F-102s were deployed to Danang AB in a more overt demonstration of PACAF deployment capabilities.

While air activities increased in Southeast Asia, the political situation began to deteriorate late in 1963. In Cambodia, Prince Norodom Sihanouk, who had been successfully wooed by the Soviets, was terminating his agreements with the Americans and being rewarded with four Soviet MiGs and 27 antiaircraft guns. Farther down the Mekong River in Saigon, President Diem, who had ruled South Vietnam for nearly a decade, was assassinated on 1 November and his government overthrown in a coup led by ARVN General Duong Van 'Big' Minh. This created a climate of confusion that encouraged the Viet Cong. Three weeks after Diem was gunned down in Saigon, American President John Kennedy was assassinated in Dallas, Texas, and succeeded by Vice-President Lyndon Johnson. Two weeks to the day after President Kennedy was interred at Arlington National Cemetery, Prime Minister Sarit Thanarat of Thailand was dead and his country ruled by General Thanom Kittikachorn. In less than six weeks leadership of all the major noncommunist powers involved in the conflict in Southeast Asia had changed suddenly and dramatically. Thailand was now under military rule. The

Below: A RVNAF A-1H Skyraider unleashes a bomb on a Vietcong target.

Above: A US Air Force A-1E Skyraider blasts a Vietcong hideout in Kin Trong Province, May 1965.

Below: Helmet in hand, RVNAF pilot Lt Duy Chanh arrives at his Bien Hoa based Skyraider, readied for a 23 November 1963 mission. The RVNAF insignia was similar to that of the USAF, but the sidebars were entirely red on yellow after the South Vietnamese flag, an abbreviated form of which appeared on the tail.

Below: B-57 Canberras, such as this pair seen over the Mekong Delta, were the first USAF jets to fly combat missions in South Vietnam.

Bottom: Defense Secretary Robert McNamara with strongman Khanh, center, at Tan Son Nhut in 1964.

change from Kennedy to Johnson was a radical shift of personalities and leadership styles, and the United States had in Lyndon Johnson the man who, more than any other, would shape America's policy in its longest and costliest war. The change in South Vietnam would also be crucial. From the reasonably stable, if corrupt, Diem regime the country drifted through a succession of erratic military governments (Minh would be ousted by Maj Gen Nguyen Khanh after less than three months in office) that would pave the way for the autocratic Thieu.

It was against this backdrop that the new Johnson Administration set about formulating the policy that would lead to major American involvement in the war in Southeast Asia.

THE GULF OF TONKIN

Through the first half of 1964 the emphasis was on winding down American involvement in South Vietnam. In May Secretary of Defense Robert McNamara was in Saigon, where he restated administration policy that US Air Force personnel would be out of the country in 'a matter of months' and that meanwhile they should limit their activities to providing 'genuine training' only and leave combat operations to the RVNAF. The capabilities of the Second Air Division were wearing thin anyway. The aging prop planes that had come in with *Farm Gate* were starting to fail. The B-26s had been grounded since 11 February when a wing on one of them failed on a combat mission. On 1 April the last of the B-26s were flown

Above: As the setting sun turns the delta rice paddies to rivers of fire, a lone USAF A-1E Skyraider wings home from a mission on the Ca Mau Peninsula south of Saigon.

Far left: A US Air Force C-123 Provider on a *Ranch Hand* defoliation mission about 48 miles east of Saigon in February 1962.

Left: A group of *Ranch Hand* C-123s of the 12th Air Commando Squadron spread their lethal load along a South Vietnam canal. Agent Orange was an amalgram of the common and long-used weed killer 2,4-D and the dioxin-riddled 2,4,5-T developed by Dow and Monsanto.

Above right: Its bomb load expended, a US Air Force A-1E Skyraider rolls down through light cloud cover to make a strafing run against Vietcong positions along the Saigon River south of the South Vietnamese capital.

out to Clark AB, their mission assumed by the T-28 fleet. The attack-modified T-28s were near the end of their usefulness too, and wing failures in combat on 24 March and 9 April led Second Air Division commander Major General J H Moore to note that his Division was 'practically out of business.' By the time of the McNamara visit in May, however, the T-28s had been largely replaced by A-1 Skyraiders, with six RVNAF Squadrons scheduled to be equipped with the newer A-1H as the USAF combat squadrons withdrew.

In June 1964 a high-level strategy conference was held at CINCPAC headquarters in Honolulu. Chairman of the Joint Chiefs of Staff General Maxwell Taylor and Ambassador Henry Cabot Lodge were there; Secretary McNamara flew in from Saigon; Secretary of State Dean Rusk attended, and General William Westmoreland who would soon replace General Harkins as MACV Commander. The conferees, representing the highest levels of the US Government and military, were walking a tightrope between their desire to resolve a conflict against communist aggression to which they were already committed and their wish to avoid getting too deeply involved in a foreign war alongside a nation governed by a revolving door of unstable military strongmen. It was decided that the United States would continue to build up South Vietnamese forces and provide air and ground support while keeping a low profile. Emphasis would be on resolving the conflict on the ground in South Vietnam rather than through use of a decisive strategic air offensive against enemy supply centers in North Vietnam, as had been proposed by USAF Chief of Staff Curtis LeMay. Though the situation would change dramatically two months later, the conference was to set the tone for the next four years based on the situation as it existed in June 1964.

On the night of 2 August 1964 the scenario changed decisively. North Vietnamese torpedo boats attacked the USS *Maddox*, an American destroyer, in the Gulf of Tonkin off North Vietnam.

Two nights later the torpedo boats tangled with the *Maddox* again, and with the destroyer USS *Turner Joy* as well. This represented a serious escalation and General LeMay used the opportunity to call again for a decisive air offensive against the North Vietnamese. The administration did not take up LeMay's idea. President Johnson announced that while 'seeking no wider war' the United States would honor its commitments and would respond to the attacks. On 5 August, under the code name *Pierce Arrow*, US Navy F-8s based on carriers in the Gulf of Tonkin retaliated by bombing North Vietnamese patrol boat bases and fuel storage dumps in southernmost North Vietnam. On the same day PACAF deployed B-57 tactical bombers and F-100s to Bien Hoa AB and Danang AB. Over the next nine days eighteen PACAF F-105 fighter bombers from the 36th Tactical Fighter Squadron at Yakota AB, Japan, deployed to Korat RTAFB, Thailand. On 7 August the US Congress passed the Gulf of Tonkin Resolution, giving the President power to 'take all necessary measures to repel any armed attack against the forces of the United States and to prevent further aggression.' The United States had traded a low profile for a wider war.

THE WIDER WAR

From an earlier prospect of containing the situation, the United States now faced a much-escalated conflict. The Pandora's Box of air raids into North Vietnam had opened, but it was still hoped that a limited response would frighten the North Vietnamese into backing off. Quite the opposite was true. A division of North Vietnamese regulars was being funneled down the Ho Chi Minh Trail infiltration route into South Vietnam. Thirty MiG-15s and -17s were deployed from China into the North Vietnamese air base at Phuc Yen. The enemy was anything but scared off.

On the night of 31 October 1964, Vietcong sappers penetrated the perimeter of Bien Hoa AB near Saigon and set up a mortar barrage in which four Americans were killed and thirty wounded. Many aircraft were destroyed, including five PACAF B-57s. Others, including 13 more B-57s, were damaged. As the acrid smoke gave way to the humid dawn of 1 November, the JCS met in Washington to ponder their options. The Defense Intelligence Agency had earlier drawn up a list of 94 strategic targets

in North Vietnam, whose destruction it was believed would cripple North Vietnam's ability to wage war. It was this list that General LeMay had advocated before Honolulu and again after the Gulf of Tonkin. The JCS decided it was time for this kind of hard-hitting action. A contingency plan was drawn up for a 16-day maximum-effort strategic air offensive against the North, and the plan was presented to Secretary of Defense McNamara and President Johnson for approval. They rejected it. Johnson and McNamara still felt it was necessary only to let the North Vietnamese know they were not immune from attack, and they would see the folly of their ways. The North Vietnamese however, unaffected by the logic of the men in Washington, saw American reluctance as an advance warning and used the time the Johnson Administration gave them to build an immense air-defense network that would cost a great many American lives as the war dragged on.

While the action against North Vietnam was the center of attention, the wider war was engulfing all Southeast Asia. In April 1964 a coup in the Laotian capital of Vientiane by an amalgam of rightists and neutralists under Prime Minister Souvanna Phouma had provoked stepped-up attacks from the North Vietnamese-sponsored Pathet Lao guerrillas. By 16 May the entire Plain of Jars region of Laos was under Pathet Lao control. American reconnaissance missions over Laos, code-named *Yankee Team*, which had been terminated 18 months earlier, were resumed. On 6 June a US Navy RF-8 reconnaissance plane from *Yankee Team* was shot down by ground fire, followed next day by an F-8 escorting an RF-8. On 8 June 14 PACAF F-100s were dispatched from Clark AB to Danang AB and Takhli RTAFB, making their first strikes against antiaircraft sites in the Plain of Jars on 9 June. On 14 December 1964 PACAF began *Operation Barrel Roll*, involving tactical fighter-bomber missions against targets in Laos. This was the beginning of continuous USAF combat operations in Southeast Asia.

Below: **This was the scene at Bien Hoa AB on the morning of 1 November 1964 after the Halloween night Viet Cong attack. Two B-57s were burned to the ground where they sat, while a third parked next to the one on the right lost a wing. Flexible fuel bladders are visible in the lower right, while A-1s are parked around the hangar at the far left. Perimeter defense would be a constant and serious problem for the US Air Force throughout the war years.**

Below: The pilot of this 19th Tactical Airlift Squadron C-123K, photographed by Staff Sargeant Andy Sarakon during a mission over South Vietnam in October 1970, has opened his window in deference to the pasty heat rippling up from the jungle below. Camouflage paint schemes on US Air Force aircraft were virtually unknown prior to 1965 when the three-tone scheme visible here was officially adopted for use in Southeast Asia.

ROLLING THUNDER

As 1965 began, the US Air Force found itself no longer an observer and sporadic participant, but deeply engaged in the wider war. The Bien Hoa AB attack had been only the worst of a series of direct attacks on American facilities in South Vietnam. On Christmas Eve 1964, Viet Cong hit the Brink Hotel BOQ in the heart of downtown Saigon with 250-lbs plastic explosive, killing two and wounding 71. The administration was coming to recognize the need for some type of air offensive against North Vietnam in the wake of these attacks. In February 1965 'tit for tat' retaliatory strikes were authorized – air attacks on the North in response to a specific attack in the South. The first of these, code-named *Flaming Dart*, came on 7 and 8 February when USAF and US Navy aircraft struck the communications center at Ninh Linh in the southern panhandle of North Vietnam.

On 1 February Vice Chief of Staff General John McConnell succeeded General LeMay as USAF Chief of Staff. He shared with his predecessor a profound belief in an immediate strategic air offensive against the North. Again the plan was endorsed by the JCS and rejected by the President and Secretary of Defense McNamara. McConnell was able, however, to convince the administration that the restrictions inherent in the strictly retaliatory *Flaming Dart* missions made them inadequate from a tactical standpoint.

The administration gave some ground by removing the 'strictly retaliatory' requirement, but the objectives of air attacks on the North were still narrowly defined by McNamara as: '(A) reduce the flow and/or increase the cost of infiltration of men and supplies from North Vietnam to South Vietnam; (B) make it clear to the North Vietnamese leadership that so long as they continue their aggression against the South they will have to pay a price in the North; and (C) raise the morale of the South Vietnamese people.'

McNamara's outline, approved by the President, paved the way for a tactical rather than strategic air offensive against the North. It would be directed principally at interdicting lines of communication and supply rather than at destroying North Vietnam's ability to wage war. This interdiction campaign would be code-named *Rolling Thunder* – the longest and largest American air operation in Vietnam.

The first *Rolling Thunder* missions were flown by US Navy aircraft of the Seventh Fleet's Task Force 77 on 11 February 1965. The first Air Force participation came with the fifth *Rolling Thunder* strike on 2 March. The bomber force included both B-57s and F-105 fighter bombers, with F-100s flying as escorts. Enemy ground fire proved to be heavier than expected over the target. Three of the F-105s and a pair of F-100s went down; Captain Hayden Lockhart had the dubious honor of being the first US Air Force pilot captured by North Vietnam.

Because of the administration's limited perception of *Rolling Thunder*, it was difficult for Second Air Division and Task Force 77 commanders to obtain clearance to attack anything but logistical targets. If the interdiction campaign were to work, North Vietnamese air defenses had to be neutralized, and the Defense Department would prove persistently timid about authorizing attacks on such targets. One bone of contention between the Navy and Air Force and the administration was Phuc Yen NVPAFB (North Vietnam People's Air Force Base) near Hanoi. Phuc Yen was the biggest interceptor base in North

Left: A *Rolling Thunder* F-105 of the 354th Tactical Fighter Squadron releases its bombs over North Vietnam.

Vietnam and virtually bristling with MiGs as well as Il-28 light bombers. As such, it was a grave hazard to *Rolling Thunder* pilots. Basic air-power doctrine dictates that the first order of business is to gain air superiority over the combat theater. By recommendation of PACAF Commander General Hunter Harris, Phuc Yen was an obvious early target in the *Rolling Thunder* campaign, and 30 B-52s were armed and ready for a scheduled night strike. The plan, however, was overridden by the authorities in Washington. It would be October 1967 before the President would finally release Phuc Yen for attack. In the intervening 30 months the Phuc Yen MiGs would not rest idle.

The first encounter of the MiG kind came on 3 April 1965. Four Navy F-8Es were flying a mission against the Thanh Hoa Bridge about 30 miles south of Hanoi when they were jumped by MiG-17s. Although one of the F-8s took battle damage, there were no losses; the first aerial combat of the Vietnam War ended in a draw. The following day the Air Force was not so lucky. A strike force of heavily laden F-105s was going north to the same target when it was attacked by a mixed flight of MiG-15s and -17s about 76 miles south of Hanoi. The sluggish F-105s, named Thunderchief but nicknamed 'Thud,' were designed as supersonic fighter bombers and traded off manueverability for speed and bomb capacity. The speedy MiGs were able to get into firing position and a pair of Thuds fell to enemy cannon fire. These were the first USAF losses from air-to-air combat in the war. Though they would be the only USAF losses during 1965, it was a blow to morale.

By this time the Air Force had deployed to Vietnam its top air-superiority fighter, the McDonnell F-4 Phantom, to fly as an escort for the fighter bombers. The Phantom's roots ran back to the Korean War years and a US Navy requirement for a carrier-based fighter/attack plane. The result was the F4H-1 in 1955. In Navy nomenclature of the day F4H translated as the fourth fighter produced for the Navy by McDonnell Douglas (manufacturer's code *H*); the -1 designated the first model F4H to be produced, corresponding exactly to an *A* in USAF nomenclature. When the Air Force expressed an interest in acquiring F4Hs, the Phantom received the USAF designation F-110A. In 1962 the Defense Department merged the Navy and Air Force nomenclature systems, scrapping the more complicated Navy system in favor of the simpler Air Force system. Thus the F4H/F-110 became the F-4 in both services.

In March 1962 the Air Force issued a Military Interdepartmental Purchase Request (MIPR) for the Phantom which it passed to the manufacturer via the Navy, acting as intermediary. The Specific Operational Requirements issued in SOR 200 called for the Air Force Phantom to function across the entire tactical mission range, air support, air superiority, etc., and to be aerial refuelable via the boom method used by the Air Force (which differed from the hose-and-drogue method used by the Navy). The first Air Force Phantoms were designated F-4C, the F-4B being the Navy production version. The first F-4Cs became operational with the 4453rd Combat Crew Training Wing at MacDill AFB, Florida, in November 1963, and with the 12th Tactical Fighter Wing at the same base in January 1964. The first deployments to Southeast Asia came early the following year, with the F-4 going on to become the top American air-superiority fighter of the war.

The first encounter between Phantoms and MiGs took place on 17 June 1965 when US Navy F-4Bs from the carrier USS *Midway* shot down a pair of MiG-17s, scoring the first American aerial victories of the war. The Air Force Phantoms got their first

Right: Another F-105 dropping 750 lb bombs on North Vietnam.

chance at the enemy on the afternoon of 10 July 1965, when a pair of MiG-17s made the mistake of tangling with a flight of F-4Cs of the 45th Tactical Fighter Squadron out of Ubon RTAFB. By now it was known that the enemy tactic for fighter escorts was to time their attack when they knew the F-4s were low on fuel. Today, four Phantoms were purposely running late, flying a *Fluid Four* pattern at an altitude that made them appear on radar like F-105s. The North Vietnamese took the bait and scrambled the MiGs from Phuc Yen. The *Fluid Four* pattern gave way to a *Loose Deuce* formation in which two of the USAF fighters would engage the enemy while the other two covered them. The MiGs broke off their intercept when they sighted the F-4s. The Phantoms lit their afterburners and gave chase, only to have the MiGs turn on them. The MiGs initially outmanuevered the heavier Phantoms and got off some cannon fire at the plane manned by Captains Ken Holcombe and Arthur Clark in the ensuing dogfight. Holcombe and Clark got inside one MiG's turn, permitting the enemy to overshoot them. They missed their first opportunity to take a shot at the MiG, but maneuvered behind him again after he made an ineffectual pass with cannons blazing. They fired all four of their AIM-9 Sidewinder air-to-air missiles; two connected, and the MiG disintegrated as it dropped into a cloud. The US Air Force had scored its first combat kill of the Vietnam War.

While Holcombe and Clark were wrapped in the contrail of their MiG, the Phantom manned by Captains Thomas Roberts and Ronald Anderson had gone into a Mach 1.4 dive to escape the other. They pulled out of the dive in a four-G (four times the pull of gravity) climb and got into a good position above the MiG. The first Sidewinder exploded off the MiG's port wingtip but did little damage; a second was hastily fired without a radar tracking lock-on and missed. The third AIM-9 exploded just

Above: Running lights ablaze, a flight of F-4Es of the 388th Tactical Fighter Wing out of Korat RTAFB line up behind a SAC KC-135 air refueling tanker to top off their tanks before heading north on a MiG CAP mission. The 388th was organized in April 1966 and earned 17 aerial victories before it was deactivated at the end of 1972.

behind the MiG, and the enemy fighter was swallowed in the blast, which marked the second kill of the war. The four airmen involved received Silver Stars, and the score had been settled for the two F-105s lost in April.

Following the early encounters of spring and summer 1965, the enemy reserved the MiGs for about nine months to reassess tactics and concentrate on building surface-to-air missiles and artillery. The MiG-15s and -17s were at a definite disadvantage against the Sidewinder-toting Phantoms despite their better maneuverability. Consequently, when the MiGs did attack it was to harass unescorted F-105s and force them to jettison their bombs before they got to the target. As of March 1966 the F-4s were flying regular *MiG CAP* (Combat Air Patrol) escort missions with the *Rolling Thunder* F-105s. In April, with northeast monsoon season over, the MiGs were ready to reopen the dogfight season.

A DARING RESCUE IN THE A SHAU

On 10 March 1966 Major Bernard Fisher became the first USAF officer to win the Congressional Medal of Honor in Southeast Asia. A US Special Forces camp in the A Shau Valley of South Vietnam was under attack by 4000 North Vietnamese troops. The northeast monsoon season was still blowing strong and the enemy knew the weather would hamper American air support. The A-1E Skyraiders that did go in faced not only the weather but withering ground fire. One of the Skyraiders was severely damaged and had to make a forced landing on the airstrip in the lower-valley camp. Fisher could see that the pilot had survived but would soon be captured and/or killed. Ignoring the fusillade of ground fire directed from the valley walls above and below, Fisher made a landing on the field, picked up his downed comrade and somehow made it into the air and back to safety.

Above: An aerial view of the A Shau camp taken on 12 March.

Left: A highway bridge 112 miles northwest of Vinh is destroyed by a 750 lb bomb from an F-105 as a second Thud (*upper left*) closes in.

Above: A pair of camouflaged Thuds at work over the southern panhandle of North Vietnam in July 1966.

US Air Force Medal of Honor Winners of the Vietnam War

Capt Steven Bennett (Palestine, Tex) 29 June 1972, Quang Tri, South Vietnam (KIA 29 June 1972)

Col George Day (Sioux City, Iowa) Conspicuous gallantry while POW. Now a retired Colonel living in Shalimar, Fla

Maj Merlyn Dethlefsen (Greenville, Iowa) 10 Mar 1967, Thai Nguyen, North Vietnam. Now a retired Colonel living in Fort Worth, Tex

Maj Bernard Fisher (San Bernardino, Calif) 10 Mar 1966, A Shau Valley, South Vietnam. Now a retired Colonel living in Kuna, Idaho

1st Lt James Fleming (Sedalia, Mo) 26 Nov 1968, Duc Co, South Vietnam. Active Duty at Randolph AFB, Texas

Lt Col Joe Jackson (Newman, Ga) 12 May 1968, Kham Duc, South Vietnam. Now a retired Colonel living in Kent, Washington

Lt Col William Jones, III (Norfolk, Va) 1 Sept 1968, Dong Hoi, North Vietnam. Killed 15 Nov 1969, Woodbridge, Va

A1C John Levitow (Hartford, Conn) 24 Feb 1969, Long Binh, South Vietnam. Now living in Plainville, Connecticut

Capt Lance Sijan (Milwaukee, Wis) Conspicuous gallantry while POW. Died while POW, Jan 1968

Lt Col Leo Thorsness (Walnut Grove, Minn) 19 Apr 1967, North Vietnam. Now a retired Colonel living in Santa Monica California

Capt Hilliard Wilbanks (Cornelia, Ga) 24 Feb 1967 Dalat, South Vietnam. KIA 24 Feb 1967

Capt Gerald Young (Anacortes, Wash) 9 Nov 1967, Da Nang area, South Vietnam. Now a retired Colonel living in Anacortes, Washington

AIR OFFENSIVE COMMAND CONTROL

With the advent of *Rolling Thunder*, the US Navy and Air Force found themselves engaged in the biggest air offensive since World War II. To integrate efforts of the two services in the massive campaign, CINCPAC established the *Rolling Thunder Coordinating Committee* rather than appointing a single overall commander for air operations. PACAF had authority to co-ordinate *Rolling Thunder* but did not receive operational control of the Navy Seventh Fleet carrier aircraft. The Coordinating Committee faced the logistical problem of two air forces under separate operational controls attacking area targets. PACAF's Second Air Division at Tan Son Nhut proposed that the area be divided by time and the two services assigned alternating three-hour intervals to hit any target in North Vietnam. The Committee, however, decided to divide North Vietnam geographically into 'Route Packages,' or navigational sectors. There were seven Route Packages (or Packs) with PACAF covering three that encompassed about 60% of North Vietnam, while the Seventh Fleet got the other four. The Air Force was assigned Route Pack 1 in the southern panhandle of North Vietnam closest to its bases in South Vietnam. Because they had more aerial refueling support, plus the proximity to bases in Thailand, the Air Force was also assigned Route Packs 5 and 6A, deeper in enemy territory. The more limited range of carrier-based aircraft gave the Navy Route Packs 2, 3, 4 and 6B, which were contiguous with the coast of the Gulf of Tonkin where the Seventh Fleet had established its *Yankee Station*.

For political reasons, the Johnson Administration opted to limit *Rolling Thunder* access to targets in the areas of Hanoi, North Vietnam's capital, and Haiphong, the largest port. Bombing would be prohibited for a ten-nautical-mile radius from Hanoi center, and four nautical miles from the center of Haiphong; it would be severely restricted out to 30 nautical miles from the center of Hanoi and ten nautical miles from mid-Haiphong. The stated purpose was to avoid civilian casualties, which it did – but it also gave the enemy an unprecedented break by turning his major strategic targets into sanctuaries. Within them, the North Vietnamese could create, undisturbed, an elaborate air-defense system that would cost the US Air Force dearly in years to come.

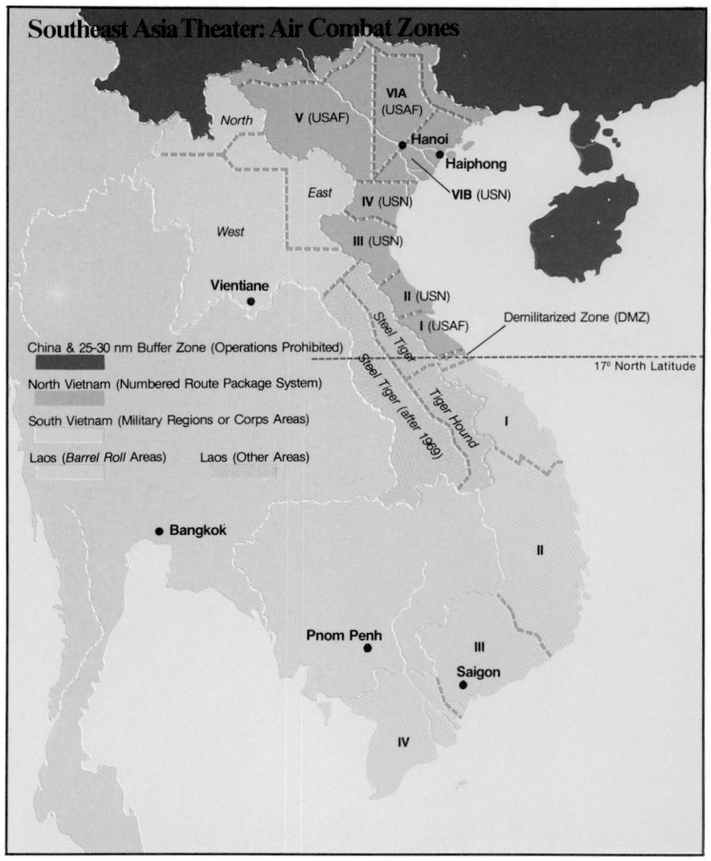

To complicate the situation, President Johnson and Secretary of Defense McNamara were taking a personal interest in the tactical air war in Southeast Asia. Split-second communications kept them abreast of the situation on the distant battlefront in a way no predecessor could have dreamed of. An unfortunate result was that administration time and energy became engrossed in making tactical decisions that better-trained field commanders should have been making. Instead of being able to get timely approval for strikes against elusive targets, Second Air Division commanders had to route their requests through MACV in Saigon to CINCPAC in Hawaii, who in turn had to pass the target 'nomination' back to the JCS in Washington, thence to the Secretary of Defense and the White House.

Left: An unarmed USAF 0-1 Bird Dog parked along with Army helicopters at a Forward Air Control base in the jungles of South Vietnam, July 1966.

Above: The F-100 Super Sabre was first introduced to Southeast Asia in a fighter-bomber role but was later used as an FAC under the code name *Misty*.

Approval or disapproval then made its way back down the chain of command. This time-lag factor was one of the heaviest burdens of the *Rolling Thunder* operation.

Rolling Thunder was the centerpiece of the interdiction campaign, but operations in Laos were an integral part of the effort to keep men and materiel in North Vietnam from reaching the South. The ongoing *Barrel Roll* operations were concentrated in route packages in north and northeast Laos, directed principally at interdicting supply lines feeding the communist Pathet Lao. On 3 April 1965 a new interdiction zone, code-named *Steel Tiger*, was established on the eastern Laotian panhandle stretching from the 17th parallel to the southernmost tip of Laos. The area was directly opposite the southern third of North Vietnam and the northern third of South Vietnam, composed of rugged jungle and mountain country bisected by the infiltration route known as the Ho Chi Minh Trail. In December 1965 the *Steel Tiger* area was divided in two, the southern half being redesignated *Tiger Hound* with interdiction operations assigned to a PACAF *Tiger Hound Task Force*.

With the rapid buildup of American aircraft in the skies over Southeast Asia during 1965 came the need for some kind of immediate on-sight command and control. Since *Farm Gate*, the basic building block of the on-sight or 'in-country' command was the Forward Air Controller (FAC), hovering over the battlefield in a single-engine light aircraft. Initially the FACs flew the tiny O-1 Bird Dog; later they graduated to the larger Cessna O-2. The FAC role was that of liaison between Army ground forces and USAF strike aircraft. Because of his relatively slow speed, the FAC had a much better view of the battlefield than faster, higher-flying jets, and could direct them to target by radio or smoke markers. In many cases the bomber pilots never saw the targets and relied entirely on the FACs. In the early years of the war the FACs were also an important tool for gathering intelligence about the enemy.

Until 1965 most air-strike command and control was located on the ground at air bases. With the ever-growing numbers of strike aircraft spreading their spider web of contrails across the Southeast Asian sky came the need for a more immediate control center to co-ordinate FACs and bombers. The answer was the Airborne Command and Control Center (ABCCC) which was located in a C-130 Hercules transport that positioned itself in a central location above the battlefield, and through which information about potential enemy targets was funneled from FACs and other sources to strike aircraft. The C-130 ABCCCs were used throughout South Vietnam and in Laos as well, where they operated under the code name *Hillsboro*.

Over North Vietnam, where there were no FACs, and where target authorization originated in Washington, command and

Above: TAC's *Big Eye* EC-121Qs were sent to Southeast Asia to fly airborne radar surveillance missions for PACAF.

control was more complex. Central control was at the Second Air Division (later Seventh Air Force) headquarters at Tan Son Nhut AB near Saigon, which relied on an advanced command/control center in the Laotian panhandle code-named *Motel*. The Navy equivalent, code-named *Red Crown*, was on a ship in the Gulf of Tonkin. A series of other radar installations was located throughout Thailand and South Vietnam, known as Control and Reporting Centers (CRC) and Posts (CRP). The northernmost, and among the busiest of the CRPs, was at Dong Ha AB north of Danang, code-named *Waterbag*. Because of its location *Waterbag* controlled all missions going into North Vietnam from bases in the south and rendezvous with refueling aircraft over the Gulf of Tonkin. *Waterbag* was also tied into the Navy Seventh Fleet radar net in the Gulf of Tonkin. The next link in the command-and-control chain was the EC-121 ABCCCs, code-named *Big Eye*. These ABCCCs, modified Lockheed Constellations, were the first AWACS (Airborne Warning and Control Systems). The EC-121 had been developed for the Air Defense Command (ADC) in the 1950s under the code name *Big Eye* to provide an airborne warning and control platform for interceptors defending North American airspace; they were first deployed to Vietnam in April 1965 as *Rolling Thunder* got underway. The *Big Eye* EC-121 ABCCCs, redesignated *College Eye* in March 1967, were initially based at Tan Son Nhut AB in South Vietnam, but transferred to Thailand in early 1967. Their stations included the areas over north central Laos and off the coast of North Vietnam, north of *Red Crown* and Task Force 77 and southeast of the port of Haiphong. The EC-121's radar was inferior to that of the later Boeing E-3 AWACS in its ability to 'see' activities close to the ground where hills and other 'ground clutter' obscured its view. Nonetheless, the airborne positioning of the *College Eye* radar so far north made it much superior to land-based radar, and an invaluable final link in the chain of command and control that guided USAF strike aircraft to their targets.

THE SEVENTH AIR FORCE

On Christmas Eve 1965, the first phase of *Rolling Thunder* closed as the US announced the first of many temporary halts to bombing raids into North Vietnam (designed to give North Vietnam a chance to reconsider, and hopefully to end their supplying of arms and materiel – and recently of regular troops – to the Viet Cong). This bombing halt, like others to follow, was used instead as an opportunity to bolster North Vietnamese air defenses. When *Rolling Thunder* resumed 37 days later (30 January 1966) it was only the beginning of an increase in the US commitment to the war. On the political front, President Johnson met a week later in Honolulu with South Vietnamese President Thieu and his Premier, the flamboyant RVNAF Marshal Ky, to discuss the war and increased American economic aid. This was one of a series of high-level contacts during 1966 that included visits to South Vietnam by both

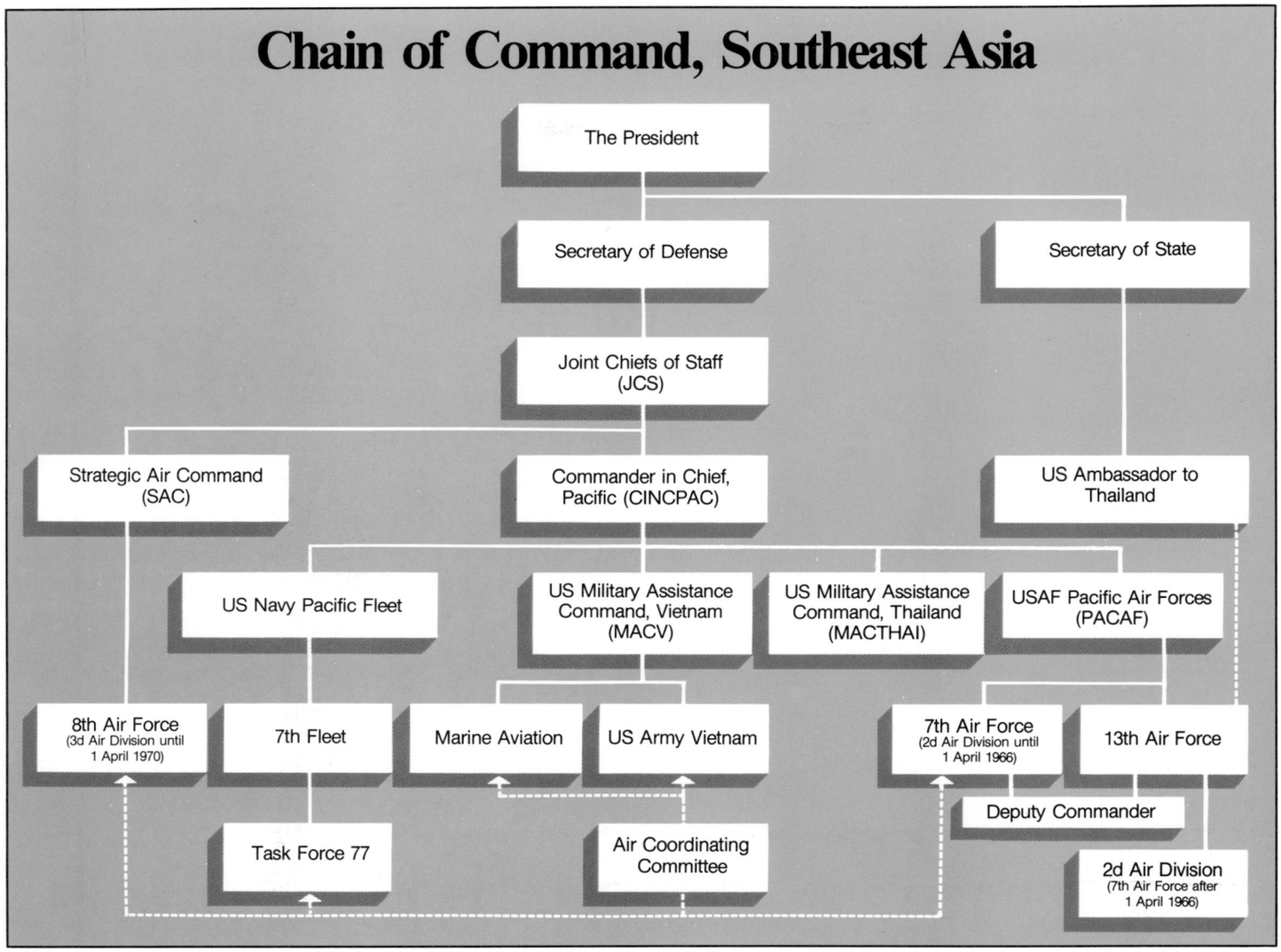

Secretary of Defense McNamara and Secretary of State Dean Rusk.

For the US Air Force, the increased commitment came with the upgrading of the Second Air Division, part of the Thirteenth Air Force, to full numbered status as the Seventh Air Force on 1 April 1966. The Seventh had been deactivated after World War II, having served with distinction in the USAAF effort, Pacific Theater. Now it was back.

In November 1965 Chief of Staff General McConnell had decided that the Second Air Division should report directly to PACAF rather than the Thirteenth Air Force. With the influx of men and aircraft, it was growing equal to a numbered air force almost the size of the Fifth during the Korean War. Meanwhile, the Thai Government had become uneasy about an arrangement that placed American forces in their country under the same command structure as those in South Vietnam. In April 1965, in the same spirit that led to creation of a MACTHAI alongside MACV, USAF forces in Thailand were put *directly* under command of the Thirteenth Air Force, while those in South Vietnam were under the Thirteenth Air Force via its Second Air Division to facilitate practical day-to-day operations, General McConnell established the simultaneous position of Deputy Commander over the Second Air Division and the Thirteenth Air Force (Thailand). With reactivation of the Seventh Air Force to assume the Second Air Division's role, the Commander changed as well, becoming Deputy Commander of both the Seventh Air Force and the Thirteenth Air Force (Thailand). Thus, US Air Force operations originating in both Thailand and South Viet-

Above: Seventh Air Force commander General Moore and an F-100 pilot confer with Air Force Secretary Harold Brown at Tan Son Nhut in January 1966. Brown later served as Defense Secretary under President Jimmy Carter.

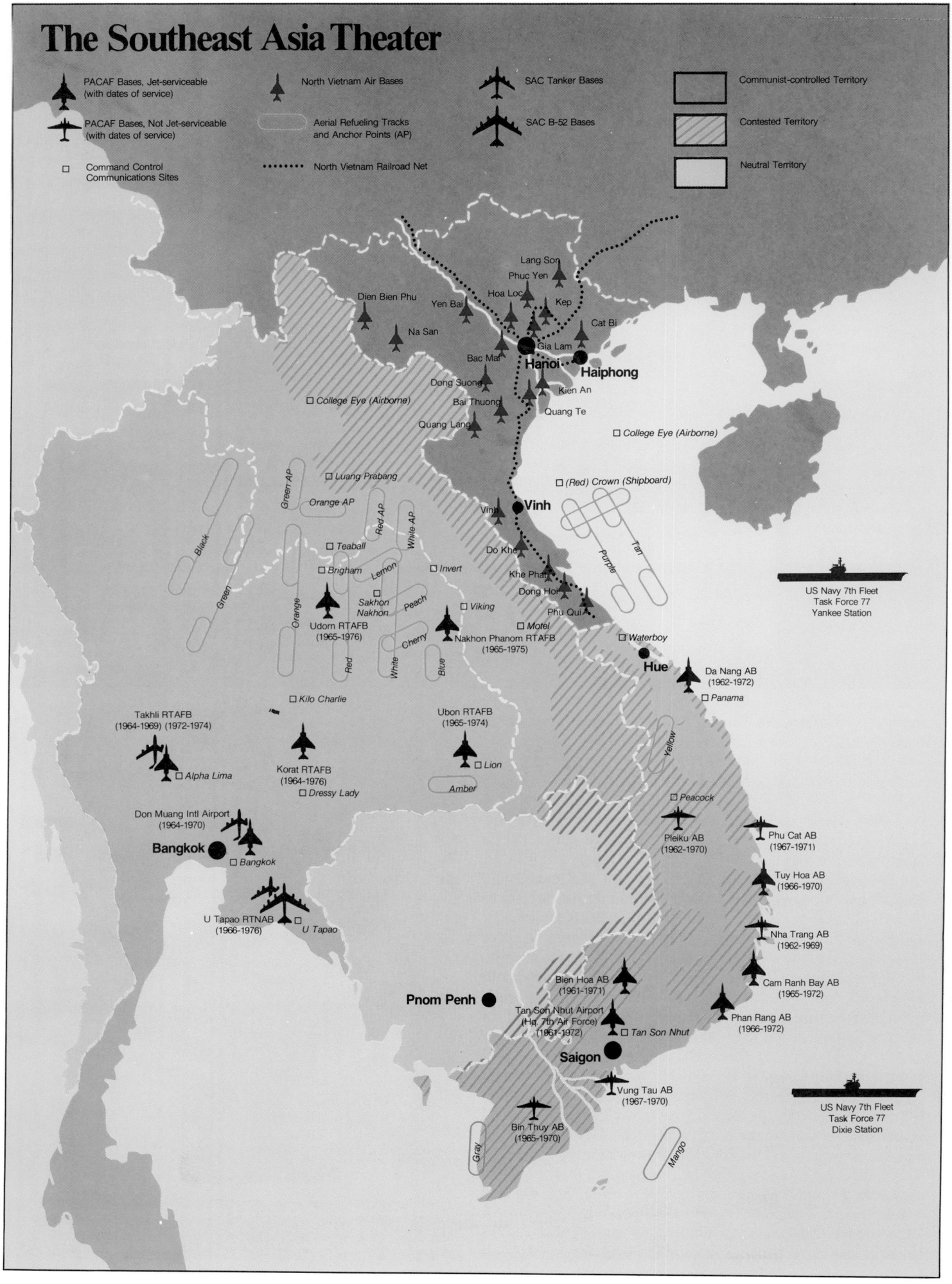
The Southeast Asia Theater
PACAF Bases, Jet-serviceable (with dates of service)
PACAF Bases, Not Jet-serviceable (with dates of service)
Command Control Communications Sites
North Vietnam Air Bases
Aerial Refueling Tracks and Anchor Points (AP)
North Vietnam Railroad Net
SAC Tanker Bases
SAC B-52 Bases
Communist-controlled Territory
Contested Territory
Neutral Territory
Lang Son
Phuc Yen
Hoa Loc
Kep
Dien Bien Phu
Yen Bai
Na San
Cat Bi
Gia Lam
Hanoi
Haiphong
Bac Mai
Dong Suong
Kien An
Bai Thuong
Quang Te
Quang Lang
College Eye (Airborne)
College Eye (Airborne)
Luang Prabang
(Red) Crown (Shipboard)
Green AP
Orange AP
Red AP
White AP
Vinh
Vinh
Black
Teaball
Do Khe
Purple
Tan
Brigham
Lemon
Invert
Khe Phat
Green
Dong Hoi
Sakhon Nakhon
Peach
Viking
Phu Qui
Orange
Udorn RTAFB (1965-1976)
Motel
Cherry
Nakhon Phanom RTAFB (1965-1975)
Waterboy
Hue
Red
White
Blue
Da Nang AB (1962-1972)
Panama
Kilo Charlie
Takhli RTAFB (1964-1969) (1972-1974)
Ubon RTAFB (1965-1974)
Yellow
Alpha Lima
Korat RTAFB (1964-1976)
Lion
Dressy Lady
Amber
Peacock
Don Muang Intl Airport (1964-1970)
Pleiku AB (1962-1970)
Phu Cat AB (1967-1971)
Bangkok
Bangkok
Tuy Hoa AB (1966-1970)
U Tapao RTNAB (1966-1976)
U Tapao
Nha Trang AB (1962-1969)
Bien Hoa AB (1961-1971)
Cam Ranh Bay AB (1965-1972)
Pnom Penh
Tan Son Nhut Airport (Hq, 7th Air Force) (1961-1972)
Phan Rang AB (1966-1972)
Tan Son Nhut
Saigon
Vung Tau AB (1967-1970)
US Navy 7th Fleet Task Force 77 Yankee Station
US Navy 7th Fleet Task Force 77 Dixie Station
Bin Thuy AB (1965-1970)
Gray
Mango

nam could be co-ordinated through the same office, although the US Ambassador to Thailand, as the senior American official, retained control of US forces based there. As part of the separation agreement, aircraft based in Thailand could be used against targets in Laos and North Vietnam, (although their use against targets in the latter would not be revealed until March 1967). South Vietnam was exempt, except in an emergency. South Vietnam-based aircraft could be used against targets in all three countries.

Because of an arrangement similar to the one in Thailand, all Seventh and Thirteenth Air Force aircraft engaged in *Barrel Roll, Steel Tiger* and *Tiger Hound* interdiction operations in Laos were nominally under direction of the US Ambassador to that country, who consulted with the Laotian Government whose ground forces, under General Vang Pao, were operating in these route packages. By extension, the US Air Attaché to the US Embassy in Laos, a USAF officer, became the US air commander for Laos, as he had the practical task of selecting targets and working with Seventh and Thirteenth Air Force commanders. Meanwhile, the Strategic Air Command's Third Air Division based on Guam maintained control of the *Arc Light* B-52 strikes in South Vietnam that had begun in June 1965. SAC did, however, continue its liaison office at Seventh Air Force Headquarters.

With reactivation of the Seventh Air Force and concomitant buildup, the USAF increased the number of bases from which jet fighters and fighter bombers could operate. When the US intervention commenced, the only jet-serviceable air bases available were Danang, Bien Hoa and Tan Son Nhut, the latter also serving as Saigon's international airport. In 1965, the big Navy facility at Cam Ranh Bay opened with its jet-serviceable field to which were assigned three squadrons of USAF F-4Cs, totaling 54 aircraft, or over half of the F-4Cs in Vietnam during the first year of their deployment. The next base to open was Phan Rang AB, which opened three days after the Seventh took over from the Second. During 1966 work began on Phu Cat AB; Tuy Hoa AB opened in November as a turnkey project whereby contractors designed and constructed a complete ready-to-use base.

THE DOGFIGHT SEASON RESUMES

On 23 April 1966 the USAF fought its first MiG battle since the victories scored the previous June. The northeast monsoon had subsided and the MiGs were back in force. Four F-4Cs of the 555th TFS were flying cover for air strikes against the Bac Giang bridge 25 miles northeast of Hanoi when a like number of MiG-17s made a head-on pass. The eight aircraft turned for another try, each attempting to outmaneuver his opposite number. When the fight ended, a pair of the MiGs had fallen victim to American air-to-air missiles.

Three days later, the first enemy MiG-21 was downed by Major Paul Gilmore and Lieutenant William Smith in an F-4C riding herd on an RB-66 reconnaissance plane over the Red River northeast of Hanoi. A second MiG-21 was encountered, but escaped when the Americans had to break off the chase because of low fuel reserves. The Soviet-built MiG-21 was, in the mid-sixties, the Russians' top fighter, as the MiG-15 had been during the Korean War. A light and highly maneuverable aircraft, the MiG-21 weighed in at 18,740 pounds versus 58,000 pounds for the F-4C. Designed as a direct result of lessons learned in the Korean War, the MiG-21 first flew in 1955 and went on to be produced in greater numbers than any combat aircraft since, serving with 33 air forces around the world. A potent adversary, the MiG-21 (NATO code-name *Fishbed*) was armed with a 23 mm twin-barrel cannon and up to four air-to-air missiles. Though 66 North Vietnamese Fishbeds would be shot down by American F-4s during the war, they took their toll on the Americans, who would not equal the ten-to-one kill superiority they achieved in the Korean War.

The first F-4 claimed by the enemy was lost to a troika of the older MiG-17s on 21 September 1966. The renewed *Rolling Thunder* Operations of 1966 (under auspices of the reactivated Seventh Air Force) saw many more sorties over the North and much higher USAF casualties. While downing 17 MiGs, five of them -21s, PACAF lost 379 aircraft during the year. Of these, the greatest number, 126, were F-105s. All but fifteen of the Thuds went down over North Vietnam or Laos, all to ground fire except for three lost to MiGs and four downed by surface-to-air missiles

Below: Air Force C-130s disgorge troops and supplies at Cam Ranh Bay AB as an F-4 makes its final approach in the distance. The sprawling complex at Cam Ranh is today a major Russian base.

Right: A shark-mouthed F-4E Phantom out of Korat RTAFB with drop tanks and bombs mounted on its external weapons pylons. The Phantom proved during Operation *Bolo* that it was the top dogfighter in Southeast Asia.

Below: Wolfpack commander Colonel Robin Olds returns from his 100th mission over North Vietnam. Olds shot down 14 Germans during World War II and four North Vietnamese MiGs.

Below right: A North Vietnamese MiG-21 photographed by USAF gun cameras during Operation *Bolo*.

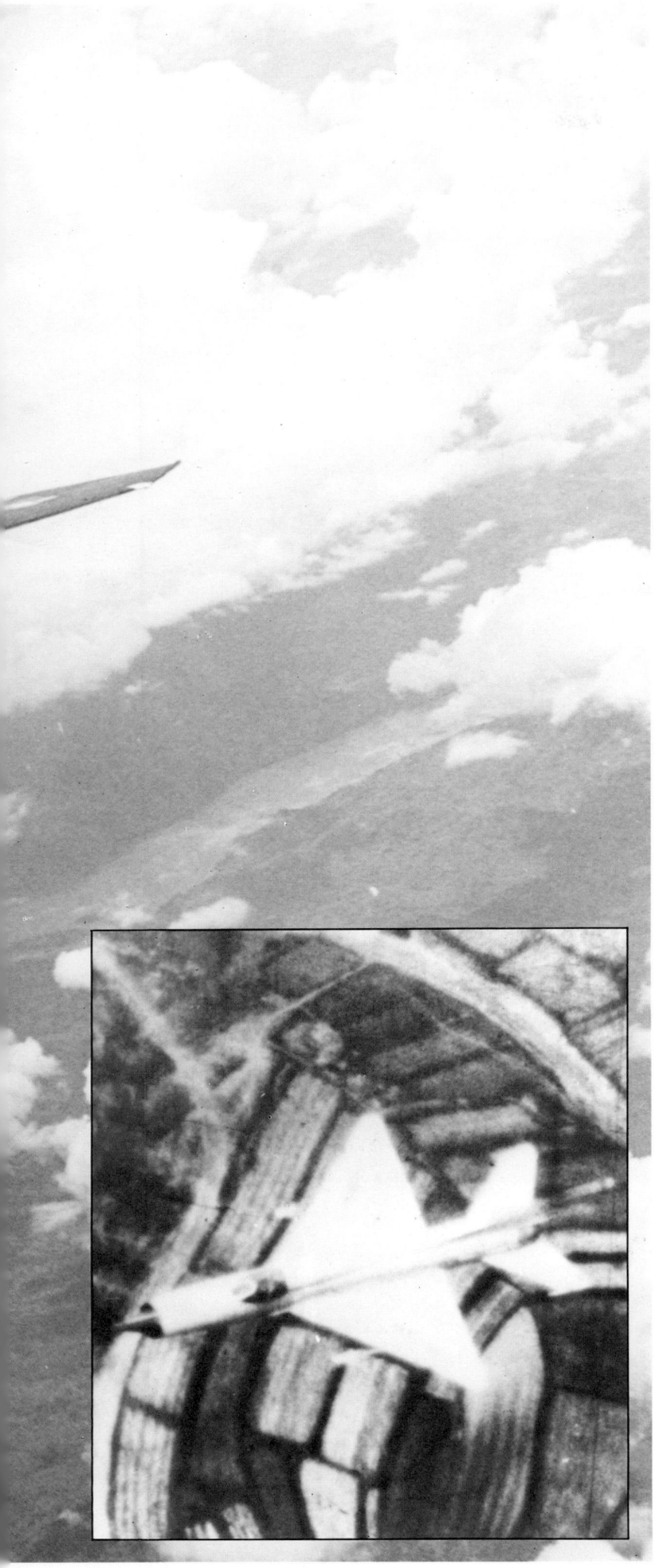

(SAMs). Fifty-six F-4s went down during the year, 42 of them in combat. PACAF also lost 41 A-1 Skyraiders, 26 F-100 Super Sabres, 17 RF-101 reconnaissance aircraft, 13 B-57s and 37 of the little O-1 Bird Dogs used by FACs. Over North Vietnam, the SAMs were the most ominous threat. Even though only 18 aircraft were lost to an estimated 1219 SAM launches in 1966, the North Vietnamese were deploying more and using them more effectively. Thanks to the restricted zones placed around Hanoi and Haiphong, the North Vietnamese had been able to increase their antiaircraft artillery (AAA) defenses eightfold. They introduced up to 25 SAM battalions between the Gulf of Tonkin incident and the end of 1966.

OPERATION BOLO AND AIR SUPERIORITY

As 1967 began PACAF had nearly 1700 aircraft, up from 1100 a year before: it was the second largest Major Command in the US Air Force. Against this backdrop of ever-escalating American presence in the Theater, the Seventh Air Force was planning for what would be the biggest air-to-air battle of the entire war. Dubbed Operation *Bolo*, the mission was responding to increased MiG harassment of F-105s. Because North Vietnamese fighter bases were still restricted from attack by American aircraft, it was determined that the next best way to destroy the maximum number of MiGs was to lure them into combat in a fighter sweep similar to those used in World War II and in MiG Alley over Korea. The man selected to lead *Bolo* was Colonel Robin Olds, commander of the 8th TFW, the 'Wolf Pack,' and a combat veteran with 10 aerial victories in World War II. The force would be drawn from four tactical Fighter Wings and consist of 14 flights of F-4Cs, 6 flights of F-105s flying *Iron Hand* missions suppressing SAM and AAA sites, and 4 flights of F-104s with support electronic-radar-jamming aircraft (EB-66s) and tankers. The *Bolo* strike force would approach North Vietnam from both east and west, creating a pincer to prevent the MiGs from breaking off and running for China where they could not be pursued.

On the morning of 2 January, the *Bolo* aircraft went north, following the usual flight and call-signs patterns of a typical *Rolling Thunder* fighter bomber mission. Because of the weather, the MiGs were slow to respond – when they did, a surprise was in store. Instead of the lumbering Thuds, they found a sky full of F-4s, armed to the teeth and ready to fight. In the massive aerial battle that ensued, seven MiG-21s (half the North Vietnamese inventory) were brought down, all of them by F-4Cs of the 8th TFW using AIM-7 Sidewinder air-to-air missiles. Not a single American aircraft was lost. The superiority of the Phantom, like the Sabre Jet in the previous war, was established. As Colonel Olds, who got his first of four MiG kills that day put it, 'We outflew, outshot and outfought them.'

Four days later a pair of F-4s from the 8th TFW was supposed to fly *MiG CAP* (escort, MiG Combat Air Patrol) for a strike force of F-105s when the mission was canceled due to weather. With the F-4s ready to go, it was decided to put on another *Bolo* type charade for the enemy. The two F-4s would go north pretending to be RF-4s on a weather-reconnaissance mission. Northwest of Hanoi, four MiGs out of Phuc Yen appeared on radar and the two Phantoms went into action. The MiGs were unprepared and outmaneuvered; what remained of North Vietnam's store of MiG-21s after *Bolo* was reduced by two. It was to be the last encounter with MiGs until April, after the monsoon season.

April 1967 was a good month for PACAF, with four MiG-17s brought down on a single day, and by F-105s to boot. April also

Below: A SAC B-52F drops a string of 750 lb general-purpose bombs during Operation *Arc Light*. The black bellies first applied to these bombers in 1965 were a forerunner to the overall camouflage scheme that was adopted when the B-52Ds entered the fray.

Above: A camouflaged B-52D during an *Arc Light* strike on Vietcong positions near Bien Hoa AB in December 1966.

Right and above right: Armorers load general-purpose bombs onto the external weapons pylons of B-52Ds at U Tapao RTAFB in Thailand. Both U Tapao and Andersen AFB on Guam were used as B-52 bases during the war, but U Tapao was much closer to targets in Southeast Asia.

Below: Perched high above the cumulus, a B-52D out of Andersen AFB on Guam releases its deadly bomb load over the target.

saw the first lifting of restrictions on attacking MiG bases. A raid was quickly launched on 24 April against the enemy base at Hoa Lac, resulting in the destruction of at least 14 MiGs. If April was a good month for the MiG hunters, May was even better. During the month 21 MiGs were destroyed in aerial combat in the North, five of them MiG-21s. The tally was more than double that of April and surpassed that for all of 1966. Particularly unlucky for the North Vietnamese was 13 May, when an unprecedented seven MiG-17s were shot down by F-4s and F-105s.

The following day marked the first aerial victory achieved by an F-4 using the newly installed SUU-16 20mm rotary-barrel 'Gatling gun' cannon mounted in a pod under the center fuselage. In Korea it had been noted that a major flaw in the otherwise superior Sabre Jet had been its light armament of .50-caliber machine guns *vis à vis* the cannons on enemy MiGs. During the years immediately following the Korean War, 20mm cannons were installed in American fighters. However, by the later fifties advances in guided air-to-air missiles caused aircraft designers to conclude that American fighters no longer needed guns. With the onset of aerial combat in Vietnam, an old lesson was being relearned. The technologically sophisticated Sidewinder and Sparrow missiles were often failing to detonate when they should have destroyed an enemy aircraft. It was back to the drawing board. While the new F-4E was being redesigned with an internally mounted cannon, the SUU-16 gun pod was produced and retrofitted on the older F-4Cs. The pilots were delighted and Captain James Craig, one of the F-4C pilots to score on 14 May 1967 with the new gun pod, was swift to point out that 'The kills with the gun mode could not have been made with a missile.'

In 1967 USAF pilots shot down 59 MiGs, including 17 MiG-21s – the greatest number of any year of the war – while losing nine F-4s and 11 F-105s in aerial combat. Colonel Olds, the 8th TFW commander, became the top-scoring pilot with four kills, three of them during May and two in one day. While Olds would not score a fifth victory to become the first USAF ace of the Vietnam War, he did become the first and only American ace to score victories in both World War II and Vietnam, retiring with a total score of 14.

Total US Air Force losses in Southeast Asia for 1967 came to 421, as against 379 for the year before; 334 of them were due to hostile action. Of the total 113 were F-105s, 95 were F-4s, and 23 were RF-4s. There were 878,771 combat sorties flown (up 69% over 1966) dropping 681,700 tons of ordnance, 87% more than the previous year.

THE TET OFFENSIVE AND THE BOMBING HALT

By the beginning of 1968, the North Vietnam People's Air Force had been virtually defeated. Constant pressure from the superior USAF forces against both aircraft and bases had sent it largely to safe bases in China. On the ground in South Vietnam, however, the situation was entirely different. On 30 January the North Vietnamese and Viet Cong launched a massive offensive designed to coincide with Tet, the lunar new year. The northern city of Hue was captured and parts of Saigon were overrun; a concerted effort was made to overrun both the Seventh Air Force bases in the Saigon area, Tan Son Nhut and Bien Hoa. While the Tet Offensive was eventually beaten back, it was done only at great cost to American and South Vietnamese forces. The price would be paid in Washington, where the Johnson Administration had a severe jolt. Tet showed an increasingly disgruntled American electorate that administration policy of the past four years had not worked. There was an enormous groundswell of public outcry for withdrawal from Southeast

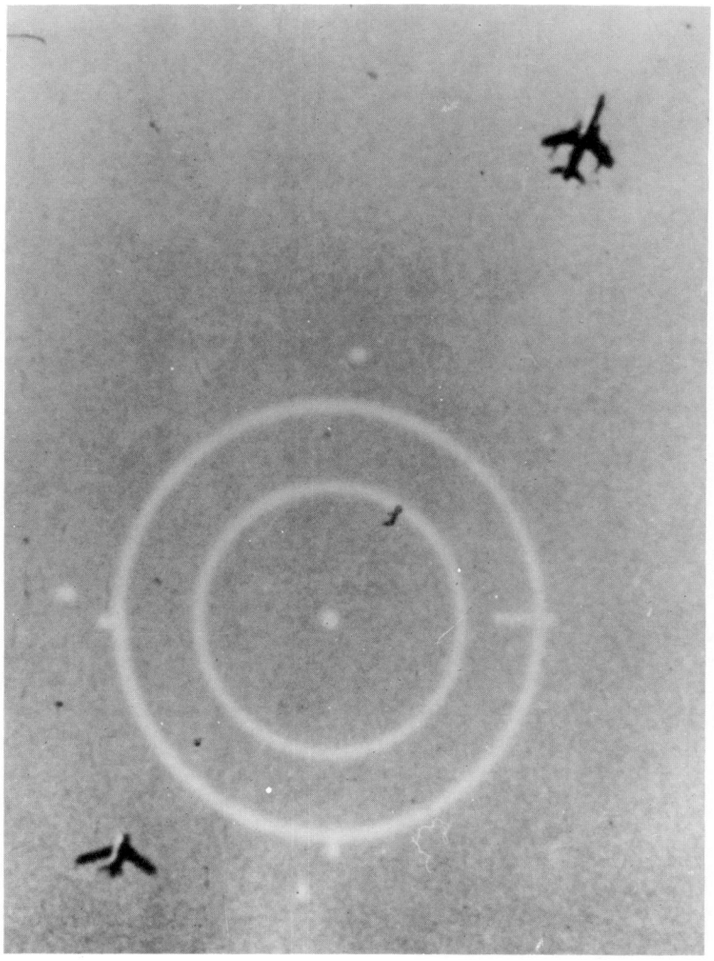

Above: Caught in a gunsight, a North Vietnamese MiG-17 closes on an F-105 during a raid on the Paul Doumer Bridge in Hanoi, December 1967.

Right: Rolling Thunder raiders blast the runway at Phuc Yen airfield in December 1967.

Asia. In a dramatic televised address, President Johnson told the American people that he would not be a candidate for re-election in 1968 and that, effective 1 April, *Rolling Thunder* bombing raids would not be made in North Vietnam above the 20th parallel. Three days later the restriction would move south to the 19th parallel. Johnson also announced that he would gradually reduce American strength in South Vietnam, and that he hoped North Vietnam would show good faith and do the same. It was announced that high-level talks would be convened to negotiate an end to the war: they began in Paris on 10 May 1968.

Air combat over North Vietnam continued for the first six weeks of the year, with eight MiGs downed by F-4Ds during that time. With the bombing halt, it would be four years before US Air Force fighters would fly against MiGs again.

On 1 November 1968, four days before the presidential election, President Johnson further de-escalated the war by announcing a halt to all bombing missions of any kind over North Vietnam – the end of *Rolling Thunder*. Armed reconnaissance flights would continue, and ultimately reveal massive rebuilding of the supply network that fed enemy forces in the South as well as a strengthening of antiaircraft defenses. It was not the good-faith de-escalation that Johnson had hoped for, but his administration was passing from the scene and the newly elected Richard M Nixon would maintain the bombing halt.

The end of *Rolling Thunder* was also that of USAF activities in the North, but the war in South Vietnam raged with renewed fury. In 90 attacks on American bases, 35 aircraft were destroyed

of a total of 392 USAF planes lost in 1968. Between them, SAMs and MiGs accounted for twelve USAF aircraft compared to 40 in 1967. Despite the end of *Rolling Thunder*, the total number of combat sorties was up to 18% over 1967 (1,034,839) with 1,092,200 tons of ordnance dropped.

NEW TACTICS OF INTERDICTION

With all hope of achieving interdiction at the source in North Vietnam dashed by the end of *Rolling Thunder*, US Air Force commanders had to turn to other means to stem enemy aggression. In November 1968 aircraft that had been part of *Rolling Thunder* turned their immense firepower to South Vietnam, where F-100s were now used as FACs under the code name *Misty*, and to Laos where a new series of interdiction operations designated *Commando Hunt* began. In *Commando Hunt I*, between November 1968 and April 1969, 67,094 PACAF and 3811 B-52 *Arc Light* sorties were flown against enemy positions and lines of communication in the *Steel Tiger* area of Laos. *Commando Hunt I* was immediately followed by a second series, then by *Commando Hunt III* on the first anniversary of Johnson's bombing halt. By that time Cessna A-37B Dragonflys, the attack version of the T-37 trainer, were being introduced to two newly activated Attack Squadrons in South Vietnam. Meanwhile, the last of an older bird, the B-57 light bomber, departed Vietnam after five years in the war zone.

Even as there was a continued emphasis on interdiction via bombing and strafing, other tactics were brought into play. The *Ranch Hand* defoliation program continued: despite the failure of *Sherwood Forest* in 1965, wishful thinking led to several more attempts to burn the forests to expose the enemy. At the beginning of 1966 two operations in January and March *Hot Tip I* and *Hot Tip II* – sought to destroy the vegetation on Cu Pong Mountain in South Vietnam. The weather, humidity, ordnance and method of delivery were described as 'satisfactory,' but the results were not. In the words of one MACV officer, 'The damn trees simply won't burn.'

Despite a record of costly failure, it would take another two years later to fully discredit the forest-fire approach. Between January and April 1968, under the code name *Pink Rose*, B-52s flew three separate offensives against a single seven-square-kilometer area of South Vietnam armed with huge quantities of incendiaries. The results were predictably poor.

Meanwhile, another unconventional weapon was being tested in the counterinsurgency war that would make bombing and forest fires appear Stone-Age-like by comparison. In late 1966 Defense Secretary McNamara, who viewed the war as something of a proving ground for high-tech theories, developed a system that came to be called *Practice Nine*. It was a surveillance system that employed seismic and acoustic sensors to be dropped into the dense jungles along the Ho Chi Minh Trail infiltration routes. The theory was that since they were hidden in the thick jungle, you could use the sensors to see and hear the enemy as he moved down the trail. The top-secret *Practice Nine* sensors, redesignated *Dye Marker* in July 1967 (after having been known briefly under the code name *Illinois City*), were sown across the area of South Vietnam just below the Demilitarized Zone (DMZ) that constituted the border with North Vietnam. In September 1967, as *Dye Marker* was being revealed to the public, the line of sensors was extending westward into Laos under the code name *Muscle Shoals*. There would be two distinct subsystems included in *Muscle Shoals*, an antivehicle system called *Mud River* and an antipersonnel system designated *Dump Truck*. The *Mud River* sensors were first positioned by air drop in December in an operation involving both Air Force and Navy aircraft, with Thailand based USAF EC-121R 'Batcats' acting as relay platforms. With the sensors in place, problems immediately arose around interpretation of the data they were picking up. As the 'bugs' were being worked out of this bugging system, the still-classified operations were renamed again (May 1968), *Dye Marker* becoming *Duel Blade* and *Muscle Shoals* becoming *Igloo White*. *Igloo White* would quickly become an integral part of the Tactical Air Control System controlling the *Commando Hunt* combat operations. As of October 1967 all the EC-121 operations, including *College Eye*, and now *Igloo White*, had been consolidated into Korat RTAFB, with the Infiltration Surveillance Center (designated *Dutch Mill* because of the shape of its antenna) located at Nakhon Phanom RTAFB to co-ordinate *Commando Hunt* and *Igloo White* under the code name *Task Force Alpha*.

By early 1969 the EC-121s flying *Igloo White* relay missions were increasingly threatened from North Vietnamese antiaircraft defenses; the proposal was to replace them with Beechcraft TQU-22A drones. This was tried between March and July under the code name *Pave Eagle I*: results left much to be desired and the TQU-22As were withdrawn for further study. Five QU-22Bs would return as *Pave Eagle II* in October 1970, but would augment *Igloo White* for only a few months before engine problems grounded them again. By the end of 1970, the two squadrons of 12 *Igloo White* EC-121Rs that had made up the 553d Reconnaissance Wing at Korat RTAFB were merged into the 553d RS; the wing was dissolved and assigned to the 388th TFW with the QU-22Bs that were now the 554th RS. In August 1971 the QU-22Bs were grounded again and the reliable C-130 ABCCCs were assigned to augment the now-obsolescent EC-121s as the *Igloo White* airborne command and control center and sensor relay system for the air war over Laos.

The next 41 month-phase saw a gradual and continuous reduction in the number of USAF sorties flown and aircraft lost in Southeast Asia. In 1969 the USAF flew 966,949 combat sorties, down from over a million in 1968. In 1970 711,440 missions were flown; in 1971 the tally was down to 450,031, less than half the number flown in 1969. In 1969 294 USAF aircraft were lost, nearly a hundred fewer than the previous year. In 1970 the number was down to 171; in 1971 it was further reduced to 87, though the total aircraft loss now stood at 1599, at a cost approaching three billion dollars.

One fact behind the figures was the termination of *Rolling Thunder*. Another was that in July 1969 the new Nixon Administration had announced the 'Nixon Doctrine,' a policy that

Above: A US Air Force EC-121R Batcat of the 553d Reconnaissance Wing taxis down the runway at Korat RTAFB in January 1969. A Thai Air Force T-6 can be seen in the background.

Top: The venerable C-47 served a variety of functions for both the USAF and the RVNAF throughout the war. The 'Delta' referred to is that of the Mekong.

Right: This RF-4C cracked up on landing at Danang AB in April 1969. The unit cost for each of the 499 RF-4Cs delivered to the USAF was $2.3 million.

MAC
50247
DELTA QUEEN
II

called for 'Vietnamization' of the war. The plan included gradual reduction of US forces with more and more of the operation to be taken over by Vietnamese forces which had theoretically become stronger over the years. On 15 August Defense Secretary Melvin Laird gave American forces the mission of helping the Vietnamese take over the war. Under the Improvement and Modernization Program that was part of Vietnamization, the RVNAF would double in size by 1972. It would be supplied with more sophisticated aircraft, including the versatile F-5 Tiger jet fighter/fighter-bomber developed by Northrop for the export trade, which was then serving with a number of smaller air forces worldwide. By the end of 1970, the RVNAF had 728 aircraft and over 700 crews organized into 30 squadrons. During the year they flew 292,523 sorties, about 41% of the number flown by the USAF.

By the end of 1972, under Projects *Enhance* and *Enhance Plus*, the RVNAF had a strength of 1817 aircraft including 135 F-5s, 245 A-37s, 540 UH-1 Huey helicopters and a variety of other, piston-engined, aircraft. Air crew strength was up to 1297 and an average of 60,000 sorties were being flown per month; 277 aircraft had been lost in 1972.

THE GUNSHIPS

Considering the abundance of weapons and tactics being supplied by the authorities in Washington, it is ironic that the most unique weapons system developed and deployed in Southeast Asia evolved by improvisation. This was the gunship, and the first platform to become one was not the latest top-secret jet but the venerable old C-47 Skytrain that had first seen service with the USAAC back in 1938.

The need from which the gunship grew was that to deliver a concentrated barrage of gunfire on a specific target. The time

Top: An AC-47 Spooky gunship banks slightly for a low, slow pass.

Above: Multi-barreled Gatling guns bark firey death from SUU-8 gun pods aboard a 'Spooky,' November 1966.

Below: A detailed sideview of an AC-47 at Bien Hoa in December 1965 showing machine guns that were used before the advent of gun pods.

Above: Airmen Ronald Snyder, James Schmisser and Allen Sims load an AC-47 minigun.

Below: The Cholon area of Saigon was raked by 'Spooky' when it was overrun by the Viet Cong during the Tet Offensive in February 1968.

frame in which even the slowest aircraft could deliver firepower to a stationary target was only a few seconds. What was needed was an aerial gun platform that could concentrate gunfire for several, or even many, minutes on such targets as enemy troop concentrations and strong points, particularly in the dead of night. It was determined that this could be achieved by mounting the guns so as to fire at a 90-degree angle to the side of the aircraft rather than straight ahead or behind. The plane would first circle, with guns aimed toward the circle's center. The circle would then become the base of an inverted cone, with the line of fire forming the cone itself; at the point of the cone where all the lines of fire converged would be the target. A transport aircraft would be the ideal platform, as it was relatively slow and had a large open fuselage in which to mount guns and ammunition. The gunships would become the most heavily armed aircraft in Southeast Asia. Most carried a sizable number of fixed-mounted guns, including several 20mm, 40mm and in some cases 75mm cannons.

The first gunships were 20 C-47 Skytrains redesignated AC-47 and deployed at the end of 1965 with the 4th Air Commando Squadron. They were initially nicknamed 'Spooky' (all gunships would have nicknames beginning with S), but came to be known as 'Puff the Magic Dragon' or 'Dragon Ship' from the fire and smoke they emitted. Puff was an immediate success: no enemy hideout could withstand the firestorm it created. With the success of a weapons system mounted in an aircraft almost thirty years in service, it was natural that the Air Force should decide to use its top-of-the-line tactical transport as a gunship. In September 1967 four AC-130 Gunship II's (later Spectre), with even greater firepower, were deployed to Laos where they achieved 'good results.' By February 1968 the 16th Special Operations Squadron at Ubon RTAFB was to join the 4th ACS, which became the 4th SOS. Because C-130s were still a first-line transport, the Air Force decided to utilize some of the fleet of Korean

Above: An AC-119G Shadow gunship off the coast of South Vietnam in July 1970. The Shadows were converted from the old C-119 Flying Boxcar transports of Korean War-era fame and were first introduced at Nha Trang AB in December 1968.

Facing page: A time exposure taken by USAF Captain Ralph Jones from a Saigon rooftop showing a pair of 'Spooky' gunships at work on Vietcong positions in Saigon during the 1968 Tet Offensive. (*See preceding page, bottom.*)

War-era C-119G transports (on the verge of retirement) as gunship platforms. The conversion was made, with the AC-119Gs modified to handle the increased weight. As part of Operation *Combat Hornet*, four AC-119G Shadows arrived at Nhu Trang AB in December 1968.

In October 1969 the first of 13 jet-augmented AC-119K Stingers of the 18th SOS arrived at Phan Rang AB in South Vietnam. By year's end there would be 29 AC-119 gunships of both types in service, with all but three of the original AC-47s being phased out. Those retained were for defense of the base at Udorn RTAFB in Thailand. The AC-130 gunships, most powerful of the lot, were modernized: 11 were returned to service by the end of 1970. A year later, as part of the Vietnamization program, the AC-119G Shadows were turned over to the RVNAF, with the USAF retaining the jet-assisted AC-119Ks, of which it now had 16 in addition to 18 AC-130s.

The gunships became one of the most-feared weapons of the war and one of its most successful tactical air weapons. A decade later the AC-130 Spectre gunships were still an important part of the Air Force, attached to the First Special Operations Wing based at Hurlburt Field, Florida.

LINEBACKER

At the beginning of 1972, American troop levels in Southeast Asia were down to 117,000, their lowest level since 1964; and President Nixon had just announced that another 70,000 would be withdrawn by May. USAF air combat had been restricted from North Vietnam for over three years, and the RNVAF was receiving a steady stream of new aircraft under *Enhance*, with an eye toward the day when they could assume the entire burden of the air war themselves. With the

American commitment dwindling and the South Vietnamese forces still building up, North Vietnamese military planners saw a window of opportunity which they decided to exploit. On 29 March 1972 North Vietnam launched a massive conventional invasion of the South, with 12 divisions of regular troops supported by artillery and tanks. It was by far the biggest conventional offensive they had ever fielded. The bombing halt had given them the respite needed to rebuild their road and rail systems, which made the present invasion possible.

The North Vietnamese air force was becoming aggressive as well. A MiG-21 had shot down a USAF HH-53 rescue helicopter over Laos with an air-to-air missile in January 1970, but they had been largely absent from combat for several years. Early in 1972 they had started to conduct combat air patrols of their own in the *Barrel Roll* areas of Laos. On the night of 21 February 1972, four years and one week since the last jet-to-jet engagement in the skies over Southeast Asia, Major Robert Lodge and Lieutenant Roger Locher of the 555th TFS were flying a *MiG CAP* mission in an F-4D over *Barrel Roll* when *Red Crown* warned them of nearby MiGs. They watched on radar as three MiGs closed on them. The F-4 crew fired three Sidewinders and watched as the missiles exploded one by one in the night sky, the last accompanied by a huge fireball. The remaining MiGs gave chase to the Phantom, but aborted the pursuit after about four minutes, sensing a trap and/or not wanting to be drawn too deep into American-controlled air space. A week later another MiG-21 attempted to intercept American aircraft over northern Laos; *MiG CAP* went into action again. Another F-4D from the 555th TFS, this time manned by Lt Col Joseph Kittenger and Lieutenant Leigh Hodgdon, closed on the MiG. Both of the aircraft fired their air-to-air missiles, but the MiG was a little too late. Kittenger watched his Sidewinder collide with the MiG and took evasive action to avoid the incoming missiles. A few days later, within days of his scheduled departure from Southeast Asia, Kittinger was the loser in another MiG encounter and became the first American POW of the renewed air-to-air war.

On the first full day of the big North Vietnamese invasion, as if to underscore the intention to renew the war on all fronts, the enemy launched another MiG sweep into Laos. The ensuing air battle sent one fewer MiG back to North Vietnam, but enemy forces were making rapid progress on the ground in the South. On 16 April 1972 the bombing halt officially ended; US Navy and Air Force fighter-bombers went North against lines of communication, rail heads and supply facilities in and around Hanoi and Haiphong. This time the antiaircraft defenses were stronger, and the MiGs more prevalent than at any time during *Rolling Thunder*. Three MiG-21s were shot down by Sidewinder-armed Phantoms on the 16th.

On 8 May the President announced the mining of Haiphong and other harbors and a new – this time largely unrestricted – air offensive against North Vietnam to be called *Linebacker*. North Vietnamese defences had been strengthened since *Rolling Thunder*, but American pilots were ready to meet the challenge. Besides the lifting of restrictions, US airmen had an arsenal of new weapons to aid them. Among these were the improved radar-guided 'smart' bombs that were used to destroy the Thanh Hoa railway and highway bridge five days after the beginning of *Linebacker*. The bridge, because of its difficult location, had withstood repeated attacks during *Rolling Thunder* and had become something of a symbol to the North Vietnamese.

A PAIR OF ACES IN THE TRIPLE NICKEL

As air-to-air combat proliferated with the onset of *Linebacker*, one squadron began to stand out. The Thailand-based 555th Tactical Fighter Squadron, called 'Triple Nickel' because of the three fives, was already almost a household word around the fighter fields of Southeast Asia because it had achieved many more MiG kills than any other USAF squadron in the theater. The 555th had been part of Colonel Robin Old's Eighth Tactical Fighter Wing (the 'Wolf Pack') at the time of operation *Bolo*; its pilots, including Colonel Olds, had accounted for four of the seven MiGs shot down during *Bolo* and both the MiGs downed four days later.

The Triple Nickel was now flying combat air patrols out of Udorn RTAFB as part of the 432nd Tactical Reconnaissance Wing, and had scored one of two victories chalked up by PACAF over Hanoi on the opening day of *Linebacker*. Two days later (10 May) the 555th was northwest of Hanoi on combat air patrol when the F-4 team of Major Robert Lodge and Captain Roger Locher, who had scored the first victory of the year and their second on 8 May, picked up two MiGs on radar. They closed on the enemy, engaged one of the MiG-21s and blew his wing off with an AIM-7 Sparrow just as they were themselves struck by an air-to-air missile. The Phantom rolled out of control, with flames beginning to melt the cockpit canopy. Locher managed to eject from the aircraft, landing in a remote jungle valley in North Vietnam where he lived off the land until he was rescued three weeks later. Moments after Locher and Lodge were hit their

Below: Claws for the MiG hunters. Sidewinder (foreground) and Sparrow air-to-air missiles are readied for loading aboard a Phantom.

Statistical Analysis of the 137 Enemy Aircraft Downed in Combat in Southeast Asia by the US Air Force

Type of USAF Aircraft Scoring Victory		Type of Weapon Credited with Each Kill				Type of Enemy Aircraft Downed	
F-4:	107½	AIM-7 Sparrow:	50	AIM-4 Falcon:	5	MiG-21:	68
F-105:	27½	Gunfire, 20mm:	41	Maneuvering Tactics:	5	MiG-17:	61
B-52:	2	AIM-9 Sidewinder:	34	Gunfire, .50 cal (B-52):	2	MiG-19:	8

Enemy Aircraft Downed in Combat by year

1965:	2	1967:	59	1969:	0	1971:	0	1973:	1
1966:	17	1968:	8	1970:	0	1972:	50		

The Final Score of Aircraft Downed in Air-to-Air Combat
137 North Vietnamese Aircraft
63 US Air Force Aircraft

Top: Captains Steve Ritchie (*left*) and Chuck DeBellevue (*right*) of the 555th Tactical Fighter Squadron, the 'Triple Nickel,' were the first USAF aces of the war and scored most of their victories while crewing together in the same F-4 Phantom.

Above: DeBellevue and Ritchie (foreground) with Lt Col Griff Baily and Captain Jeff Feinstein at Udorn RTAFB. The slogan of the 432nd Tactical Recon Wing (which contained the 555th) was: 'Protect the Force, Get the Pictures . . . and Kill MiGs.'

Above: A SAC tanker gasses up two 388th TFW F-4Es while three 354th TFW A-7s wait their turn.

Below: Captain Jeff Feinstein killed five MiG-21s to become the last USAF ace of the war.

wingmen, Lieutenant John Markle and Captain Stephen Eaves, engaged what may well have been the same MiG. They fired a pair of Sparrows and a second MiG went down. Meanwhile a third MIG was trying to get into firing position when he fell into the sights of another F-4 manned by Captains Steve Ritchie and Chuck De Bellevue. The 555th had lost a flight leader that day, but they had also sent three MiGs into the jungle below.

In the next two days the Triple Nickel scored twice more, giving it six victories in five days and 26 for the year to date. The victory on 12 May was particularly notable because the two crewmen involved, Wayne Frye and James Cooney, were both Lieutenant Colonels. As Cooney remarked later, they had 'probably set a world's record for the total age of an air crew in an F-4 for a MiG kill.' He was right: their combined age was 85.

The four MiGs destroyed during the remainder of May included the second for Captain Ritchie and a second for Captain Jeffrey Feinstein of the 13th Tactical Fighter Squadron. On 8 July Ritchie was teamed with De Bellevue again to make a formidable team that shot down two of the three MiGs to fall to the Air Force that day. On the 18th and 29th of July Feinstein scored his third and fourth kills, making him the third USAF pilot in the war (after Olds in 1967 and Ritchie earlier in the month) to score four confirmed victories. Both Ritchie of the 555th and Feinstein of the 13th had a probable fifth kill disallowed during June by the Seventh Air Force Enemy Aircraft Claims Evaluation Board, so competition was developing over

Above: Four 388th TFW F-4E Phantoms return to Korat RTAFB after a mission over North Vietnam.

Below: Major Ralph Kuster in a 388th TFW F-105 drills a MiG-17 with 20 mm cannon fire, 3 June 1967.

which would be first to achieve the coveted fifth confirmed kill, making him the first USAF ace of the war.

On 28 August Ritchie and De Bellevue were in the lead Phantom of a four-plane flight providing MiGCAP for a *Linebacker* strike mission over North Vietnam when a MiG-21 was picked up on radar. They rolled the big F-4 into firing position and fired two Sparrows to entice the MiG into a turn. As the enemy took evasive action, the Phantom fell into his six o'clock position and fired two more air-to-air missiles – Steve Richie became the first fighter pilot in Southeast Asia to join the ranks of USAF aces.

The victory also gave De Bellevue his fourth score and further enhanced the 555th's position as the top-scoring squadron in the war. On 9 September De Bellevue, now teamed with Captain John Madden, was part of a flight of 555th TFS Phantoms flying MiGCAP west of Hanoi. A MiG-21 was sighted visually and the pair made a pass, firing two Sparrows that failed to guide properly and missed. Captain Calvin Tibbett and Lieutenant William Hargrove were observing and promptly jumped into the fray. They fired two Sidewinders which, like the Sparrows before them, failed to guide, so they opened fire with their 20mm cannon. A stream of tracers cut into the MiG, the pilot ejecting just as the plane turned nose down. The flight was beginning to re-form when several MiG-19s jumped them. Madden and De Bellevue went into a low-speed 'yo-yo' maneuver behind the MiGs as they tried to evade the Phantom. As the three aircraft

Below: The F-111 had disastrous teething troubles when first introduced in 1968 but was a potent fighting machine when reintroduced in 1972.

Right: Letting Saigons be bygones: an aerial view of Tan Son Nhut a couple of weeks before the final collapse.

rolled across the muggy late-summer sky, the F-4 crew fired two Sidewinders, both of which found their mark. The Americans came out of the maneuver at 1500 feet as one of the MiG-19s exploded into the runway at the Phuc Yen air base. The encounter not only made De Bellevue the second USAF ace of the war, it gave him a sixth kill that made him the highest-scoring American ace of the war. There would also be two US Navy aces, with five kills each. On 13 October Captain Feinstein was flying with 13th TFS Commander Lt Col Curtis Westphal over Hanoi when they encountered a MiG-21 out of Kep. If the Triple Nickel was lucky for Ritchie and De Bellevue, the 'Double 13s' were unlucky for the MiG pilot when an AIM-7 Sparrow made Jeffrey Feinstein the third and final USAF ace in the skies over Southeast Asia.

THE ELEVEN-DAY WAR

While their MiGCAPs duelled in the clouds, the *Linebacker* fighter bombers pummeled North Vietnam with fewer and fewer of the target restrictions that had hamstrung the *Rolling Thunder* campaign. While the smart bombs represented a technological advance over their predecessors, aircraft technology was advancing too. The F-111 had been deployed to Takhli RTAFB in 1967 under the code name *Combat Lancer* as an experimental fighter bomber, but had been recalled to the drawing board, so to speak, when several crashed. The problem was not so much in the aircraft but in one of its systems – terrain-avoidance radar. When perfected and reintroduced in September 1972 as part of *Linebacker*, it made the F-111 a highly feared and potent weapon. They called it 'Whispering Death,' because the terrain-avoidance radar permitted the plane to fly very close to the ground, far below enemy radar coverage; thus it arrived over the target before it could be seen, heard or detected in any way.

The venerable Thuds were joined by the F-111s and the MiGCAPs swept the skies. By October the exhausted North Vietnamese let it be known that they would be willing to allow the stalled Paris Peace Talks to go forward. With some hope for a negotiated settlement in the air, *Linebacker* was terminated on 23 October.

By December, however, it seemed that North Vietnam saw *Linebacker*'s termination as a repeat of the bombing halt of 1968; it began to drag its feet again in peace talks. The United States was prepared. After eight inconclusive years of limited air warfare, it was decided to launch the unrestrained air offensive against North Vietnam that had been proposed again and again since 1964. Beginning on 18 December, the B-52s, which had been used only occasionally in southernmost North Vietnam, would be used against Hanoi and Haiphong, the targets once restricted even for fighter bomber operations. Over a hundred of the enormous strategic bombers were available for the campaign, which would be designated *Linebacker II*. Original strategy called for a three-night maximum effort, with the huge bombers of SAC's Eighth Air Force flying from U Tapao RTNAFB, Thailand and Andersen AFB on Guam. Their vast firepower would be augmented by both PACAF and Seventh-Fleet fighter bombers who would hit the same targets by day. All strike aircraft would be supported by *MiG CAP* provided again by both PACAF and Seventh Fleet. It would be the largest air operation of the war.

For three nights the vast armada had thundered over the most important strategic targets in North Vietnam, when the decision came down to continue the maximum effort indefinitely. With a standdown on Christmas Day, *Linebacker II* ran for eleven punishing days, during which time no target of importance was spared – railyard, airfield or petroleum-storage complex. At the end North Vietnam was, for the first time, a beaten nation: by 29 December 1972 their means of waging war had been virtually

destroyed. The SAM missiles that had knocked down 15 B-52s early in the campaign had been used up, and most of the MiGs were either destroyed on the ground or sitting on inoperable runways. The North Vietnamese had little choice but to return to the peace talks and to bargain in good faith. In less than a month, a cease-fire had been signed and that phase of the long and bloody conflict which had involved the United States so deeply was over.

THE LAST FLIGHT OUT

The war in Southeast Asia did not end with *Linebacker II*. Limited tactical operations would continue against parts of North Vietnam until 15 January 1973, and in South Vietnam until the 27th; B-52 *Arc Light* raids continued until the following day, officially ending as the peace accords were being signed in Paris.

Under operation *Countdown*, USAF personnel were withdrawn from South Vietnam, reaching a manpower ceiling of 12 military and 28 civilians by 29 March. All PACAF/Seventh Air Force aircraft had been flown out or turned over to the RVNAF a month earlier. The first American prisoners of war in North Vietnam, mostly USAF and Navy pilots, were released on 12 February with the USAF given the task of flying C-141 transports to Hanoi to bring the men out to Clark AB in the Philippines.

USAF air operations continued from the bases in Thailand against communist insurgents in Laos and Cambodia until 15 August when Congress passed a resolution banning the bombing. On 7 November the Senate and the House of Representatives overrode a presidential veto and passed the War Powers Resolution, which made it impossible to commit American forces to combat for more than sixty days without Congressional approval. The US had not only gotten out of the war in Vietnam, it had closed the door on going back.

During the dozen years it spent fighting the war in Southeast Asia, the US Air Force had flown 5,226,701 combat sorties and suffered casualties of 2118 killed, 3460 wounded and 599 still missing in action. Aircraft lost to combat and other factors totaled 2257, including 445 F-4s, 397 F-105s, 243 F-100s and 30 B-52s, at an estimated cost of $3,129,948,000. During their missions the USAF dropped 6,162,000,000 tons or ordnance, twelve times the total dropped in Korea and nearly three times that expended in World War II. In aerial combat the USAF shot down 137 MiGs with the last, a MiG-21, downed on 8 January 1973. In turn the USAF lost 67 aircraft to the MiGs for a loss rate of 2 to 1.

The United States was now out of Vietnam, the Seventh Air Force relocated to the Philippines; forces in Thailand were gradually being phased out. Against this backdrop, North Vietnamese and Viet Cong went back to business as usual throughout 1974, with South Vietnam fighting back. On 28 February 1975 they launched an offensive like that which had precipitated *Linebacker I* three years earlier, but this time there was no American response. One by one, South Vietnamese units crumbled as province after province fell to the tank- and artillery-supported North Vietnamese offensive. USAF transports, meanwhile, were operating a continuous evacuation airlift of Americans and South Vietnamese from Tan Son Nhut and Bien Hoa.

On 21 April South Vietnamese President Thieu resigned and fled the country. Eight days later a joint US military operation involving PACAF units and designated *Frequent Wind* evacuated 395 Americans and 5205 others from a surrounded Saigon, the last flight out being made by a helicopter from the roof of the US Embassy. Next day, 30 April 1975, North Vietnamese armored units occupied Saigon. Both South Vietnam and the NLF ceased to exist, Hanoi now controlled all of Vietnam and the war was over at last.

TACTICAL AIR POWER IN THE US AIR FORCE

TACTICAL AIR POWER

Tactical air power is the basic building block of every air force and indeed the reason for their existence. Of more than 140 air forces in the world, barely half a dozen have a strategic air-power capability, while all have some form of tactical capability.

Tactical air power, by definition, involves the use of aerial combat and support in warfare toward an immediate tactical goal, either defensively or offensively. Tactical airpower includes support of land or sea forces in battle, interception of enemy aircraft attacking one's homeland or one's forces behind the lines, interdiction of enemy forces and supply routes behind *his* lines and achieving air superiority over a battlefield or theater. Tactical air power also includes reconnaissance, which can be defined as intelligence gathering (from the air) to support land, sea or air combat operations. Tactical air power has been used by hundreds of air forces in wars and skirmishes all over the world since the early 20th century. In our own troubled times, hardly a month goes by without some news of tactical air operations somewhere in the world.

If tactical air power is the basic building block of an air force, the fighter aircraft is the keystone of such air power. Fighters, generally known as pursuit planes up to World War II, are relatively small, fast and highly maneuverable compared to bombers, the other major type of combat aircraft. The fighter's primary mission is to fight other aircraft, whether in duelling for air superiority or intercepting enemy bombers. The interceptor is a fighter designed primarily to attack intruding enemy aircraft. The fighter's secondary mission of ground support is to attack enemy ground positions with bombs, rockets or guns. Fighters engaged in this type of mission are called fighter bombers and are distinguished from the other principal tactical aircraft (light bombers or attack planes, including such subtypes as dive bombers and torpedo bombers) by the fact that they could convert themselves to fighters at any time by jettisoning their bombs.

Attack aircraft, or light bombers, are usually in the same size and weight class as fighters, but often trade the speed and maneuverability required of a fighter in air-to-air combat for the ability to carry a heavier load of air-to-ground ordnance. Tactical ground support is the primary mission of attack aircraft or light bombers. Of the basic aircraft in the tactical arsenal, fighters, interceptors and fighter bombers may be different versions of the same basic aircraft, while attack aircraft or light bombers are designed specifically for ground support or interdiction.

Right: **An F-15 pilot climbs into his bird on the flight line at Holloman AFB, New Mexico.**

THE TACTICAL AIR COMMAND

Tactical air power has been an important part of the US Air Force and its predecessors since World War I. Today the Tactical Air Command (TAC) and the Strategic Air Command (SAC) are roughly equal in personnel strength as the two largest USAF Major Commands, each with just over 100,000. While SAC is the only strategic air command, TAC has more aircraft and is the centerpiece of USAF tactical air power, which also includes three major regional Commands, with additional personnel and aircraft: the Alaskan Air Command (AAC), The Pacific Air Forces (PACAF) and The United States Air Forces in Europe (USAFE). TAC is responsible for training the pilots and developing the weapons and tactics that are rotated into the front-line regional Commands. TAC's importance is seen in the fact that two Major Commands with tactical missions were integrated into it in the late 1970s. The United States Air Forces Southern Command (USAFSO), headquartered at Albrook AFB in the Panama Canal Zone, became the USAF Southern Air Division under TAC control, with Division headquarters relocated to Howard AFB, Canal Zone. In June 1979 the Aerospace Defense Command (ADCOM or ADC), responsible for the nation's air defense and the major American component in the joint US-Canadian North American Air Defense Command (NORAD), became part of TAC; its commander became TAC Deputy Commander for Air Defense. In the trend of that era toward absorbing USAF tactical air power into TAC, PACAF was scheduled to be disbanded and its assets incorporated into TAC by 1 July 1975, but the order was postponed and, 11 months later, rescinded. It would not, however, be improbable to envision all tactical Commands being ultimately incorporated into TAC.

The Tactical Air Command and the Aerospace Defense Command (known as the Air Defense Command until 1 January 1968), the core of today's TAC, were both founded as Major Commands on 21 March 1946 along with the Strategic Air Command. These three Major Commands were designed to incorporate the heart of USAAF combat air power and become the basic structure of the new USAF, which would come into being 18 months later. TAC basic organization consisted of the major tactical numbered Air Forces from the European Theater of World War II – the Ninth and Twelfth – being brought stateside and stretched over the installations, training and organization framework of the Third Air Force (in the Southeast quadrant of the continental US). In May 1946 TAC headquarters was established at Langley Field, Virginia (Langley AFB after 1947), where it has remained ever since.

Because of the precipitous drop in both personnel and first-line aircraft strength in the late forties, as well as a drop in funding, both ADC and TAC were cut back drastically in December 1948, losing their Major Command status. They became components of a newly created umbrella Command, the Continental Air Command (CONAC). Two years later, in December 1950, with Chinese intervention in the Korean War and the obvious need to build up American air power, both TAC and ADC were restored to Major Command status, retaining it until they merged into a single Major Command in 1979.

The USAF Southern Command (USAFSO), which was to become TAC's Southern Air Division, originally became a Major Command – the Caribbean Air Command – in November 1947, redesignated USAFSO in July 1963. Created from the World War II-era Sixth Air Force, the Caribbean (like the Joint US-Brazil Air Command) indicated US emphasis on the South Atlantic during that period because of the southern route's importance during the war. With the June 1979 merger, TAC had control not only of all the USAF tactical air assets in the continental United States but those as far south as the Panama Canal and as far east as Iceland (where US Air Forces, Iceland, had been part of ADC).

TAC's mission is to organize, train, equip and maintain a highly mobile tactical air force capable of deployment anywhere in the world either on its own, through one of the three major regional Commands (as through PACAF in Southeast Asia), or through the Rapid Deployment Force (RDF). The mission includes all the classic elements of tactical air power: air superiority; interdiction; close air support; reconnaissance; electronic combat countermeasures (jamming etc) and tactical air control (control of tactical combat aircraft). To quote directly, 'TAC is the US Air Force's mobile strike force . . . able to deploy US general purpose air forces anywhere in the world on a moment's

The Commanders of the Tactical Air Command

Lt Gen E R Quesada 21 Mar 1946-23 Nov 1948
Maj Gen Robert Lee 24 Dec 1948-20 June 1950
Maj Gen Glenn Barcus 17 July 1950-25 Jan 1951
Gen John Cannon 25 Jan 1951-31 Mar 1954
Gen O P Wayland 1 Apr 1954-31 July 1959
Gen Frank Everest 1 Aug 1959-30 Sept 1961
Gen Walter Sweeney, Jr 1 Oct 1961-31 July 1965
Gen Gabriel Disosway 1 Aug 1965-31 July 1968
Gen William Momyer 1 Aug 1968-30 Sept 1973
Gen Robert Dixon 1 Oct 1973-30 Apr 1978
Gen W L Creech 1 May 1978-

The Commanders of the Air Defense Command

Lt Gen George Stratemeyer	21 Mar 1946–30 Nov 1948
Maj Gen Gordon Saville	1 Dec 1948–31 Dec 1950
Lt Gen Ennis Whitehead	1 Jan 1951–25 Aug 1951
Gen Benjamin Chidlaw	25 Aug 1951–31 May 1955
Maj Gen Frederick Smith, Jr (acting)	31 May 1955–19 July 1955
Gen Earle Partridge	20 July 1955–17 Sept 1956
Lt Gen Joseph Atkinson	17 Sept 1956–15 Aug 1961
Lt Gen Robert Lee	15 Aug 1961–31 July 1963
Lt Gen Herbert Thatcher	1 Aug 1963–31 July 1967
Lt Gen Arthur Agan	1 Aug 1967–31 Dec 1967

The Commanders of the Aerospace Defense Command

Lt Gen Arthur Agan	1 Jan 1968–28 Feb 1970
Lt Gen Thomas McGehee	1 Mar 1970–1 July 1973
Gen Seth McKee	1 July 1973–1 Oct 1973
Gen Lucius Clay, Jr	1 Oct 1973–31 Aug 1975
Gen Daniel James, Jr	1 Sept 1975–5 Dec 1977
Gen James Hill	6 Dec 1977–30 Nov 1979

The Commanders of the Aerospace Defense Center, Tactical Air Command

Gen James Hill	1 Dec 1979–1 Jan 1980
Gen James Hartinger	1 Jan 1980–31 Aug 1980

(With creation of the Space Command on 1 Sept 1982, the functions of the Aerospace Defense Center were absorbed by Space Command, and the ADC Commander became SPACECOM Commander)

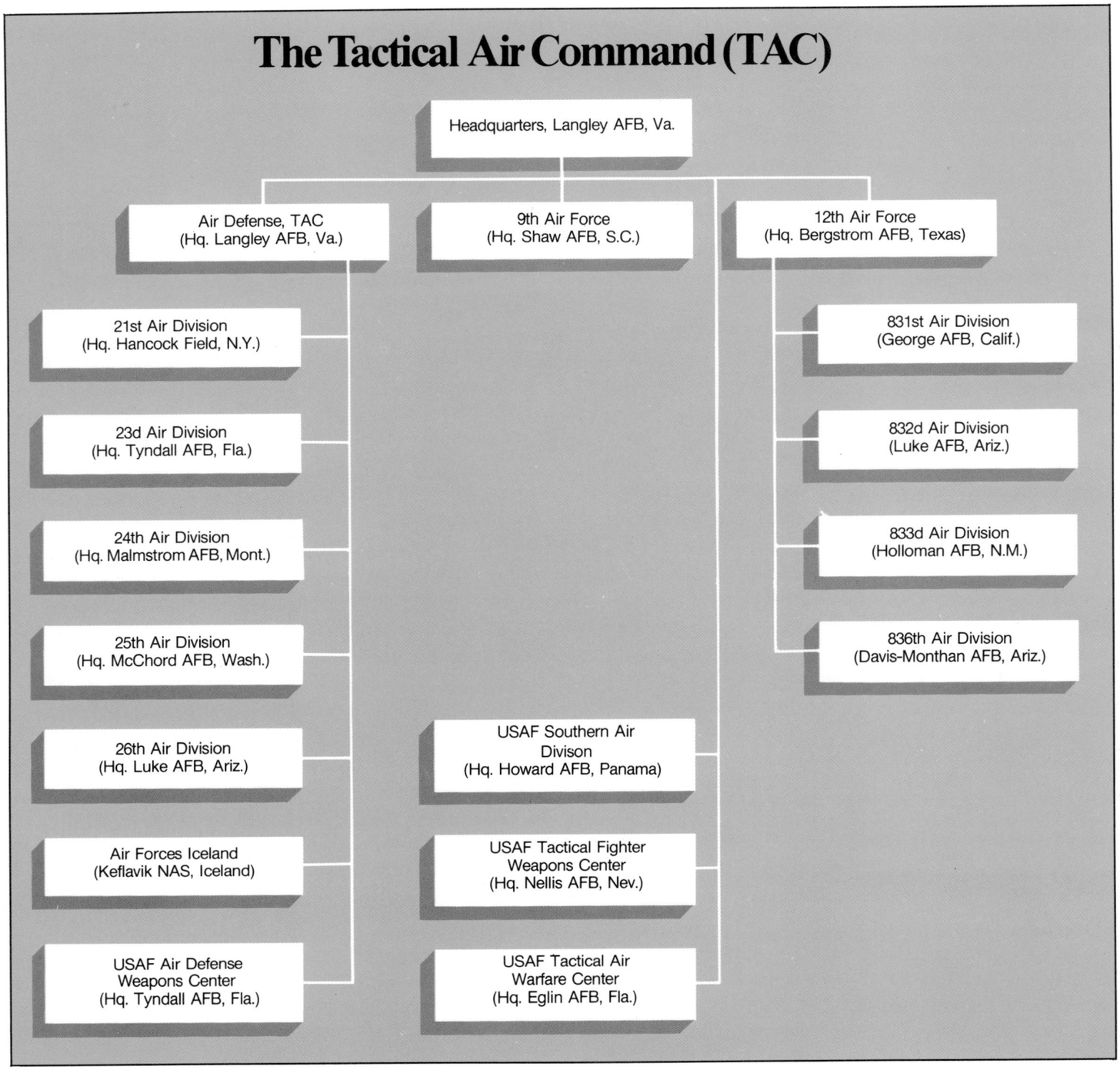

notice for tactical air operations in support of national security, and to provide combat ready forces to defend North America against aerospace attack.'

TAC is also a component of several joint multiservice military commands like the US Readiness, US Atlantic and US Southern Commands. Through the TAC Deputy Commander for Air Defense (ADTAC), TAC replaced ADC as the US component in NORAD until creation of the Space Command (SPACECOM) in 1982.

As part of its mission, TAC is involved in dozens of realistic tactical air exercises in the United States annually (including the joint US-Canada air defense exercise code-named *William Tell*); Canada, Egypt (*Bright Star*), Germany, Italy and Korea are other sites for such exercises. A vital part of TAC training is a series of exercises designed by General Robert Dixon (TAC Commander 1973-78). Known as 'Flags', these were developed in the late seventies to give USAF personnel practical, highly realistic training to prevent repetition of the mistakes that had plagued Air Force operations during the war in Southeast Asia. *Red Flag*, the best-known, occurs several times a year for six-week periods at the huge Air Force Bombing and Gunnery Range north of Nellis AFB in the tip of Nevada. Its objective is to provide fighter pilots with realistic air-to-air combat missions. War in the skies over Vietnam had proved that despite training prior to actual combat, fighter pilots still had a lot to learn, and that most of their mistakes occurred during their first ten missions. If a pilot survived his tenth mission the odds improved vastly, showing that he had mastered the necessary skills. But what of the airman who didn't survive ten missions? Air Force training had produced great *pilots*, but it seemed to take experience to produce great *combat pilots*. General Dixon conceived *Red Flag* as a way of giving pilots ten combat missions under controlled conditions. TAC created an 'enemy' in its 4440th Tactical Fighter Training Group formed at Nellis AFB, against which pilots flying in *Red Flag* do mock battle. Calling themselves Aggressors, the pilots of 4440th fly the Northrop F-5,

Above: AFRES C-130s on the line at TAC's Howard AFB, Panama.

Below: Keflavik NAS; Iceland-based TAC Phantoms intercept a Russian Tu95 over the North Atlantic.
Right: A flight of 49th TFW F-15 Eagles out of Holloman AFB. The Eagle is TAC's top fighter.

similar in size, appearance and radar signature to the MiG-21, the commonest Soviet-bloc tactical aircraft. The F-5s are even painted with Soviet and Warsaw Pact camouflage schemes. The name *Red Flag* implies the nature of the 'enemy.' Opposing aircraft are shot down by computers rather than guns, but in other respects *Red Flag* is realistic, with the Aggressors flying Soviet and Warsaw-Pact tactics as well as markings. *Red Flag* also involves units from the US Navy, Canada and various NATO air forces.

Black Flag is the maintenance counterpart of the more visible *Red Flag*. Its maintenance crews practice keeping aircraft flying under frantic wartime conditions.

Blue Flag trains command-control and communications (C^3) personnel to ply their vital trade under wartime conditions. Training is tailored to simulate theaters in which the C crews might have to operate – Europe, Korea or the Persian Gulf.

Checkered Flag is the exercise under which TAC units from stateside deploy to overseas bases, usually of other tactical Commands, from which they would have to operate in an emergency. Crews learn the peculiarities of a given base, runways, local weather, facilities available, etc.

Copper Flag is the TAC Air Defense (ADTAC) equivalent of Red Flag in which air-defense crews, both air and ground-based, practice defending against enemy tactical or strategic air attack.

Green Flag trains tactical air forces in the use of Electronic Warfare (EW) and Electronic Countermeasures (ECM). It is the Electronic Warfare counterpart of the other *Flags* and a *Green Flag* exercise is held annually at Nellis AFB in co-ordination with a *Red Flag*.

Silver Flag was designed to prepare TAC ground personnel in such fields as civil engineering, air-base ground defense, law enforcement and medical services to function under wartime conditions. *Silver Flag* has three principal elements. WARSKIL trains noncombat TAC personnel to do their jobs under a wartime scenario. WARFIL trains selected personnel from bases in the United States whose skills or specialties would require their deployment to the front in wartime. The Base Augmentation Programs of *Silver Flag* have the task of providing smooth and efficient transportation of TAC personnel under emergency conditions.

HO
AF 77 112
HO
AF 77 128
HO
AF 77 099

TACTICAL AIR COMMAND BASES

Langley AFB (TAC Headquarters)
Location: 3 miles north of Hampton, Virginia
Area: 3500 acres
Altitude: 10ft
Personnel: 9258 Military
1710 Civilian
The base was activated 30 December 1916 as Langley Field, and is the oldest continually active AFB in the country. It was named for aviation pioneer and scientist Samuel Pierpont Langley, who died in 1906. The host unit is the 1st Tactical Fighter Wing flying F-15s. Tenants include 5th Weather Wing (MAC), 2d Aircraft Delivery Group (TAC), 480th Reconnaissance Technical Group (TAC), 48th Fighter Interceptor Sqdn (TAC) and the US Army TRADOC Flight Detachment. The NASA Langley Research Center is located across base.

Bergstrom AFB
Location: 7 miles SE of downtown Austin, Texas
Area: 3998 acres
Altitude: 541ft
Personnel: 5050 Military
915 Civilian
The base was activated on 22 September 1942, named for Captain John Bergstrom, the first Austin serviceman to die in World War II (8 December 1941 in the attack on Clark Field in the Philippines). The base is headquarters for both the 12th Air Force (TAC) and the 10th Air Force (AFRES), and is the site of the TAC NCO Academy West. Also located on base are the 67th Tactical Recon Wing with RF-4Cs and the 924th Tactical Fighter Gp (AFRES) flying F-4Ds.

Cannon AFB
Location: 7 miles west of Clovis, New Mexico
Area: 25.663 acres
Altitude: 4295ft
Personnel: 3900 Military
418 Civilian
The base was activated in August 1942 and was named for General John K Cannon, commander of Allied Air Forces in the Mediterranean area in World War II. It is the home of the 27th Tactical Fighter Wing flying F-111s.

Davis-Monthan AFB
Location: Outskirts of Tucson, Arizona
Area: 11,000 acres
Altitude: 2620ft
Personnel: 6489 Military
1327 Civilian
The base was activated in 1927 and named for 1st Lt Samuel Davis, and 2nd Lt Oscar Monthan (died 1921 and 1924 respectively). The base is the headquarters of the 836th Air Div and home to the 355th Tactical Training Wing (A-10 combat training), 602d Tactical Control Wing, 41st Electronic Combat Sqdn, 868th Tactical Missile Training Sqdn, and SAC's 390th Strategic Missile Wing responsible for Tital IIs based in Arizona. The base is also the site of AFLC's Military Aircraft Storage and Disposition Center, where several thousand aircraft are mothballed in the dry desert air for possible future use (see page 208).

England AFB
Location: 5 miles west of Alexandria, Louisiana
Area: 2282 acres
Altitude: 89ft
Personnel: 3173 Military
540 Civilian
The base was activated in October 1942 and later named for Lt Col John England, a World War II ace (17.5 victories) who was killed in an F-86 crash on 17 November 1954. The base is home to the 23d Tactical Fighter Wing flying A-10s.

George AFB
Location: 6 miles NW of Victorville, California
Area: 5347 acres
Altitude: 2875ft
Personnel: 5842 Military
450 Civilian
The base was activated in 1941, and renamed for World War I ace Brig Gen Harold George, who was killed on 29 April 1942. Headquarters of the 831st Air Div, the base is the home of 37th Tactical Fighter Wing (the Wild Weasel F-4Gs), 35th Tactical

Above: The base headquarters building at Langley AFB in Virginia.

Fighter Wing (Pave Spike F-4Es), F-4 transitional training, German Luftwaffe F-4 training and a TAC F-106 group.

Hancock Field
Location: Ten miles NNE of Syracuse, New York
Area: 765 acres
Altitude: 421ft
Personnel: 818 Military
315 Civilian
Activated in 1942 as Syracuse Army Air Base, it was renamed in 1952 for US Congressman Clarence Hancock (1885-1949) of Syracuse. The 4789th Air Base Group is host to the 21st NORAD Region, 21st TAC Air Div, 3513th USAF Recruiting Sqdn, 174th Tactical Fighter Wing (ANG).

Holloman AFB
Location: 6 miles SW of Alamogordo, New Mexico
Area: 50,697 acres
Altitude: 4093ft
Personnel: 5934 Military
1104 Civilian
The base was activated in 1942 and renamed for missile pioneer Col George Holloman, who was killed on 19th March 1946. The base is the headquarters of the 833d Air Div, playing host to 49th Tactical Fighter Wing (F-15), 479th Tactical Training Wing (AT-38), 4449th Mobility Support Sqdn (*Harvest Bare*), 82nd Tactical Control Flight and 40th Aerospace Rescue and Recovery Sqdn among others. The AFSC 6585th Test Group conducts aircraft and missile-system tests and evaluation, and operates the Central Inertial Guidance Test Facility, High Speed Test Track Facility and the Radar Target Scatter (RATSCAT) site.

Homestead AFB
Location: 5 miles NNE of Homestead, Florida
Area: 3491 acres
Altitude: 7ft
Personnel: 5814 Military
1150 Civilian
Activated in April 1955, the base is home to TAC's 31st Tactical Training Wing (F-4D), 726th Tac Control Sqdn (TAC), 482d Tactical Fighter Wing (AFRES), and the 301st Aerospace Rescue and Recovery Sqdn (AFRES).

Hurlburt Field, Eglin AFB
Location: 5 miles west of Fort Walton Beach, Florida
Area: 464,980 acres (entire Eglin AFB)
Altitude: 35ft
Personnel: 3602 Military
315 Civilian
Located on AFSC's Eglin AFB reservation, Hurlburt Field was activated in 1943 and is a TAC base named for Lt Donald Hurlburt who was killed in a crash here on 2 October 1943. The field is the headquarters of the 2nd Air Division, the focal point of all Air Force Special Operations. Under the 2nd Air Division are the 1st Special Operations Wing equipped with MC-130E Combat Talon, AC-130H Spectre Gunship, HH-53 Pave Low III and the UH-1N; the USAF Special Operations School; Special Operations Combat Control Team; and Special Operations Weather Team. The 2nd Air Div also has units based at Clark AB, Philippines; Rhein-Main AB, Germany and Howard AFB in Panama. Assigned as tenant units at Hurlburt Field are the 4442d Tac Fighter Control Group (USAF Ground Operations School) and the 823d Civil Engineering Sqdn (*Red Horse*).

Luke AFB
Location: 20 miles WNW of Phoenix, Arizona
Area: 5631 acres
Altitude: 6ft
Personnel: 6242 Military
1350 Civilian
Activated in 1941, the base was named for Lt Frank Luke, the 'Arizona Balloon Buster' who was the first airman to receive the Medal of Honor in World War I. He was killed in action near Murvaux, France, on 29 September 1918. Luke AFB, the largest fighter-training base in the world, is headquarters for both the 26th and 832d TAC Air Divisions as well as the 405th and 58th Tactical Training Wings, conducting training in both F-16 and F-15. The headquarters of the 26th NORAD Region is also at Luke AFB.

MacDill AFB
Location: Tampa, Florida
Area: 5631 acres
Altitude: 6ft
Personnel: 6242 Military
1350 Civilian
Activated on 15 April 1941, the base was named for Col Leslie MacDill who had been killed in a plane crash on 8 November 1938. The base is headquarters for the US Readiness Command and the US Central Command, as well as the 56th Tactical Training Wing, conducting F-16 replacement training.

Moody AFB
Location: 10 miles NNE of Valdosta, Georgia
Area: 6050 acres
Altitude: 233ft
Personnel: 3470 Military
629 Civilian
The base was activated in June 1941 and named for Major George Moody, who had been killed on 5 May while test-piloting a Beech AT-10. Moody is home to the 347th Tactical Fighter Wing flying F-4Es.

Mountain Home AFB
Location 56 miles SE of Boise, Idaho
Area: 6639 acres
Altitude: 3000ft
Personnel: 4175 Military
699 Civilian
Activated in April 1942, the base is home to the 366th Tactical Fighter Wing flying the F-111 fighter and EF-111 Electronic Countermeasures variant.

Below: An F-4E Phantom of the 347th Tactical Fighter Wing based at Moody AFB, Georgia. TAC and the other tactical commands use the two-letter tailcode first introduced in Southeast Asia to identify aircraft with their bases.

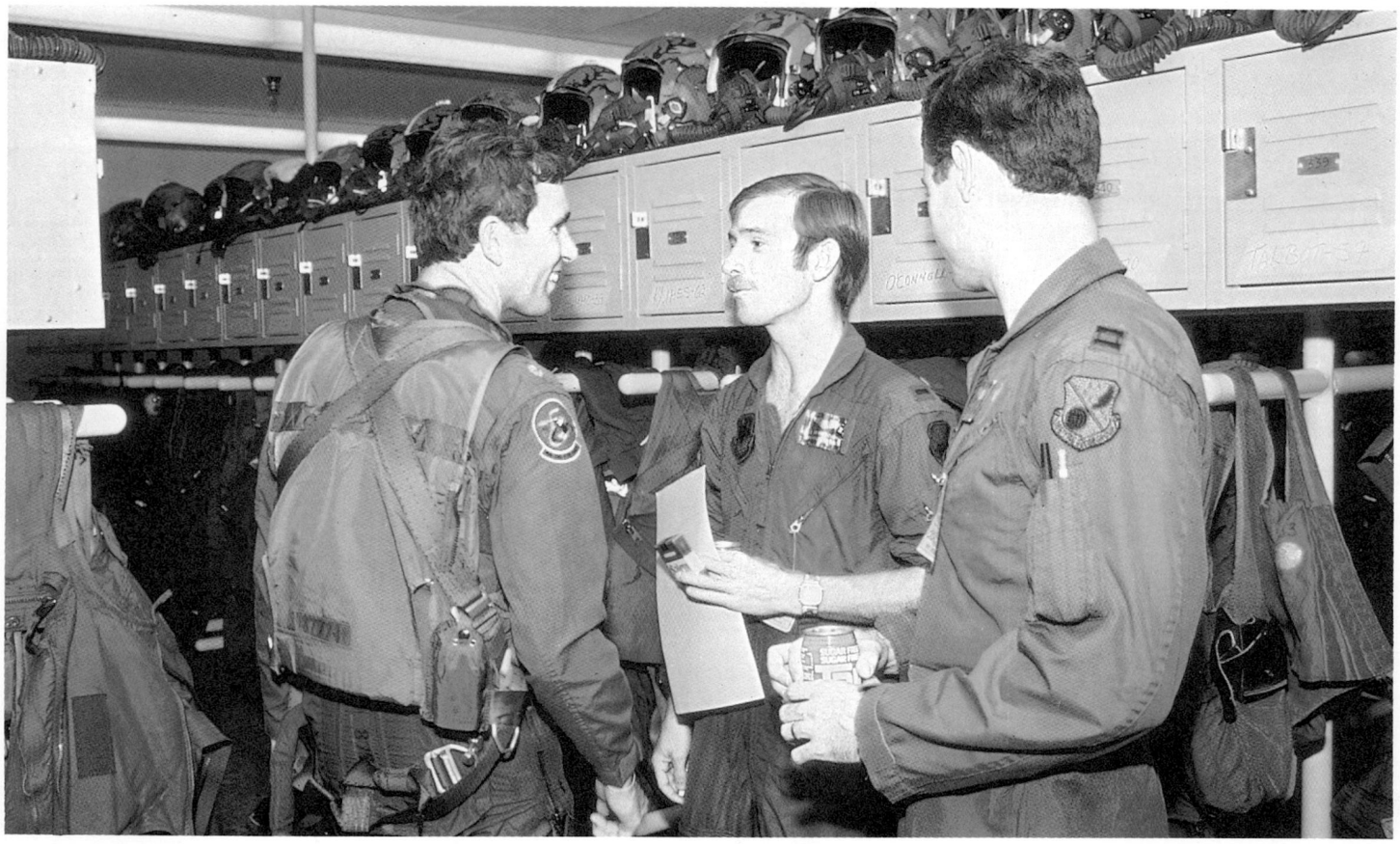

Above: A group of fighter pilots sip diet cola and recap the day's activities in a Nellis AFB locker room after a gruelling *Red Flag* exercise over the parched Nevada desert.

Myrtle Beach AFB
Location: Just south of Myrtle Beach, South Carolina
Area: 3793 acres
Altitude: 25ft
Personnel: 3270 Military
455 Civilian
Sharing a runway with the Myrtle Beach Airport, the base was an Army Air Field between 1941 and 1947. It was reactivated by the USAF in 1956. Current operations are by the 354th Tactical Fighter Wing flying A-10s.

Nellis AFB
Location: 8 miles NE of Las Vegas, Nevada
Area: 11,274 acres (base alone)
3,012,770 acres (with attached USAF ranges)
Altitude: 2171ft
Personnel: 9266 Military
1083 Civilian
With its attached USAF gunnery and bombing ranges, Nellis is the largest USAF base, in fact, larger than some of the foreign countries whose pilots sometimes attend exercises here. Activated in July 1941, the base is named for Lt William Nellis, a fighter pilot killed on 27 December 1944 over Europe. The host unit is the Tactical Fighter Weapons Center, which conducts advanced tactical fighter training and realistic combat training (such as Operation *Red Flag*) for the USAF and US Navy as well as NATO and other allied countries. Units include the 57th Fighter Weapons Squadron, 4440th Tactical Fighter Training Group (*Red Flag*), 474th Tactical Fighter Wing and the USAF Thunderbirds Air Demonstration Squadron.

Indian Springs AF Auxiliary Field (Nellis AFB)
Location: 45 miles NW of Las Vegas
Area: 1652 acres
Altitude: 3124ft
Personnel: 343 Military
13 Civilian
Activated in 1942 the base is now home to the 554th Combat Support Squadron of the 554th Range Group who provide bombing and gunnery range support for tactical operations out of Nellis AFB, as well as US Department of Energy nuclear-weapons testing.

Seymour Johnson AFB
Location: Goldsboro, North Carolina
Area: 4281 acres
Altitude: 109ft
Personnel: 5155 Military
837 Civilian
The base was activated on 12 June 1941 and named for Navy Lt Seymour A Johnson of Goldsboro, who had been killed in a crash on 4 March. The base is one of several for the 4th Tactical Fighter Wing F-4Es with a dual-based commitment to NATO. It is also home to SAC's 68th Air Refuelling Group and AFCC's 2012th Communications Squadron.

Shaw AFB
Location: 10 miles WNW of Sumter, South Carolina
Area: 11,645 acres
Altitude: 244ft
Personnel: 5408 Military
709 Civilian
Activated on 30 August 1941, the base is named for 2nd Lt Ervin Shaw, killed in action with the Air Service on 9 July 1918. It is the headquarters of the 9th Fighter Wing (flying F-16s and RF-4Cs) as well as the 507th Tactical Air Control Wing.

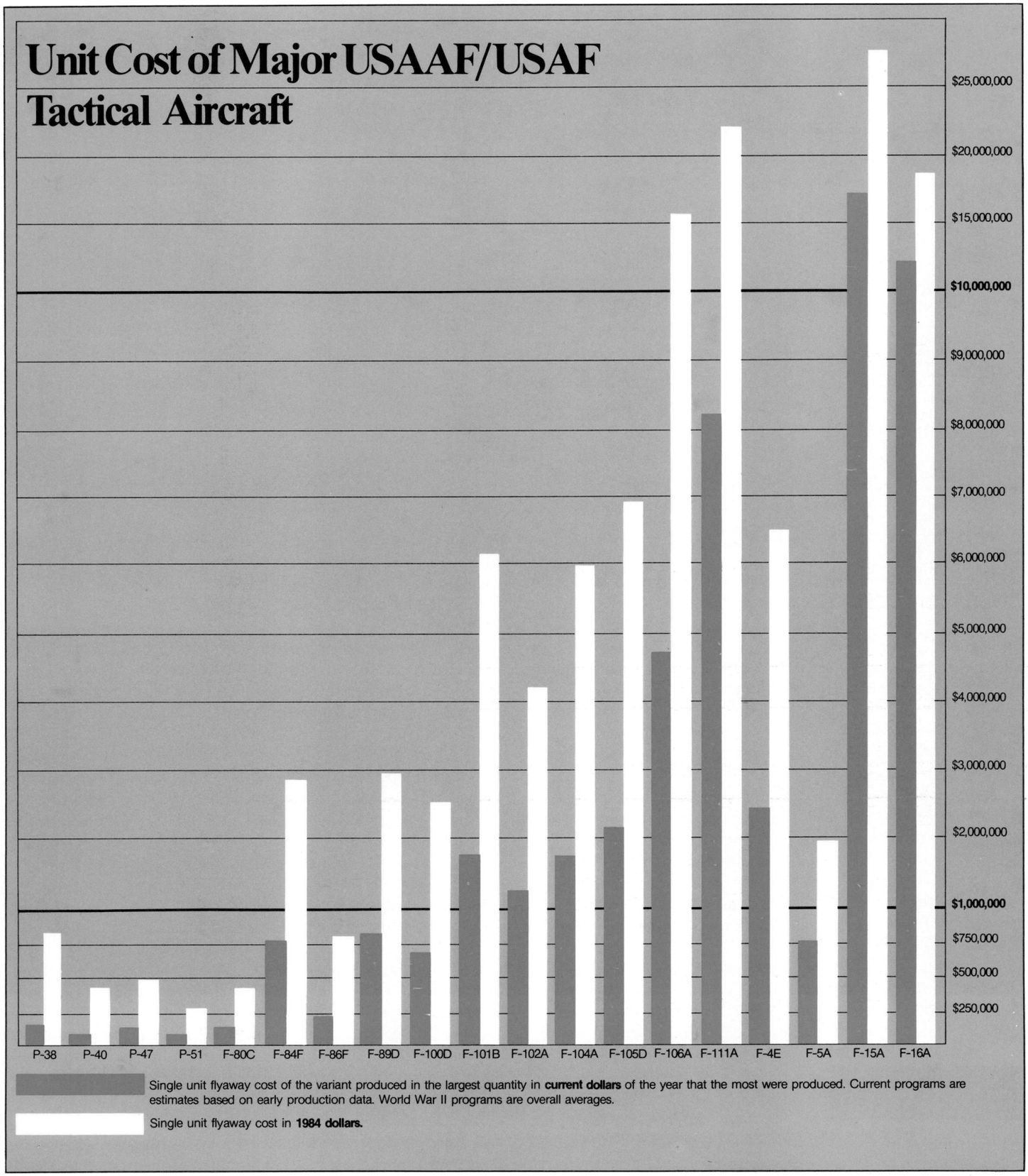

Tyndall AFB
Location: 13 miles east of Panama City, Florida
Area: 28,000 acres
Altitude: 18ft
Personnel: 4250 Military
1198 Civilian

The base was activated on 7 December 1941, the day Pearl Harbor was attacked, and named for Lt Frank Tyndall, a World War I fighter pilot killed on 15 July 1930. The base is the home of the USAF Air Defense Weapons Center and the focal point of operational and technical expertise in the area of air defense for all services. The center conducts testing and evaluation of pilots, tactics and weapons, including the biennial Project *William Tell* interceptor meet to test the skills of the best Air Defense interceptor units from the US and Canada. The base is also home to the TAC/NCO Academy East, the 23d NORAD Region headquarters, ATC's 3625th Technical Training Squadron and AFCC's 2021st Communications Squadron.

US AIR FORCES IN EUROPE

Since the end of World War II Europe has been seen as the likeliest locale for a major power confrontation that could lead to World War III. To meet this threat, the US Air Forces in Europe (USAFE) were organized as a Major Command of the new USAF in 1947. USAFE was formed from the tactical air assets left in Europe after postwar demobilization and is today the second largest (after TAC) tactical Command. USAFE operates nearly 800 tactical aircraft and has over 1500 TAC aircraft in the United States preassigned to it – these could be in place in Europe within 30 days. The aircraft are assigned to bases on both continents through the Co-located Operating Base (COB) program. USAFE is the largest regional Command, with over 50,000 uniformed personnel. Headquartered at **Ramstein AB** in Germany, it is the American contribution to the Allied Air Forces Central Europe (AAFCE), the tactical air component of the North Atlantic Treaty Organization (NATO). USAFE is composed of three numbered Air Forces, the Third, Sixteenth and Seventeenth.

The USAFE Seventeenth Air Force, based at **Sembach AB** along with the Luftwaffe of the German Federal Republic (Bundesrepublik Deutschland, BRD), is the major air element in NATO defense of Central Europe. The area is critical because it faces the largest concentrations of Soviet and Warsaw Pact land and air power. All bases of the Seventeenth are located in the BRD with the exception of the 32d Tactical Fighter Squadron, based at **Camp New Amsterdam** near Soesterberg in the Netherlands. Flying F-15s, the 32d TPS is under joint operational control of the Seventeenth Air Force and the Netherlands Air Defense Center, as its primary role is to work with the Royal Netherlands Air Force (Koninklijk Luchtmacht Nederland, KLN) to maintain allied air superiority over the Netherlands in the event of war. There are six fighter wings assigned to the Seventeenth Air Force, all headquartered in the BRD and flying A-10s, F-4s, F-15s, F-16s and RF-4s. Also in Germany, historic **Tempelhof Central Airport** in Berlin is maintained as an American support base, and the Military Airlift Command (MAC) has its 435th Tactical Airlift Wing at **Rhein-Main AB** across the runway from Frankfurt's Rhein-Main Airport, Germany's major international air hub. Rhein-Main AB is also the MAC air-cargo hub for supplies being delivered to American forces in Germany, but much of the traffic is now going into Ramstein AB because of growing civilian operations at Rhein-Main airport.

The Third Air Force, headquartered at **RAF Mildenhall** in England, is USAFE's largest in terms of personnel and facilities. While the Seventeenth has the bulk of USAFE's tactical combat aircraft, the Third provides support facilities through nine RAF bases in southern England. Besides supporting rotational MAC airlift operations and SAC strategic reconnaissance and air refueling operations, the Third has two Tactical Fighter Wings flying F-111 fighter bombers, one with A-10 attack aircraft and a Tactical Recon Wing with RF-4s. The latter has an 'Aggressor' Squadron, the 527th TFTS flying F-5s in *Red Flag*-type exercises. The Third Air Force also has a civil engineer and heavy-repair squadron at **RAF Wethersfield**; its 501st Tactical Missile Wing at **RAF Greenham Common** supports the deployment of the BGM-109G Ground Launched Cruise Missile (GLCM).

USAFE units across southern Europe and into Asia Minor are under the Sixteenth Air Force Command headquartered at **Torrejon AB** in Spain. The Sixteenth has a Tactical Fighter Training Wing (the 406th) at Zaragoza AB, Spain, and a Tactical Fighter Wing (the 401st), flying F-16s at its home base of Torrejon. In addition there are three bases in Italy: **San Vito AS**, a support and communications station; **Comiso AS**, where the 487th Tactical Missile Wing supports the Ground Launched Cruise Missile; and **Aviano AB** in northern Italy, a major support and refueling base. Aviano AB's refueling function is important for USAFE and other NATO aircraft, because combat aircraft are not permitted to routinely overfly neutral Austria and Switzerland and routing them over France eats up a lot more fuel than would a direct Germany-to-Italy flight. Bases in Greece and Turkey support both USAFE tactical operations and electronic surveillance of military activities in the southwestern Soviet Union and the southern flank of the Warsaw Pact. The bases in Turkey are administered by TUSLOG (The Turkey/United States Logistics Group) headquartered at **Ankara AB** and provide support services for a wide range of USAFE, NATO and MAC aircraft operating in the area on a rotational basis. MAC

Above: Two F-15 Eagles over Germany during the 1982 *Reforger/Crested Cap* exercise.
Below: A 52d TFW USAFE F-4G out of Spangdahlem AB, Germany, armed with AGM-45 Shrike missiles (*see pages 148-9*).

Above: USAFE ground crewmen in chemical warfare gear prepare to land Mk82 bombs onto an A-10 attack plane at Sembach AB. A crucial element of USAFE training is preparation for doing one's job in an environment contaminated by enemy chemical weapons.

units providing airlift for TUSLOG operate out of **Incirlik AB** to nine sites around the country in an ongoing operation code-named *Turkey Trot*.

NATO operations in the eastern Mediterranean have always been complicated by tension between NATO members Greece and Turkey over Cyprus. Turkey's 1974 invasion of Cyprus resulted in a US arms embargo (since lifted) aimed at Turkey. Recently, there was the threatened withdrawal of Greece from NATO and the cancellation of USAFE base rights there.

Prior to 1966, another major concentration of USAFE air power was located in northern France with USAFE units based at Chaumont AB, Dreux AB, Evreux Fauville AB, Laon AB, Etain AB, Chambley AB, Toul Rosieres AB, Phalsbourg AB and Chateauroux AS; rotational units operated through bases in

French Morocco, such as Nouasseur AB, until 1956. In 1966 French President Charles de Gaulle ended USAFE's nearly two-decade presence in France by withdrawing his country from the NATO military command structure and expelling all NATO units from the country, including NATO headquarters and USAFE units. Shortly thereafter, the United States lost another major base in the theater – Wheelus AFB in Libya – when King Idrus was overthrown by the sinister but charismatic Muammar Quaddafi.

USAFE's mission today is to work with other NATO air forces to provide for air defense of Western Europe and to support NATO ground forces defending Western Europe in the event of a Soviet and/or Warsaw-Pact invasion. USAFE also monitors Soviet and Warsaw-Pact activities during peacetime and provides support for MAC and SAC units operating in Europe. In 1977 USAFE was the first regional Major Command to receive the F-15 Eagle air superiority fighter and the A-10 'Warthog' tactical air-support attack aircraft, both the top of their respective lines. In 1980 the first of the G-model F-4 Phantom, the 'Wild Weasel' or SAM suppressor version, made its appearance with USAFE units. Two years later the F-16 fighting Falcon, a fighter/fighter-bomber with the advanced capabilities of the F-15, made its debut with USAFE.

USAFE participates with other NATO air forces as well as US Army units in a number of training exercises such as *Reforger* and *Crested Cap* from Norway to the Mediterranean every year. USAFE is, of course, also a participant in the *Flag* exercises. In recent years these exercises have included training personnel to perform ground operations in chemical warfare protection suits and the development of procedures for Rapid Runway Repair.

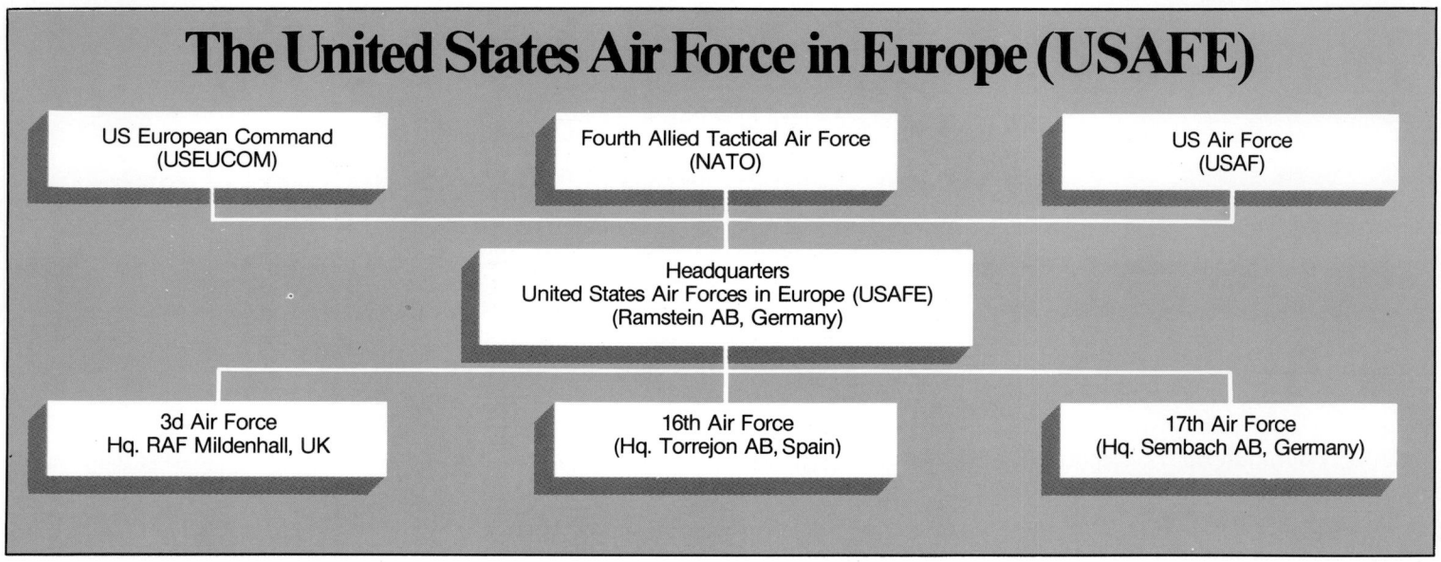

THE PACIFIC AIR FORCES

The Pacific Air Forces (PACAF), the air component of the US Pacific Command, were originally called the Far East Air Forces (FEAF), the name being changed in July 1957. The FEAF was created during World War II by a merger of the Fifth and Thirteenth Air Forces (the Seventh being added later in the war). The FEAF became the air component of General MacArthur's Far East Command; at the end of the war it was joined by the previously independent Twentieth Air Force. With the defeat of Japan FEAF headquarters was moved to Tokyo. The onset of the Korean War in 1950 made FEAF the principal air element of the United Nations Command, with the front-line Fifth and Twentieth Air Forces augmented by a FEAF Bomber Command composed largely of SAC B-29s on temporary assignment.

On 1 July 1957 FEAF officially became the Pacific Air Forces (PACAF), the single USAF Command for the Pacific Theater, with two numbered Air Forces – the Fifth in Japan and the Thirteenth in the Philippines. Both the other numbered Air Forces, the Seventh in Hawaii and the Twentieth on Okinawa, had been dissolved since 1955. Command headquarters was moved to Hickam AFB adjacent to the Navy's base at Pearl Harbor, Hawaii, while the Fifth Air Force moved from its headquarters at Moriyama near Nagoya, Japan, to the plush former FEAF headquarters at Fuchu AS near Tokyo. Fuchu AS was also close to Tachikawa AB and Yokota AB, two of the major Fifth Air Force bases in Japan. PACAF began with 89,679 personnel and 959 aircraft (including 152 F-100s and 249 F-86s), but by the time PACAF was called upon for sustained operations in Southeast Asia in 1964, personnel strength had been reduced to 65,155 with 582 aircraft (including 110 F-102s and 153 F-105s) in the inventory. The rapid escalation of the war in Southeast Asia, and PACAF's new responsibility for USAF air operations there, sent Command strength to a peak of nearly 170,000 personnel and 2100 aircraft prior to the bombing halt in 1968. The Seventh Air Force was reactivated at Tan Son Nhut AB in South Vietnam and PACAF found itself operating from 18 bases in Southeast Asia, including ten in South Vietnam, seven in Thailand and Ching Chuan Kang AB (Republic of China) on Taiwan. As more and more responsibility for the conduct of the air war was turned over to the South Vietnamese, and tactical aircraft assigned to PACAF were gradually returned to TAC and reserve units, PACAF sank back to its prewar strength. By 1975 the Seventh Air Force had ceased to exist. In May PACAF flew

The Commanders of the US Air Forces in Europe

Brig Gen John McBain	15 Aug 1947–20 Oct 1947
Lt Gen Curtis LeMay	20 Oct 1947–15 Oct 1948
Lt Gen John Cannon	16 Oct 1948–20 Jan 1951
Gen Lauris Norstad	21 Jan 1951–26 July 1953
Lt Gen William Tunner	27 July 1953–30 June 1957
Gen Frank Everest	1 July 1957–31 July 1959
Gen Frederic Smith, Jr	1 Aug 1959–30 June 1961
Gen Truman Landon	1 July 1961–31 July 1963
Gen Gabriel Disosway	1 Aug 1963–31 July 1965
Gen Bruce Holloway	1 Aug 1965–31 July 1966
Gen Maurice Preson	1 Aug 1966–31 July 1968
Gen Horace Wade	1 Aug 1968–31 Jan 1969
Gen Joseph Holzapple	1 Feb 1969–31 Aug 1971
Gen David Jones	1 Sept 1971–30 June 1974
Gen John Vogt	1 July 1974–31 Aug 1975
Gen Richard Ellis	1 Sept 1975–31 July 1977
Gen William Evans	1 Aug 1977–1 Aug 1978
Gen John Pauly	1 Aug 1978–1 Aug 1980
Gen Charles Gabriel	1 Aug 1980–30 June 1982
Gen Billy Minter	1 July 1982

The Commanders of the Far East Air Forces

Lt Gen George Kenney	15 June 1944–30 Dec 1945
Lt Gen Ennis Whitehead	30 Dec 1945–25 Apr 1949
Lt Gen George Stratemeyer	26 Apr 1949–20 May 1951
Lt Gen Earle Patrtridge (acting)	21 May 1951–9 June 1951
Gen O P Weyland	10 June 1951–25 Mar 1954
Gen Earle Partridge	26 Mar 1954–31 May 1955
Gen Laurence Kuter	1 June 1955–see below

The Commanders of the Pacific Air Forces

Gen Laurence Kuter	1 June 1955–31 July 1959
Gen Emmett O'Donnell, Jr	1 Aug 1959–31 July 1963
Gen Jacob Smart	1 Aug 1963–31 July 1964
Gen Hunter Harris	1 Aug 1964–31 Jan 1967
Gen John Ryan	1 Feb 1967–31 July 1968
Gen Joseph Nazzaro	1 Aug 1968–31 July 1971
Gen Lucius Clay, Jr	1 Aug 1971–30 Sept 1973
Gen John Vogt	1 Oct 1973–30 June 1974
Gen Louis Wilson, Jr	1 July 1974–31 May 1977
Lt Gen James Hill	1 June 1977–14 June 1978
Lt Gen James Hughes	15 June 1978–1 July 1981
Lt Gen Arnold Braswell	1 July 1981–

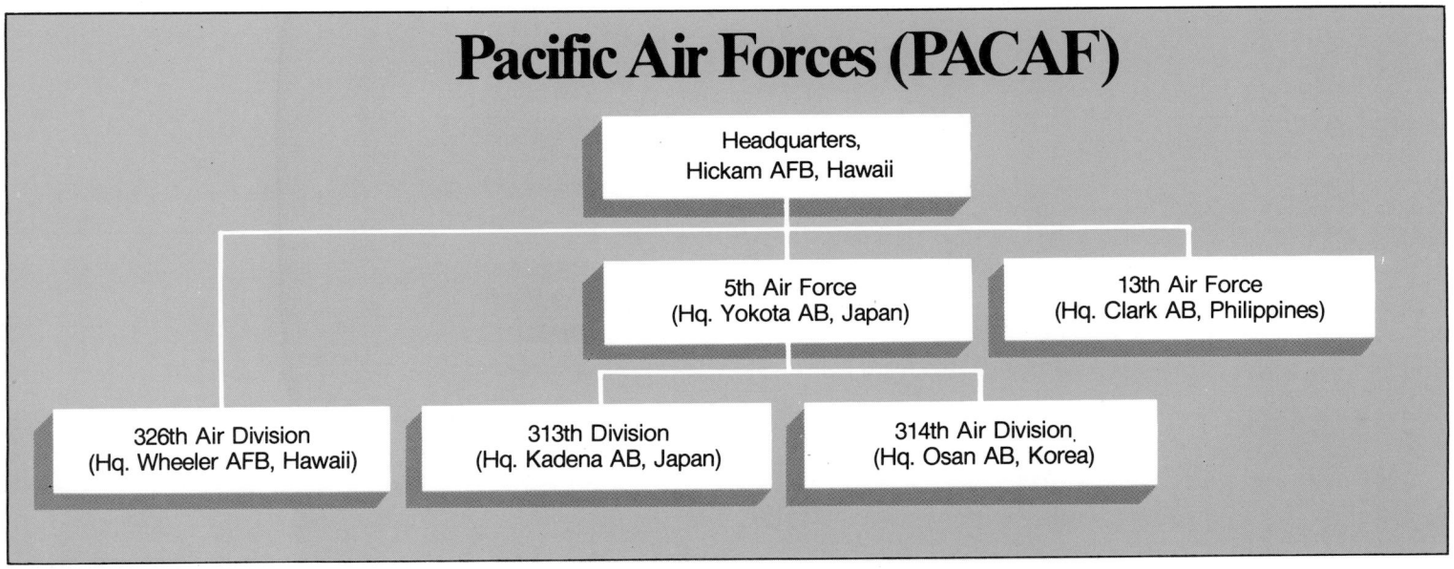

its last missions in Southeast Asia, evacuating personnel from Saigon under operation *Frequent Wind* and helping to rescue the crew of the American merchant vessel SS *Mayaguez*, which had been hijacked by Cambodian revolutionaries in international waters. In 1976 PACAF strength declined to 34,111 personnel and 255 aircraft, as the last bases in Thailand were returned to the Thai Government.

Today PACAF strength has stabilized slightly above the 1976 level, with qualitative improvements in aircraft strength in the form of F-15 aircraft now assigned to the 313th Air Division on Okinawa and F-16s to the 314th Air Division in Korea. While its numbers have stabilized, PACAF's area of responsibility has increased beyond the Pacific The Pacific Command and PACAF now have responsibility for the Indian Ocean region as well, an area that stretches from the east coast of Africa to the west coast of the Americas, covering more than a hundred million square miles or half the surface of the earth.

PACIFIC AIR FORCES BASES

Hickam AFB, Hawaii
Location: West of Honolulu, adjacent to Honolulu Airport
Area: 2731 acres
Altitude: 3ft
Personnel: 5116 Military
1957 Civilian

PACAF headquarters is still at Hickam, a stone's throw from the Pacific Command Headquarters at Pearl Harbor. The base was activated in September 1937 and named for Lt Col Horace Hickam, killed in a crash at Fort Crockett, Texas, on 5 November 1934. The base is home to the 154th Tactical Fighter Group of the Hawaii Air National Guard as well as MAC's 834th Airlift Division and First Weather Wing. The base also serves as headquarter site for Air Force Communications Command and Electronic Security Command activities in the Pacific.

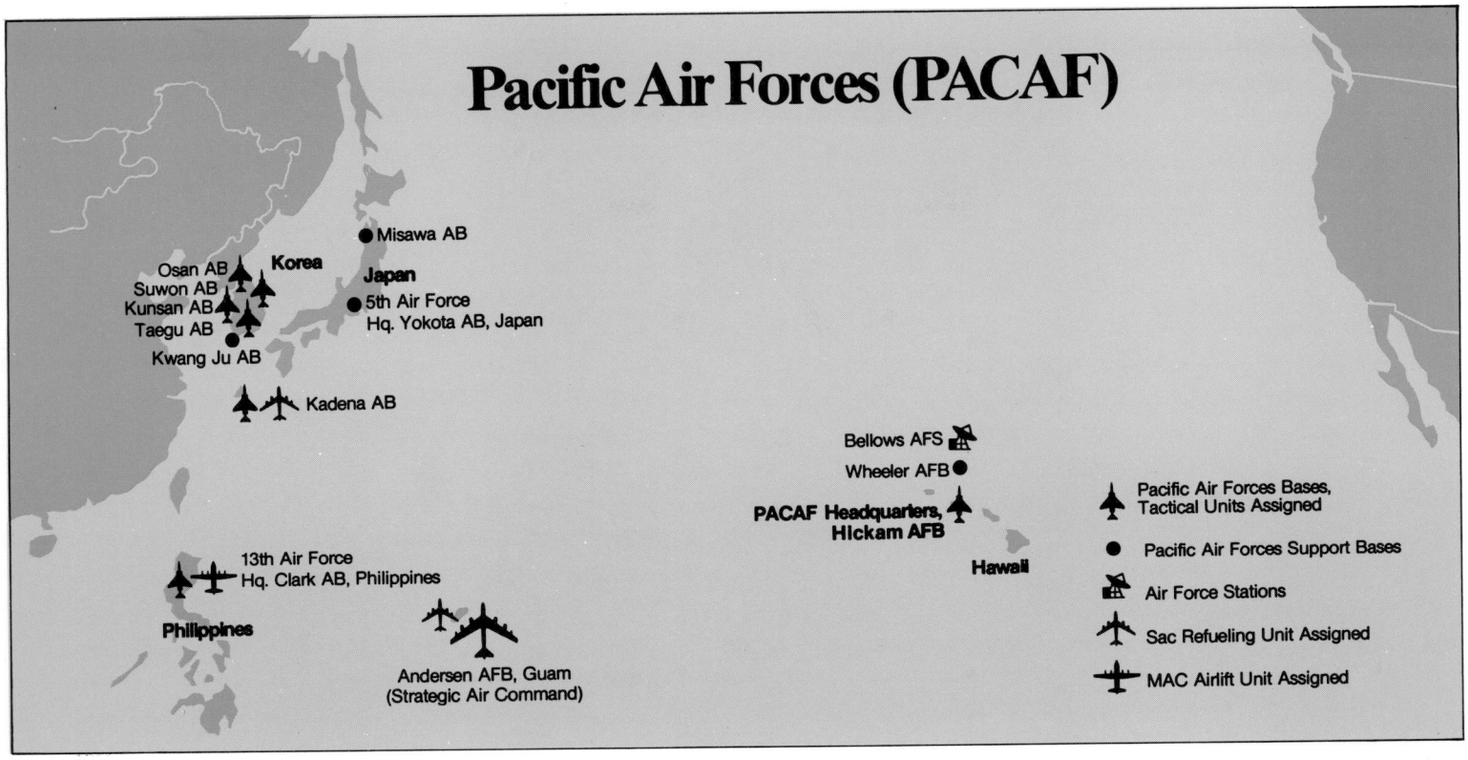

Above: An F-16 'Commando' Falcon prepares for refueling over the Pacific enroute to Hickam AFB for a *Cope Elite* exercise.

Left: PACAF Eagles from Kadena AB with Royal Singapore Air Force and Royal Australian Air Force aircraft during the *Kangaroo 81* exercise.

Wheeler AFB, Hawaii
Location: At the center of Oahu, north of Hickam AFB
Area: 1369 acres
Altitude: 845ft
Personnel: 720 Military
112 Civilian

The oldest active air base in Hawaii, Wheeler was activated in February 1922 and named for Major Sheldon Wheeler, Commanding Officer of Luke Field, Hawaii, killed in a crash there on 13 July 1921. Wheeler AFB is the headquarters of PACAF's 326th Air Division, which operates the Air Defense Control Center, the operational control facility for the interceptors of the Hawaii Air National Guard that provide the air defense umbrella for Hawaii.

Clark AB in the Philippines, two hours north of Manila (now technically a Philippine air force base), the oldest and largest American air base outside the United States, continues to be home to the Thirteenth Air Force and its Third Tactical Fighter Wing. The largest concentration of PACAF air power is under the Fifth Air Force, with the Fifth's air power focused in Korea with the 314th Air Division at **Osan AB. Yokota AB**, Fifth Air Force headquarters, serves as a support base. Meanwhile, the combat aircraft assigned by Fifth Air Force to augment the air defense capabilities of the Japanese Air Self-Defense Force (JASDF), are located with the 313th Air Division at **Kadena AB** on the Japanese Island of Okinawa. In the Indian Ocean, Air Force activites center on the large secret Navy base on the British island of Diego Garcia.

PACAF READINESS EXERCISES

To prepare for its role in defending the vast region under its charge, PACAF, like USAFE and TAC, engages in numerous annual and semiannual training exercises. The largest is *Team Spirit*, held in Korea and not only PACAF but the US Army, US Navy, US Marine Corps and Republic of Korea forces. *Cope Thunder* is the PACAF equivalent of TAC's *Red Flag*, a series of realistic tactical warfare exercises held seven times a year on the Crow Valley Gunnery Range near Clark AB in the Philippines, with the 26th Tactical Fighter Training Squadron's F-5s in the role of Aggressors. *Cope Thunder* involves units from all the American services throughout the Pacific as well as Philippine Royal Australian and Royal New Zealand Air Force units. In 1982 Royal Thai Air Force units participated in *Cope Thunder* for the first time. A corollary exercise, *Combat Sage*, uses realistic combat scenarios to evaluate the effectiveness of air-to-air weapons systems.

The northern counterpart of *Cope Thunder*, code-named *Cope North*, is flown out of Misawa AB in northern Japan as a joint exercise with Japan's JASDF. *Cope North* provides integrated training for the two forges in air defense, including airborne command and control, as well as air-to-ground missions. The need to tighten up Japanese air defense was clearly demonstrated in 1976, when Russian pilot Lt Viktor Belenko successfully penetrated Japanese air space in a MiG-25 Foxbat interceptor. Belenko's objective was to land and defect, but had he been on an attack mission he would not have been intercepted. *Cope North* is designed to train PACAF and JASDF pilots to prevent such penetrations. PACAF exercises include joint maneuvers with other Asian allies such as the joint Royal Australian Air Force (RAAF/USAF *Pacific Consort* and *Kangaroo*.

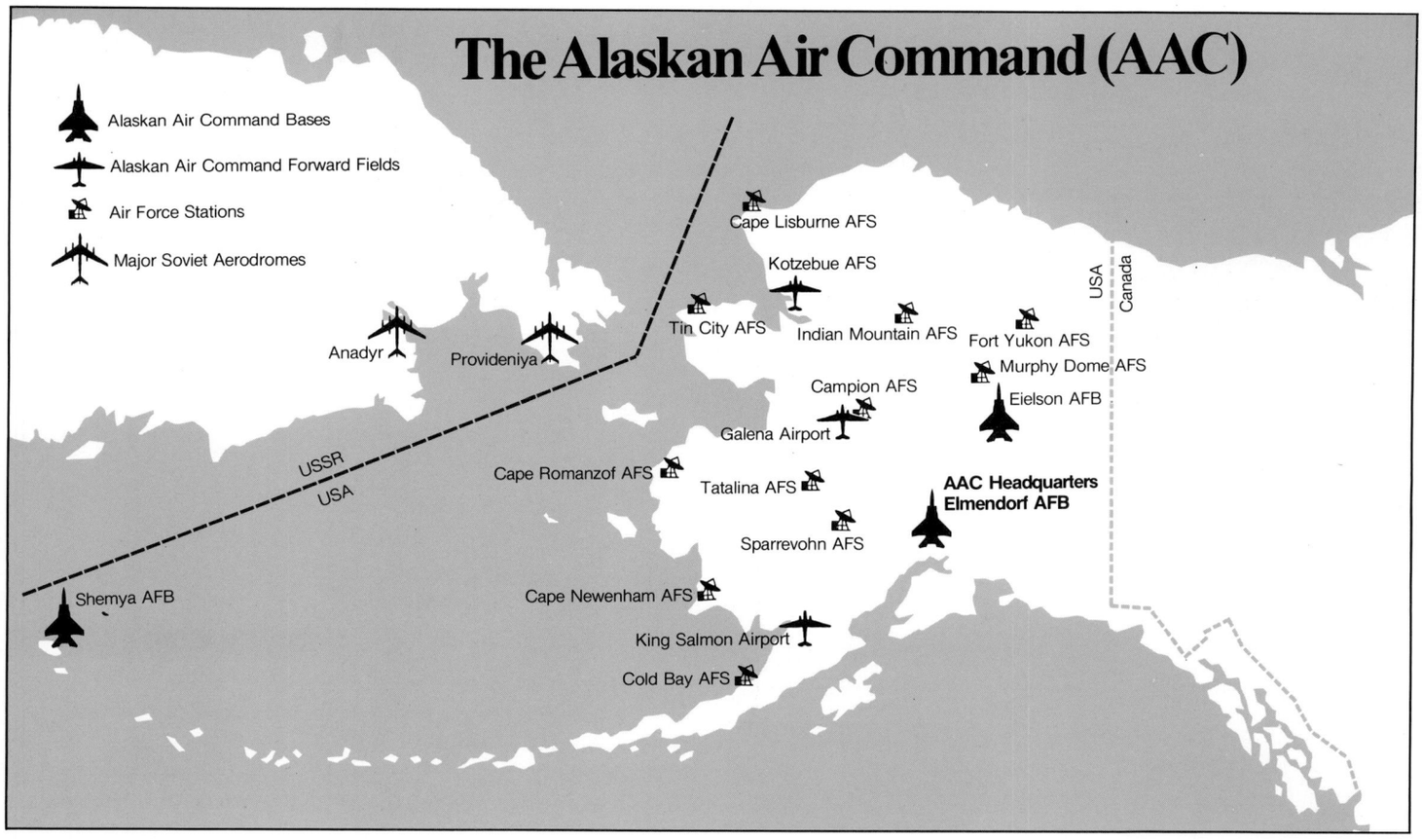

THE ALASKAN AIR COMMAND

Just below the Arctic Circle in the Bering Strait, there is a place where one can stand in one of the fifty United States and see Soviet Union territory only two miles away. This site is on Little Diomede Island, Alaska, where only a thin strip of water (in winter, passable ice) separates the world's two superpowers. This proximity of Alaska to the Soviet Union underscores the importance of the Alaskan Air Command to overall security of the United States. Cold and loneliness make Alaska's remote corners a cruel and forbidding place, but also one of stark and awesome beauty. As the prophet of air power, Billy Mitchell, said in 1935, 'Alaska is the most strategic place in the world.'

The Alaskan Air Command (AAC) was created on 18 December 1945 by redesignation of the World War II-era Eleventh Air Force. AAC headquarters was moved from Adak Island to Elmendorf Field (Elmendorf AFB since 1947) near Anchorage on 1 October 1946 where it has remained since. With the onset of the cold war, the AAC's primary mission was to provide early warning of possible Russian air attack over the Polar route and to shoot down Russian bombers. With the mission of flying Combat Air patrol over the roof of the North American continent, AAC has taken the motto 'Top Cover for America.' The AAC interceptor units were initially equipped with P-51s, replaced in succession by F-80s, F-94s, F-89s, F-102s F-4s (1970) and in 1983, F-15s. AAC reached peak aircraft strength (200) in 1957 (when F-89s were the first-line interceptor); it has declined steadily ever since.

In 1947 the Navy's Hoge Board, studying national defense, and an AAC study, independently recommended establishment of radar stations in Alaska to answer the need for early warning of possible Russian attack. Plans called for between 22 and 58 Aircraft Control and Warning System (AC&W) sites, but because of the same budget restrictions that were plaguing the entire Defense Department, only ten sites and two control centers were funded in the 1949 budget. AAC began a design for a permanent system with five coastal sites at Cape Lisburne, Cape Newenham, Cape Romanzof, Tin City (closest to Little Diomede Island) and Northeast Cape (St Lawrence Island). In addition to the coastal sites, there would be five Ground Control Intercept (GCI) radar sites in the interior of Alaska at Campion, Tatalina, King Salmon Airport, Fire Island and Murphy Dome. They would be divided into two sectors, with the Southern Sector Control Center at Elmendorf AFB and the Northern at Ladd AFB (now the Army's Fort Wainwright) near Fairbanks. When the latter was turned over to the Army in 1960, both control centers were consolidated at Elmendorf.

Construction began on the AC&W system in 1950, but with the outbreak of the Korean War five temporary sites were quickly established at Elmendorf AFB, Ladd AFB, King Salmon Airport, Nome and Gambell on St Lawrence Island. The emergency sites went on-line on 27 June 1950, marking 24-hour-a-day operation of the Alaskan air defense system, which has been continuous ever since. Meanwhile, construction continued on the permanent sites, with Murphy Dome, Fire Island and King Salmon opening in 1951. Tatalina and Campion opened the following year, Cape Lisburne, Cape Romanzof, Northeast Cape and Tin City in 1953. As a result of the Korean War, two additional sites were funded: the first, at Indian Mountain, opened in 1935; the other, at Sparrevohn, became operational in 1954 along with the site at Cape Newenham. The following year construction began on six additional GCI sites at Middleton Island, Ohlson Mountain, Bethel, Fort Yukon, Kotzebue and Unalakleet, all of which were completed in 1958.

On 12 September 1957 the joint US-Canada North American Air Defense Command (NORAD) was established (and the Alaskan NORAD region a year later). Campion and King Salmon became NORAD Control Centers, each with responsibility for the GCI sites in its area. In 1957 JCS approved extend-

Above: Two squadrons of Elmondorf-based all-weather F-102s were AAC's only interceptors from 1960 to 1969.

ing the Distant Early Warning (DEW) Line of radar stations out from Alaska into the Aleutian Islands. Six such sites were authorized at Cold Bay (the main site), Nikolski, Port Heiden, Port Moller, Cape Saridref and Driftwood Bay, all of which went into service under AAC control in 1959.

The final system of 18 AC&W/GCI and six DEW Line Stations was in place for only four years when AAC closed the sites at Middleton Island, Ohlson Mountain and Bethel for reasons of economy. In 1969 the Joint Chiefs of Staff ordered a cutback in air defense forces, which resulted in closing the NORAD sites at Northeast Cape, Fire Island and Unalakleet as well as the DEW Line sites in the Aleutians. Of the latter, Cold Bay remained open and was converted to a NORAD Surveillance Station. In 1973 Campion was downgraded from a NORAD Control Center to a GCI site and Kotzebue from a GCI site to a surveillance station.

In 1970 further cutbacks were made in the fabric of Alaskan air defense. The Nike Hercules surface-to-air missiles batteries around the city of Fairbanks and Eielson AFB were deactivated, and rotational assignments of Aerospace Defense Command F-106s to AAC from bases in the 'lower 48' states under the code name *College Shoes* were terminated. In 1979 the Nike Hercules system was deactivated in the Anchorage-Elmendorf AFB area, marking the first time since 1940 that the area had not ground-to-air artillery or missile air defense.

In 1971 the traditional air defense role of AAC gradually began to give way to tactical air support with activation of the 25th Tactical Air Support Squadron and establishment of the Yukon and Blair Lakes Electronic Warfare Ranges. In 1973 USAF Chief of Staff John Ryan commissioned a study code-named *Saber Yukon* to verify the need for the now-outdated Alaskan AC&W system. The following year, the need verified, AAC began the *Seek Igloo* program, the first major modernization of the system. In 1979 General Electric received the contract to build the first *Seek Igloo* AN/FPS-117 Minimally Attended Radar system at King Salmon. By 'minimally attended' was meant that the sites would be automated, requiring fewer operating personnel in these often isolated regions. The *Seek Igloo* program was completed in 1984 with the Air Stations at Tin City, Tatalina, Sparrevohn, Murphy Dome, Indian Mountain, Fort Yukon, Cold Bay, Cape Romanzof, Cape Newenham and Cape Lisburne as well as King Salmon coming on-line as Minimally Attended Radar sites. The former radar has been replaced by state-of-the-art, three-dimensional (range, azimuth,

The Commanders of the Alaskan Air Command

Brig Gen Joseph Atkinson	1 Oct 1946–25 Feb 1949
Brig Gen Frank Armstrong, Jr	26 Feb 1949–27 Dec 1950
Maj Gen William Old	27 Dec 1950–14 Oct 1952
Brig Gen W R Agee	27 Oct 1952–26 Feb 1953
Maj Gen George Acheson	26 Feb 1953–1 Feb 1956
Lt Gen Joseph Atkinson	24 Feb 1956–16 July 1956
Maj Gen Frank Armstrong, Jr	17 July 1956–23 Oct 1956
Maj Gen James Davis	24 Oct 1956–27 June 1957
Lt Gen Frank Armstrong, Jr	28 June 1957–18 Aug 1957
Brig Gen Kenneth Gibson	19 Aug 1957–13 Aug 1958
Maj Gen C F Necrason	14 Aug 1958–19 July 1961
Maj Gen Wendell Bowman	26 July 1961–8 Aug 1963
Maj Gen James Jensen	15 Aug 1963–14 Nov 1966
Maj Gen Thomas Moore	15 Nov 1966–24 July 1969
Maj Gen Joseph Cunningham	25 July 1969–31 July 1972
Maj Gen Donavon Smith	1 Aug 1972–5 June 1973
Maj Gen Charles Carson, Jr	18 June 1973–2 Mar 1974
Maj Gen Jack Gamble	19 Mar 1974–30 June 1975
Lt Gen James Hill	1 July 1975–14 Oct 1976
Lt Gen M. L. Boswell	15 Oct 1976–30 June 1978
Lt Gen Winfield Scott, Jr	1 July 1978–1 Apr 1981
Lt Gen Lynwood Clark	1 Apr 1981–

height) radar which will remote-track data to the Elmendorf Region Operations Center at Elmendorf AFB. The highly automated nature of the equipment has reduced staffing requirements at the sites by up to 80% or more.

As an indication of the Alaskan Air Command's renewed importance, its commander, since 1975, has been designated senior military officer for Alaska, Commander of the Joint Task Force, Alaska, in time of war and Commander of the Alaska NORAD Region.

ALASKAN AIR COMMAND BASES

Elmendorf AFB (AAC Headquarters)
Location: Adjacent to Anchorage, Alaska
Area: 13,400 acres
Altitude: 118ft
Personnel: 6120 Military
1483 Civilian

Activated in 1940 as Elmendorf Army Air Field at Fort Richardson, the base is named for Captain Hugh Elmendorf, who was killed on 13 January 1933 at Wright Field, Ohio. The 18th Pursuit Squadron arrived in February 1941. In early 1942, shortly after the American entry into World War II, the Eleventh Air Force was established here. Elmendorf and the Eleventh played an important part in the Aleutian Campaign during the war and in later air operations against the Kurile Islands north of Japan. Always the principal fighter base in Alaska, Elmendorf used the slogan 'Top Cover for America' before it was adopted in 1969 as the AAC motto. Beyond being a fighter base, Elmendorf has been an important stop for MAC flights between the United States and the Far East.

The Elmendorf AFB host unit is the 21st TFW with its 43d TFS and 5021st Tactical Operations Squadron. The base is also home to the NORAD Alaska Region Control Center, the 1931st Communications Group (AFCC), the 6981st Electronic Security Squadron (ESC), the 616th Military Airlift Group and such MAC units as the 17th Tactical Airlift Squadron, the 11th Weather Squadron, the 71st Aerospace Rescue and Recovery Squadron and the AAC Rescue Coordination Center that has accounted for more than 3600 rescues since it was established in 1961.

Eielson AFB
Location: 26 miles SE of Fairbanks, Alaska
Area: 35,000 acres
Altitude: 534ft
Personnel: 3233 Military
343 Civilian

Activated in October 1944, the base is named for the Arctic aviation pioneer Carl Ben Eielson, first man to fly across the Arctic Basin (Point Barrow to Spitzbergen) and the first to fly airmail in Alaska. He was killed in a crash near Siberia on 9 November 1929. The field was originally planned and built as a satellite to nearby Ladd Field (later Ladd AFB), which was a way station for Lend-Lease delivery flights to Russia during World War II. In 1947 Eielson became full-fledged AAC base and has since survived the deactivation of Ladd AFB as an Air Force installation. In the late 1950s and early 1960s Eielson, now with one of the longest runways in North America, became a forward base for SAC B-36s and B-52s as well as SAC tankers. Eielson is still an important base for SAC tankers and for SAC RC-135 electronic reconnaissance aircraft that fly regular missions to the periphery of Russian air space near the Kamchatka Peninsula, the site of several top-secret Soviet military installations. It was an Eielson-based SAC RC-135 that crossed paths with the Korean Air Lines 747 shot down by Soviet interceptors on 1 September 1983 (and which the Russians later claimed they had confused with the 747).

The Eielson host unit is the 343d Composite Wing incorporating the 343d Combat Support Group, the 25th Tactical Air Support Squadron and the 18th TFS. The units conduct Air Support training on the nearby Blair Lakes conventional bombing and gunnery range and Yukon Electronic Warfare Range. SAC tanker operations at Eielson are under control of SAC's Sixth Strategic Wing. The Air Training Command has also located its Arctic Survival School at Eielson.

Shemya AFB
Location: On the western tip of the Aleutian Island chain.
Area: 11.25 sq miles
Altitude: 270ft
Personnel 570 Military
0 Civilian

Above: A group of Alaskan Air Command A-10 Thunderbolts of the 18th Tactical Fighter Squadron out of Eilson AFB, May 1982.

Shemya is the westernmost part of the United States, so located that the International Date Line had to be routed around it so it would be in the same day as the rest of the United States. Known as 'The Black Pearl,' the 4.5-mile-long island was captured by the Japanese early in World War II and wrested from their control on 28 May 1943, in the final days of the battle to retake the larger nearby island of Attu. A 10,000-foot runway, still the centerpiece of the base, and birchwood hangers were built at Shemya to accommodate B-29 strategic bomber attacks against Japan (which were ultimately flown from the Marianas south of Japan and not from Shemya). The base was kept busy during the war as an Eleventh Air Force B-24 and B-25 base. After the war it became an air refueling site on the Great Circle Route between Anchorage and the Far East, playing an important part in airlift operations during the Korean War. In July 1954 Shemya was declared surplus, deactivated and turned over to the Civil Aeronautics Authority (forerunner of the Federal Aviation Administration – FAA) who in turn leased it to Northwest Orient Airlines, which maintained its presence there until 1961. The Air Force resumed operations on Shemya in 1958, in support of various strategic intelligence activities as well as aircraft refueling. Shemya recovered importance steadily until 21 June 1968, when it was redesignated from an Air Force Station to an Air Force Base.

In August 1977 the new *Cobra Dane* AN/FPS-108 Phased Array Radar facility became operational at Shemya, replacing the older AN/FPS-17 Detection and AN/FPS-80 Tracking Radars monitoring space and missile activity in eastern Siberia and Kamchatka. The *Cobra Dane* facility is now under SPACECOM control, having been operated successively by ADC and SAC. AAC Tactical aircraft, now including F-15s based at the other AAC bases, are regularly rotated through the 10,000-foot runway on the Black Pearl of the frigid North Pacific – 1600 miles from Anchorage but only 600 miles from Petropavlovsk.

Left: **An AAC ground crew chief refuels an F-111A at Elmendorf AFB during Operation *Brim Frost 81.***

Above: **Three AAC F-89 Scorpions in flight over Alaska's Mt McKinley in July 1954. Scorpions were the premier US Air Force all-weather interceptor throughout the mid-fifties. The last F-89 left AAC service in July 1960, leaving F-102s providing 'Top Cover for America'. Standard Air Force markings during this era included insignia red wingtip and tail surfaces, which show as a neutral grey in this photo. By 1959 the insignia red was giving way to vivid fluorescent orange. The purpose of the high-visibility markings was the need to locate the aircraft should it be downed in some trackless wilderness, such as this one presided over by AAC.**

TACTICAL AIRCRAFT

The tactical fighter aircraft in service with the US Air Force fall into three eras or generations. The first generation were those early jets in operational service during the first decade following World War II, 1945-1955. These included the F-80, the F-84 and the F-86 Sabre Jet. In the second generation were the larger, more sophisticated jets of the Century Series, so named because they began with the F-100 and were numbered sequentially through F-106. They were followed by the F-110, which became the famous F-4 Phantom, the premier American fighter from 1965 to 1975. The third generation incorporated lessons learned by the Air Force in Southeast Asia and the best of the microelectronics, high-technology boom of the seventies. Third-generation aircraft include the Air Force's F-15 and F-16 and the Navy's F-14 and F-18.

THE FIRST GENERATION

The fighters of the Korean War era began with much of the same technology that had marked World War II fighters and culminated in North American's F-86. The swept-wing F-86 was the superior fighter over Korea and the most successful jet fighter produced until that time. The **F-86** (A, E, & F models) **Sabre Jet** was really the ultimate USAF air superiority fighter of the period and would remain so long after the cease-fire in Korea.

The three most important USAF tactical aircraft to follow the F-86 were of a new type, predicated on improved technology and necessitated by a growing threat of Russian bomber attack. The type was the all-weather air defense interceptor, the most important of which would be the Northrop F-89 Scorpion. In the late 1940s the only all-weather interceptors in the USAF inventory were the propellor-driven (now out-moded) F-82 and F-61. Early in 1949, because of delays in the F-89 program, two other types were procured to supplement the F-89. In March 1949, with their F-86A going into active service, North American proposed an all-weather interceptor version of the F-86. The new interceptor would be based on the F-86 airframe and would have a single crewman. The single-seat configuration was a radical departure for an all-weather interceptor – it was customary in such aircraft to have a second crewman to back up the pilot in navigation and weapons-system operation. North American believed the sophisticated electronics it was developing would compensate for the absence of the second crewman and the Air Force went along, ordering 124 aircraft. The converted F-86A, incorporating a Hughes Fire-Control System, was designated XF-95 and first flew in September 1949. When the Russians were known to possess the atomic bomb, the Air Force ordered an additional 31 of the new aircraft (7 October) which was redesignated YF-86D.

The first YF-86D, with a J47-GE-17 turbo jet engine developing 6650lb of thrust with afterburner, flew on 22 December 1949 less than a year after the program got underway.

Procurement of the **F-86D** became, despite early program slippage, a high-priority Air Force program. In April 1953 (nearly two years behind schedule) the F-86D finally entered service with active Air Defense Command squadrons. By the end of the year ADC had 600 of them; by June 1955 1026 (or 73%) of the Command's 1405 interceptors were F-86Ds, the remainder being F-94Cs and F-89Ds. Few F-86Ds served overseas. The FEAF in Korea received a few but they were withdrawn as unsuitable for the short fields available there. Six years later, in 1959, two squadrons (the 431st and 437th FIS) went to Spain in support of SAC bombers at Torrejon and Zaragoza. In all there were 2504 F-86Ds built for service with the USAF and the Air National Guard: they would serve until June 1961. Some F-86Ds were converted to F-86L standard with advanced electronics, and 120 of an advanced F-86D, redesignated F-86K, were also built.

Above: **The all-weather interceptor version of the Sabre Jet, designated F-86D, with its distinctive nose radome.**

Above right: **The F-84F, carrying fuel tanks in its role as a SAC escort fighter, was a swept-wing development of the F-84 Thunderjet.** ***Below:*** **A lineup of F-84Fs at Elmendorf AFB, Alaska.**

F-86D Sabre Jet
Manufacturer: North American Aviation
First year of service: 1951
Aircraft type: Single-seat interceptor
Wingspan: 37ft 1in
Length: 40ft 4in
Weight: 17,000lb (gross)
Range: 836 miles
Service ceiling: 54,600 feet
Top/Cruising speed: 707mph
Powerplant: (1) 5700lb thrust (7630lb with afterburner) General Electric J47-GE-17 turbojet
Armanent/Capacity: (24) 2.75 inch FFAR rockets

F-84F Thunderstreak (RF-84F called Thunderflash)
Manufacturer: Republic Aviation
First year of service: 1954
Aircraft type: Single-seat fighter, fighter-bomber, tactical reconnaissance aircraft (RF-84F)
Wingspan: 33ft 7in
Length: 43ft 5in
Weight: 13,800lb (gross)
Range: 2200 miles (with drop tanks)
Service ceiling: 46,000 feet
Top speed: 695mph
Powerplant: (1) 7200lb thrust Wright J65-W-3 turbojet
Armament/Capacity: Six .50 caliber machine guns

The second of the postwar interceptors was **Lockheed's F-94 Starfire**, which was based on their earlier F-80 Shooting Star. A lot of hopes were being pinned on the F-89 Scorpion, but it was an all-new design and the F-94, like the F-86D, would work from existing technology and give the Air Force interim all-weather interceptors. The first of the two-man F-94s, 14% longer than the one-man F-80s, entered service in May 1950 and served in Korea beginning late the following year. The Starfires were based at Suwon AB to provide fighter interceptor cover (replacing the old F-82s) for the American bases in South Korea and escort for B-29 strikes against the North. Although not too successful against low-flying aircraft, few planes proved as reliable as the F-94 against the enemy in the Korean War, especially in nasty weather and darkness, for which the F-94 was designed. The F-94s flew when most other aircraft were grounded by bad weather. Most Korean veterans praised the plane: it was rugged and could rack up a lot of flying hours without maintenance. The Air Force received a total of 854 Starfires, including 356 F-94Bs and 387 F-94Cs, with the latter serving USAF units until 1959 and ANG units until 1960.

Throughout this time, the interceptor the USAF had been waiting for was **Northrop's F-89 Scorpion**, so named because the upsweep of its tail resembled that of an angry scorpion ready to strike. During World War II Northrop had built the P-61 Black Widow (also named for a poisonous invertebrate) which resembled the Scorpion in being a multi-seat, twin-engine night fighter that was the largest American fighter to see service during its time.

The F-89, like the F-80, F-84 and F-94, was of straight-winged design, lacking the swept-wing characteristic that made the F-86 such a radical design. The XF-89 first flew in August 1948, with the first F-89A going into service in September 1950. Only 48 F-89A and B models were delivered due to problems with airframe and engine design. The C version of this long-awaited interceptor was also plagued with structural deficiencies that resulted in a series of disastrous crashes during flight-testing in 1952, which in turn resulted in the grounding of the whole program for several months.

Eventually 163 F-89Cs were delivered, but the bugs were finally worked out of the system with the F-89D, of which 682 were delivered. Entering operational service with ADC in January 1954, the F-89D was the first USAF fighter to abandon guns in favor of missiles. The F-89D was also the first to have permanently mounted wing-tip pods from which missiles would be fired. The missiles were the Hughes GAR-1 (originally designated XF-98, later designated AIM-4) Falcon supersonic (Mach 3) radar-guided, air-to-air, solid-fuel rockets with a range of about four miles. Beginning in November 1956, 350 F-89Ds were redesignated F-89J, having been modified to carry the Douglas MB-1 (later designated AIR-2) Genie unguided rockets, the first air-to-air rocket to carry a nuclear warhead. The first firing of a live-armed Genie took place on 19 July 1957, when an ADC F-89J fired the rocket over the northern part of the range at Yucca Flat, Nevada, detonating the nuclear warhead at 15,000 feet. The F-89J was an important part of the ADC arsenal in the late fifties, reaching a peak inventory of 286 in June 1958. With the advent of the Genie-capable F-101 and F-106, ADC began turning its F-89s over to the Air Guard, with whom nuclear armed F-89Js served until 1968.

Below: **The Lockheed F-94 Starfire, a supersonic outgrowth of the F-80 program, carried 24 rockets in a firing ring around the nose, operated above 45,000 feet, had nose radar, and provided ejection seats for both crewmen. It was 41 feet 4 inches long and had a span of 37 feet 6 inches.**

Above: An F-89J in flight with its full armament of two MB-1 Genie nuclear-armed rockets and four Hughes GAR-2 (later AIM-4) Falcon guided missiles. (Tactical missiles are discussed on pages 148-9).

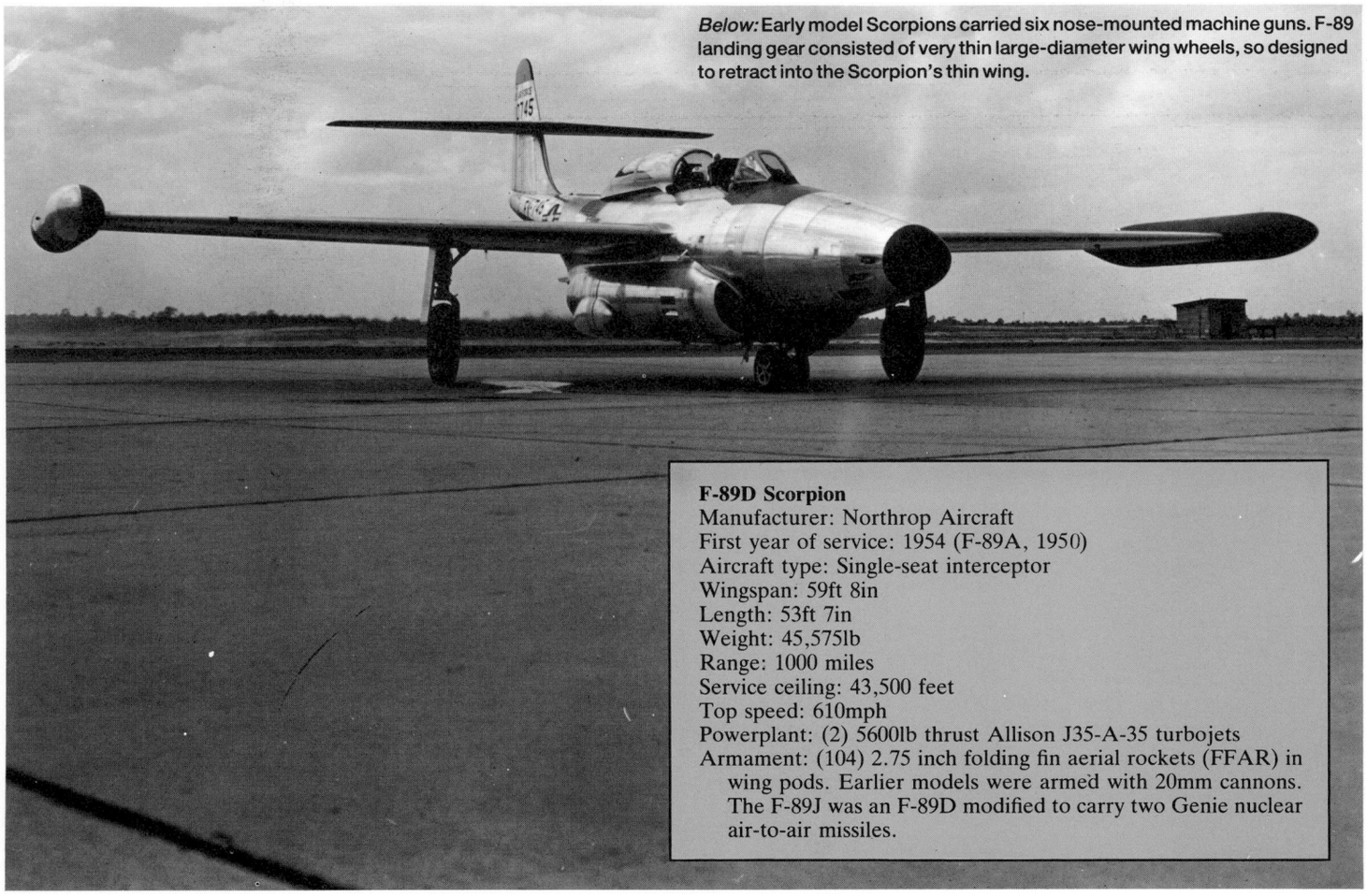

Below: Early model Scorpions carried six nose-mounted machine guns. F-89 landing gear consisted of very thin large-diameter wing wheels, so designed to retract into the Scorpion's thin wing.

F-89D Scorpion
Manufacturer: Northrop Aircraft
First year of service: 1954 (F-89A, 1950)
Aircraft type: Single-seat interceptor
Wingspan: 59ft 8in
Length: 53ft 7in
Weight: 45,575lb
Range: 1000 miles
Service ceiling: 43,500 feet
Top speed: 610mph
Powerplant: (2) 5600lb thrust Allison J35-A-35 turbojets
Armament: (104) 2.75 inch folding fin aerial rockets (FFAR) in wing pods. Earlier models were armed with 20mm cannons. The F-89J was an F-89D modified to carry two Genie nuclear air-to-air missiles.

Major USAAF/USAF Fighters
and their Periods of Service

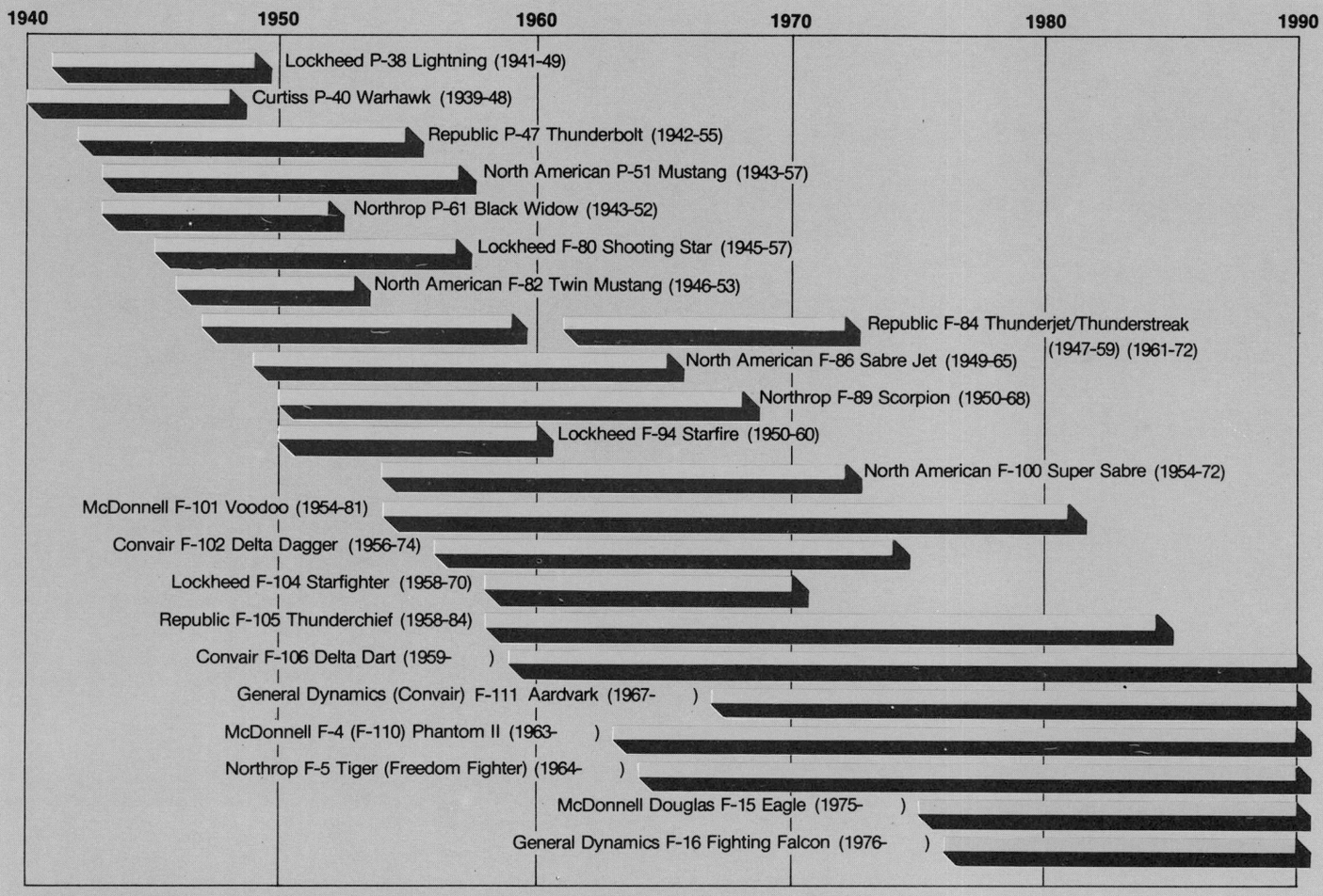

Data for USAAF/USAF aircraft only, excludes aircraft delivered directly to foreign air forces without USAAF/USAF service.
Periods begin with operational service, not first recorded flight. Periods include service with Air National Guard, but do not include mothballed aircraft.

Major USAAF/USAF Attack Aircraft
and their Periods of Service

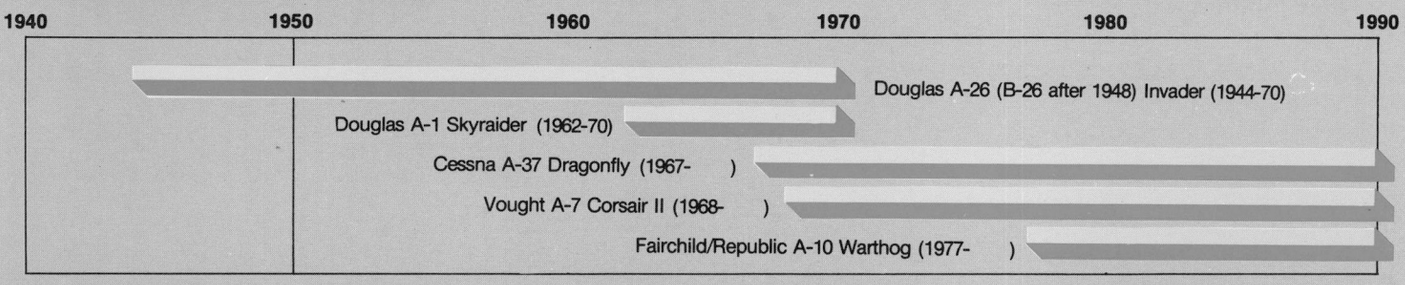

Data for USAAF/USAF aircraft only, excludes aircraft delivered directly to foreign air forces without USAAF/USAF service.
Periods begin with operational service, not first recorded flight. Periods include service with Air National Guard, but do not include mothballed aircraft.

Major USAAF/USAF Fighters

Total Number Delivered

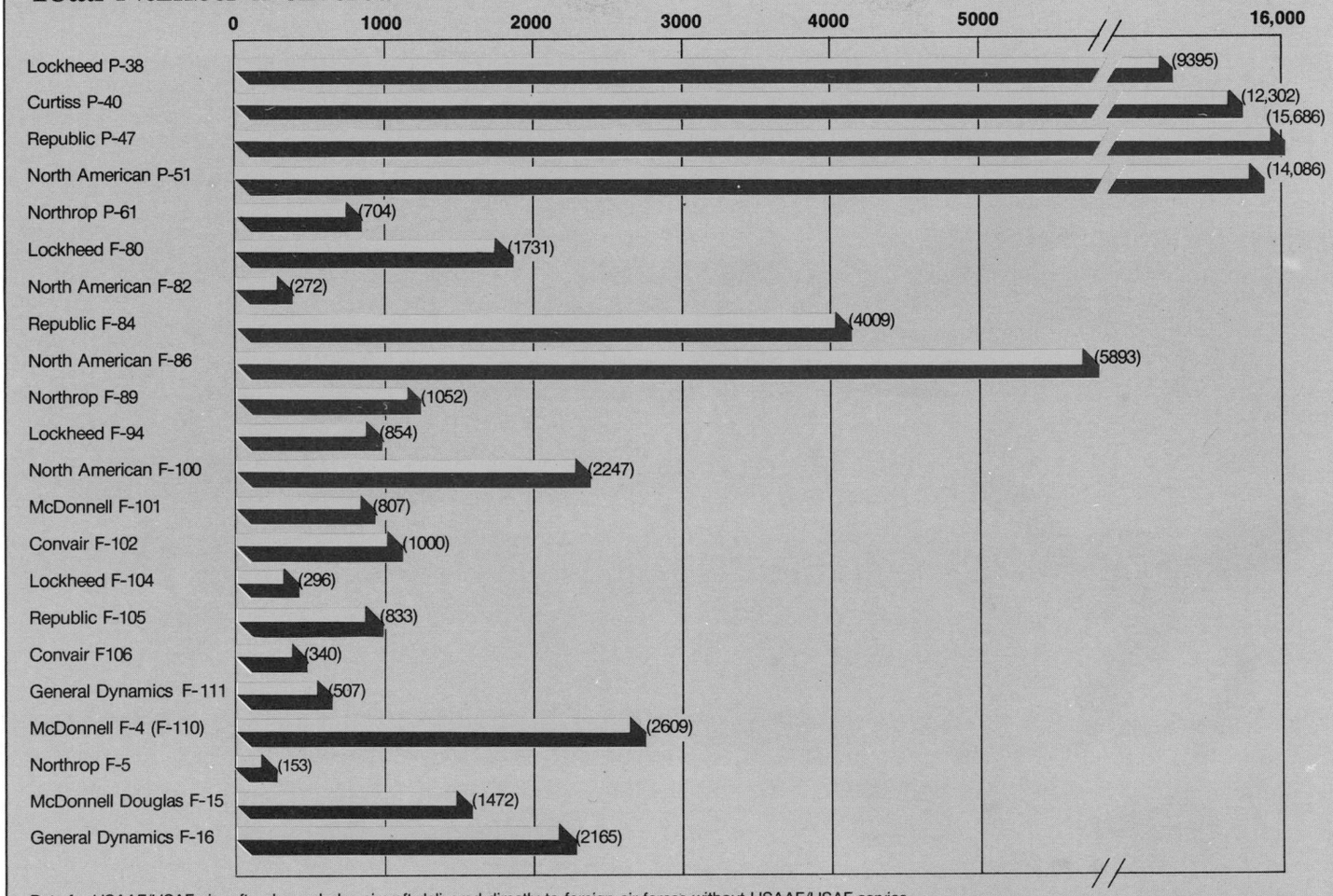

Data for USAAF/USAF aircraft only, excludes aircraft delivered directly to foreign air forces without USAAF/USAF service.

Major USAAF/USAF Attack Aircraft

Total Number Delivered

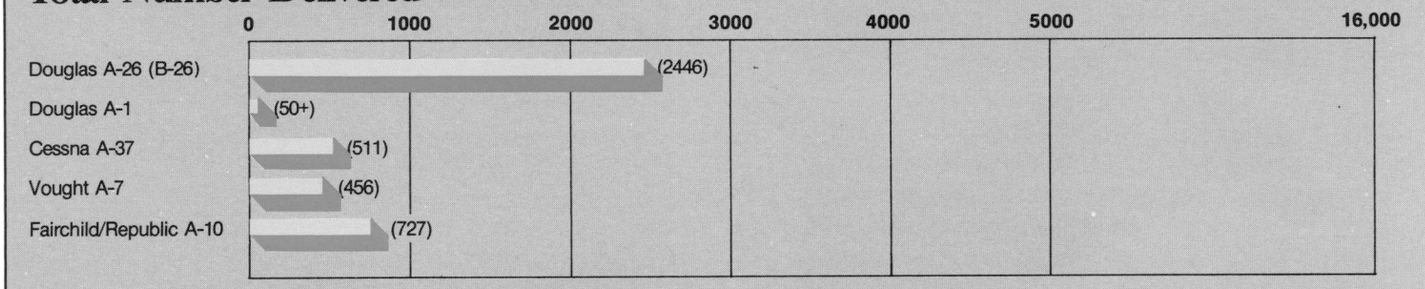

Data for USAAF/USAF aircraft only, excludes aircraft delivered directly to foreign air forces without USAAF/USAF service.

THE CENTURY SERIES

The first of the Century Series was, of course, the **F-100**. It was North American Aviations' attempt to provide a successor to its very successful F-86 Sabre Jet. Called Super Sabre (what else?), the F-100 was also a swept-wing, single-seat, all-purpose fighter. The prototype first flew in May 1953, with the first operational F-100As going into service in September 1954. The F-100C became operational in July 1955, the F-100B becoming the prototype for the third Sabre, the F-107, which would never get past the prototype stage. The F-100C differed from the F-100A in that it had underwing pylons for ordnance and fuel tanks, and that it was aerial refuelable.

While the 205 F-100As and 476 F-100Cs were designed as fighters, the 1274 F-100Ds were built to function primarily as fighter-bombers, a role that was secondary with the earlier Super Sabres. The F-100D was first delivered to operational units in June 1956; these were rapidly deployed to overseas bases to

A Century series family portrait. Clockwise from below: Lockheed's F-104 Starfighter, North American's F-100 Super Sabre, Convair's F-102 Delta Dagger, McDonnell's F-101 Voodoo and the Republic F-105 Thunderchief. Of those not pictured, the Republic F-103 and North American F-108 were Mach 3 interceptor designs that were never built. Two examples of the needle-nosed North American F-107 Super Super Sabre (with top-mounted intake that started life as F-100B) were built and the VTOL (Vertical Take-off and Landing) Ryan F-109 never made it past the experimental stage. The Convair F-106 arrived later, serving the Air Force for 30 years, and the F-110 and F-111 belonged to another era.

replace F-84s. FEAF received 46 at Itazuke AB in Japan, while USAFE received 70 at Etain AB and Chaumont AB in France and Boulihaut AB and Sidi Slimange AB in Morocco. F-100s were introduced into combat operations over Laos in May 1962. F-100 operations over North Vietnam began in 1965; two years later most had been deployed to Southeast Asia, with only five F-100 squadrons remaining in the United States.

The F-100F was a two-seat development of the F-100C originally intended as a trainer. It was armed with only two of the 20mm M-39 cannons of which the F-100D carried four. It first entered TAC inventory in January 1958 and was quickly deployed to PACAF and USAFE squadrons. In Southeast Asia F-100Fs were modified as 'Wild Weasel' aircraft, assigned to destroying North Vietnamese SAM sites. A total of 294 F-100Fs served with the USAF, the last ones being phased out along with the last F-100D in 1972.

McDonnell's F-101 Voodoo began on the drawing board as a long-range bomber escort with the designation F-88. The Air Force cancelled the F-88 program in 1950 shortly after the first flight of the second prototype because of budget constraints. The F-88, however, turned out to be a good plane despite the cancellation and the enormous success of the parallel North American F-86 Sabre Jet. In January 1952 the Air Force contracted with McDonnell to build an updated version of the F-88, now designated F-101. Flight testing began in 1954 and the first F-101A entered operational service with TAC in July 1957. The Air Force also contracted for a reconnaissance version, designated RF-10A, which became operational in May 1957. The RF-101A initially incorporated the long focal-length Fairchild KA-1 and KA-2 framing cameras and the Fairchild CAI KA-18 strip camera. An updated recon version, the RF-101C, entered operational service the same year and became the reconnaissance workhorse of the Air Force. Refitted with newer high-resolution cameras by 1962, RF-101Cs were used for surveillance over Cuba and provided irrefutable evidence that the Russians were installing offensive missiles there. The RF-101 was also the only Voodoo to see action in Southeast Asia, being used for reconnaissance and strike evaluation from 1961 through 1970 when they were replaced by RF-4Cs. The Voodoo is also remembered for its interceptor version, the two-place F-101B which entered ADC service in January 1959. Later interceptors built after 1961 were designated F-101F and there were a total of 480 F-101B/F interceptors in a total of 887 Voodoos of all types.

F-100D Super Sabre
Manufacturer: North American Aviation
First year of service: 1954 (F-100A)
Aircraft type: Air superiority fighter and fighter-bomber
Wingspan: 38ft 9in
Length: 47ft 0in
Weight: 34,832lb (gross)
Range: 1500 miles (with external tanks)
Service ceiling: 35,000 feet
Top speed: Mach 1.3
Powerplant: (1) 17,000lb thrust Pratt & Whitney J57-P-21A turbojet
Armament: Four 20mm guns and underwing pylons for six 1000lb bombs, 2 Sidewinder or 2 Bullpup air-to-air missiles

Above: The first flight of Kelly Johnson's F-104 Starfighter over Edwards AFB in February 1956.

F-101B Voodoo
Manufacturer: McDonnell Aircraft Corp (now McDonnell Douglas)
First year of service: 1957
Aircraft type: Fighter-bomber and all-weather interceptor
Wingspan: 39ft 8in
Length: 67ft 4¾in
Weight: 46,500lb (gross)
Range: 1550 miles
Service ceiling: 51,000 feet
Top speed: Mach 1.85
Powerplant: (2) 14,990lb thrust Pratt & Whitney J57-P-55 turbojets
Armament: Three AIM-4D Falcon air-to-air missiles carried internally, and two AIR-2A Genie nuclear-warhead unguided rockets under the fuselage

F-104A Starfighter
Manufacturer: Lockheed Aircraft
First year of service: 1958
Aircraft type: Single-seat fighter, interceptor
Wingspan: 21ft 11in (without tip tanks)
Length: 54ft 9in
Weight: 28,779lb (gross)
Range: 1300 miles with external fuel tanks
Service ceiling: 55,200 feet
Top/Cruising speed: Mach 2
Powerplant: (1) 14,800lb thrust General Electric J79-GE-3 turbojet
Armament/Capacity: (1) 20mm cannon plus various combinations of FFAR rockets, AIM-9 Sidwinder missiles and gravity bombs.

The **Lockheed F-104 Starfighter**, known familiarly as the 'missile with a man in it,' was designed by Kelly Johnson and submitted to the Air Force by Lockheed on its own initiative. Based on Korean War experience, Lockheed knew the Air Force might be looking for a high-speed light-weight fighter capable of operating from forward fields. The Air Force hesitantly issued a contract to Lockheed in 1953 and XF-104 flight testing began the following year. The first F-104A entered operational service with ADC (not TAC as originally intended) in January 1958. The two-seat F-104B was similar, with the addition of a 20mm Vulcan cannon to the Sidewinder missiles provided for earlier. Incorporating aerial refueling capabilities, the F-104C and D were designed for tactical air support, and several served in Southeast Asia. The US Air Force accepted a total of 663 F-104s but retained only 296 for its own use, the rest being transferred to allied countries under the Military Assistance Program. In addition, many were produced under Lockheed license in Canada, Japan and Germany.

The **F-105 Thunderchief** was Republic Aviation's Mach 1.5 successor to the F-84 Thunderstreak. The Thunderchief, or 'Thud' as it came to be known during the Vietnam War, began life as a nuclear-capable tactical bomber and became the most commonly used fighter-bomber of the war. The first flight of the YF-105A prototype occurred in October 1955, with the first operational Thud, an F-105B, entering TAC service in August 1958. Only 80 F-105As and Bs were delivered, the principal production model being the F-105D. There were 610 F-105Ds built, followed by 143 F-105Fs, some of which were modified as F-105Gs. A total of 833 F-105s were delivered, 355 fewer than authorized by Congress.

Convair's F-102 Delta Dagger and F-106 Delta Dart both had their roots in the theories of the German scientist Dr Alexander Lippisch. During World War II Lippisch had developed several aircraft designs with delta-configuration wing types, among them the Messerschmitt Me-163. After the war, while the Messerschmitt-designed swept wing was being used by Boeing and North American, Consolidated Vultee (later Convair) enlisted the assistance of Dr Lippisch in the design of its tailless, pure-delta-winged research aircraft, the Model 7002 – the first of this type. First flown in 1948, the 7002 (later designated XF-92) led to an Air Force requirement for a supersonic delta-winged interceptor that came to be known as the '1954 Ultimate Interceptor.' The contract was won by Corvair and was designated F-102. The first YF-102 flew in October 1953, but design changes and changes in requirements delayed delivery of the first production

Left: Notable Century-birds, a 351st TFW F-105 (*top*) and a sleek ADC F-102.

F-102A Delta Dart ('Deuce')
Manufacturer: Convair Division of General Dynamics
First year of service: 1956
Aircraft type: Single-seat all-weather interceptor
Wingspan: 38ft 4½in
Length: 68ft 4½in
Weight: 28,000lb gross
Range: 1350 miles
Service ceiling: 54,000 feet
Top/Cruising speed: Mach 1.3
Powerplant: (1) 17,000lb thrust Pratt & Whitney J57-P-23/25 turbojet
Armament/Capacity: Three AIM-4 Falcon and one AIM-26 Nuclear Falcon missile carried internally. Earlier provision for unguided HVAR rockets had been deleted by the early 1970s. No guns.

F-102A until June 1955; the first did not enter operational service until the following April. The F-102 was delivered to AAC, PACAF and USAFE in 1958 and served for nearly a decade. The F-106 began as the F-102B, a much improved aircraft in which all the lessons learned the hard way in the F-102A program would be put to use. The designation of the new 'ultimate Interceptor' was changed to F-106 in April 1956, and the prototype flew in December 1956, only three years after the first F-102. The first F-106As entered ADC service in May 1959 and have continued in USAF and Air Guard service for well over a quarter of a century – longer than any other US Air Force fighter. Given this longevity of service, the F-106, with its continual modernization programs, may be the closest the Air Force could have come in the mid-1950s to developing the 'Ultimate Interceptor.' The F-106 was the last production aircraft in the Century Series, and with the retirement of the F-105 in 1984 it remains the only one still in active service.

Above: ***College Shoes*** **F-106s with ADC insignia on their tails over Alaska's Mt McKinley.**

Below: **TAC F-104s, one equipped with an air refueling probe.**

F-105D Thunderchief ('Thud')
Manufacturer: Fairchild Industries, Fairchild Republic Division
First year of service: 1961 (F-105B, 1958)
Aircraft type: Single-seat all-weather fighter-bomber
Wingspan: 34ft 11¼in
Length: 67ft ¼in
Weight: 52,546lb (gross); 27,500lb (empty)
Range: 1842 miles
Service ceiling: 52,000 feet
Top speed: Mach 2.1
Powerplant: (1) 26,500lb thrust Pratt & Whitney J75-P-19W turbojet
Armament: One 20mm multibarrel rotary cannon plus more than 14,000lb of stores underwing and underfuselage.

F-106A Delta Dart
Manufacturer: Convair Division of General Dynamics
First year of service: 1959
Aircraft type: Single-seat all-weather interceptor
Wingspan: 38ft 3½in
Length: 70ft 8¾in
Weight: 42,400lb (gross); 25,300lb (empty)
Range: 1200 miles
Service ceiling: 65,000 feet
Top speed: Mach 2
Powerplant: (1) 24,500lb thrust Pratt & Whitney J57-P-17 turbojet
Armament: One 20mm cannon on most F-106As plus one Genie missile and four AIM-4 Falcon missiles carried internally

F-111F ('Aardvark')
Manufacturer: General Dynamics
First year of service: 1967
Aircraft type: Two-seat variable-geometry fighter-bomber (see FB-111A)
Wingspan: 63ft 0in (spread); 31ft 11.4in (fully swept)
Length: 73ft 6in
Weight: 100,000lb (gross); 47,481lb (empty)
Range: 2925 miles without external fuel
Service ceiling: 59,000 feet
Top speed: Mach 2.5
Powerplant: (2) 25,100lb thrust Pratt & Whitney TF30-P-9 turbofans
Armament: One 20mm multibarrel cannon plus up to 25,000 pounds of bombs, missiles or fuel tanks

F-5E Tiger II
Manufacturer: Northrop
First year of service: 1972 (F-5A, 1964)
Aircraft type: Single-seat air superiority fighter
Wingspan: 26ft 8in
Length: 47ft 4¾in
Weight: 24,722lb (gross); 9723lb (empty)
Range: 1543 miles with external fuel tanks
Service ceiling: 51,800 feet
Top speed: Mach 1.64
Powerplant: (2) 5000lb thrust General Electric J85-GE-21B turbojets
Armament: Two 20mm cannons plus up to 7000lb of mixed ordnance on 4 underwing and one underfuselage pylons

THE TRANSITION YEARS

The **General Dynamics F-111 Aardvark** began with the controversial Defense Department Tactical Fighter Experimental (TFX) program in 1960. The desired plane was a tactical aircraft that could do everything and do it for both the Air Force and the Navy. The TFX was given the designation F-111 in 1961, with the F-111A destined for the Air Force and the F-111B for the Navy. The problems inherent in designing a plane that could be all things to all people were enormous, and serious difficulties arose. The Navy dropped out of the program but the Air Force continued. The first flight of the resulting variable-geometry F-111A took place on 21 December 1964, 22 months after the program began and 2 weeks ahead of schedule; it was not until 16 October 1967 that the F-111s entered operational service with TAC. They were rushed into service in Southeast Asia during the following March under the code name *Combat Lancer*. Problems with the plane's Terrain Following Radar resulted in several losses and it was returned to the drawing board and not redeployed until the fall of 1972. After the war the F-111D and E, and ultimately the F-111F, continued in production as fighter bombers. The original F-111 F had a range of 2925 miles without external fuel and a service ceiling of 59,000 feet: top speed, Mach 2.5. Meanwhile two other distinctive aircraft types have used the basic F-111 airframe. First, SAC has taken advantage of the inherent long-range and heavy-load-carrying capability of the airframe for its strategic medium bomber

version, the FB-111. Beginning in 1979 TAC began to deploy a Grumman-developed electronic warfare version, designated EF-111. The EF-111 is designed to provide barrier surveillance jamming, suppression of SAM threats during close air support operations and escort jamming for deep strike missions.

No single fighter aircraft epitomized the US Air Force during the war in Southeast Asia – and the following decade – better than **McDonnell's F-4 Phantom II.** More Phantoms have been produced for the Air Force than any other plane since the Sabre Jet. They provided the backbone of AAC, USAFE, PACAF and TAC from the late sixties until the early eighties when the F-15 began to come on-line in large numbers. The F-4s, however, will continue to serve as second- and even first-line fighters with Air Force units around the world well into the nineties. Since the war in Southeast Asia, the multirole F-4E has been continually updated with such hardware as Northrop's TISEO (Target Indentification System, Electro-Optical) and the Pave Tack system, which provides the F-4 with nighttime and all-weather capabilities to track and target ground targets for laser, infrared and electro-optically guided weapons. Some F-4Es have been modified as F-4G 'Wild Weasels' equipped to detect, locate and destroy enemy missile sites and tracking radar by means of programable electronic warfare software and antiradar missiles such as the new AGM-88 HARM.

The RF-4C, the high-speed reconnaissance version of the Phantom, was brought into service during the war in Southeast Asia to replace the RF-101 which could function only in daylight. The basic RF-4 package includes standard optical cameras for daytime use and infrared sensors for nighttime operations. Seventeen of the 505 originally constructed have been retrofitted with Side-Looking Airborne Radar (SLAR) for all-weather standoff surveillance; 24 RF-4s are equipped with a Tactical Electronic Reconnaissance (TEREC) sensor for locating sources

F-4E Phantom II
Manufacturer: McDonnell Douglas
First year of service: 1967 (F-4C, 1963)
Aircraft type: Two-seat multi-role fighter, reconnaissance aircraft (RF-4C)
Wingspan: 38ft 7½in
Length: 63ft 0in
Weight: 61,795lb (gross); 30,328lb (empty)
Range: 1300 miles
Service ceiling: 40,000 feet
Top speed: Mach 2
Powerplant: (2) 17,900lb thrust General Electric J79-GE-17A turbojets
Armament: One 20mm rotary multibarrel cannon, up to 4 Sparrow, Shrike or Sidewinder missiles on 4 underwing and 4 underfuselage pylons (up to 16,000lb of external stores)

Transition-era fighters clockwise from upper left: A USAFE F-111 'Vark' out of RAF Lakenheath; the plucky and economical Northrop F-5 (*see graph on page 113*); and the McDonnell Phantom, as F-110A prototype in 1962 and as F-4C in Vietnam in 1965.

Above: Wild Weasel F-4Gs of the 35th Tactical fighter Wing out of George AFB on the Nellis AFB flight line during *Red Flag*. (Please note F-4G reference on page 212.)

Top right: An F-4E ready to roll. The multi-barrelled 20 mm cannon under the F-4E's chin made a difference in Vietnam and became an integral design element of both the F-15 and F-16.

WW
AF
69
273
WW
AF
69
272

of electronic emissions. Other modernization programs include the Pave Tack Infrared system for enhanced all-weather target locating.

Developed as a light, uncomplicated, low-cost fighter for the export trade in the 1950s, **Northrop's N-156 Freedom Fighter** found its way into Air Force inventory in 1964 under the designation F-5 Tiger. Over the years, the US Air Force has accepted delivery of over 1000 F-5s, nearly all of them transferred or sold to such countries as South Vietnam, South Korea, the Philippines, Turkey, Iran, Greece, Norway and Nationalist China under the Military Assistance Program or the Foreign Military Sales Program. Those few which are retained in USAF service are used principally by Aggressor squadrons in dissimilar air-to-air combat training exercises like TAC's *Red Flag* because their size and shape approximates that of the Eastern Bloc's MiG-21. By and large, when its performance is considered against its very economical cost, the F-5 is an excellent aircraft. It is, however, less sophisticated technologically than the larger and more expensive aircraft that the USAF has tended to purchase for its own first-line fighter squadrons. Northrop has sought to address this problem through the introduction (early 1980s) of a much-improved version designated F-20 (originally F-5G) Tigershark.

THE NEW GENERATION

The Century Series fighters were designed in the 1950s for supersonic combat high in the stratosphere in new kinds of dogfights. In the late 1960s and early 1970s the Air Force found itself in a shooting war in which real dogfights demonstrated that aircraft design had strayed from the practical lessons of earlier combat. The axiom that the more complicated the weapons system, the less likely it was to work, proved at least partially true. Sophisticated air-to-air missiles were seen to be no substitute for good old-fashioned guns, and the F-4 had to be retrofitted with 20mm cannons. Maneuverability (as had been proven in earlier air wars) was more important than speed, but the Century Series had generally traded maneuverability for ever-higher speeds. Most dogfights were waged at the same speeds as in the Korean War.

F-15A Eagle
Manufacturer: McDonnell Douglas
First year of service: 1974
Aircraft type: Single-seat high-performance air superiority fighter
Wingspan: 42ft 9¾in
Length: 63ft 9in
Weight: 68,000lb (gross); 27,300lb (empty)
Range: 2878 miles without external fuel
Service ceiling: 65,000 feet
Top speed: mach 2.5
Powerplant: (2) 23,930lb thrust Pratt & Whitney F100-PW-100 turbofans
Armament: One 20mm multibarrel rotary cannon plus 4 Sparrow and 4 Sidewinder missiles on underside pylons (up to 16,000lb of external stores)

Discussion of an air superiority fighter to replace the F-4 began in the late 1960s. It culminated in a contract award to the McDonnell division of McDonnell Douglas to build this new experimental fighter designated FX. The contract was signed in January 1970, the first flight of the resulting **YF-15 Eagle** taking place in July 1972. Deliveries of operational aircraft followed in 1973. In early 1975 a specially prepared F-15 nicknamed 'Streak Eagle' set eight world time-to-height speed records, six of which remain unbroken, including *Climb to 20,000 meters* (65,616ft) in 2 minutes 2.94 seconds. The Eagle is armed with both guns and

F-16A Fighting Falcon ('Viper,' 'Electric Jet')
Manufacturer: General Dynamics
First year of service: 1979
Aircraft type: Single-seat air superiority and multirole fighter
Wingspan: 32ft 10in
Length: 49ft 6in
Weight: 35,400lb (gross); 15,586lb (empty)
Range: 2000 miles
Service ceiling: 50,000 feet
Top speed: Mach 2
Powerplant: (1) 25,000lb thrust Pratt & Whitney F100-PW-200 (3) turbofan
Armament: One 20mm multibarrel rotary cannon plus 2 wingtip mounted Sidewinder missiles and 7 other external pylons for fuel tanks, air-to-air or air-to-surface weapons

Above left: Their missile racks empty after a training mission, two McDill AFB Eagles roll out to return to base.

Above: This Hill AFB F-16 is armed with AIM-9L and J Sidewinders, 2000-lb Mk 84bombs,and anALQ-110 ECM pod on its centerline (*see pages 148 and 212*).

air-to-air missiles, whose effectiveness is enhanced by an IFF (Identification, Friend or Foe) system that distinguishes aircraft that can be seen visually but not identified. The lightweight Hughes radar system has 'look-down' capability, meaning that it can track small high-speed objects even at tree-top level. The Eagle cockpit is also enhanced by a 'head up' display (HUD) that projects all the data from the control panel onto the windshield – in a dogfight the pilot doesn't have to look down to read altitude, airspeed or other data. The first units to receive F-15s were TAC's 1st TFW at Langley AFB and USAFE's 36th TFW at Bitburg AB, followed by TAC's 49th TFW at Holloman AFB and PACAF's 18th TFW at Kadena AB in 1979. By 1982 the Eagle was flying with all four Major Tactical Commands as well as TAC's Air Defense interceptor squadrons.

In 1972 the Air Force began to test, under its Lightweight Fighter Prototype program, two prototype aircraft designed to incorporate such emerging technologies as decreased structural weight through the use of composites to replace metal, blended body aerodynamics, fly-by-wire electronic controls and automatically variable wing leading edges to enhance the already outstanding maneuverability entailed by the lighter weight. The two planes selected to flight-test these new technologies were the YF-17 designed by Northrop Aviation, maker of the lightweight F-5, and the YF-16 by General Dynamics, which hadn't been involved with a USAF fighter program since Convair (whom General Dynamics had since acquired) had produced the highly successful F-106 over a decade earlier. Two prototypes of each design were built and flight-tested, with the production contract awarded to General Dynamics in April 1975. The first **F-16A Fighting Falcon** (the F-16B is the two-seat trainer version) flew in December 1976, with the first operational unit, the 388th TFW at Hill AFB, receiving their first Falcons in January 1979. Meanwhile, the F-16 was selected for co-production by four NATO countries in Europe: Belgium, Norway, Denmark and the Netherlands. The Belgian air force also accepted the first European-built F-16 in January 1979. USAFE's 50th TFW became the first overseas USAF Tactical Wing to receive the Falcon in 1982, with the 8th TFW at Kunsan AB, Korea, the first PACAF unit equipped with the F-16. In addition to the NATO countries producing it, the plane is also in service with Egypt, Pakistan, Venezuela, Korea, and Israel, which has used it in live combat since 1981. Like the F-15, the F-16 is equipped with both 'look down' radar and 'head up' display; built-in structural and

Left: F-16s of the Thunderbirds, the US Air Force aerobatic demonstration team. Since their creation in the 1950s, the Thunderbirds have used F-84s, F-100s and T-38s. With the transition to F-16s in the 1980s, the Thunderbirds for the first time flew jets that could be made combat-ready in a matter of hours.

wiring provisions and systems allow its expansion to precision-strike, night-attack and long-range intercept missions as well as air superiority and combat air patrol. Beginning in 1984 the F-16C (the F-16D is its two-seat trainer version) added such improvements as provisions for the AMRAAM air-to-air missiles and the LANTIRN navigation and attack system.

General Dynamic's Convair Division was the first to design and build operational delta-winged aircraft for the Air Force, and General Dynamics is reviving that tradition with the **F-16XL.** The F-16XL is essentially a delta-winged 'cranked arrow' F-16 providing improved range, payload, speed and maneuverability. This version began flight testing in July 1982 as a possible candidate for the Air Force's next-generation air superiority/deep interdiction fighter.

THE WARTHOG

Since the Air Force was created in 1948, most of its attack planes had their start somewhere else. The A-1 and A-7 were both born as US Navy carrier-based attack bombers. The A-26/B-26 was a World War II light bomber. The A-37 Dragonfly was developed from a Cessna T-37 trainer and thrown into combat in Southeast Asia. It was not until the war in Vietnam that the Air Force began to think seriously about designing an entirely new aircraft specially for ground attack and close air support. The program was called AX for Attack, Experimental: like the two-plane competition in the Lightweight Fighter Prototype program, the AX would involve a two-plane fly-off. The competition was held from October through December 1972 between Northrop's A-9 and Fairchild Republic's A-10, with the latter winning the production contract.

The **Fairchild Republic A-10** is a unique aircraft to say the least. It was nicknamed by its maker Thunderbolt II, for Re-

Right: An F-16A escorts a delta-winged F-16XL through its paces at the 1982 Farnborough Air Show. For the demonstration both aircraft were equipped with the visible AIM-9 missiles as well as AIM-7s on the undercarriage. The F-16 is the first USAF aircraft to operate experimentally with voice-activated controls.

Below: A flock of F-16 Falcons on a training mission. The blue color coding on the wing-tip mounted Sidewinders indicates that their warheads are inert.

Above: Its engines mounted high and aft to confuse ground-launched heat-seeking missiles, the A-10 Thunderbolt II is equipped with underwing Multiple Ejection Racks (MER) and in this case an AGM-65 Maverick air-to-ground missile (*see pages 148-9*).

public's P-47 Thunderbolt, used in the ground-attack role in World War II (and because Republic tactical aircraft had always had the prefix 'Thunder'). Because of its unusual appearance – called ugly even by the pilots who know and love it – the A-10 is universally known in the Air Force as the 'Warthog.'

Fighters are easily the most glamorous aircraft in any air force. Their mission is to fly high and fast and to maneuver smoothly and gracefully. Attack planes are the other side of the tactical air-power coin. They are built to fly low, fly slow and carry a big load.

The Warthog was not designed for supersonic flight, and certainly not to win any beauty contest; it was designed to kill tanks. Its speed, barely 400mph, is entirely sufficient for its primary mission. There is a popular cartoon posted in A-10 squadron locker rooms that shows a Russian tank head-on with an A-10 looming up behind him, also head-on. The caption is the Russian tank commander urging his driver to 'Step on it, Ivan, I think he's gaining on us.'

The real beauty of the A-10 is in the way it is designed to fulfil its primary mission. It incorporates such modern technology as a head up display, but it is primarily designed for survival and firepower. Its survivability is enhanced by heavy armor, particularly in the cockpit area, and by the redundancy of its systems – whole portions of the plane may be shot away without its becoming unflyable. The A-10's firepower begins with its huge GAU-8/A 30mm, seven-barrel rotary cannon. The gun is located in the bottom centerline of the forward fuselage, with the nose wheel offset for the sake of the gun. The GAU-8/A fires up to 4200 rounds per minute of armor-piercing ammunition designed with nonradioactive uranium slugs for heavier impact. While this ferocious cannon is itself enough to destroy a tank or similar target, the A-10's arsenal also includes various bombs and rockets as well as the Maverick air-to-ground missile. For target designation the A-10 carries a Pave Penny laser system pod.

The first A-10 squadron became operational with TAC at Myrtle Beach AFB in 1977; since then Warthog squadrons have joined USAFE, PACAF, AAC and the Air Force Reserve.

A-10 Thunderbolt II ('Warthog')
Manufacturer: Fairchild Industries, Fairchild Republic Div
First year of service: 1977
Aircraft type: Single-seat close air-support attack aircraft
Wingspan: 57ft 6in
Length: 53ft 4in
Weight: 50,000lb (gross); 24,959lb (empty)
Range: 288 miles (with 110 minute loiter over target and 20 min fuel reserve)
Cruising speed: 439mph without ordnance
Powerplant: (2) 9065lb thrust General Electric TF34-GE-100 turbofans
Armament: One 30mm multibarrel cannon plus 8 underwing and three underfuselage attachments for 16,000lb of bombs, missiles, gun pods and jammer pods

Below: A Maverick-armed 81st TFW (USAFE) Warthog lands at Sembach AB in Germany.

Below: Neither a fighter nor an attack plane, the E-3A with its skunk-striped radome is an essential part of the TAC fleet, providing Airborne Warning And Control Systems (AWACS) services for TAC in complex air-combat scenarios.

Above: The Vought A-7 Corsair II is based on a US Navy carrier-based attack plane and had its baptism of fire with the USAF in Southeast Asia in 1968, where it turned in an outstanding performance.

Above: Inside a TAC E-3A AWACS, controllers can manage a large number of combat aircraft on various operations over a wide geographic area. The AWACS would be essential in Central Europe if war broke out.

A-7D Corsair II
Manufacturer: LTV Vought
First year of service: 1968
Aircraft type: Single-seat subsonic attack aircraft
Wingspan: 38ft 9in
Length: 46ft 1½in
Weight: 42,00lb (gross); 19,781lb (empty)
Range: 2871 miles with external fuel tanks
Top speed: 698mph
Powerplant: (1) 14,500lb thrust Allison TF41-A-1 non-after-burning turbofan
Armament: One 20mm multibarrel cannon plus up to 15,000lb of air-to-air or air-to-surface missiles, bombs, or gun pods on six underwing and two underfuselage attachments

E-3 Sentry (former designation EC-137)
Manufacturer: Boeing Commercial Airplane Company/Boeing Aerospace Company
First year of service: 1977
Aircraft type: Airborne Warning And Control System (AWACS)
Wingspan: 145ft 9in
Length: 152ft 11in
Weight: 325,000lb
Endurance: 11 hours+ (unrefueled)
Service ceiling: 29,000 feet
Cruising speed: 600mph
Powerplant: (4) 21,000lb thrust Pratt & Whitney TF33 turbofans
Surveillance radar: AN/APV-1 with IFF and data link fighter-control (TADIL-C) antennae

Above: An F-15 Eagle and A-10 Warthog of TAC's Tactical Fighter Weapons School at Nellis AFB, Nevada. Air Force blue with yellow markings is standard color for all USAF ground vehicles (*upper left*) except flight-line emergency vehicles (*bottom center*). (*See photos pages 14 and 15.*)

WA
AF 77 083

TACTICAL MISSILES

The first tactical air-to-air missiles in USAF service were those that evolved from World War II technology, like the **High Velocity Aerial Rocket (HVAR)** and **Folding Fin Aerial Rocket (FFAR)** that were relatively inexpensive unguided rockets that armed the early jet fighters. The growing sophistication of aerial rockets in the 1950s led to the discontinuance of guns in fighter aircraft.

Many of the early tactical rockets are still in use, such as the **AIR-2 (Air Intercept Rocket) Genie** nuclear-armed unguided rocket that was first deployed aboard the F-89J in the late 1950s. Many thousands were produced through 1962, and Genies still remain in service aboard USAF F-106 and Canadian F-101 interceptors.

The Hughes **AIM-4 (Air Intercept Missile) Falcon** was the first air-to-air guided missile to be adopted by the Air Force, becoming the standard armament on all USAF all-weather interceptors. Original versions were the radar homing AIM-4A and infrared homing AIM-4C, of which around 21,500 were produced between 1956-9. The AIM-4D is a 'cross-bred' version combining the infrared homing system of the AIM-4G Super Falcon with the airframe of the AIM-4C. Thousands of early Falcons were converted to AIM-4 D standard. The AIM-4F and G Super Falcon, less susceptible to electronic countermeasures than the Falcon, were introduced beginning in 1960. Both also had increased performance, with the AIM-4F using a Hughes semi-active radar homing guidance system, and the AIM-4G using an infrared homing system. A nuclear-capable version, the AIM-26 Nuclear Falcon, was introduced in 1960 but is no longer in service.

The Raytheon **AIM-7 Sparrow** is a supersonic radar-homing, long-range, all-weather, all-altitude air-to-air missile. It became standard on the F-4 Phantom and was used extensively in Vietnam. About 34,000 first-generation AIM-7Cs through Es were produced. The AIM-7F was introduced in the 1970s, followed by the AIM-7M in 1980. About 5400 AIM-7Fs and 4300 AIM-7Ms have been produced incorporating larger motors, doppler guidance and improved electronic countermeasures. The monopulse seeker introduced on the AIM-7M provides an improved cost-performance ratio and adds a look-down capability.

Above: An F-86 unleashes a salvo of HVARs over Nellis AFB.

The **AIM-9 Sidewinder**, with fewer than 24 moving parts, is one of the simplest and cheapest (less than half the cost of a Sparrow) air-to-air guided missile in the Air Force. The first AIM-9B was successfully fired in 1953; since then many thousands have been produced by General Electric and Philco for the Air Force as well as the US Navy and many foreign countries. A total of 3000 of the early AIM-9Es are still in Air Force inventory, along with 800 AIM 9Hs (principally a Navy version) and 14,000 AIM-9Js, which were brought on-line for the F-15. The AIM-9P is an improved version of the highly maneuverable AIM-9J, produced by conversion of AIM-9Js and Es. The AIM-9L is a 'third-generation' Sidewinder with new engines, im-

AIR-2A Genie
Manufacturer: McDonnell Douglas Astronautics
First deployment: 1957
Missile type: Nuclear-tipped air-to-air missile
Length: 9ft 7in
Maximum diameter: 1ft 5½in
Launch weight: 820lb
Speed: Mach 3
Range: 6 miles
Guidance: None (Fired automatically by Hughes Fire Control System in launching aircraft)
Warhead: Nuclear 1.5KT
Powerplant: (1) 36,000lb thrust Thiokol SR49 TC-1 solid-fuel

AIM-4G Super Falcon
Manufacturer: Hughes Aircraft
First deployment: 1960 (AIM-4A/C)
Missile type: Air-to-air missile
Length: 6ft 9in
Maximum diameter: 6.6in
Launch weight: 145lb
Speed: Mach 2.5
Range: 7 miles
Guidance: Infrared homing system
Warhead: 40lb high explosive
Powerplant: First stage: (1) 6000lb thrust Thiokol M46 solid fuel; Second stage: (1) 6000lb thrust Thiokol M46 solid fuel

AIM-7F/M Sparrow
Manufacturer: Raytheon/General Dynamics (Pomona)
First deployment: 1963, AIM-7D ; 1974, AIM-7F
Missile type: All-weather air-to-air missile
Length: 12ft
Maximum diameter: 8in
Launch weight: 500lb
Speed: Mach 3.5+
Range: 26 miles+
Guidance: Raytheon semiactive Doppler radar homing system
Warhead: High explosive
Powerplant: Hercules Mk58 Mod 0 boost-sustained

AIM-9L Sidewinder
Manufacturer: Naval Weapons Center
First deployment: 1953
Missile type: Close-range air-to-air missile
Length: 9ft 5in
Maximum diameter: 5in
Launch weight: 190lb
Speed: Mach 2.5
Range: 4.35 miles
Guidance: Solid-state infrared homing system
Warhead: 25lb high explosive
Powerplant: Rocketdyne/Bermite Mk36 Mod 7/8 solid-fuel

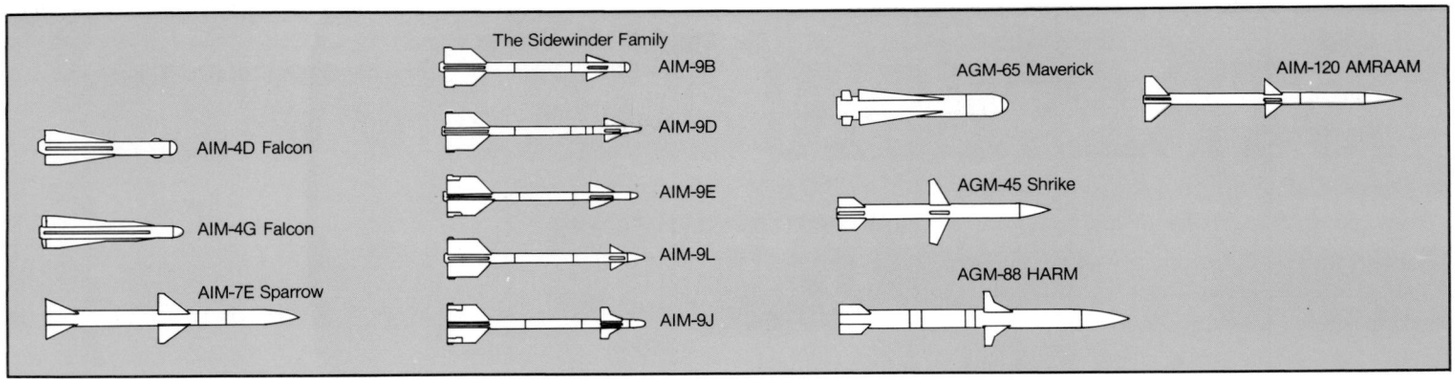

proved performance and maneuverability and improved tracking stability. The first of 15,000 of the new AIM-9M, an improved AIM-9L, went into production in 1982.

The **AGM-45 (Air-to-Ground Missile) Shrike** antiradiation missile, designed to automatically zero in on enemy radar sites, first entered service in 1965 against targets in North Vietnam. Since then more than 13,000 have been supplied to the Air Force.

The **AGM-65 Maverick** is a television-guided ground-attack missile with a 'launch and leave' capability, meaning that it can find the target on its own once launched. The Maverick was first used in Vietnam in 1972 and still equips all of TAC's first-line fighter-bomber and attack aircraft from the A-7 and A-10 to the F-111 and F-16.

The Texas Instruments **AGM-88 HARM (High Speed Anti-Radiation Missile)**, like the Shrike, is used against enemy radar sites and can cover a wide range of radar frequencies through programable digital processors in the avionics systems of both the missile and the launching aircraft. The HARM was designed for the F-4G 'Wild Weasel' but can also be used on the F-15 and F-16 as well as the B-52.

The General Dynamics **AGM-109H Tomahawk** is based on the Tomahawk cruise missile and is used in tactical nonnuclear operations where a subsonic standoff weapon is required for attacking heavily defended, high-value targets like enemy airbase runways.

The Hughes **AIM-120 AMRAAM (Advanced Medium Range Air-to-Air Missile)** is a radar-guided, all-environment intercept missile which will begin to replace the AIM-7 Sparrow as of 1986 aboard the F-15 and F-16. The AMRAAM has an inertial mid-course guidance system and active radar terminal homing, providing launch-and-manuever and launch-and-leave capabilities. The AIM-120 is superior to the earlier AIM-7 with respect to its warhead, velocity, range, low-altitude capability and electronic countermeasures.

Rockwell International's **GBU-15 (Glide Bomb Unit)** is described as an air-launched cruciform-wing glide bomb fitted with a television/infrared guidance system. It is basically a 'smart bomb,' whose guidance system gives it pinpoint accuracy whether dropped from five miles or a few hundred feet. The GBU-15 is a mid-1970s development of the earlier Pave Strike GBU-8 used in Vietnam. The GBU-15 offers two trajectories, a line-of-sight direct trajectory and an indirect trajectory in which the mid-course glide capability is brought into play. In this mode, the bomb can actually be guided to the target.

The latest twist in the arsenal of air-launched tactical missiles is the Vought **ALMV (Air Launched Miniature Vehicle)**, designed as an Anti-Satellite (ASAT) weapon that can be carried and launched by an F-15. Certain designated F-15s at designated TAC Air Defense bases will be equipped with this two-stage nonnuclear missile capable of destroying orbital altitude satellites in outer space.

AGM-45A Shrike
Manufacturer: Naval Weapons Center
First deployment: 1965
Missile type: Air-to-ground missile
Length: 10ft
Maximum diameter: 8in
Launch weight: 400lb
Speed: (classified)
Range: 3.5 miles
Guidance: Texas Instruments passive homing head
Warhead: 145lb high explosive/fragmentation
Powerplant: (1) Rocketdyne Mk39 Mod 7 or Aerojet General Mk53 solid-fuel

AGM-65A Maverick
Manufacturer: Hughes Aircraft
First deployment: 1971
Missile type: Air-to-ground 'launch & leave' missile
Length: 8ft 1in
Maximum diameter: 1ft
Launch weight: 462lb
Speed: (classified)
Range: (classified)
Guidance; Self-homing electro-optical system
Warhead: High explosive
Powerplant: Thiokol TX-481 solid-fuel

AIM-120A (AMRAAM)
Manufacturer: Hughes Aircraft
First deployment: 1985
Missile type: Advanced medium-range air-to-air missile
Length: 12ft
Maximum diameter: 7in
Launch weight: 327lb
Guidance: Inertial midcourse, with active radar terminal homing
Warhead: High explosive

AGM-88A HARM
Manufacturer: Texas Instruments
First deployment: 1983
Missile type: High-speed anti-radar missile
Length: 13ft 8½in
Maximum diameter: 10ft
Launch weight: 807lb
Speed: (classified)
Range: 10 miles
Guidance: Passive homing system, homes on radar emissions
Warhead: High explosive
Powerplant: First stage:dual thrust Thiokol smokeless solid-fuel

STRATEGIC AIR POWER IN THE US AIR FORCE

STRATEGIC AIR POWER

Strategic air power contrasts with tactical in that it is used against long-range targets that affect an enemy's *will* to wage war or long-term *ability* to wage war. Largely theoretical before World War II, strategic air power played a key role in the defeat of Germany and Japan. During the war, Britain's RAF and the USAAF were the major practitioners of strategic air power: the USAAF organized three numbered air forces, the Eighth and Fifteenth in Europe and the Twentieth in the Pacific, to carry out strategic bombing offensives.

After the war, to perpetuate its strategic bomber superiority, the USAAF created the Strategic Air Command (SAC) in 1946. Since then, while tactical air warfare has been a major part of nearly all postwar conflicts, strategic air power has been applied only sparingly. It was used by SAC in the 1972 *Linebacker II* operations over North Vietnam and by the RAF in the Falklands War of 1982, but scarcely anywhere else. Perhaps the main reason is that strategic air power has come, since World War II, to be associated with the massive strategic nuclear arsenals of the Soviet Union and the United States. It has taken on the aura of a 'doomsday' strategy. All the destructive power delivered by all the strategic bombing offensives of World War II could be matched in a few seconds by a nuclear exchange between the superpowers. So massive is the potential firepower of these two arsenals that it could destroy not only the principals, but most of the known world as well. The world has been spared strategic nuclear warfare through US-Soviet recognition of the concept of Mutual Assured Destruction, with its appropriate acronym MAD. Nuclear war has been avoided, thus far, by balancing one arsenal against the other.

On the American side, the nuclear arsenal is in three parts, known as the *Triad*. One of these parts, Submarine Launched Ballistic Missiles (SLBM), is under control of the US Navy; manned bombers and Intercontinental Ballistic Missiles (ICBM) are under control of the US Air Force's Strategic Air Command.

THE STRATEGIC AIR COMMAND

The Strategic Air Command was created at the same time as the Tactical Air Command and the Air Defense Command (21 March 1946). It is the US Air Force's long-range strike force, deterring nuclear war by its readiness to fight a nuclear war and supporting other operations by maintaining heavy bombers for conventional bombing missions. SAC has

Below: SAC maintains bombers and missiles for long-range strike missions, but it also manages a fleet of high-performance reconnaissance aircraft, such as this super-secret SR-71 photographed by the author at Beale AFB, to gather the information needed to develop and update the strategic war plan.

provided bombers for service in both Korea and Southeast Asia, with bombers in Korea under FEAF Bomber Command control, but those in Southeast Asia under direct SAC control. Beginning in the 1980s some of SAC's bombers have been organized into a Strategic Projection Force (SPF) to provide massive conventional bombing capabilities in support of the Rapid Deployment Force (RDF).

With nearly 110,000 uniformed personnel, SAC is the largest single Major Command in the Air Force. In addition, it is the gaining command for 15,800 members of the Air National Guard and Air Force Reserve. The SAC Force is composed of over 1000 ICBMs, nearly 400 B-52 and B-1 long-range bombers, 60 FB-111 medium-range bombers and nearly 100 sophisticated U-2, TR-1 and SR-71 strategic reconnaissance aircraft. In addition to these, SAC manages the Air Force's entire fleet of over 600 KC-135 and KC-10 aerial refueling tankers.

About 30% of the bomber and tanker fleet are on a 24-hour ground alert, ready to react immediately in time of war. At the same time, SAC's ICBM force also maintains a 24-hour alert posture.

SAC is composed of three major components, the Eighth and Fifteenth Air Forces and the First Strategic Aerospace Division. Of the three major strategic air forces of World War II, the Eighth and Fifteenth were both assigned to SAC within six weeks of its creation while the Twentieth, having gone from direct JCS control to part of FEAF, remained under that Command until permanently disbanded in March 1955. The Second Air Force, one of the four continental numbered air forces of World War II, was reactivated in November 1949 and assigned to SAC as the home-front Third Air Force had been assigned to TAC. Until 1950 the three SAC numbered air forces were divided by type of aircraft. The Second was in charge of reconnaissance aircraft, the Eighth heavy (B-36) and some medium (B-29) bombers, and the Fifteenth medium bombers. In April 1950 SAC forces were realigned geographically. The Fifteenth (March AFB, California) would be in charge of SAC forces in the west, the Eighth (MacDill AFB, Texas) would supervise the central region while the Second (Barksdale AFB, Louisiana) controlled the east. In 1951 seven SAC Air Divisions were established under numbered-air-forces control, including two overseas, the Fifth at Rabat, French Morocco, and the Seventh at South Ruislip, England. In June 1954, with deactivation of the FEAF Bomber Command, SAC's Third Air Division was established at Andersen AFB on Guam, although the base was not transferred from FEAF to SAC until the following year.

In June 1955 Eighth Air Force Headquarters was moved to Westover AFB in Massachusetts, giving it control over SAC assets in the central and northeast states while the Second retained the southeast. In July 1957 the Sixteenth Air Force at Torrejon AB near Madrid, Spain, was assigned to SAC, assuming control of SAC operations in Spain and sharing with the Second control of Fifth Air Division operations in North Africa, which were fully integrated into the Sixteenth, as the Fifth was deactivated in 1958. The Seventh Air Division in England was also dissolved, but not until 1965. In April 1966, after nine years with SAC, the Sixteenth was transferred to USAFE; on 31 March 1970 the illustrious Eighth was deactivated at Westover AFB with all SAC's assets in the United States divided between the Second and Fifteenth Air Forces. It was the first time since 1949 that SAC had only two numbered air forces in the continental United States.

While the idea had been to eliminate the Eighth entirely, the plan was changed out of deference to the Eighth's long history, going back to its exploits during World War II in the skies over Germany. Instead, the Eighth Air Force was re-established on 1 April 1970 at Andersen AFB, incorporating the Third Air Division, and given jurisdiction over the B-52 *Arc Light* raids against Southeast Asia that originated there. In January 1975 the Eighth was moved back to Barksdale AFB, where it replaced the Second Air Force which was deactivated.

The third building block of the present SAC, the First Strategic Aerospace Division (1STRAD), like the numbered air forces, reports directly to SAC headquarters. On 21 July 1961 the former First Missile Division became the first Strategic Aerospace Division based at Vandenberg AFB, California. The original concept had called for the First Missile Division to function as the keystone of the SAC ballistic missile force, comprised of a diverse conglomeration of missile units based around the country and operating various types of missiles. However, the Thor and Jupiter missiles had been deactivated, and by 1961 the Atlas and Titan units assigned to the First had been transferred to the Fifteenth Air Force.

Thus when the First Strategic Aerospace Division was born, its function was to control the missile test launches taking place at Vandenberg and to train missile crews for SAC. Since 1958 over 1500 launches have taken place at Vandenberg, largely under the auspices of 1STRAD. These have included the huge Titan IIID space booster, many Minuteman launches and recently the MX test program. As the host unit at Vandenberg, 1STRAD is host to the Air Force's Space and Missile Test Organization, an agency of the Air Force Systems Command (AFSC), conducting missile tests over the Pacific Ocean from its Western Space and Missile Center (WSMC). The WSMC's Western Test Range extends from Vandenberg across the Pacific and into the Indian Ocean. The Shuttle Activation Task Force (SATAF) at Vandenberg is responsible for the program making the base the western launch site for the Space Shuttle program.

The Commanders of the Strategic Air Command

Gen George Kenney
21 Mar 1946–15 Oct 1948
Gen Curtis LeMay
16 Oct 1948–30 June 1957
Gen Thomas Power
1 July 1957–30 Nov 1964
Gen John Ryan
1 Dec 1964–31 Jan 1967
Gen Joseph Nazzaro
1 Feb 1967–31 July 1968
Gen Bruce Holloway
1 Aug 1968–30 Apr 1972
Gen John Meyer
1 May 1972–31 July 1974
Gen Russell Dougherty
1 Aug 1974–31 July 1977
Gen Richard Ellis
1 Aug 1977–1 Aug 1981
Gen Bennie Davis
1 Aug 1981–

STRATEGIC AIR COMMAND BASES

Offutt AFB (SAC Headquarters)
Location: 8 miles south of Omaha, Nebraska
Area: 1914 acres
Altitude: 1048ft
Personnel: 12,880 Military
3348 Civilian (including 740 contract personnel)

The US Army's Fort Crook was activated on the site in 1888; in 1924 the landing field was renamed in honor of Lt Jarvis J Offutt, an Air Service pilot who died 13 August 1918 of injuries suffered during combat in World War I. In addition to being SAC's headquarters, the base is home to the 55th Strategic Recon Wing and the 544th Strategic Intelligence Wing – as such it is also home base for the *Looking Glass* Airborne Command Post. USAF Global Weather Central (MAC) is also at Offutt, as well as MAC's 3d Weather Wing.

Andersen AFB
Location: 16.8 miles north of Agana, Guam
Area: 20,500 acres (including off-base facilities)
Altitude 535ft
Personnel: 3801 Military
645 Civilian
Activated as North Field in 1945 just after the island was retaken from the Japanese in World War II, the base was one of a string established on Guam and the neighboring Marianas Islands for conducting the B-29 strategic offensive against Japan. Another field on Guam, Northwest Field, still exists on the Andersen reservation but is not in use. Named for Brig Gen James Roy Andersen, reported missing in a flight from Guam to Hawaii in February 1945, the base was the headquarters of SAC's 8th Air Force during the Vietnam War and one of two B-52 bases active in that war. Today it is the headquarters of SAC's 3d Air Division and its 43d Strategic Wing, flying B-52s and KC-135s.

Barksdale AFB
Location: Bossier City, Louisiana
Area: 22,000 acres (20,000 reserved for recreation)
Altitude: 166ft
Personnel: 5864 Military
1334 Civilian
Activated on 2 February 1933, the base was named for Lt Eugene Barksdale who was killed in August 1926. The base is the present headquarters of the 8th Air Force and its 2d Bomb Wing, flying B-52s, KC-135s and KC-10s. It also houses the 1st Combat Evaluation Group and the SAC NCO Academy. The ATC's 14th Flying Training Wing is here, and MAC operations include the 26th Weather Squadron and elements of the 1401st Military Airlift Squadron. AFRES activities include a detachment of the 307th Civil Engineering Squadron (*Red Horse*), the 917th Tactical Fighter Group (A-10s) and the 78th Air Refueling Squadron (KC-10s).

Beale AFB
Location: 13 miles east of Marysville, California
Area: 22,944 acres
Altitude: 113ft
Personnel: 4250 Military
551 Civilian
Named for Brig Gen Edward Fitzgerald Beale, an Indian agent in California prior to the Civil War, the base was originally US Army's Camp Beale. It was transferred to the USAF in November 1948 and became an AFB three years later. As headquarters of SAC's 14th Air Div and its 9th Strategic Recon Wing, Beale is home base for all the USAF's highly sophisticated SR-71, U-2

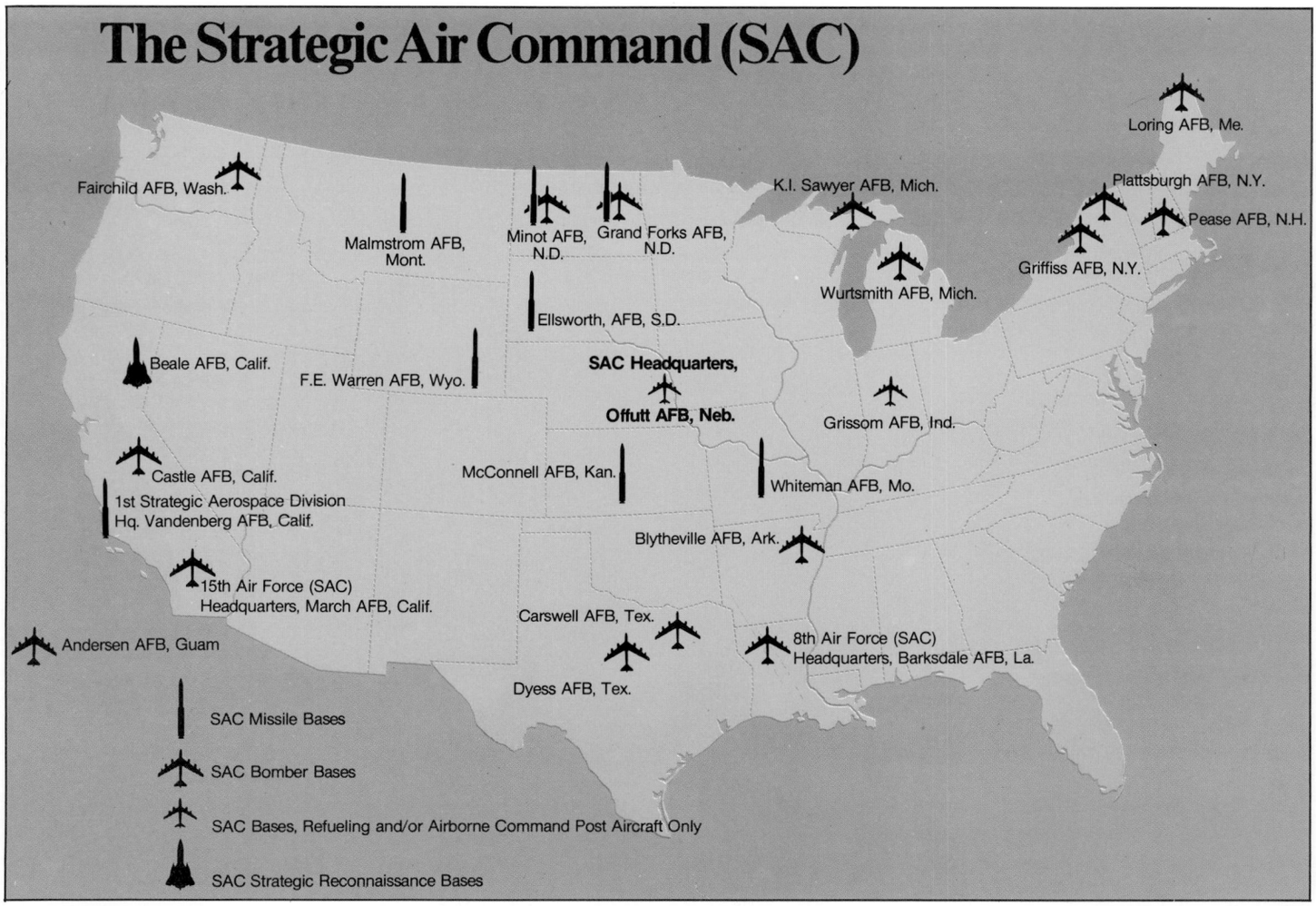

and TR-1 reconnaissance aircraft. Also housed on the base are the 100th Air Refueling Squadron, the 7th Missile Warning Squadron and AFCC's 1883d Communications Squadron.

Blytheville AFB
Location: 4 miles NW of Blytheville, Arkansas
Area: 3092 acres
Altitude: 254ft
Personnel: 2992 Military
340 Civilian
Active between June 1942 and February 1947 as a USAAF Field, the base was reactivated as an AFB in August 1955. It is the home of SAC's 42d Air Division and 97th Bomb Wing.

Carswell AFB
Location: 7 miles WNW of downtown Fort Worth, Texas
Area: 2750 acres
Altitude: 650ft
Personnel: 5010 Military
944 Civilian
The base was activated in August 1942 and named on 30 January 1948 for Maj Horace Carswell Jr, a native of Fort Worth who was a World War II B-24 pilot and posthumous recipient of the Medal of Honor. The base is the headquarters of SAC's 19th Air Division and the 7th Bomb Wing. The AFRES 301st Tactical Fighter Squadron is also housed here.

Castle AFB
Location: 8 miles NW of Merced, California
Area: 2700 acres
Altitude: 188ft
Personnel: 5024 Military
400 Civilian
Activated in September 1941, the base is named for Brig Gen Frederick Castle, World War II B-17 pilot and recipient of the Medal of Honor. The first unit to fly B-52s in 1955, the 93d Bomb Wing is today responsible for crew training for B-52G, B-52H, and KC-135 aircraft. TAC's 84th Fighter Interceptor Squadron flying F-106s is also based here, having moved from Hamilton AFB north of San Francisco when that installation closed. The base is also the site of the Castle Air Museum, which has many important aircraft on static display including the B-17, B-29, the British Vulcan Bomber and one of a few rare B-45 Tornados.

Dyess AFB
Location: Abilene, Texas
Area: 6058 acres
Altitude: 1789ft
Personnel: 5184 Military
430 Civilian
The base served as a USAAF Field from April 1942 until 1945, being reactivated as Abilene AFB ten years later. In March 1956 it was renamed for Lt Col William Dyess, a World War II pilot who made a daring escape from a Japanese prison camp only to die in Burbank, California, in a 1943 P-38 crash. Dyess houses SAC's 12th Air Division and 96th Bomb Wing as well as MAC's 463d Tactical Airlift Wing, ATC's 417th Field Training Detachment and AFCC's 1993d Communications Squadron.

Ellsworth AFB
Location: 11 miles ENE of Rapid City, South Dakota
Area: 4906 acres

Altitude: 3200ft
Personnel: 6192 Military
560 Civilian
Activated in July 1954, the base is named for Brig Gen Richard Ellsworth, killed 18 March 1953 in the crash of an RB-36. The base is home to the 44th Strategic Missile Wing and the 28th Bomb Wing, including SAC's Post Attack Command and Control System Squadron.

Fairchild AFB
Location: 12 miles WSW of Spokane, Washington
Area: 6127 acres
Altitude: 2462ft
Personnel: 4022 Military
814 Civilian
Activated in January 1942, the base was named for Gen Muir Fairchild, USAF Vice-Chief of Staff at the time of his death in 1950. It is home to SAC's 47th Air Division, 92d Bomb Wing and Det 7 of the 4000th Aerospace Applications Group. Fairchild also houses ATC's 3636th Combat Crew Training Wing, a detachment of MAC's 40th Aerospace Rescue and Recovery Squadron, AFCC's 2039th Communications Squadron and the 141st Air Refueling Wing of the Washington ANG.

Grand Forks AFB
Location: 16 miles West of Grand Forks, North Dakota
Area: 6912 acres (plus Minuteman III sites spread across 7500 square miles)
Altitude: 911ft
Personnel: 5123 Military
484 Civilian
The base was activated in 1956 after the citizens of the city for which it is named raised the money to buy the land for the Air Force. The base houses the 321st Strategic Missile Wing which manages the missile sites, and the 319th Bomb Wing flying B-52Gs and KC-135s.

Griffis AFB
Location: One mile NE of Rome, New York
Area; 3896 acres
Altitude: 504ft
Personnel: 3871 Military
2870 Civilian
Activated on 1 February 1942, the base was named for a US airman who became the first killed in action in Europe two weeks later. The host unit is SAC's 416th Bomb Wing; the major tenant is AFSC's Rome Air Development Center. Other tenants include AFCC's Continental Communications Division and 485th Engineering and Installations Group and TAC's 49th Fighter Interceptor Squadron.

Malmstrom AFB
Location: One and a half miles east of Great Falls, Montana
Area: 3573 acres (plus a 23,000 square mile Minuteman Missile complex)
Altitude: 3525ft
Personnel: 3925 Military
453 Civilian
Activated on 15 December 1942, the base was later named for Col Einar Malmstrom who was killed on 24 August 1954. The 341st Strategic Missile Wing based at Malmstrom was SAC's first Minuteman wing and today presides over its largest missile complex.

McConnell AFB
Location: 5 miles SE of Wichita, Kansas
Area: 3066 acres
Altitude: 1371ft
Personnel: 4381 Military
698 Civilian
The base was activated on 5 June 1951 and is named for Lt Thomas McConnell, a B-24 pilot killed during the 10 July 1943 raid on the Japanese base at Bougainville, and his brother Capt Fred McConnell, killed in a plane crash on 25 October 1945. The base is home to SAC's 381st Strategic Missile Wing and 384th Air Refueling Wing, as well as the 184th Tactical Fighter Group of the Kansas ANG.

Minot AFB
Location: 13 miles north of Minot, North Dakota
Area: 5050 acres (plus 19,324 acres of missile sites)
Altitude: 1650ft
Personnel: 5784 Military
550 Civilian
Activated in February 1957, the base is home to SAC's 57th Air Division, 91st Strategic Missile Wing and 5th Bomb Wing, as well as TAC's 5th Fighter Interceptor Squadron.

Francis E Warren AFB
Location: Cheyenne, Wyoming
Area: 5872 acres (plus 200 Minuteman III sites located in a 12,600-square-mile area of Wyoming, Colorado and Nebraska)
Altitude: 6142ft
Personnel: 3516 Military
533 Civilian
Named for Francis Emory Warren, Wyoming governor and later Senator, the base was a US Army installation for over 80 years until it was turned over to the USAF in 1947. It was the home of the first Atlas-D ICBM (1960-65) and is the headquarters of the 4th Air Division and the 90th Strategic Missile Wing.

Pease AFB
Location: 3 miles west of Portsmouth, New Hampshire
Area: 4374 acres
Altitude: 101ft
Personnel: 3580 Military
551 Civilian
Named for Capt Harl Pease Jr, a B-17 pilot posthumously awarded the Medal of Honor, who was killed in the 7 August 1942 raid on the Japanese base at Rabaul. Activated in 1956, the base is the home of SAC's 45th Air Division and 509th Bomb Wing and the NYANG's 157th Air Refueling Group.

Plattsburgh AFB
Location: Plattsburgh, New York
Area: 3388 acres
Altitude: 235ft
Personnel: 3700 Military
745 Civilian
Established in 1814, the base is the second oldest active military installation in the US. (The oldest is the Presidio of San Francisco, dating from 1776.) An Air Force Base since 1955, Plattsburgh is home to the 380th Bomb Wing flying FB-111s and KC-135s. The 4007th Combat Crew Training, also based here, trains all of SAC's FB-111 crews.

K I Sawyer AFB
Location: 20 miles south of Marquette, Michigan
Area: 5224 acres
Altitude: 1220ft
Personnel: 3999 Military
482 Civilian
The base was named for Kenneth I Sawyer, who had proposed the site for a county airport before his death in 1944. The base was activated in 1959 and is the home of SAC's 410th Bomb Wing and 46th Air Refueling Squadron and TAC's 87th Fighter Interceptor Squadron.

Vandenberg AFB
Location: 8 miles NNW of Lompoc, California
Area: 98,400 acres
Altitude: 400ft
Personnel: 6415 Military
6400 Civilian (including NASA)
Activated in October 1941 as US Army Camp Cooke, the base was transferred to the Air Force on 7 June 1957 and renamed for Gen Hoyt Vandenberg, the second USAF Chief of Staff. Vandenberg is the only launch site for USAF Ballistic Missiles and has, since 1958, witnessed over 1500 launches. The base is also the alternative launch site for the Space Shuttle. The host unit is SAC's 1st Strategic Aerospace Division.

Whiteman AFB
Location: One and a half miles south of Knob Noster, Missouri
Area: 3384 acres (plus a missile complex comprising about 10,000 square miles)
Altitude: 869ft
Personnel: 3182 Military
392 Civilian
The base is named for Lt George Whiteman, a fighter pilot shot down over Wheeler Field, Hawaii, during the Japanese attack on Pearl Harbor. Activated in 1942, it is now the headquarters of the 351st Strategic Missile Wing, which manages sites throughout the lower Midwest.

Wurtsmith AFB
Location: 3 miles NW of Oscoda, Michigan
Area: 5213 acres
Altitude: 634ft
Personnel: 3074 Military
417 Civilian
Activated in 1924 as Camp Skeel, a gunnery range for nearby Selfridge Field (now Selfridge ANGB), the base became Oscoda Army Air Field in 1942. After the war it was renamed for Maj Gen Paul Wurtsmith, killed in a B-25 crash in 1946. Becoming a SAC base in April 1960, Wurtsmith is home to the 40th Air Division and 379th Bomb Wing.

US AIR FORCE BOMBERS

Bombers are generally classed by weight (i.e., light, medium, heavy) with ranges and payload generally increasing with weight and size. Light bombers have generally been classified with attack bombers as tactical aircraft. Medium bombers, as a rule, could be considered either as tactical or strategic, while heavy bombers are usually designed as strategic aircraft. At the end of World War II, the USAAF had 3063 light bombers (including 1906 A-26s), 5576 medium bombers (including 2039 B-25s and 760 B-26s) and 12,883 heavy bombers (including 3972 B-17s and 5267 B-24s) with its 2242 B-29s classed as Very Heavy Bombers. With postwar demobilization and reliance on the deterrent power of America's monopoly on nuclear weapons for defense, the vast majority of these bombers were scrapped. For example, when the USAF was created (1947) only *fifteen* B-24s remained in inventory. Most of the B-29s (2112 in 1947) were retained because they included the only planes capable of carrying the atomic bomb and had the longest range of any bomber in the world. In the development stage, however, was a bomber so large that when it came into service the B-29 would be reclassed from Very Heavy to Medium Bomber.

This new plane was the **Consolidated-Vultee (later Convair) B-36 Peacemaker**. It was half again larger than the B-29 and propeller-driven by six huge Pratt and Whitney R-4360 engines. The first YB-36A began tests at Wright Field (soon to become Wright-Patterson AFB) in August 1947, just as the US Air Force was about to come into being. Thus the B-36 became synonymous with the US Air Force in those early days. The first B-36A became operational with SAC on 26 June 1948; by the end of 1947 there were 36 in SAC's inventory. The B-36 was originally conceived during World War II as a strategic bomber with sufficient range to bomb Germany from the United States. With the onset of the cold war, the B-36 became the bomber that would strike the Soviet Union with nuclear weapons if World War III broke out.

The B-36 was not only the largest bomber in the world, it was by far the largest item in the budget of the new US Air Force. The first 95 production models had a unit cost of over $6 million, and the total program cost over half a billion. When the Soviet Union first displayed its MiG-15, making the B-36 potentially vulnerable, a storm of controversy broke out over the cost-versus-vulnerability issue. Congressional hearings (the 'B-36 Hearings') addressed charges that political favoritism (Defense Secretary Louis Johnson had served on Convair's Board of Directors) had allowed the Air Force to procure a 'costly sitting duck.' The B-36 survived the hearings and ultimately the Air Force took delivery of 385 of the huge bombers. The B-36D, first flown in July 1949, augmented the six big prop engines with four 5200lb-thrust

Above: The enormous B-36 represented the ultimate in World War II ideas about strategic bombers. Too late for the war, this controversial giant came to symbolize the new US Air Force in its early days.

General Electric J47 jet engines. The SAC inventory hit its peak number of Peacemakers – 209 B-36s and 133 RB-36s – in 1954; the last of them was retired in May 1958.

A lot of unusual aircraft designs came out of the aviation boom of the postwar period, but probably no more unusual airplanes got past the single prototype stage than **Northrop's B-35 and B-49**. Flying Wings were the stuff of fiction and fantasy back to the early years of powered flight, and there were a number of them on the drawing boards in the 1930s and 1940s. Northrop had been experimenting with small flying wings in the early 1940s and presented a proposal for a four-engine flying-wing bomber to the USAAF during the war. The USAAF was intrigued and gave the go-ahead for two flying-wing bomber prototypes under the designation XB-35. The new plane did not come on line in time to serve in World War II but made its first flight in June 1946, less than a year after its end. The B-35 had a crew of nine in its pressurized center section and enough room left over for a six-man relief crew. Its span was thirty feet greater than that of the B-29 and it was powered by four Pratt and Whitney Wasp Majors. Despite its lack of a fuselage, the B-35 had a bomb capacity twice that of the B-29 and nearly equal to that of the B-36. Even before the first flight of the XB-35, it was decided that jet propulsion was the wave of the future and that the B-35 program would evolve in midstream into a jet-propelled flying wing under the designation B-49.

The first XB-49 flew on 21 October 1949 powered by eight 4000lb-thrust Allison J35s. Its bomb capacity was less than that of the B-35 and its range of about 4000 miles was less than half the B-35's. Nevertheless, the XB-49's top speed was about 500mph against 390 for the B-35 and the Air Force contracted for 30 YRB-49s and the conversion of ten existing B-35s to YRB-49As. Because of its inferiority to the B-36 in terms of bomb capacity and range, the B-49 program was cancelled after the flight of the first YRB-49A on 4 May 1950.

The B-36 and the B-35/B-49 Programs were all heavy-bomber

Above: Faster than many fighters when it was first introduced, the sleek B-47 was a technological marvel in the early 50s.

Top: Technology ahead of its time. Northrop would revive the flying wing design of the B-49 for its 'Stealth' bomber in the 1980s.

Below: North American's jet-propelled B-45 Tornado.

B-36B Peacemaker
Manufacturer: Consolidated (Convair)
First year of service: 1948
Aircraft type: Long-range heavy bomber
Wingspan: 230ft
Length: 162ft
Weight: 278,000lb gross
Range: 8175 miles (with bomb load)
Service ceiling: 42,500 feet
Top speed: 381mph
Powerplant: (6) 3500hp Pratt & Whitney R-4360-41 Wasp Major radials
Armanent/Capacity: Sixteen 20mm cannons in eight remote-controlled turrets, plus up to 84,000lb of bombs

programs with SAC as the understood client. Meanwhile, a flurry of activity centered around development of light and medium jet bombers to replace the piston-engined Martin B-26, Douglas A-26 and North American B-25 of World War II fame. A pair of experimental aircraft in that size range were brought on line in the late forties. First there was the twin-engined Douglas XB-43, followed by the larger four-engined **North American XB-45 Tornado.** Flying on 15 March 1947, the B-45 became the first jet bomber to go into production in the United States. A total of 139 B-45s were produced, culminating in 33 RB-45Cs which were first delivered in 1949 and which saw limited service in the Korean War.

At the same time another set of jet bombers, in the same size and weight class as the B-29 – now considered a medium bomber – were being produced and test flown. First among them was the four-engined Consolidated XB-46 which first flew on 2 April 1947, followed by the six-engined Martin XB-48 on 14 June 1947 and Boeing's six-engined **XB-47 Stratojet** on 17 December 1947. Both the Consolidated and Martin Aircraft had straight wings like the B-43, B-45 and all the prop-driven bombers of the war era. The B-47, on the other hand, had the then-revolutionary swept wing that would soon make the F-86 Sabre Jet such an outstanding fighter.

Above: The B-49 Flying Wing and the B-45 medium bomber during flight testing.

Below: The 1000th Stratojet, a tail-gun-equipped B-47E.

B-47E Stratojet
Manufacturer: Boeing Military Airplane Company
First year of service: 1951 (B-47A)
Aircraft type: Medium Bomber
Wingspan: 116ft
Length: 107ft
Weight: 206,700lb
Range: 4100 miles
Service ceiling: 40,500 feet
Top speed: 606mph
Powerplant: (6) 7200lb thrust General Electric J47 turbojets
Armament: (2) 20mm cannons in radar-directed tail turret, with a bomb capacity of 20,000lb

Above: **Two tactical bombers with B-prefixes that served with TAC rather than SAC. Many B-57s such as this B-57B *(left)* were painted gloss black (with red trim) for nighttime operations, while the Douglas B-66B *(right)* appeared in natural metal finish. Later B-66s used in Vietnam were camoflaged in typical TAC/PACAF Southeast Asia camoflage.**

While most of its meager budget was being devoted to the B-36 program, the Air Force cautiously decided to go ahead with production of the B-47, which so far had the most outstanding performance of any bomber yet proposed. The B-47's speed – over 600mph – was better than any other jet bomber's and even than many jet interceptors in service. The high performance of the B-47 was attractive to the Air Force and helped offset criticism that the B-36 was too slow. With the Stratojet in SAC's arsenal, it was the end of piston-engined strategic bombers in the US Air Force. Even the huge B-36 that had symbolized, had almost *been*, the Air Force for half a dozen years was now doomed. Committed to production in 1949, the first B-47 entered SAC service on 23 October 1951. At the end of 1952 there were only 62 B-47s in service with SAC; by the end of the following year their number had risen to 329, surpassing the B-36 fleet by seven planes..

The B-47E was the standard production version of the B-47, accounting for nearly 80% of the 2040 B-47s produced. It incorporated ejection seats, 20mm cannons, JATO (Jet Assisted Take-Off) pack and upgraded engines. Included among the B-47Es were 240 RB-47Es, a few of which saw brief service in Southeast Asia in a reconnaissance role. Although it was produced in vastly greater numbers than any other US Air Force bomber since World War II, and was deployed at SAC bases worldwide for over a decade, the B-47 was retired without ever having fired a shot in anger. The peak number of in-service B-47s (1367 B-47s, 176 RB-47s) was reached in 1958; from there it declined until the last 114 B-47s were finally retired in 1965.

All the postwar experimentation with exotic jets promised state-of-the-art strategic bombers and high performance fighters, but the onset of the Korean War demonstrated that light-bomber technology had progressed little since World War II. The B-29 was ill-designed for tactical operations, and the F-84s had high performance and were good tank-killers but were certainly not bombers. Thus it was that the old Douglas A-26 Invader (it had been redesignated a bomber, B-26, in 1948 when the original Martin B-26 was retired) filled the bill. The Invader had proven itself in the earlier war, but the Air Force clearly saw the need for a light bomber with higher performance than the B-26 or even the B-45. Martin, who had produced the original B-26 – the Marauder – during World War II and the ill-fated XB-48 medium bomber, was at work on just such an aircraft. Originally designated with an 'Attack' prefix as A-45, but later redesignated B-51, it was an unusual design. It had swept wings (unusual in itself in the late 1940s) and three engines, one molded into the tail and the other two mounted on short pylons below the *front* of the fuselage in the manner of the German Ju 287 medium jet bomber of World War II. The Air Force did not like the B-51 and rejected it in favor of another light bomber of foreign design – the English Electric Canberra. Martin obtained a consolation prize in the form of a license to produce the Canberra in the United States.

The first Martin-built **Canberra**, designated **B-57A** flew on 20 July 1953, four years after the first English version. Most of the B-57s were B-57 B, C, and E light bombers, some of which were the first American jet combat aircraft deployed to Southeast Asia in 1964. During that war the B-57 proved an effective light bomber, flying both day and nighttime strike mission, mostly in South Vietnam. The RB-57D was the reconnaissance version, vastly different in appearance from the other B-57s. While the standard B-57s had a 64-foot wingspan, the RB-57D had a span

B-57B Canberra ('Cranberry')
Manufacturer: Martin (from earlier English Electric model)
First year of service: 1954
Aircraft type: Light attack bomber
Wingspan: 64ft
Length: 65ft 6in
Weight: 26,800lb
Range: 2100 miles
Service ceiling: 48,000 feet
Top/Cruising speed: 582mph
Powerplant: (2) 7220lb thrust Wright J65-5 turbojets
Armanent/Capacity: Provision for four 20mm or eight .50 caliber wing-mounted guns, plus an internal bomb load of 5000lb and other ordnance carried underwing

EB-66E Destroyer
Manufacturer: Douglas Aircraft
First year of service: 1958
Aircraft type: Electronic reconnaissance and countermeasures version of B-66 bomber
Wingspan: 72ft 6in
Length: 75ft 2in
Weight: 70,000lb gross
Range: 2000 miles
Service ceiling: 43,000 feet
Top/Cruising speed: 620mph
Powerplant: (2) 10,200lb thrust Allison J71-A-13 turbojets
Armament/Capacity: Two 20mm cannons in tail turret (generally on B-66 version, rarely found on EB-66)

Above: Convair's delta-winged B-58 Hustler was the USAF's first supersonic bomber.

of 106 feet and enormous wing area, giving it the kind of upper-atmosphere gliding ability enjoyed by the U-2.

A final type of light bomber was the **Douglas B-66 Destroyer**, an Air Force version of the Navy's A-3 Skywarrior. The A-3, which first saw service in 1956, was designed as a bomber to carry nuclear weapons and fly from an aircraft carrier, but ultimately found itself also in service as a reconnaissance aircraft and air refueling tanker. Fewer than half the B-66s built for the Air Force were the B-66B bomber version. Instead, most served as RB-66B and C reconnaissance aircraft and WB-66D weather reconnaissance aircraft. A number of them were modified as EB-6E electronic warfare aircraft. Over North Vietnam during the war, the EB-66Es provided electronic countermeasures and radar jamming for the *Rolling Thunder* strikes.

The first supersonic bomber was the **Convair B-58 Hustler**, a delta-winged aircraft like Convair's F-102 and F-106 that first flew in 1956 (the same year as the F-106). A medium bomber, it was a long sleek ship capable of a top speed in excess of Mach 2 and able to carry its ten-ton weapons pod (armed with nuclear or conventional bombs) over a range of 5000 miles. Unlike other bombers, the B-58 did not have a bomb bay; rather it carried the aerodynamically streamlined weapons pod attached under its fuselage. The weapons pod was designed so that it could be dropped on the target in its entirety, leaving the bomber much smaller and lighter, thus capable of the fastest possible escape from the nuclear blast. The B-58 first entered operational service with SAC's 43 Bomb Wing at Carswell AFB on 1 August 1960. The SAC B-58s went on to set a number of world's speed records including *Tokyo to London* in 8 hours, 35 minutes (average speed 938mph), *Anchorage to London* in 5 hours, 25 minutes (average speed 827mph) and *Tokyo to Anchorage* in 3 hours, 9 minutes (average speed 1094mph). A lot of hopes had ridden with the B-58, but despite its outstanding performance, it was not the right plane at the right time. It had been designed to fly its mission at high altitude, but advances in Soviet SAM technology made that sort of mission impossible. Rather than adapt it for low-level penetration, it was retired. The number of Hustlers in SAC reached a peak of 94 in 1964 and remained above 76 until the deactivation program got underway (1968). On 16 January 1970 the last two B-58s were flown to the AFLC storage and disposition facility at Davis Monthan AFB where they were unceremoniously cut up for scrap. Three B-58s remain in existence: one is at the US Air Force Museum (Wright Patterson AFB, Ohio), one at the SAC Aerospace Museum (Offutt AFB, Nebraska) and one at the Pima County Air Museum adjacent to Davis Monthan AFB.

B-58A Hustler
Manufacturer: Convair
First year of service: 1960
Aircraft type: Supersonic bomber
Wingspan: 56ft 10in
Length: 98ft 9in
Weight: 163,000lb
Range: 5125 miles
Service ceiling: 64,000 feet
Top speed: 1385mph
Powerplant: (4) 15,600lb thrust General Electric J-79-5B/C turbojets
Armament/Capacity: One 20mm remote-controlled tail cannon, plus underfuselage weapons pod for various nuclear or conventional bombs. Normal payload weight, 19,450lb

Major USAAF/USAF Bombers

Total Number Delivered

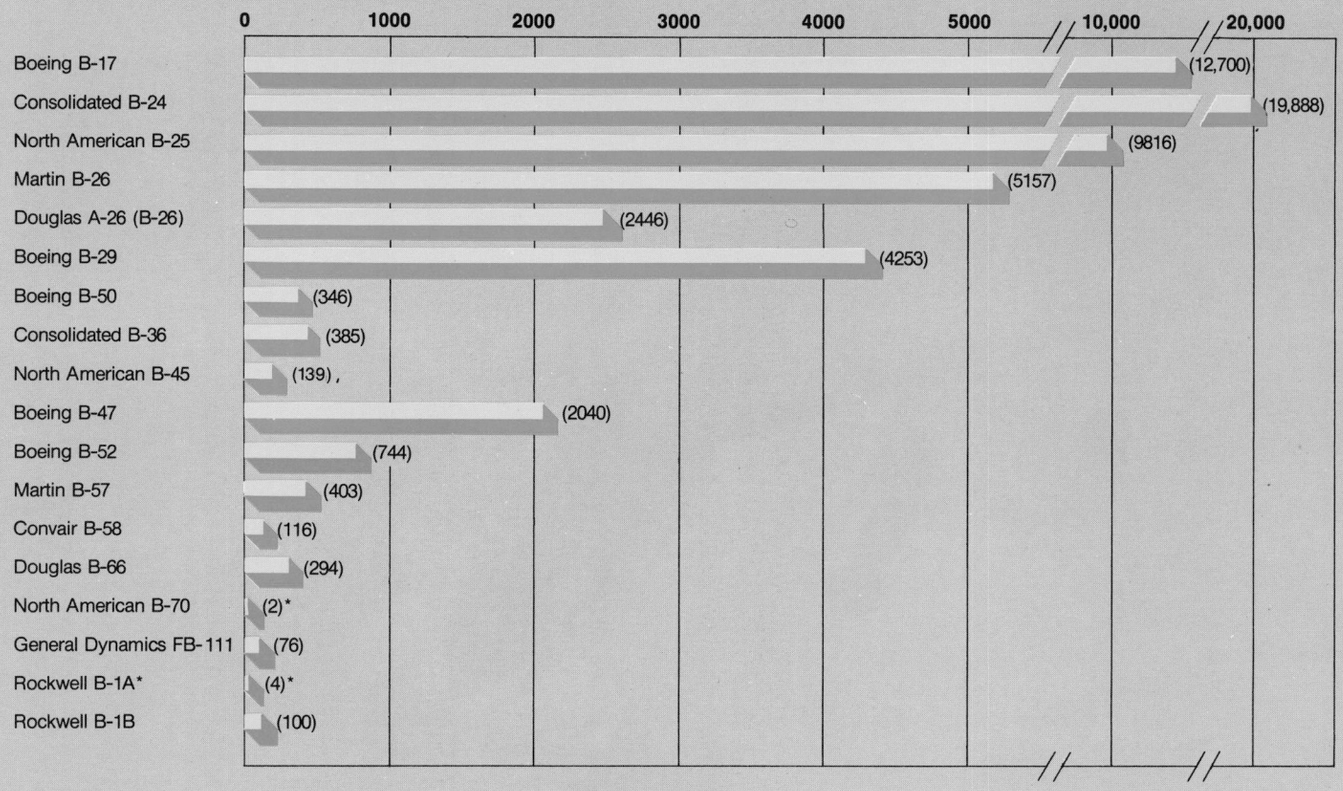

Major USAAF/USAF Bombers

and their Periods of Service

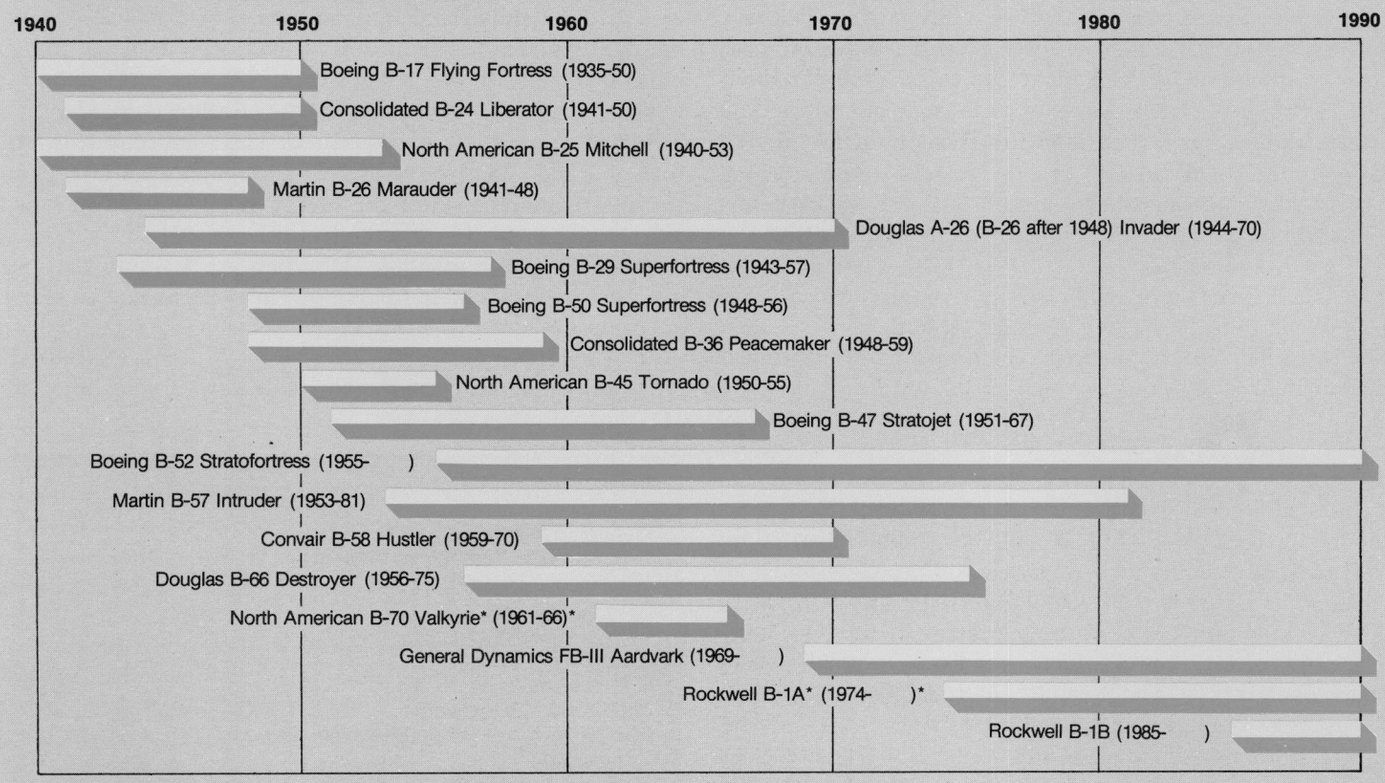

Data for USAAF/USAF aircraft only, excludes aircraft delivered directly to foreign air forces without USAAF/USAF service.

Periods begin with operational service, not first recorded flight. Periods include service with Air National Guard, but do not include mothballed aircraft.

*Neither the B-70 nor B-1A were production aircraft. Data for them is given only as a point of interest.

Above: **A 93rd Bomb Wing B-52G based at Castle AFB in California. The 93d Bomb Wing was the first to receive B-52s in 1955.**

Right: **Elaborate retrofitting, including intricate forward-looking sensors, has kept the B-52 fleet up to date.**

The most famous bomber to serve with the US Air Force, and the longest in service, was described by Secretary of the Air Force Donald Quarles (1955-1957) as 'the most formidable expression of air power in the history of military aviation' – **Boeing's B-52 Stratofortress**. When Boeing's B-47 medium bomber was outclassing the big B-36 heavy bomber, the Seattle-based planemaker was working on a heavy bomber of its own. It would be powered by eight Pratt & Whitney J57 turbojets. It would be nearly as large as a B-36 and would exceed it in both speed and range. First flown in 1952, the Stratofortress entered service on 29 June 1955 with SAC's 93d Bomb Wing at Castle AFB. Between 16 and 18 January 1957 three 93d Bomb Wing B-52s undertook Operation *Power Flight*, a nonstop flight around the world, aided by five in-flight refuelings. With aerial refuelings the B-52 had a proven intercontinental range, but on 10 January 1962, a B-52H took off from Kadena AB, Okinawa, and flew *unrefueled, nonstop*, to Madrid, setting a world distance record of 12,532 miles.

The total number of B-52s in SAC service reached a peak of 639 in 1962, and declined thereafter as the new shorter-tailed B-52G and H came on line and the earlier models were retired. The B-52 was introduced into combat in Southeast Asia on 18 June 1965, when 27 stateside-based B-52Fs flying from Andersen AFB on Guam struck Viet Cong positions in South Vietnam. It was the beginning of the *Arc Light* operations that would see B-52s in almost continuous operation over Southeast Asia until 15 August 1973. SAC's B-52 operations were under operational control of the Third Air Division at Andersen AFB until 1 April 1970 when the Eighth Air Force was activated at Andersen. When the B-52s went into combat, they were almost exclusively B-52Fs. As this was happening, SAC initiated a program called *Big Belly* in which the bomb bay capacity of the B-52Ds increased dramatically. Gradually the B-52Fs were withdrawn from service and replaced by the *Big Belly* B-52Ds whose bomb capacity increased fourfold over all other B-52 models. Most of the B-52 missions in Southeast Asia were the *Arc Light* carpet bombing missions, which were principally tactical. In December 1972, however, the B-52Ds (augmented by B-52Gs from stateside bases) carried out the strategic bombing offensive against North Vietnam code-named *Linebacker II*.

B-52D Stratofortress
Manufacturer: Boeing Military Airplane Company
First year of service: 1955
Aircraft type: Long-range heavy bomber
Wingspan: 185ft
Length: 157ft 7in
Weight: 450,000lb
Range: 7500 miles
Service ceiling: 50,000 feet
Top speed: 585mph
Powerplant: (8) 10,000lb thrust Pratt & Whitney J47-29W turbojets
Armament: (4) .50 caliber machine guns in manned tail turret, with a bomb capacity of 54,000lb

B-52H Stratofortress
Manufacturer: Boeing Military Airplane Company
First year of service: 1960
Aircraft type: Long-range heavy bomber
Wingspan: 185ft
length: 160ft 11in
Weight: 488,000lb
Range: 11,000 miles
Service ceiling: 55,000 feet
Top speed: 650mph
Powerplant: (8) 17,000lb thrust Pratt & Whitney TF33 Turbofans
Armament: (1) six barrelled 20mm Vulcan cannon in radar-operated tail turret, with a bomb capacity of 13,500lb

Above: One of the four B-1As during early testing at Rockwell's Palmdale, California, facility in 1974.

Right: When the B-1 program was reactivated, a B-1A prototype was modified to B-1B standards for pre-production flight testing at Edwards AFB in 1983.

Below: An FB-111 Aardvark with six Mk 117 bombs on each of its underwing pylons.

FB-111A ('Aardvark')
Manufacturer: General Dynamics
First year of service: 1969
Aircraft type: Medium-range high-altitude strategic bomber (see F-111F)
Wingspan: 70ft (spread); 33ft 11in (fully swept)
Length: 73ft 6in
Weight: 100,000lb
Range: 4100 miles with external fuel
Service ceiling: 65,000 feet
Top speed: Mach 2.5
Powerplant: (2) 20,350lb thrust Pratt & Whitney TF-30-P7 turbofans
Armament: Four SRAM missiles on external weapons pylons plus two in bomb bay; or six nuclear bombs; or combination; or 31,500lb of conventional bombs

B-1A
Manufacturer: Rockwell International, North American Aircraft Operations
First year of service: 1974
Aircraft type: Strategic bomber
Wingspan: 136ft 8½in (fully spread); 75ft 2½in (fully swept)
Length: 150ft 2½in
Weight: 389,800lb (gross)
Range: 6100 miles
Service ceiling: 50,000 feet
Top speed: Mach 2.1
Powerplant: (4) 30,000lb thrust General Electric F101-GE-100 turbofans
Armament: Three internal weapons bays, accommodations for 24 AGM-69B SRAMs on three rotary dispensers or 75,000lb of free-fall bombs; plus provision for 8 SRAMs or 40,000lb of bombs externally.

B-1B
Manufacturer: Rockwell International, North American Aircraft Operations
First year of service: 1985
Aircraft type: Strategic Bomber
Wingspan: 136ft 8½in (fully spread); 78ft 2½in (fully swept)
Length: 147ft
Weight: 477,000lb (gross)
Top/Cruising speed: High subsonic
Powerplant: (4) 30,000lb thrust General Electric F-102-GE-102 turbofans
Armament: Similar to B-1A with additional ability to carry Air Launched Cruise missiles.

Above: A SAC KC-10A Extender refuels a B-52G. Because they are designed around a basic commercial DC-10 airframe, KC-10s can receive maintenance at civilian airports in an emergency.

Above right: A KC-135 Stratotanker in flight. SAC has been the sole manager of the Air Force's tanker fleet since 1965.

Below: A KC-135 of the 100th Air Refueling Wing during takeoff from Beale AFB.

KC-135 Stratotanker
Manufacturer: Boeing Military Airplane Co
First year of service: 1956
Aircraft type: Aerial refueling tanker (see C-135)
Wingspan: 130ft 10in
Length: 135ft 3in
Weight: 297,000lb (gross); 98,466lb (empty)
Range: 1150 miles (fully loaded); 9200 miles (ferry range)
Service ceiling: 50,000 feet
Top speed: 585mph
Powerplant: (4) 13,750lb thrust Pratt & Whitney J57-P-59W turbojets
Capacity: An average of 120,000lb of transfer fuel

KC-10A Extender
Manufacturer: McDonnell Douglas
First year of service: 1981
Aircraft type: Aerial refueling tanker
Wingspan: 165ft 4.4in
Length: 181ft 7in
Weight: 590,000lb (gross)
Range: 4370 miles (with max payload)
Service ceiling: 42,000 feet
Top speed: 528mph
Powerplant: (3) 52,500lb thrust General Electric CF6-50C2 turbofans
Capacity: Maximum cargo or transfer fuel payload is 169,529lb

U.S. AIR FORCE
00314

80074

After the war the B-52Ds were retained in the Air Force as conventional bombing platforms and were not phased out until 1984. The higher-performance B-52G and H continued in their role of nuclear weapons carriers. To move into the next decade with a mission for which they were designed in the 1950s, the B-52G and H have now undergone extensive modifications. Their avionics systems now include Advanced Capability Terrain-Avoidance Radar (ACR) and the AN/ASQ-152 Electro-optical Viewing System (EVS) with Low Light TV (LLTV) and Forward-Looking Infrared (FLIR) cameras. The big B-52s will continue in service until the new B-1 Strategic bomber, to be introduced in 1985, reaches full strength in SAC Bomb Wings. Modifications to their weapons delivery potential have included the capability to operate with the new strategic air-launched missiles.

The first all-new long-range strategic bomber to enter service in the USAF arsenal since the B-52 was introduced in 1955 is the **Rockwell B-1**. The B-1 would be produced by Rockwell's North American Division – formerly the North American Aviation Company – which produced such planes as the B-25 Mitchell bomber and F-86 Sabre Jet. The first proposal for the B-1 arose in response to the Air Force Advanced Manned Strategic Aircraft (AMSA) program of the mid-1960s. The idea was for a supersonic low-altitude penetration bomber to replace the B-52 in lieu of the recently cancelled Mach 3 B-70. In 1976 the Air Force budgeted for 244 of the B-1s to be delivered by 1981, but the program was abruptly cancelled in 1977 by then-President Jimmy Carter. The first prototype B-1A had flown in December 1974; it would continue in flight testing with three others, but these four would be research aircraft only, with no production follow-up. When President Ronald Reagan was elected in 1980, he promptly revived the B-1 program. The production B-1 (designated B-1B) is similar to the B-1A, but will have a greater payload (also greater than the B-52G and H), smaller radar signature and slower speed. Where the B-1A had exceeded Mach 2 in flight-testing, the B-1B is rated only at speeds in the 'high subsonic' range. Delivery of operational B-1Bs is scheduled for 1985, four years later than the Initial Operating Capability (IOC) projected in the original B-1 program. Avionics systems will include extensive electronics countermeasures, Terrain-Avoidance Radar, an extremely accurate Inertial Navigation System (INS) and tie-in with the Air Force Satellite Communications (AFSATCOM) system.

Offensive weaponry on the B-1B will include many types of weapons now in use with the B-52G and H. There are three internal weapons bays with rotary launchers that have a capacity of eight AGM-86 Air-Launched Cruise Missiles (ALCM), 24 AGM-69 Short-Range Attack Missiles (SRAM), twelve B-28 and B-43, or 24 B-61 and B-83, free-fall nuclear bombs. In the conventional mode, the internal rotary launchers can carry up to 84,500lb Mk 82 or 24,2000lb Mk 84 bombs. The B-1B also has the potential of carrying ordnance under its wings, including 14 SRAMs or ALCMs and various gravity-fall nuclear or conventional bombs.

STRATEGIC RECONNAISSANCE AIRCRAFT

Because SAC has responsibility for carrying out the nation's strategic war plan, it is also charged with planning. Since planning requires information, SAC operates for the Air Force a fleet of the most sophisticated reconnaissance aircraft in the world. The **Lockheed U-2**, designed for very high altitude reconnaissance, was introduced secretly in the 1950s and used to monitor ICBM sites within the Soviet Union – until one piloted by Francis Gary Powers was brought down by a Russian SAM over Sverdlovsk in 1960, creating an international incident. The early U-2s remained an important part of the USAF reconnaissance arsenal through the 1960s and '70s over Cuba, Vietnam and other trouble spots. The basic U-2A and B have been modified into such diverse types as the electronic patrol version designated U-2EPX and the weather reconnaissance version (some of which have been transferred to NASA) designated WU-2. All these aircraft had basically the same airframe until introduction of the much broader-winged U-2R, which served as the prototype for Lockheed's newest reconnaissance aircraft, the **TR-1**, which first flew in 1981. The TR-1, like the U-2R, has a 103-foot wingspan and operates at extremely high altitudes equipped with cameras and sensors for day or night all-weather reconnaissance.

Above: The B-52Gs based at Griffiss AFB in New York were the first to become operational with the ALCM.

The **SR-71 Blackbird**, another Lockheed product, is a unique aircraft of extremely high performance. Designed in the 1960s, it incorporates technology that is not known to have been equalled or surpassed since. Wearing flight suits made from the same mold as the lunar mission and Space Shuttle suits, the SR-71 pilots take their aircraft to the edge of space, to over 100,000ft, at speeds well in excess of Mach 3. The SR-71 combines a unique fuselage and wing contour and enormously powerful engines to achieve speeds that no other aircraft has been able to touch since the Blackbird set the *World's Absolute Speed* record of 2193.167mph in July 1976. As the pilot says about his amazing plane, 'The real beauty is in what you can't and will never see.' He is referring to the extremely sensitive electronic and photographic gear within the SR-71: its sophisticated battlefield surveillance systems have the capability of covering 100,000 square miles in a single hour.

AGM-86 ALCM Air Launched Cruise Missile
Manufacturer: Boeing Aerospace
First deployment: 1982
Missile type: Air-to-ground cruise missile
Length: 20ft 9in
Maximum diameter: 2ft ½in (wingspan: 12ft)
Launch weight: 2825lb
Speed: 500mph
Range: 1550 miles
Guidance: Inertial plus Tercom terrain contour matching
Warhead: W-80-1 Nuclear
Powerplant: First stage (1) 600lb thrust Williams International F107-WR-100 turbofan

Above: A Boeing AGM-86B Air Launched Cruise Missile with its wings extended in flight over the Air Force test range south of Hill AFB.

STRATEGIC AIR LAUNCHED MISSILES

The B-52G and H and the B-1B are equipped to carry both the **Short Range Attack Missile (SRAM)** and the **Air Launched Cruise Missile (ALCM)**. Both these missiles were developed by Boeing and are designed to carry nuclear warheads. The SRAM, first deployed in 1972, has a short range and is designed to be used by the bomber to destroy obstacles encountered on the way to the target, such as SAM batteries and radar sites.

The ALCM, first deployed in 1982, has a much longer range and is used as an offensive weapon. The ALCMs, released in quantity by the bombers, then use their Terrain-Avoidance Radar to fly very close to the ground under enemy radar, striking targets a thousand miles apart. The bomber's effectiveness is multiplied by its ability to drop its weapons out of the range of enemy target defenses and against several targets at once.

INTERCONTINENTAL BALLISTIC MISSILES

The first ICBM in service with the USAF was the 118-foot **Atlas**, beginning in February 1958: the last of these was retired by April 1965, making the 103-foot **LGM-25 Titan** the oldest ICBM in SAC's arsenal. The Titan was first deployed in 1963, with final deactivation scheduled for 1987. Nearly twice the size of the newer Minuteman, the Titan also carries a larger nuclear warhead.

AGM-69 SRAM Short Range Attack Missile
Manufacturer: Boeing Aerospace
First deployment: 1972
Missile type: Air-to-ground ballistic missile
Length: 14ft
Maximum diameter: 1ft 5½in
Launch weight: 2230lb
Speed: Mach 2.5
Range: 100 miles
Guidance: General Precision/Kearfot inertial system, permitting high or low altitude over dogleg trajectory
Warhead: Nuclear 175KT
Powerplant: Lockheed Propulsion LPC-415 solid-fuel restartable

The **LGM-30 Minuteman** was first deployed in 1962 and has been the backbone of SAC's ICBM force ever since. The Minuteman force reached the level of 1000 missiles in April 1967, and has subsequently remained at that level, although updated versions have been substituted as older missiles are deactivated. The LGM-30F Minuteman II, with its increased range, payload and accuracy, began to replace the Minuteman I in 1965 and the Minuteman III became operational in 1970. The force now includes 450 Minuteman IIs and 550 Minuteman IIIs, the latter with multiple warheads or MIRVs (Multiple Independently Targeted Re-entry Vehicles). Both the Titan and Minuteman forces are based in hardened underground concrete silos located across the central United States. The *Upgrade Silo* program, completed in January 1980, improved the silo launch sites and increased their protection against blast, shock, radiation and electro-magnetic pulse. Other modifications to the Minuteman III have included a Command Data Buffer System that provides a capability for remote targeting. The incorporation of the Guidance Improvement Program and deployment of the Mk 12A re-entry vehicle have greatly increased both accuracy and warhead yield.

The newest member of the SAC ICBM force is the **MGM-118A Peacekeeper**, developed under the Missile, Experimental (MX) program. The MGM-118A has ten multiple warheads in its MIRV system, making it a considerably more potent weapon than the Minuteman. The method by which the Peacekeeper would be based and launched was the object of some controversy in the late 1970s and early 1980s. The existing Minuteman sites – hardened silos – were thought vulnerable to Soviet attack because they were stationary. Several plans evolved by which the MX could become mobile, thus harder to target. The original plan proposed by the Carter Administration (the *Racetrack* system) would have placed the missiles in mobile launchers and shuttled them around a huge network of underground tracks. When this plan was discarded, it was replaced by another 'deceptive basing' scheme called Multiple Protective Shelters

Above left: The bat-like SR-71 Blackbird routinely flies at altitudes above 80,000 feet and at speeds in the Mach 3 range.

Below: An SR-71 screams into the air from the runway at Beale AFB. All of the Air Force's fleet of SR-71s are assigned to the 9th Strategic Reconnaissance Wing at Beale, but they operate from bases around the world.

Above: The TR-1, outwardly identical to the U-2R, is similar to the earlier model U-2s except for the longer nose and much greater wingspan. Both of the former aircraft are painted the same flat black color (known officially as indigo blue) as the SR-71. Also like the SR-71, the TR-1s are assigned to the 9th SRW but serve temporary duty all over the world.

U-2B
Manufacturer: Lockheed
First year of service: 1954 (U-2A)
Aircraft type: High-altitude strategic reconnaissance aircraft
Wingspan: 80ft
Length: 49ft 7in
Weight: 17,270lb (gross)
Range: 4000 miles
Service ceiling: 80,000 feet
Cruising speed: 528mph
Powerplant: (1) 17,000lb thrust Pratt & Whitney J75-P-13 turbojet

SR-71 Blackbird
Manufacturer: Lockheed
First year of service: 1965
Aircraft type: Strategic reconnaissance aircraft
Wingspan: 55ft 7in
Length: 107ft 5in
Weight: 170,00lb (gross); 60,000lb (empty)
Range: 2982 miles
Service ceiling: over 80,000 feet
Top speed: Mach 3+ (holds absolute world speed record of 2193.167mph, Mach 3.3)
Powerplant: (2) 34,000lb thrust Pratt & Whitney JT11D-20B(J58) turbojets

TR-1
Manufacturer: Lockheed
First year of service: 1981
Aircraft type: Strategic and tactical reconnaissance aircraft
Wingspan: 103ft
Length: 63ft
Weight: 40,00lb (gross)
Range: over 3000 miles
Service ceiling: 90,000 feet
Cruising speed: 430mph
Powerplant: (1) 17,000lb thrust Pratt & Whitney J75-P-13B turbojet

Left and above: The 10-story-tall Tital II. The Titan was the largest ICBM in US Air Force inventory for two decades.

Above: A Minuteman ICBM is test fired. The 550 multiple-warhead Minuteman IIIs were SAC's only multiple-warhead missiles for two decades.

LGM-25C Titan II
Manufacturer: Martin Marietta Aerospace
First deployment: 1963
Missile type: Two-stage liquid-fuel ICBM
Length: 103ft
Maximum diameter: 10ft
Launch weight: 330,000lb
Speed: 17,000mph
Range: 6300 miles
Guidance: Inertial
Warhead: Thermonuclear 9MT, in GE Mk6 reentry vehicle
Powerplant: First stage 430,00lb thrust Aerojet General LR87; Second stage: 100,000lb thrust Aerojet General LR91

(MPS). Under MPS, the missiles would be transported between launching shelters. In this 'shell game' concept, as with *Racetrack*, the enemy could never be sure exactly where the missiles were: he would have to expend a lot of ICBMs on empty shelters to be sure of destroying all those that actually housed an MX. The Reagan Administration, recognizing the cost involved in the deceptive-basing scenarios, proposed putting all the missiles together in one field under a plan called the Closely Spaced Basing (CSB) System of *Dense pack*. The idea here was that at least *some* missiles would survive almost any attack. Ultimately all of these plans were rejected because none could guarantee more protection for the MX fleet than was provided for the Minuteman fleet by their concrete silos. In 1983, as flight testing of the MGM-118 Peacekeeper got underway, a final decision was made to base the new missile in existing Minuteman and Titan silos – a simple, workable, cost-effective solution to the controversy.

LGM-30F Minuteman II, LGM-30G Minuteman III
Manufacturer: Boeing Aerospace
First deployment: 1965 (Minuteman II) 1968 (Minuteman III)
Missile type: Three-stage solid-fuel ICBM
Length: 59ft 10in
Maximum diameter: 5ft 6in
Launch weight: 78,000lb (Minuteman III)
Speed: 15,000mph
Range: 7000 miles (Minuteman III)
Guidance: Inertial (Rockwell International)
Warhead: Single thermonuclear (Minuteman II); Three thermonuclear 175KT or 340KT in Avco Mk12 or Mk12a reentry vehicle (Minuteman III)
Powerplant: First stage: (1) 210,000lb thrust Thiokol M-55E; Second stage: (1) 60,300lb thrust Aerojet General SR19-AJ-1; Third stage: (1) 34,400lb thrust Aerojet General SR73-AJ-1 (Minuteman III)

MGM-118A Peacekeeper (MX)
Manufacturer: Martin Marietta, Denver Aerospace
First deployment: 1984-85
Missile type: Four-stage solid-fuel ICBM
Length: 70ft
Maximum diameter: 7ft 8in
Launch weight: 192,00lb (approx)
Speed: (Classified)
Range: 7000 miles+
Guidance: Inertial
Warhead: Ten Thermonuclear 350 KT in General Electric Mk12a reentry vehicle
Powerplant: First stage: Thiokol solid-fuel; Second stage: Aerojet General solid-fuel; Third stage: Hercules solid-fuel; Fourth stage: Rocketdyne liquid-fuel

MILITARY AIRLIFT IN THE US AIR FORCE

MILITARY AIRLIFT

In the early days of the USAAS and USAAC, when the aircraft were of short range and modest speed, most of those services' own supplies and personnel moved from base to base by train. Flying was generally something you went to the base to do, not a means of getting to the base. World War II changed all this. By the 1940s civilian transports had evolved into aircraft that could carry large numbers of people, not just a couple of hardy souls. General Hap Arnold called World War II a war of logistics, and an important part of logistical transport was by air. From a prewar airlift capacity of practically nil, the USAAF developed an extensive system serving land forces as well as its own needs that would be a model of postwar military airlift. The war in China, for example, would have been lost had it not been for the stream of transports flying over the 'Hump.'

As with strategic bombers, the USAAF was one of the the pioneers of military airlift. The British did not develop as extensive an airlift network because the distances between the British Isles and the front were relatively much shorter than the globe-circling American supply lines. German airlift capacity was mostly in the durable little tri-motored Ju-52, which had been a prewar airliner and had served widely as a paratroop (*Fallschirmjaeger*) plane during the early years of the war when the Germans were on the offensive. Germany also developed the huge six-engined Me-323, which incorporated front-opening clamshell doors through which trucks, horses and light armor could be directly loaded. The Me-323, though incredibly slow, had a large cargo capacity and participated in the airlifts that helped prolong the German stands at Stalingrad and in North Africa.

Today most air forces have a small short-range tactical airlift capacity and rely on civilian airliners for long-range support. Because most nations now have a government-owned state airline, it is relatively easy to put one of its planes on temporary duty with the air force. Most of the world's major airlines operate Boeing 747s, whose cargo capacity is greater than that of tactical airlifters. Thus nations with state-owned airlines using 747s can make money with their heavy airlifters when they are not in military service. British Airways and Aerolinas Argentinas airliners were used as military transports during the 1982 Falklands War, and France used UTA 747s to transport troops and materiel during the 1983 Chad-Libya conflict. In the Soviet Union, the air force airlift command and the state airline, Aeroflot, operate the same types of aircraft and their activities often overlap.

The United States has arrangements to use civilian airliners in time of crisis, and used chartered airliners from Seaboard,

Above: **A 63d Military Airlift Wing C-141 Starlifter.**

Transamerica, World Airways etc during the war in Southeast Asia. But generally speaking the US relies on its own military 'airline' to provide airlift support to all its military forces. This is the US Air Force's Military Airlift Command (MAC), and if ranked with civilian airlines, it would be one of the biggest in the world.

THE AIR TRANSPORT COMMAND

The forerunner of MAC was the Air Corps Ferrying Command (ACFC), created on 29 May 1941 to co-ordinate the ferrying of Lend Lease supplies to England. The ACFC became the Air Transport Command (ATC) on 20 June 1942; this became the Military Air Transport Service (MATS) on 1 June 1948, then the Military Airlift Command (MAC) on 1 January 1966.

With the fall of France, policy turned toward helping England against Germany: one step was the supplying of war materiel, especially aircraft, to England, most of which were Douglas Bostons and Lockheed Hudsons. These were manufactured in California and flown by company pilots to eastern Canada, where they were picked up by pilots of the British Atlantic Ferrying Organization and flown to Scotland. With increased aircraft production and the need for British pilots at the front, President Franklin D Roosevelt ordered that the USAAC (soon to be the USAAF) take charge of the delivery program. This led to the creation of the ACFC in May 1941, under the control of Air Corps Chief General Hap Arnold, after whom the Command was nicknamed 'The Arnold Line.' Soon the ferry service expanded to a full-fledged transportation service (flying transport planes as well as ferrying bombers) because the sea lanes took valuable time and were by now heavily infested with German U-boats. With the expansion of routes across the South Atlantic as well as the North, the general increase of air traffic and America's entry into the war, the USAAF redesignated the ACFC as the Air Transport Command (ATC) on 20 June 1942.

The ATC quickly became the official 'airline' for all War Department operations, responsible for transporting people, materiel and mail to wherever in the world American forces were operating. By the end of the year the ATC had eight operational Wings, North Atlantic, South Atlantic, Caribbean, Africa/Middle East, Alaskan, South Pacific and India/China, plus a Domestic Transportation Wing within the US. One of the ruggedest operations ATC undertook was the India/China Wing's airlift across the Himalayas. By 1942 land and sea access to Chinese and American forces fighting in China had been cut off, so the India/China Wing of ATC took over the job of

supplying them. In the flights over the 'hump,' as it came to be known, ATC pilots had to contend with 16,000-foot ridges, limited visibility, violent turbulence, severe icing and Japanese fighters. During December 1942 ATC hauled 1227 tons of supplies over the Hump. By July 1943 tonnage was up to 3451; by July 1945 it had risen to 71,000 tons. The last flights were in November 1945, by which time ATC had delivered 650,000 tons of materiel to China.

Throughout the War ATC and its civilian contractors hauled 2,702,861,000 ton-miles of mail and materiel across both the long intercontinental air lanes and shorter intratheater routes. Evacuation of sick and wounded rose from 3260 in 1943 to 86,407 in 1945. Passenger operations also reached a peak in 1945 – five billion passenger-miles. The ATC personnel strength had risen to an August 1945 level of 209,201 uniformed and 104,667 civilian. After the war The Airways & Air Communications Service, The Air Weather Service, The Air Rescue Service and Flight Service were transferred to ATC control along with responsibility for aeronautical charting. However, even with its newly assigned tasks, ATC declined to a personnel strength of 42,090 uniformed and 17,590 civilian by the end of 1946. In December 1944 ATC aircraft strength had reached its peak of 10,456, which included 1278 Curtis C-46 Commandos, 4901 of the ubiquitous Douglas C-47 and C-53 (paratroop version) Skytrains, and 356 of the big four-engined Douglas C-54s. By the end of 1946, total strength was down to 4310, including 689 C-46s, 2218 C-47s and 489 C-54s.

THE MILITARY TRANSPORT SERVICE

With the creation of the US Air Force in 1947, recommendations came in from all quarters in favor of unifying the Navy and Air Force airlift capabilities. The new Defense Secretary, James Forrestal, directed creation of such an entity on 15 January 1948 and put Major General Laurence Kuter in charge of organizing the program. Kuter became the first commander of the Military Air Transport Service (MATS) on 1 June 1948. MATS was directed to absorb the 'property and facilities presently assigned to the Naval Air Transport Service (NATS).' These included three squadrons of C-47s (Navy designation R4D) and C-54s (Navy designation R5D), as well as 2818 uniformed personnel.

The ink was no sooner dry on Kuter's first batch of orders when MATS found itself facing its first crisis. When the war in Europe had ended three years before, the victorious Allies had divided Germany into four zones of occupation, with the city of Berlin, in the heart of the Russian zone, divided into four zones as well. In June 1948 the Russians sealed off all ground transportation routes between the Western zones of Germany and western Berlin, in an effort to force the Americans, British and French out of the city. USAFE immediately undertook flying supplies to American forces there with its own transports, but President Harry S Truman quickly decided that the United States should help supply the entire population of beleagured Berlin. MATS went into action. All available C-54s, R5Ds and C-82s from as far away as Japan and Guam were brought to Germany to take part in the airlift. Commercial carriers were contracted to haul supplies from the States, and the military airlifters set up a 24-hour-a-day aerial bridge between Wiesbaden and Rhein-Main air bases in Western Germany and Berlin. Air bases at Fassberg and Celle on the western end were quickly added; by the first of July aircraft were arriving in Berlin at the rate of one every three minutes, a rate which was maintained until the Russians withdrew the blockade on 12 May 1949 and reopened land links to the city.

Code-named Operation *Vittles*, the Berlin airlift saw the Combined Airlift Task Force (CALTF) under MATS Major General William Tunner fly over 150,000 sorties through rain,

Left: Ferrying Command pilots from the USAAF, the US Navy and two commercial airlines discuss an approaching weather front, prior to making a hazardous North Atlantic crossing to the beleagured British Isles during the winter of 1941-42.

Below: MATS C-54s prepare to take off from Tempelhof Airport on the morning of 1 March 1949. During the night, the worst snowstorm of the winter with high winds and icing conditions forced a temporary halt to operations, but tonnage was near normal again by the end of the day.

sleet, snow and fog. CALTF delivered 2,325,000 tons of food, fuel and other supplies and suffered only twelve crashes. *Vittles* proved to the Russians and to the world the capability of an organized airlift, and in the end it was the Russians who gave up, conceding an Allied presence in Berlin. The Berlin Airlift stands as the first action taken by MATS and by the new US Air Force in the cold war, an action which they managed to win without a shot being fired.

Two years later a hot war broke out in Korea, and the first USAF plane to be lost was a MATS C-54, destroyed by the North Koreans at Kimpo Airport near Seoul in the war's first hours. MATS now undertook to airlift supplies to UN forces, mostly American, across the Pacific in Korea. Korea was 30 hours (by C-54) away by the Great Circle route through Alaska and 34 hours away by the more practical Mid-Pacific route.

General Tunner was also put in command of this operation, and again transports were brought in from throughout MATS and supported by commercial cargo planes under contract. The airlift operation was of two parts connecting at bases in Japan. One was the Trans-Pacific leg, delivering supplies to Japan, the other being the intratheater phase between there and forward bases in Korea. The C-47s took the biggest share of the intratheater operations, but C-54s were also used. C-54s on the Trans-Pacific run were augmented by the newer Boeing C-97s and (after 1952) by the huge Douglas C-124 Globemasters with their 45-ton cargo capacity.

During the Korean War, MATS delivered 80,000 tons of cargo and 214,000 troops to Korea. From the Korean experience, airlift came to be recognized as one of the Air Force's four primary tasks and MATS learned valuable lessons that would be milestones in its future and that of MAC. First among these was that the airlift force must be an active force, ready to go at the *beginning* of a crisis. Among others were the Tunner Doctrine of centralized control – the notion that larger transports were indeed preferable and more cost effective – and that air (Aeromedical) evacuation was by far the best means of handling wounded personnel.

Despite these lessons, the post-Korea period was one of stagnation for MATS. Between World War II and the late 1950s, the C-124 was the only major new type of long-range transport introduced, and that had been in 1951. MATS was also withdrawing from intratheater transport, delivering supplies to central aerial ports and letting the theater commands pick up from there. On 1 January 1953, for example, Wheelus AFB, Libya, and Dhahran AB, Saudi Arabia, were turned over to USAFE.

On 1 July 1958 General Tunner, who had commanded both the Berlin and Korea Airlift operations, as well as the Hump airlift in World War II, became commander of MATS. He began to systematically promote both military airlift in general and MATS in particular. When American peacekeeping forces were sent into Lebanon in 1958, MATS and USAFE airlifters moved the troops and supported the operation. Concurrently, when the Taiwan Straits crisis broke, MATS delivered men and materiel and used its big C-124s to deliver partially disassembled F-104s to PACAF units in Taiwan.

In 1960 (and again in 1964) MATS found itself flying a massive rescue and relief action into Central Africa. When Belgium granted independence to the Belgian Congo in 1960, a firestorm of anarchy and bloodshed swept the entire region. On 14 July the United Nations Security Council called on member nations to support evacuation of Europeans and other foreigners whose lives were endangered. MATS established an Air Transport Wing at Chateauroux AS in France to co-ordinate and control the Congo Airlift. Three routes were set up between Chateauroux and Leopoldville. The western route ran 5700 miles through Morocco, Dakar and Accra; the central route 4000 miles through Wheelus AB and Kano, Nigeria; the eastern 4800 miles through

Above: A formation of Fairchild C-119 Flying Boxcars of the 483d Troop Carrier Wing enroute to the Korean front in October 1952. Deliveries of C-119s began in 1949 and their total number reached 1052.

Below: Wings for an F-84 fighter are removed from a huge C-124 at a base in Japan in June 1952. A MATS C-54 and C-47 are seen in the background. The cargo capacity of the C-124 dwarfed that of the earlier planes.

Above: Two MATS Pacific Division transports, a C-54 (foreground) and a C-97, arrive at Hickam AFB, Hawaii, carrying combat casualties from Korea. Aeromedical evacuation saved many lives in the Korean War.

Below: A huge Douglas C-124 Globemaster II wings its way eastward over the city of San Francisco on 16 February 1955. Based on the earlier C-74 Globemaster I, the C-124 was for a decade the largest airlifter in the US Air Force. MATS received 243 of the big planes and they continued in service through the Vietnam War, with the last one being retired in 1975.

Wheelus AB, Ethiopia, and Stanleyville in the Congo. Twenty-six hundred people were evacuated by MATS through September 1960. By 4 January 1964 MATS had flown 63,798 passengers (refugees out, peacekeeping troops in) and 18,593 tons of cargo in 2128 missions.

Since the late 1950s MATS and later MAC forces have supported the Army in a number of overseas readiness exercises. In 1960 General Tunner proposed a massive airlift exercise to test the MATS' ability to supply a large number of Army troops in a very short time, sustaining a high rate of aircraft utilization as in wartime or emergency conditions. The exercise was code-named *Big Slam/Puerto Pine* and would involve airlifting 20,000 troops and equipment from the US to Puerto Rico and back in the space of two weeks. It helped to demonstrate the need for a new generation of airlifters. The result was Congressional authorization to develop long-range jet transports and provide MATS with more C-135s (the transport version of the KC-135 air-refueling tanker) and longer-range C-130s. The first of the new long-range jet transports was Lockheed's C-141 Starlifter (to come on line in 1965) followed by the huge C-5 four years later.

Meanwhile other big joint Army/MATS exercises were in the works. In 1963 plans were drawn up for Operation *Big Lift*, which would involve airlifting the entire Second Armored Division from Fort Hood, Texas, to Germany in 60 hours. On 22 October troops began to board MATS C-124s and C-135s in Texas, as other MATS aircraft began collecting their support equipment and that of four USAF fighter squadrons which were also being deployed to Europe as part of *Big Lift*. The longer-range transports flew directly to Germany; smaller aircraft used staging bases in Bermuda, Greenland and at the MATS base at Lajes Field in the Azores. The 15,000 men and 450 tons of equipment of the Second Armored Division were delivered to Rhein-Main AB, Sembach AB and Ramstein AB and were in action within 60 hours of their departure.

The Congo Airlift and exercises like *Big Slam* and *Big Lift* demonstrated both the practical airlift capabilities and theoretical airlift potential of the US Air Force, and in 1965 Congress authorized upgrading the status of MATS: on 1 January 1966 it became the Military Airlift Command (MAC).

C-119G Flying Boxcar
Manufacturer: Fairchild Engine and Airplane Corporation
First year of service: 1952
Aircraft type: Transport
Wingspan: 109ft 3in
Length: 86ft 6in
Weight: 74,400lb (gross)
Range: 2280 miles
Service ceiling: 23,500 feet
Cruising speed: 200mph
Powerplant: (2) 3500hp Wright R-3350-85 piston engines
Capacity: 62 troops or 28,000 pounds of cargo

C-124C Globemaster II
Manufacturer: Douglas Aircraft Company
First year of service: 1951
Aircraft type: Heavy lift transport
Wingspan: 174ft 2in
Length: 130ft 5in
Weight: 194,500lb (gross)
Range: 4030 miles
Service ceiling: 18,400 feet
Top speed: 304mph
Powerplant: (4) 3800hp Pratt & Whitney R-4360-63A piston engines
Capacity: 200 troops, 127 litters or 68,500 pounds of cargo

Below: A C-141 Starlifter takes off from Danang AB in June 1970. An HH-53B rescue helicopter is on the ramp in the foreground.

THE MILITARY AIRLIFT COMMAND AT WAR

The biggest challenge to the Air Force's airlift capabilities began on the eve of the metamorphosis of MATS into MAC. The war in Southeast Asia, like the Korean War, was fought at the end of a 10,000-mile logistics pipeline, but Southeast Asia was far more demanding and lasted three times as long. Both the Great Circle route through Alaska and Japan and a Trans-Pacific route through Clark AB in the Philippines were used, with the principal terminus at Tan Son Nhut AB near Saigon. Once supplies were delivered to Southeast Asia, MAC and PACAF operated intratheater airlift in South Vietnam, Laos and Thailand. The new long-range jet transport, the C-141 Starlifter, made its first flight to Vietnam on 5 August 1965, shortly after becoming operational with MAC. The C-141 flying time from Travis AFB to Tan Son Nhut was 18 hours 15 minutes (compared to 30 hours 30 minutes for the turboprop C-130). A milestone for MAC's C-141s came during the North Vietnamese offensive in April 1972, when a Starlifter was sent into the Central Highlands to evacuate refugees, mostly women and children. The C-141 is designed to carry a normal load of 90 passengers, but this one came out of the Highlands with a record 394 passengers plus crew.

During the war MAC transported more than two million passengers and two million tons of cargo. MAC's Air Rescue Service personnel saved 4120 lives, including 2780 in combat. The last MAC actions in the Southeast Asia War included operation *Homecoming*, beginning January 1973, when MAC C-141s flew into the North Vietnamese air base at Gia Lam near Hanoi to evacuate 566 American military and civilian prisoners of war to Clark AB. MAC's final action in Vietnam came in April 1975. In the controversial Operation *Babylift*, MAC and civilian contract carriers evacuated 1794 Vietnamese and Cambodian war orphans to the United States just prior to the fall of Saigon to the communists. During the same month, under the code name *Frequent Wind*, MAC evacuated 50,493 other refugees from Saigon to the Philippines and Guam in 201 C-141 and 174 C-130 missions. Most of these final missions were flown by C-141s and C-130s and the majority went smoothly: Operation *Babylift* was marred by the 4 April 1975 crash of a C-5 on takeoff from Tan Son Nhut. Of the 326 passengers – Vietnamese orphans, their escorts and American citizens from Saigon – 206 were killed.

THE MILITARY AIRLIFT COMMAND NOW

Since the war MAC has remained the prime agent for global airlift for both the US Air Force and the entire US Defense establishment. Until 1965 the Major Theater Commands had their own short-range Tactical Airlift Wings. Since March of that year, all tactical and aeromedical intratheater airlift resources in the USAF have been assigned to MAC.

MAC is headquartered at Scott AFB, Illinois, and is composed of three numbered air forces. The 21st, out of McGuire AFB, New Jersey, controls airlift operations eastward through Canada, Greenland, Iceland, NATO Europe, Africa and the Middle East and southward into the Caribbean and South America. The 22nd Air Force, out of Travis AFB, California, controls airlift operations in the entire Pacific area, Antarctica, Diego Garcia and westward to the Arabian Peninsula, where its area meets that of the 21st. The 23d Air Force is based at MAC headquarters, Scott AFB. It has no geographic boundary and is the focal point of MAC Special Operations and the Aerospace Rescue and Recovery Service (ARRS), which began as the Air Rescue Service (ARS) in December 1946 with the mission to search for and rescue downed pilots. The ARS (ARRS since 8 January 1966) saved numerous pilots in both Korea and Southeast Asia, many of the rescues accomplished under enemy fire. ARS and ARRS have also played a key contingency role in the recovery of capsules for the manned spaceflight program. ARRS operates a fleet of about 200 airplanes and helicopters, including UH/HH-1s, CH/HH-3s, CH/HH-53s and various types of C-130s. ARRS has also participated with other MAC units in global humanitarian airlift operations like the October 1980 operation in which ARRS saved 65 people from the sinking civilian cruise ship *Prinsendam* in the Gulf of Alaska.

Global humanitarian airlift is a tradition with MAC that goes back to the Berlin Airlift. Disaster finds MAC on hand to deliver food and medical supplies and to evacuate the wounded and refugees. Some of the key operations span the globe and MATS/-MAC history. In 1952 Operation *Magic Carpet* delivered 3763 stranded Moslem pilgrims from Beirut to Jidda, Saudi Arabia. In 1973 MAC helicopters evacuated a hospital in Iceland endangered by an erupting volcano. In Operation *Sno-Go* in February 1977, MAC airlifted 2 million pounds of snowplows and 600 relief workers to the Buffalo, New York, area in the wake of

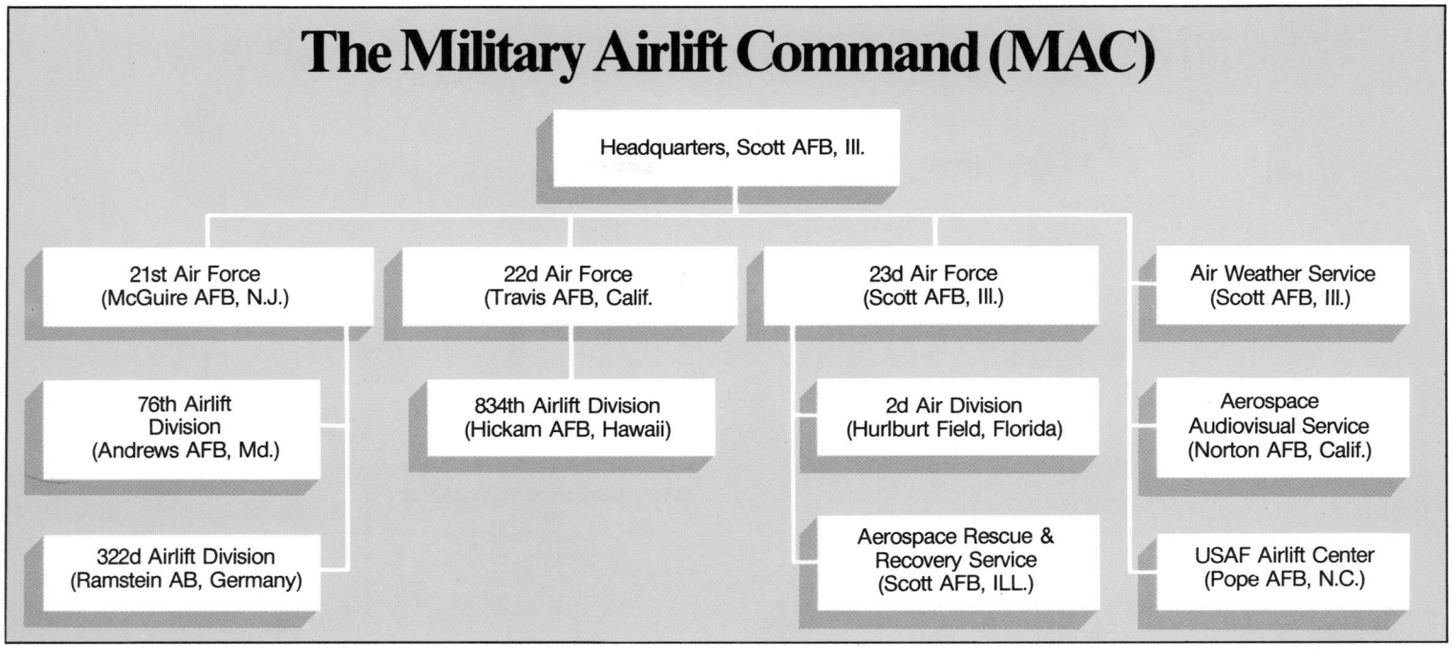

what was called the 'Blizzard of the Century.' In March 1979 MAC airlifted a 115-ton water filtration system and other equipment to Harrisburg, Pennsylvania, after the nuclear power-plant emergency at Three Mile Island. In May 1980, when Mount St Helens erupted in Washington State, MAC provided communications and rescue services, saving 61 lives.

In addition to these unique operations, MAC planes and helicopters have airlifted aid to victims of typhoons, floods, earthquakes and other natural disasters on every continent, in locales ranging from Peru to Yugoslavia and from Alaska to Iran.

MAC's Air Weather Service (AWS) headquartered at Scott AFB operates a network of weather observation and forcasting facilities to support Army and Air Force units worldwide. AWS works with ARRS on tropical-storm reconnaissance and providing weather forecasts prior to aircraft deployments, missile and satellite launches and other military operations. AWS also monitors and reports relevant solar activity and other space phenomena. It has a demonstrated operational capability to provide aerial and ground base weather modification services.

MAC AS AN AIRLINE

MAC is a military command, but the nature of its mission makes it a lot like a civilian airline. It has an established worldwide route structure serving 21 *Intertheater* Aerial Ports and 22 *Intratheater* Operating Locations, with Commercial Gateway Operating Locations (OL) at 13 major commercial airports around the world. MAC also has regular passenger and cargo schedules and provides executive transport for members of the Legislative and Executive Branches of the Federal Government (including the President) through the 89th Military Airlift Wing (of the 21st Air Force) based at Andrews AFB outside Washington DC.

MAC is also like an airline in that its users have to pay for it. Since 1958 any agency using MAC has to allocate money from its own budget to the Airlift Service Industrial Fund (ASIF). The ASIF rate schedule is established by an Assistant Secretary of Defense, and like a commercial rate schedule, it reflects fuel and manpower costs, etc. The ASIF system has interjected a good deal of 'dollar cost discipline' into airlift operations over the years. All MAC users, even those using the 89th MAW at Andrews, have to pay their airlift bills. Users have a choice of 'buying' a few seats on a scheduled MAC flight to send a few of their personnel overseas, or of 'chartering' a whole C-5 to deliver a tank.

The Commanders of the Military Air Transport Service

Lt Gen Laurence Kuter	1 June 1948–28 Oct 1951
Lt Gen Joseph Smith	15 Nov 1951–30 June 1958
Lt Gen William Tunner	1 July 1958–31 May 1960
Gen Joe Kelly, Jr	1 June 1960–18 July 1964
Gen Howell Estes, Jr	19 July 1964–31 Dec 1965

The Commanders of the Military Airlift Command

Gen Howell Estes, Jr	1 Jan 1966–31 July 1969
Gen Jack Catton	1 Aug 1969–12 Sept 1972
Gen Paul Carlton	20 Sept 1972–31 March 1977
Gen William Moore, Jr	1 Apr 1977–30 June 1979
Gen Robert Huyser	1 July 1979–26 June 1981
Gen James Allen	26 June 1981-

MILITARY AIRLIFT COMMAND BASES

Scott AFB (MAC Headquarters)
Location: 6 miles ENE of Belleville, Illinois
Area: 3000 acres
Altitude: 453ft
Personnel: 6704 Military
3582 Civilian

Activated 14 June 1917, the base was named for Cpl Frank Scott, the first US airman to die in a crash (28 September 1912). In addition to being the headquarters of MAC (the host unit being the 375th Aeromedical Airlift Squadron), it is also headquarters for Air Force Communications Command (AFCC). Among reporting units based at Scott are MAC's 23d Air Force, AFCC's Airlift Communication Division, headquarters of the Aerospace Rescue and Recovery Service, the headquarters of the Air Weather Service, the Environmental Technical Applications Center, 7th Weather Wing, 932d Aeromedical Airlift Group and the USAF Medical Center, Scott.

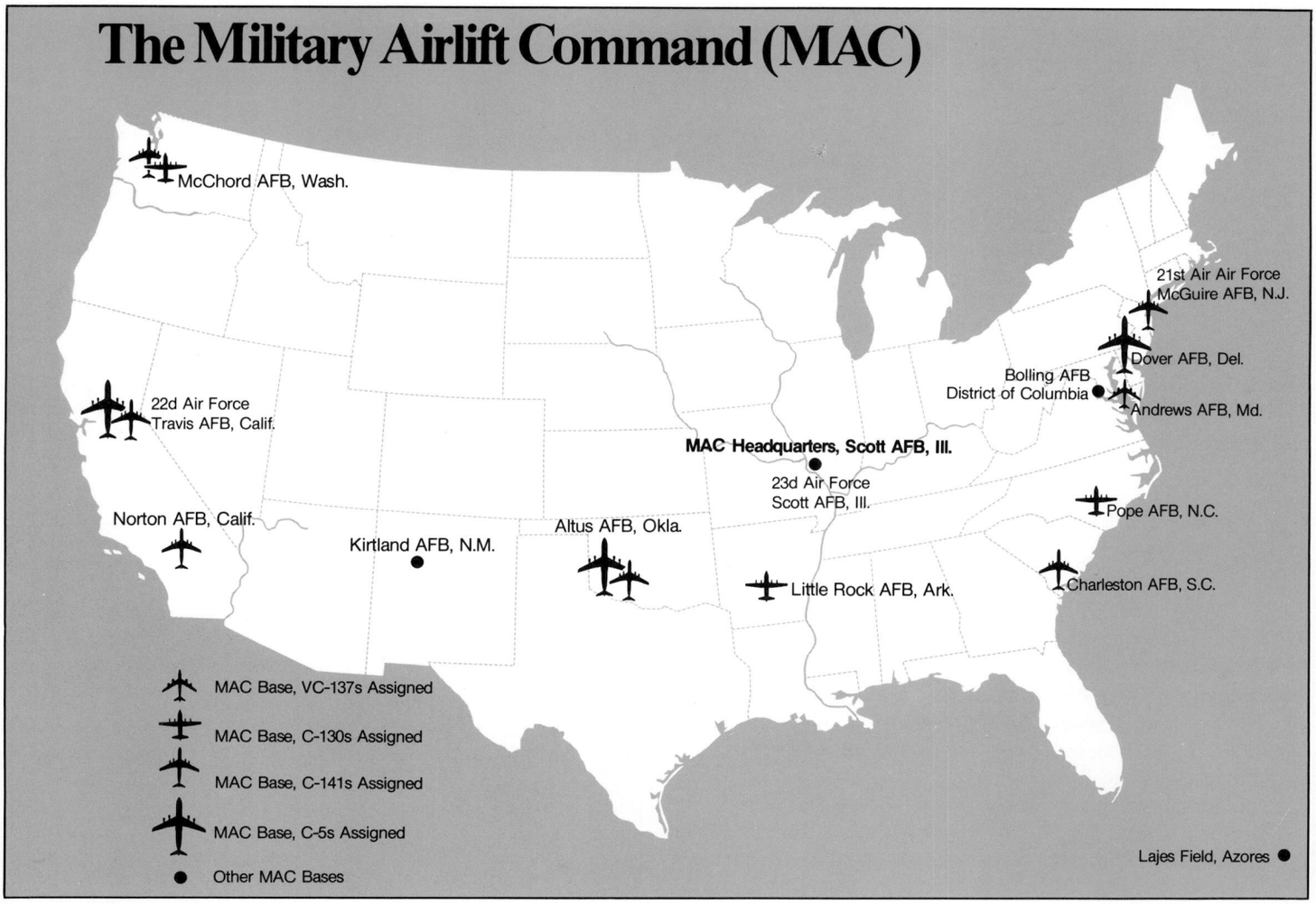

Altus AFB
Location: Altus, Oklahoma
Area: 4113 acres
Altitude: 1376ft
Personnel: 3569 Military
786 Civilian
Active as a USAAF Air Field between January 1942 and May 1945, the base was reactivated as an AFB in January 1953. Altus is the home of MAC's 443d Military Airlift Wing, providing crew training for C-141 and C-5 transport aircraft, and SAC's 340th Air Refueling Group.

Andrews AFB
Location: 11 miles SE of Washington, DC, in the State of Maryland
Area: 4216 acres
Altitude: 279ft
Personnel: 5542 Military
5453 Civilian
Activated in June 1943, the base is named for air-power pioneer and USAAF European Theater Commander Lt Gen Frank Andrews, killed in a 3 May 1943 plane crash in Iceland. A Military Airlift Command base, Andrews is the headquarters of the Air Force Systems Command (AFSC). The best-known tenant of the base, however, is the 89th Military Airlift Wing flying VC-137 VIP executive transports including *Air Force One,* the executive transport used by the President of the United States. The transports are also at the service of other members of the executive branch as well as Congress. The base is also home to the Maryland Air National Guard's 113th Tactical Fighter Wing and the Air Force Reserve 459th Tactical Airlift Wing.

Bolling AFB
Location: In the District of Columbia, 3 miles south of the US Capitol building.
Area: 604 acres
Altitude: 16ft
Personnel: 1562 Military
1157 Civilian
Activated in October 1917 the base was renamed for Col Raynal Bolling, Air Service Assistant Chief, who was killed in World War I. Because of its proximity to the seat of government, Bolling has been an important base, headquarters for many units and Commands including those of SAC, the largest. After the war Bolling lost many of its functions to Andrews AFB with its longer runway. Today the base serves many activities of the Headquarters USAF, located across the Potomac at the Pentagon, and is the site of AFSC's Air Force Office of Scientific Research, the Air Force Reserve Personnel Center and the Air Force Chief of Chaplains.

Charleston AFB
Location: North Charleston, South Carolina
Area: 3772 acres
Altitude: 45ft
Personnel: 6821 Military (including reserve)
1641 Civilian
Active between June 1942 and February 1946 as a USAAF field, the base was reactivated as an AFB in August 1953. The joint-use airfield is shared by the 437th Military Airlift Wing (MAC), the 315th Military Airlift Wing (AFRES) and the 48th Fighter Interceptor Squadron (TAC).

Dover AFB
Location: 4 miles SE of Dover, Delaware
Area: 3734 acres
Altitude: 28ft
Personnel: 5067 Military
1416 Civilian
The base served as a USAAF Field between December 1941 and the end of World War II; it was reactivated as an AFB in February 1951. Since then Dover has become the largest air cargo port on the US East Coast. The 436th Military Airlift Wing is one of only two operational units in the Air Force flying the huge C-5 Galaxy, the world's largest transport aircraft. The other unit operational with the C-5 is the 60th MAW at Travis AFB in California. The 443d MAW at Altus AFB also flies C-5s, but in a crew-training role. The C-5s of Dover are responsible for American outsize airlift requirements from the Mississippi River east to New Delhi, while the C-5s from Travis cover the other half of the globe.

Kirtland AFB
Location: Just south of Albuquerque, New Mexico
Area: 51,330 acres
Altitude: 5532ft
Personnel: 4881 Military
13,634 Civilian
Activated in 1941, the base was named for pioneer aviator and Langley Field Commandant Col Roy Kirtland. MAC units include the 1606th Air Base Wing (the host unit) and the 1550th Aircrew Training and Test Wing. Other installations at Kirtland include the Defense Nuclear Agency Field Command, the Air Force Test and Evaluation Center, the Naval Weapons Evaluation Facility, the Scandia Laboratories, the Lovelace Biomedical and Environmental Research Institute, the Department of Energy's Albuquerque Operations Office, and the Air Force Directorate of Nuclear Security. The Air Force Systems Command is a major tenant at the base with its Air Force weapons Laboratory, Air Force Contract Management Division and the AFSC NCO Academy. The New Mexico Air National Guard's 150th Tactical Fighter Group is also based at Kirtland.

Little Rock AFB
Location: 12 miles NE of Little Rock, Arkansas
Area: 6894 acres
Altitude: 310ft
Personnel: 6300 Military
650 Civilian
Activated in 1955, the base is home to the 314th Tactical Airlift Wing and provides C-130 crew training for all branches of the US Armed Forces and many foreign countries. Tenants include the 22nd Air Force Leadership School and SAC's 308th Strategic Missile Wing, one of the three Titan II Wings in the Air Force.

McChord AFB
Location: 8 miles south of Tacoma, Washington
Area: 4609 acres
Altitude: 322ft
Personnel: 5703 Military
1703 Civilian
The base was activated on 5 May 1938 and named for Col William McChord, killed making a forced landing at Maidens, Virginia, on 18 August 1937. It is headquarters for MAC's 62nd Military Airlift Wing and the AFRES 446th Military Airlift Wing, as well as TAC's 25th Air Division and 318th Fighter Interceptor Squadron.

McGuire AFB
Location: 18 miles SE of Trenton, New Jersey
Area: 3552 acres
Altitude: 133ft
Personnel: 4886 Military
1714 Civilian
Adjoining the US Army's Fort Dix, the base was originally the Fort Dix Army Air Field. Activated as an AFB in 1949, it is named for Major Thomas McGuire Jr, America's second-ranking ace in World War II (38 kills); he was killed in action in the Philippines on 7 January 1945. The base is headquarters of MAC's 21st Air Force, 438th Military Airlift Wing, the AFRES 514th Military Airlift Wing and the MAC NCO Academy East. It is also headquarters for the New Jersey Civil Air Patrol and Air National Guard, the latter with its 170th Air Refueling Group and 108th Tactical Fighter Wing.

Norton AFB
Location: 59 miles east of Los Angeles, California in San Bernardino County
Area: 2407 acres
Altitude: 1156ft
Personnel: 5519 Military
3010 Civilian
The base was activated 2 March 1942 and named for San Bernardino native and A-20 bomber pilot Capt Leland Norton, killed in action in France on 27 May 1944. It is home to the 63d Military Airlift Wing and AFRES 445th Military Airlift Wing, as well as the MAC NCO Academy West and 22d Air Force NCO Leadership School. Norton is also headquarters for the Air Force Inspection and Safety Center, the Air Force Audit Agency, the Aerospace Audiovisual Service and AFSC's Ballistic Missile Office.

Pope AFB
Location: 12 miles NNW of Fayetteville, North Carolina
Area: 1750 acres
Altitude: 318ft
Personnel: 3942 Military
618 Civilian
Activated in 1919, the base is named for Lt Harley Pope, an Air Service flyer during World War I who was killed 6 January 1919 in a crash near Fayetteville. Adjoining the US Army's Fort Bragg, Pope is the USAF Airlift Center and home to the 317th Tactical Airlift Wing, 1st Aeromedical Evacuation Squadron and the AFRES 5th Mobile Aerial Port Squadron.

Travis AFB
Location: 50 miles NE of San Francisco at Fairfield, California
Area: 6170 acres
Altitude: 62ft
Personnel: 9016 Military
2347 Civilian
Activated on 25 May 1943, the base is named for Brig Gen Robert Travis, killed here 5 August 1950 in a B-29 crash. Travis is the headquarters of MAC's 22nd Air Force and 60th Military Airlift Wing, as well as the AFRES 349th Military Airlift Wing and SAC's 307th Air Refueling Group. The 60th MAW is one of only two units in the Air Force operational with the C-5 Galaxy heavy-lift transport plane, the other being the 436th MAW at Dover AFB. Travis is also the site of the David Grant Medical Center.

THE MAC AIRLIFT FLEET

Of the roughly 1000 aircraft in MAC's fleet, about 60% are divided between C-141s and C-130s, 17% are helicopters of various types, 12% are CT-39 Sabreliners and the balance are of other types, notably the C-9 Nightingale and huge C-5 Galaxy.

The bulk of MACs *airlift* operations are carried out by three transports with distinctly different size and weight characteristics, which complement one another. They could almost be designated 'medium,' 'large' and 'extra large.' All three were designed and built by Lockheed-Georgia: the C-130 Hercules (medium), the C-141 Starlifter (large) and the C-5 Galaxy (extra large).

The **C-130 Hercules** entered operational service in 1956 and has become, during its three decades, the real workhorse of American Military Airlift. It has served everywhere in the world where the US Air Force, the Air Force Reserve or the Air Guard are active, from Europe to Antarctica, and in a wide variety of roles. Basically, the turbo-prop powered Hercules is an intratheater tactical airlifter; it is also used as a paratroop plane, an air ambulence, or a long-range transport. C-130s have been modified to fight forest fires and for air-snatch recovery of satellites and reconnaissance drones.

The MC-130 has been outfitted with *Combat Talon* equipment to recover objects or persons from the ground by cable in a low-level pass. It is equipped with terrain-following radar, precision navigation, airdrop avionics and in-flight refueling capability. The AC-130 Spectre Gunship is one of the most heavily armed aircraft in the Air Force. The HC-130 is the principal fixed-wing aircraft in service with the ARRS and Air Guard and Reserve Rescue squadrons. The WC-130 is equipped for weather reconnaissance including penetration of tropical storms to obtain data for forecasting storm movements.

Top: Lockheed's C-130 Hercules is MAC's workhorse intratheater airlifter.

Above: A 7th Special Operations Squadron MC-130E Combat Talon aircraft during a training mission with US Army Special Forces in Germany.

Right: A lineup of 60th Military Airlift Wing C-5A Galaxies on the ramp at Travis AFB in California.

Below: A 63d Military Airlift Wing C-141B out of Norton AFB comes in for a landing at Travis AFB. The Air Force has taken delivery of 284 C-141s since 1965.

USAF
59414

Above: A pair of MAC C-130s with a pair of TAC A-10s on the ground at Texas Lake, Nevada, during a *Red Flag* exercise. The Air Force has received 964 C-130s since 1956.

The **C-141 Starlifter** is the next size up from the C-130 and is also in service with MAC around the world as both transport and paratroop plane supporting Army and Air Force activities. The C-141A became operational in April 1965 and immediately began daily supply missions to Southeast Asia. After a decade in service, the entire fleet of C-141s went back to Lockheed for modification as C-141Bs. This involved making the planes aerial refuelable, lengthening the fuselage by 15 feet. The C-130 carries six standard 463L cargo pallets (the C-141A could carry ten); now the C-141B carries thirteen. Modification of the fleet of 270 aircraft is equivalent to building 90 new C-141As. The first C-141B flew in 1977, with the last completed and put into squadron service in 1982. Like the smaller C-130 and larger C-5, the C-141 has the wing mounted high on the fuselage to minimize cabin obstruction and to give the planes more clearance when operating from rough remote landing fields.

The **C-5 Galaxy** is the largest plane of any type in service in the world, carrying 36 of the standard 463L pallets in a cargo hold that reminds one of a gymnasium interior. The payload of these turbofan-powered monsters is in excess of 100 tons, which translates as two Army M-60 main battle tanks or three CH-47 helicopters. With aerial refueling the C-5 gives MAC the ability to move any item of equipment in the Army's arsenal anywhere in the world in a matter of hours. The first C-5A became operational with MAC in December 1969, with all 81 delivered by May 1973. Like the smaller airlifters, the C-5 provides airlift support for Army and Air Force activities and readiness exercises world-

C-130 Hercules
Manufacturer: Lockheed Georgia
First year of service: 1956
Aircraft type: Multirole transport
Wingspan: 132ft 7in
Length: 97ft 9in
Weight: 175,000lb (gross)
Range: 2100 miles
Service ceiling: 25,000 feet
Top speed: 386mph
Powerplant: (4) 4508hp Allison T56-A-15 turboprops
Capacity: Up to 92 troops or 6 standard cargo pallets

C-141B Starlifter
Manufacturer: Lockheed Georgia
First year of service: 1979 (C-141A, 1965)
Aircraft type: All-weather transport
Wingspan: 159ft 11in
Length: 168ft 3½in (C-141A, 145ft)
Weight: 343,000lb (gross)
Range: 4080 miles
Service ceiling: 41,600 feet
Top speed: 466mph
Powerplant: (4) 21,000lb thrust Pratt & Whitney TF-33-P-7 turbofans
Capacity: Cargo on 13 standard pallets (instead of 10 for C-141A), maximum payload is 90,200lb

wide. Though there are now only 77 in service, their enormous size makes their presence felt. In 1980 the C-5As began to undergo wing-strengthening modifications to extend their service life to 30,000 hours. In 1984 the Air Force accepted the first of 50 all-new C-5Bs.

In addition to its airlift duties, MAC is also in the business of executive transportation. First there are the five **Boeing VC-137s** (the VIP version of the basic Model 707 jetliner) of the 89th MAW that include *Air Force One*. Next are over one hundred **Rockwell CT-39 Sabreliners**, small four- to seven-passenger executive jets used for shuttling small numbers of personnel between bases. The CT-39s are a basic utility aircraft and virtually identical to the commercial Sabreliner. As the *T* prefix indicates, the Air Force uses the Sabreliners for training as well as transport. While most of the USAF Sabreliners are in service with MAC, a few are with PACAF, AFSC and AFCC. The balance of MAC's fixed-wing fleet includes such other light executive transports as the **Lockheed Jetstar** (Air Force Designation **C-140**), the **Beechcraft Super King** (Air Force Designation **C-12**) and finally the **McDonnell Douglas C-9A Nightingale**.

The C-9 is the military version of the standard McDonnell Douglas DC-9 commercial jetliner, converted for use as an aeromedical airlift transport, or air ambulance. The C-9 became operational in August 1968, with delivery of 21 of them to MAC's 375th Aeromedical Airlift Wing at Scott AFB completed in February 1973. Most are still based at Scott, but three are assigned to Clark AB in the Pacific and three to Rhein-Main AB in Europe. Among the facilities aboard the C-9 are refrigeration; a medical supply work area; oxygen systems; a hydraulic folding ramp for efficient loading of stretchers and supplies; a special ventilation system for isolating an intensive care section; and provision for electrical power for cardiac monitors, respirators, incubators and infusion pumps at any location in the cabin. The Nightingale's interior configuration is easily modified to accept various combinations of stretcher or ambulatory patients. The C-9 fleet flies over 3000 missions annually, airlifting over 60,000 patients.

Most of the over 200 helicopters in service with the Air Force are with MAC. There are over 125 of the **Bell UH-1 Hueys** used by the Army in huge numbers and first delivered to the Air Force in 1964. In Vietnam they were used for classified psychological warfare operations; today they serve as utility transports and on short-range search and rescue missions. The **Sikorsky CH-3** and **HH-3 Jolly Green Giants** were also introduced during the War in Southeast Asia for use on long-range pilot rescue missions, often deep into North Vietnam. Similar to, but more powerful than the HH-3, is **Sikorsky's HH-53**, used in Southeast Asia as a rescue helicopter; it remains in first-line service with MAC ARRS units. The HH-53H *Pave Low III* is modified for 'Special Operations' with Forward Looking Infrared (FLIR), Inertial Navigation System (INS) and a computer-projected map display.

SPECIAL OPERATIONS

One of the two major components of MAC's 23d Air Force – along with the ARRS – is the MAC Second Air Division, based at TAC's Hurlburt Field, Florida, with a Detachment at Howard AFB in Panama. The Second Air Division contains the First Special Operations Wings at Hurlburt Field, the First Special Operations Squadron based at Clark AB and the Seventh Special Operations Squadron at Rhein-Main AB. The Second Air Division is the US Air Force's commando team, conducting 'special operations' like unconventional warfare, foreign internal defense and psychological warfare. It was created in the wake of the disastrous attempt to rescue American hostages in Iran in 1980. Its aircraft include HH-53 and UH-1N helicopters, MC-130 transports and the AC-130 Spectre Gunships born in Vietnam. By 1982 infrared-equipped Spectres were flying nighttime surveillance missions over war-torn El Salvador from Howard AFB.

The Second works in close conjunction with the elite commandos of such other services as the Army's Green Berets and the Navy's SEALS (Sea/Air/Land). It provides their airlift capability and assists them in operations like *Urgent Fury*.

URGENT FURY

The tiny Caribbean island nation of Grenada received its independence from Great Britain in 1974. Five years later the government was taken over by a pro-Castro Marxist strongman named Maurice Bishop. He was gradually but successfully wooed by the Soviet Union and concluded a number of secret deals with them. Grenada was rapidly becoming a Cuban arms dump, with quantities of armor, small arms and antiaircraft weapons being stored there. Most important, a deal was struck whereby Cuba would build a new 10,000-foot runway at Point Salines, Grenada, for civilian use and the Russians, under a May 1980 treaty, would get landing rights for their Tu -95 bomber/reconnaissance aircraft, as well as airlift transports, at the airport. The airport would not be – as some would later charge – a tactical operations base, but rather a stop-over point for long-range reconnaissance operations between Soviet bases in Cuba and Angola. It would also serve as a refueling stop for the Russian arms airlift going into Nicaragua from places like Libya. In early 1983 several Russian airlift aircraft were impounded in Brazil when it was discovered they were loaded to the gills with weapons and ordnance for Cuban/Nicaraguan covert offensive actions in Central America. A stopping place in Cuban-held Grenada would avoid such difficulties.

C-5A Galaxy
Manufacturer: Lockheed Georgia
First year of service: 1969
Aircraft type: Heavy lift transport
Wingspan: 222ft 9in
Length: 247ft 10in
Weight: 769,00lb (gross); 372,500lb (empty)
Range: 3450 miles
Service ceiling: 34,000 feet
Top speed: 571mph
Powerplant: (4) 43,000lb thrust General Electric TF39-GE-1C turbofans
Capacity: Crew of 5, plus a rest area for 15 (relief crew etc), 73 fully equipped troops plus 36 standard pallets or assorted vehicles; or 343 fully equipped troops

C-9A Nightingale
Manufacturer: McDonnell Douglas
First year of service: 1968
Aircraft type: Aeromedical airlift transport
Wingspan: 93ft 5in
Length: 119ft 3½in
Weight: 108,00lb (gross)
Range: over 2000 miles
Service ceiling: 35,000 feet
Top speed: 565mph
Powerplant: (2) 14,500lb thrust Pratt & Whitney JT8D09 turbofans
Capacity: Over 40 ambulatory patients, 30 to 40 litters or a combination plus 5 medical staff

Below: **Two C-9 Nightingales prepare to depart Rhein-Main AB, Germany to pick up 52 American hostages freed by Iran, 19 January 1981.**

Below: **A MAC HH-53B helicopter rescues a downed pilot in Southeast Asia, 16 June 1970.**

By October 1983 the situation in Grenada was deteriorating rapidly. The runway was just finished, but the political situation had unraveled completely. Bishop had been arrested, then executed, by factions of his Marxist-style army which itself had disintegrated into what could best be described as a street gang. The thugs had imposed a 24-hour-a-day shoot-on-sight curfew, and people were being gunned down on the street. Neighboring Caribbean nations, including Jamaica and Barbados, urgently requested the United States to do something. With a thousand Americans in a medical school there, and a strong indication that taking them hostage was next on the gang's agenda, the US decided to act. On 24 October MAC began ferrying men and supplies into the airport at Bridgetown, Barbados.

At 5:36 on the morning of 25 October, Operation *Urgent Fury* began in the skies over Grenada. While the Marines conducted a helicopter assault on Pearls Airport on the north side of the island, MAC was dropping Army Ranger paratroopers onto the new Cuban airport at Point Salines in the south. American forces were going into offensive combat operations for the first time in ten years. For the first time since 1945, American troops were being committed to action with a clear objective and strategic plan that included *winning* a war.

The MAC-dropped paratroops were quickly reinforced by other Rangers in Army UH-60 and CH-47 helicopters, but by now Cuban troops guarding the airfield had opened up with their Soviet-made 23mm antiaircraft guns. Going got tough and several helicopters were hit and went down.

Urgent Fury was certainly a 'special operation' and the Second Air Division was on hand with its AC-130 Spectre Gunships, with their two 20mm (100 rounds per second) Vulcan cannons, two 7.62 (also 100 rps) miniguns, 40mm Cannon and awesome 105mm howitzer. In the words of an Administration spokesman, 'AC-130s were called in to hose down the (Cuban antiaircraft) positions, and they effectively silenced them.' Within a matter of hours MAC C-130s from Pope AFB near Fort Bragg, North Carolina and C-141s from the 437th Military Airlift Wing out of Charleston AFB, staging through Bridgetown, Barbados, became the first planes to use the barely completed Cuban runway.

The 437th was flying in troops of the Army's 82nd Airborne Division to reinforce the Marines and Rangers who had gone in at and just after H-hour, but the Second Air Division still wasn't through. As Army units moved out to capture Cuban positions north of the airport on the road to the capital at St George's, Spectre was overhead spitting the deadly hail of fire and lead that silenced enemy guns.

Meanwhile the enemy had surrounded the Grand Anse Campus of the St George's Medical College and with it a number

Above: **Paratroopers of the US Army's 82d Airborne Division watch as a MAC C-141 sets down at the Cuban-built Point Salines Airport on the island of Grenada in October 1983.**

of American students. They had set up gun emplacements atop the Spice Island and Grenada Beach Hotels to fire on American helicopters, should they attempt an assault. At 4:30 PM the assault came, but the helicopters were accompanied by Navy A-6 and A-7 attack planes from the carrier USS *Independence* and by the AC-130s. The horrifying 15-minute barrage laid down by the AC-130s destroyed the two hotels and with them the enemy gun positions. The helicopters landed and the students were airlifted to Point Salines, where C-141s of the 437th MAW airlifted them to safety.

The next objective for American forces was the Cuban headquarters at Calvigny. Supported by the AC-130s, the 82nd Airborne captured this final Cuban stronghold by the 27th; within a week *Urgent Fury* was over, with the last of the Cubans scuttling out of the bush to give themselves up to American forces.

MAC airlift units continued the airlift, taking out the wounded and troops that were no longer needed. MAC aircraft also airlifted the defeated Cubans to neutral airports and brought in a Congressional delegation, which came to be critical and left supporting the intervention, after seeing the Cuban arms dump.

For the first time in 38 years, the United States had fought and won. To top it off the troops were enthusiastically greeted by the people of Grenada, who welcomed them as liberators.

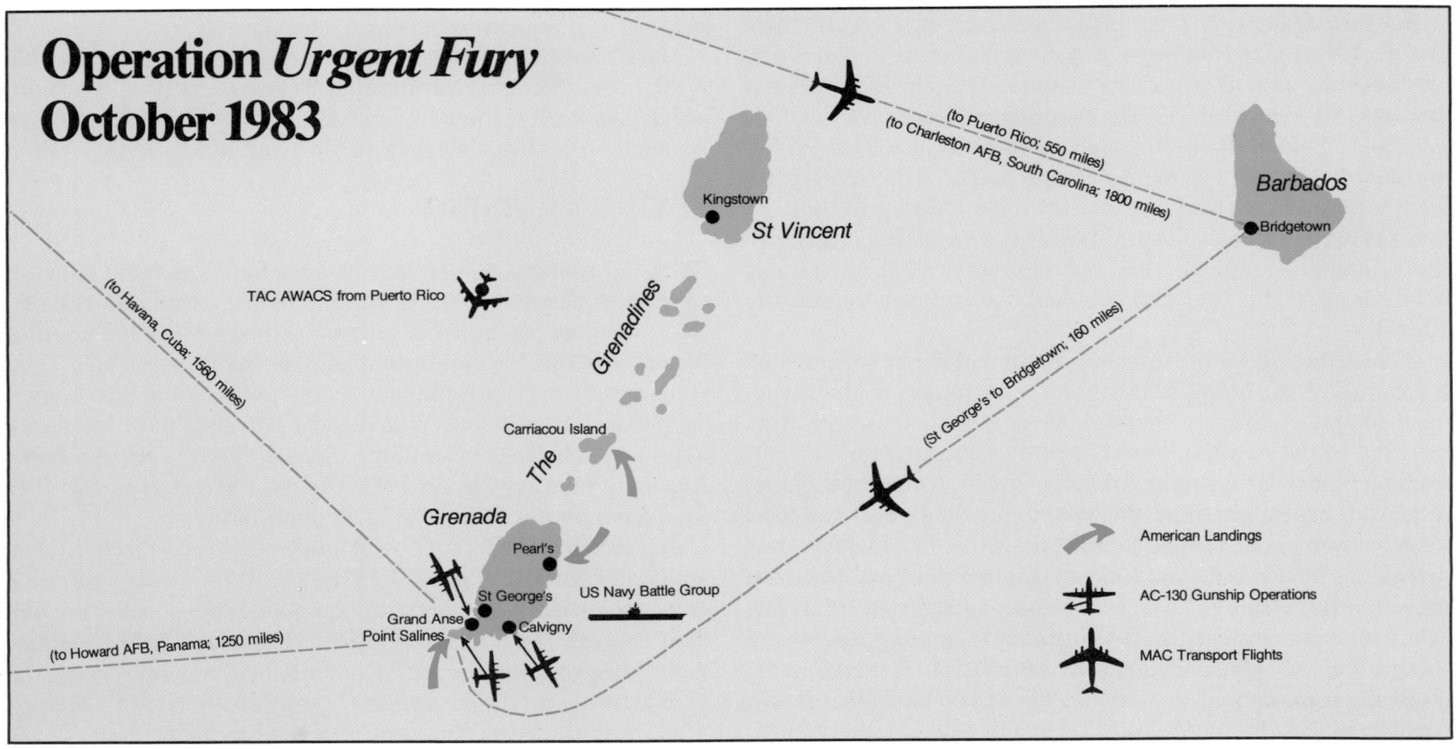

US Air Force Training

THE AIR TRAINING COMMAND

The Air Training Command (ATC) was established as the Army Air Forces Training Command on 7 July 1943, and redesignated Air Training Command on 15 April 1946. Before 1943 flight training was not organized or standardized service-wide, and other training was in the hands of such entities as the Army War College. The first Signal Corps pilots of 1909 got their 'flight training' through correspondence with Wilbur and Orville Wright. In World War I potential USAAS pilots were sent to France and England for flight training. It took the massive requirements of World War II to bring about creation of the Training Command: 1939 requirements called for training only 300 pilots; by 1942 that goal had been adjusted upward to 30,000.

When General Arnold directed creation of the new Command there was 'an air of breathless haste' in response to the urgent need to train pilots for the war. Over a million people were assigned to the new Command, and a crash program built 609 training bases (375 for flying training, 234 for technical training) practically overnight. For the first time, flying and technical training were under a single Command, whose first headquarters was in the Texas & Pacific Railway Building in Fort Worth. It moved to Barksdale Field in 1946 and up to Scott AFB in 1949. After the war most of the more than 600 training bases were turned over to other Commands or civilian agencies; ATC gradually consolidated its activities to the few bases that it now occupies.

Today ATC is headquartered at Randolph AFB near San Antonio, Texas, where it moved in 1957 when MAC took over Scott AFB. It is responsible not only for flying and technical training, but recruiting, basic military training, professional military training and specialized education as well.

The Community College of the Air Force is contained within ATC, as is the Air University at Maxwell AFB in Alabama, which was itself a Major Command until 1978. The Air Force Academy is a Direct Reporting Unit and is not part of ATC.

FLYING TRAINING

Pilot training in ATC is a 49-week undergraduate program conducted for officers selected to become pilots. Training includes 500 hours of ground instruction and 175 hours of flying, 74 in the T-37 jet trainer and 101 in the Supersonic T-38. Undergraduate pilot training is conducted at Columbus, Laughlin, Reese, Vance and Williams AFBs, with pilot instructor training conducted at Randolph. Senior cadets at the Air Force Academy take part in an Indoctrination Program in the T-41 conducted by the 557th Flying Training Wing.

Beginning in 1988 ATC will introduce Specialized Undergraduate Pilot Training (SUPT). In SUPT, all trainees will have the same primary training in fundamental flying skills, but will then enter different training tracks. These will be the Fighter/Attack/Reconnaissance (FAR), which will continue to use the T-38 as its trainer, or the Tanker/Transport/Bomber (TTB) track which will use another trainer with a larger flight deck.

Left: This neoclassical building at Scott AFB served as ATC's headquarters from 1949 to 1957.

Above: The Lockheed T-33 'T-Bird' has served as one of ATC's principal trainers for over 30 years. There have been 5871 of this durable trainer version of the F-80 fighter delivered to the USAF since 1949.

Navigator training is a 28-week undergraduate program conducted only at Mather AFB near Sacramento. Ground instruction covers airmanship; basic navigation procedures and equipment; celestial, radar and low-altitude environment navigation; map reading and weather. Undergraduate navigator flying training is conducted aboard T-37s and T-43s.

Graduate courses offered by ATC at Mather include a 4-week advanced navigation program, a 5-week tactical navigation program, a 14-week navigator-bombardier program and a 21-week electronic warfare training program. Four specialized programs are also offered: electronic warfare operations and staff officer training, senior officer electronic warfare training, electronic warfare refresher training and an electronic warfare course for US Army air defense officers.

RECRUITMENT

The Air Force Recruiting Service is a unit of ATC, also headquartered at Randolph AFB. Its responsibility is to seek eligible young people who can be trained as US Air Force personnel. The Recruiting Service is also responsible for recruiting health care professionals like doctors, dentists, nurses, biomedical scientists and veterinarians.

The Commanders of the Air Training Command

Lt Gen Burton Yount	7 July 1943–14 Apr 1946
Lt Gen John Cannon	15 Apr 1946–15 Oct 1948
Lt Gen Robert Harper	14 Oct 1948–30 June 1954
Maj Gen Glenn Barcus	1 July 1954–25 July 1954
Lt Gen Charles Myers	26 July 1954–31 July 1958
Lt Gen Frederic Smith, Jr	1 Aug 1958–31 July 1959
Lt Gen James Briggs	1 Aug 1959–31 July 1963
Lt Gen Robert Burns	1 Aug 1963–10 Aug 1964
Lt Gen William Momyer	11 Aug 1964–30 June 1966
Lt Gen Sam Maddux, Jr	1 July 1966–30 Aug 1970
Lt Gen George Simler	1 Sept 1970–9 Sept 1972
Lt Gen William McBride	9 Sept 1972–31 Aug 1974
Lt Gen George McKee	1 Sept 1974–31 Aug 1975
Gen John Roberts	1 Sept 1975–1 Apr 1979
Gen Bennie Davis	1 Apr 1979–29 July 1981
Gen Thomas Ryan	29 July 1981–22 June 1983
Gen Andrew Iosue	23 June 1983–

BASIC MILITARY TRAINING

Once recruited, new enlisted personnel report to Lackland AFB for a six-week basic military training program that also includes academic training, physical conditioning and marksmanship. The Officer Training School, also at Lackland, prepares selected college graduates and college-educated enlisted personnel to be USAF officers. The OTS program includes both military and academic training as well as marksmanship and physical training. Students scheduled for pilot training enter a three-week flight screening program conducted in T-41 Mescaleros.

TECHNICAL TRAINING

Technical Training is conducted at five ATC Technical Training Centers at Keesler, Chanute, Lowry, Sheppard and Goodfellow AFBs, and at 90 field locations. Technical training is an ongoing process throughout one's Air Force career, with 300,000 students graduating annually from more than 2800 courses, including supply services, personnel, medical services, maintenance and communications, computer operations and of course aircraft and missile-systems operation.

SURVIVAL TRAINING

Basic survival training is given annually to about 5000 aircrew members at Fairchild AFB, with a water-survival course at Homestead AFB, Florida, and an arctic survival course at Eielson AFB in Alaska. ATC also monitors survival training conducted by the Air Force Academy and by AFSC's School of Aerospace medicine at Brooks AFB. The ATC Environmental Information Division at Maxwell AFB collects, evaluates and publishes data on natural and cultural environments that are potentially pertinent to survival and life-support training. During TAC's *Red Flag* exercises, ATC survival-training instructors conduct evaluation of search-and-rescue and escape-and-evasion exercises.

OTHER ATC ACTIVITIES

Located at Sheppard AFB, the School of Health Care Sciences offers 178 courses in such departments as medicine, dentistry, nursing, biomedical science and health services administration. A two-week orientation course for the majority of newly commissioned Air Force medical ser-

vice officers is given at the school prior to their assignments to active duty.

The Defense Language Institute English Language Center at Lackland AFB conducts English Language Training programs for the Department of Defense. The 3500 students who attend the Center annually are mostly military officers from 41 countries in Europe, Africa, Asia, the Middle East and Latin America who are being trained in the US; some will eventually undergo ATC pilot training. The average course is 16 weeks, but can range from 4 weeks to a year. The center also provides a 27-week English language instructor course and a 13-week advanced instructor course to foreign students.

The Civil Air Patrol is a civilian volunteer organization headed by a USAF officer selected by the Secretary of the Air Force; it became an official USAF auxiliary in 1948. Its services include air search and rescue operations and other emergency operations, communications, and youth motivation through aerospace education and leadership training.

The Community College of the Air Force was established in 1972 with headquarters at Maxwell AFB. The College provides both on and off-duty academic and technical education for enlisted personnel at many USAF locations. It is accredited by the Southern Association of Colleges and the School's Commission on Colleges and is the only federal agency with the authority to award associate degrees.

In 1980 ATC became the host of the EURO-NATO Joint Jet Pilot Training (ENJJPT) Program. The 55 week NATO-sponsored training program will take place at Sheppard AFB and be very similar to the West German Luftwaffe undergraduate

Below: **A ground crewman removes safety pins from a T-33 at Eielson AFB, Alaska during the *Jack Frost 75* exercise.**

Above: The Northrop T-38 Talon is ATC's first-line supersonic trainer, but some, like this one, serve other commands such as SAC.

training program formerly conducted at Sheppard. The Luftwaffe will be represented again in ENJJPT, as well as fighter pilot trainees from the air forces of Belgium, Canada, Denmark, Greece, Holland, Norway, Portugal, Turkey and the United Kingdom. The course will involve 452 classroom hours in 17 academic courses, and 216 flying training days. Flying training will include 110.6 hours flying time with 26.4 solo hours in the T-38. Students enrolled will reach a maximum of 254 in 1985, with a ratio of 144 foreign to 110 USAF personnel.

THE AIR UNIVERSITY

Established in 1946, and functioning as a Major Command until absorbed by ATC in 1978, the Air University at Maxwell AFB prepares officers and senior non-commissioned officers (NCO) to command and staff duties. Important components of the Air University include the Air War College, Air Command and Staff College, Squadron Officers School and the Leadership and Management Development Center. The University also manages the Air Force Senior NCO Academy, the Air Force Institute of Technology at Wright-Patterson AFB and the Air Force Reserve Officer Training Corps (ROTC), which has detachments at colleges and universities nationwide.

US AIR FORCE TRAINERS

The oldest trainer in service with ATC is the **T-33 T-Bird**, the trainer version of Lockheed's F-80 Shooting Star – the first American jet fighter – which was introduced 40 years ago. About 200 T-33s are still in use for combat support, proficiency and radar target evaluation training. Introduced in the mid-1950s, the **Cessna T-37** was the first jet to be ordered specifically as a trainer. Whereas the T-33 is based on a combat aircraft, the T-37 had a combat aircraft, the AT-37 Dragonfly (an attack plane first introduced during the Vietnam War) based on *it*. The T-37 has a side-by-side seating arrangement and is ATC's standard primary trainer.

The supersonic **Northrop T-38 Talon** entered operational service with ATC in March 1961. Almost identical to the F-5 tactical fighter except for the addition of a second seat, the Talon is ATC's advanced trainer. More than 900 are in operation with the Air Force, most with ATC; a small number are also in service with TAC, SAC and NASA. The T-38, like the F-5, has proven to be an outstanding aircraft and is expected to serve ATC well past the turn of the century.

The **Cessna T-41 Mescalero**, the standard Cessna Model 172, entered ATC service in 1964. It serves as a preliminary flight screening training and for cadet flight training at the Air Force Academy.

The **Boeing T-43** is a navigation trainer based on the Boeing model 737 commercial jetliner. ATC received 19 of them in 1974 and has passed four of them along to the Air National Guard. Based at Mather AFB, with the 323d Flying Training Wing, ATC's T-43s provide navigator training with the same advanced navigational avionics found in operational Air Force aircraft. Systems include celestial, inertial and radar navigational, as well as LORAN (Long Range Navigation) and various radio systems. The interior configuration of the T-43 can accommodate twelve students (or four advanced students) plus three instructors.

The **Fairchild Republic T-46** was selected for development under the Next-Generation Trainer (NGT) Program, and will replace the T-37 as ATC's primary trainer. While retaining the side-by-side seating of the T-37, the T-46 incorporates pressurization, adverse weather capability and increased range. This will permit training flights at higher, less crowded altitudes and in weather that would have precluded such flights in earlier primary trainers.

AIR TRAINING COMMAND BASES

Randolph AFB (ATC Headquarters)
Location: 20 miles ENE of San Antonio, Texas
Area: 2901 acres
Altitude: 761ft
Personnel: 5532 Military
2354 Civilian

The base was activated in June 1930 and named for Capt William Randolph, who was killed two years earlier when his AT-4 crashed on takeoff. It is hosted by the ATC's 12th Flying Training Wing providing instructor training in T-37s and T-38s. Randolph is home to the Air Force Manpower and Personnel Center, Occupational Measurement Center and Office of Civilian Personnel Operations; it is also headquarters for the USAF Recruiting Service.

Chanute AFB
Location: 14 miles north of Champaign, Illinois
Area: 2125 acres
Altitude: 735ft
Personnel: 6700 Military
1700 Civilian
Activated in May 1917, the base was named for Octave Chanute, a glider pilot and engineer who had died seven years earlier. It is the site of the Chanute Technical Training Center, which provides training for USAF personnel in many technical fields including metallurgy, aircraft and missile mechanics, weather forecasting, life support and fire protection and rescue.

Columbus AFB
Location: 10 miles NNW of Columbus, Mississippi
Area: 6013 acres
Altitude: 214ft
Personnel: 3079 Military
648 Civilian
Activated in 1941 as a center for pilot training, the base retains that function through the 14th Flying Training Wing, which provides undergraduate pilot training.

Goodfellow AFB
Location: Two miles SE of San Angelo, Texas
Area: 1127 acres
Altitude: 1877ft
Personnel: 1137 Military
443 Civilian
Named for Lt John Goodfellow Jr, a fighter pilot killed in action on 17 September 1918, the base was activated in January 1941. It is home to the 3480th Technical Training Wing and the Air Force Technical Training School.

Gunter AFS
Location: 4 miles NE of Montgomery, Alabama
Area: 348 acres
Altitude: 220ft
Personnel: 1430 Military
1048 Civilian
The base was activated on 27 August 1940 and named for former Montgomery Mayor William Gunter, an enthusiastic supporter of military aviation. The site is the headquarters of the Air Force Data Automation Agency, and is also home to the Air Force Data Systems Design Center, Logistics Management, Center Extension Course Institute and Senior NCO Academy.

Keesler AFB
Location: Biloxi, Mississippi
Area: 3600 acres
Altitude: 26ft
Personnel: 12,646 Military
3650 Civilian
Named for Lt Samuel Keesler Jr, an aerial observer killed during World War I, the base was activated on 12 June 1941. It is the headquarters of the Keesler Technical Training Center (communications, electronics, personnel and administration), and the Keesler Air Force Medical Center. Tenants include a TAC Airborne Command and Control Squadron and the AFCC NCO Academy Leadership School. Given its position on the edge of the turbulent Gulf of Mexico, the base is also home to Weather Reconnaissance units of both MAC and AFRES.

Lackland AFB
Location: 8 miles WSW of San Antonio, Texas
Area; 6783 acres (including the Lackland Training Annex)
Altitude 787ft
Personnel: 20,628 Military
5724 Civilian
Activated in 1941, the base is named for Brig General Frank Lackland, an early Commandant of the nearby Kelly Field flying school. It provides basic training for airmen, as well as advanced courses for Security Police, police-dog handlers, instructors, drug abuse counselors and recruiters. Lackland is also the site of the Defense Language Institute English Language Center, the Air Force Officer Training School and Wilford Hall Medical Center.

Laughlin AFB
Location: Six miles east of Del Rio, Texas
Area: 4008 acres
Altitude: 1080ft
Personnel: 2973 Military
550 Civilian
The base was activated in October 1942 and named for Lt Jack Laughlin, a B-17 pilot killed over Java on 29 January of that year. It is home to the 47th Flying Training Wing offering undergraduate pilot training.

Lowry AFB
Location: Six miles east of Denver, Colorado
Area: 1863 acres (plus a 3833-acre training annex 25 miles away)
Altitude: 5400ft
Personnel: 9810 Military
5312 Civilian
Activated on 26 February 1938, the base is named for Lt Francis Lowry, killed in action over France on 26 September 1918. A Technical Training Center, it provides courses in avionics, aerospace munitions, air intelligence, audiovisual and logistics. Both the Air Force Accounting and Finance Center and the Air Reserve Personnel Center are at Lowry, as well as the 3320th Correction and Rehabilitation Squadron.

Mather AFB
Location: 12 miles ESE of Sacramento, California
Area: 5800 acres
Altitude: 96ft
Personnel: 5300 Military
2000 Civilian
The base was activated in 1918 and named for Lt Carl Mather, killed in a mid-air collision in January of that year. Mather is exclusive Defense Department training center for navigators, providing instuction for the Navy and Marines as well as the Air Force. The base is also home to SAC's 320th Bomb Wing and the Air Force Reserve's 940th Air Refueling Group.

Maxwell AFB
Location: One mile west of Montgomery, Alabama
Area: 2523 acres
Altitude: 168ft
Personnel: 4582 Military
1603 Civilian
Activated in 1918, the base is named for Lt William Maxwell, who died in a crackup in the Philippines on 12 August 1920. Today it is the USAF Professional Education Center, with headquarters for the Air University, Air Force ROTC, the Air War College, Squadron Officer School, Community College of the Air Force, Foreign Officer School, Civil Air Patrol, the Leadership and Management Development Center and the Air University Center for Aerospace Doctrine.

Reese AFB
Location: Six miles west of Lubbock, Texas
Area: 3502 acres
Altitude: 3338ft
Personnel: 2663 Military
763 Civilian
The base was activated in 1942 and named for Lt Augustus Reese Jr, a P-38 pilot killed in Sardinia on 14 May 1943. It is home to the 64th Flying Training Wing providing undergraduate pilot training.

Sheppard AFB
Location: 4 miles north of Wichita Falls, Texas
Area: 5000 acres
Altitude: 1015ft
Personnel: 7829 Military
1524 Civilian
Activated on 14 June 1941, the base is named for US Senator from Texas Morris E Sheppard, who died earlier that year. The 80th Flying Training Wing provides undergraduate training for pilots and navigators for 12 NATO countries under the EURO-NATO Joint Jet Pilot Training Program. The Sheppard Technical Training Center provides courses in such disciplines as aircraft maintenance, engineering, communications and missile transportation. The 3785th Field Training Group provides advanced training through 72 detachments at 18 field locations around the world. The School of Health Care Sciences offers courses in medicine, dentistry, nursing, biomedical sciences and health service administration.

Vance AFB
Location: 3 miles SSW of Enid, Oklahoma
Area: 1811 acres
Altitude: 1307ft
Personnel: 1300 Military
1300 Civilian
The base was activated in November 1941 and later renamed for Lt Col Leon Vance Jr, a native of Enid and a 1939 West Point graduate who had received the Medal of Honor for his actions over Wimereaux, France, on 5 June 1944. Lt Col Vance was killed six weeks later when the transport returning him to the States went down in the Atlantic off Iceland. The base is the home of ATC's 71st Flying Training Unit.

Williams AFB
Location: 16 miles SE of Mesa, Arizona
Area: 4762 acres
Altitude: 1385ft
Personnel: 3300 Military
1070 Civilian
Activated in July 1941, the base is named for Lt Charles Williams, killed in a bomber crash near Fort De Russy, Hawaii, on 6 July 1927. Williams is the largest undergraduate training base in the Air Force. Home of the 82nd Flying Training Wing, it provides F-5 combat-crew training for foreign pilots. Also at the base, the Human Resources Laboratory of AFSC's Flying Training Division is conducting extensive research into flight simulators.

RESERVE POWER FOR THE US AIR FORCE

THE AIR NATIONAL GUARD

The Air National Guard (ANG), along with the Air Force Reserve (AFRES), provide America's 'shadow air force,' a pool of trained reserve personnel who can be called up to augment the regular Air Force in time of crisis, national emergency or war. While AFRES is a Separate Operating Agency of the US Air Force, the Air National Guard (known familiarly as the 'Air Guard,' like the Army's National Guard) is under command of the Governors of each of the fifty states, Puerto Rico, Guam, the Virgin Islands, and the Commanding General for the District of Columbia. The Governors may call up elements of the National Guard to protect lives in time of natural disaster and civil unrest. Hardly a winter storm season goes by without an ANG helicopter rescuing someone from a rooftop somewhere in the country. In time of war the President may 'nationalize' the National Guard, at which time they join the regular Army and Air Force units overseas.

Meanwhile, ANG units train with, and are assigned to, USAF Major Commands, called 'Gaining Commands,' that would 'gain' the ANG units assigned to them in time of war. MAC is the Gaining Command for ANG airlift units, SAC for ANG aerial refueling units and TAC for ANG fighter and interceptor units (except for the Hawaii Air National Guard, which would be gained by PACAF). The Air Guard has over 100,000 people organized in 24 wings, 67 groups, 91 flying squadrons and 242 nonflying units. These units constitute 17% of SAC's aerial refueling capability, 26% of TAC's tactical fighter force, 32% of MAC's tactical airlift, 54% of the Air Force's tactical reconnaissance assets and 66% of the TAC Air Defense interceptor force.

The idea of the National Guard goes back to the militias of the Revolutionary War era, with the term 'National Guard' first used in 1824. The designation became official under the Dick Act of 21 January 1903. Under the National Defense Act of 1920, the Militia Bureau of the War Department became the National Guard Bureau. In World War II units of the nationalized National Guard were among the first to see action; after the war they were turned back to the states. The Aviation Group, National Guard Bureau, was formed at the end of the war and its

Above right: **An F-106 of the 194th Fighter Interceptor Squadron, California ANG, fires a training missile over the Tyndall AFB gunnery range.**

Right: **A California Air Guard HC-130 refuels a pair of Air Guard HH-3s over the Pacific coast just south of San Francisco.**

90146
FORCE

U.S. AIR FORCE
RESCUE
60224
U.S. AIR FORCE
8

Below: A pair of the Ohio Air Guard F-84s.

designation changed to Air Force Division, National Guard Bureau, when the US Air Force was created. Ultimately it became the Air National Guard.

The Air Guard traditionally has been equipped with aircraft classed generally as 'second line.' Nearly all their aircraft were Air Force hand-me-downs. At the beginning of the Korean War, the Air Force fighter wings were equipped with jets, while the Air Guard units were flying F-51s. The Guardsmen in their F-51s still turned in an outstanding performance when they went into action in Korea. After that war, the Guard didn't get F-86D interceptors until the Air Force had F-89s. The F-89s did not pass into Air Guard colors until the F-102 and F-106 became operational. This writer remembers that his first experience aboard a fighter aircraft was in the back seat of a Montana Air National Guard F-89 based at Great Falls IAP.

Ultimately, ANG received F-106s, but by then the Air Force had F-4s and was getting F-15s. In the early 1980s this hand-me-down practice began to change, as the South Carolina Air National Guard's 169th Tactical Fighter Group received brand new F-16s along with regular Air Force units. The theory now is that if ANG is to be part of the first line of defense it should have first-line aircraft. Though they are called 'weekend warriors,' the Guardsmen are some of the best-trained personnel in the Air Force. Many are former active-duty pilots; they often participate in as many readiness exercises (over a longer period of years) as current active-duty personnel.

THE AIR FORCE RESERVE

Formerly a USAF Direct Reporting Unit (DRU), and since 1983 a Separate Operating Agency (SOA), the Air Force Reserve (AFRES) has the mission of training reserve Air Force personnel to be ready for mobilization. The manpower administration support required for the mobilization of the

Below: Hawaii ANG F-86 interceptors on alert at Hickam AFB, March 1960. The Hawaii Air Guard still provides the first-line air defense for the island state.

AFRES is provided by the Air Reserve Personnel Center in Denver, which is now also an SOA. Reservists, like Guardsmen, are part-time personnel or 'weekend warriors,' but unlike ANG, which is under the jurisdiction of State governors, the AFRES is part of the Air Force. AFRES is headquartered at Robins AFB, Georgia, and organized into three (formerly ADC active-duty) numbered air forces. These are the Fourth and Fourteenth, for whom MAC is the Gaining Command, and the Tenth, whose units are mostly assigned to TAC as a Gaining Command, but which has five Aerial Refueling Squadrons assigned to SAC.

Like ANG, AFRES participates in many annual readiness exercises including *Reforger* in Europe, *Brim Frost* in Alaska, *Team Spirit* in the Pacific, and *Red Flag*. AFRES crews and units assigned to MAC are constantly present on MAC's global airlift routes. AFRES units constitute 10% of the Air Force's fighter squadrons and are consistently represented among top units in fighter weapons competitions.

Like the Air Guard, the Reserve has generally found itself receiving aircraft in service for a while with the regular Air Force. Like the Guard, however, AFRES is changing. Beginning in 1981 with the introduction into SAC of the new McDonnell Douglas KC-10 Extender aerial refueling tanker, AFRES was designated to supply 50% of the crews. The tanker is identical in almost all respects (save for the aerial refueling systems) to the commercial DC-10 jetliner, and many of the AFRES pilots have regular jobs flying DC-10s for the airlines. AFRES units are also receiving A-10s at the same time as regular Air Force units, plus 'factory-fresh' C-130s. Because of their long-term training and prior service, the Reservists are like the Guardsmen in being among the best military airmen available. Generally called the best reserve air force in the world, AFRES, like ANG, provides a highly competent and economical backup to the regular Air Force.

The Chief of the Aviation Group, National Guard Bureau

Col William Robertson	28 Nov 1945-Oct 1948

The Chiefs of the Air Force Division, National Guard Bureau

Maj Gen George Finch	Oct 1948–25 Sept 1950
Maj Gen Earl Ricks	13 Oct 1950–4 Jan 1954
Maj Gen Winston Wilson	26 Jan 1954–5 Aug 1962
Maj Gen Brown	6 Aug 1962–30 Nov 1969

The Directors of the Air National Guard

Maj Gen Brown	1 Dec 1969–19 Apr 1974
Maj Gen Pesch	20 Apr 1974–31 Jan 1977
Maj Gen Guice	1 Feb 1977–1 Apr 1981
Maj Gen Conaway	1 Apr 1981–

The Chiefs of Air Force Reserve

Maj Gen Tom Marchbanks, Jr	18 Jan 1968–1 Feb 1971
Maj Gen Rollin Moore, Jr*	2 Feb 1971–26 Jan 1972
Brig Gen Alfred Verhulst (acting)	27 Jan 1972–15 Mar 1972
Maj Gen Homer Lewis	16 Mar 1972–8 Apr 1975
Maj Gen William Lyon	16 Apr 1975–16 Apr 1979
Maj Gen Richard Bodycombe	17 Apr 1979–31 Oct 1982
Maj Gen Sloan Gill	1 Nov 1982

*Gen Moore was also Commander, Headquarters Air Force Reserve, from 1 Aug 1968 until the two jobs were officially merged on 16 March 1972.)

LOGISTICS AND RESEARCH IN THE US AIR FORCE

A COMMON HISTORY

Two vital support functions for any air force are Supply or Logistics and Research and Development (R&D). Since 1 April 1961 these activities have been under the respective direction of the Air Force Logistics Command (AFLC) and the Air Force Systems Command (AFSC). These commands had common origins near Dayton, Ohio, in the early years of the century; for a period before and again after World War II, they were actually part of the same Command.

Until the early days of American involvement in World War I, military aviation support was small-scale, easily handled by existing Army agencies. The war brought expanding needs, and on 4 December 1917 the Signal Corps Equipment Division established the Airplane Engineering Department, the first forerunner to AFSC, as an experimental laboratory organization, at McCook Field near Dayton. A month later, AFLC's first forerunner, the Fairfield Aviation General Supply Depot, was established at nearby Wilbur Wright Field. When the Aviation Section of the Signal Corps became the US Army Air Service (USAAS), the Airplane Engineering Department became its Airplane Engineering Division. After the war the new USAAS moved its logistical depot system from Washington to Wilbur Wright Field; the Fairfield Supply Depot was incorporated into the new logistics section, called Property, Maintenance and Cost Compilation, which would be renamed Field Services Section in 1924.

In July 1926 the USAAS became the more independent US Army Air Corps (USAAC), and the new USAAC Materiel Division was established. It would be headquartered at McCook Field and combine the Field Services Section and the former Engineering Division. The new Materiel Division would have six sections: Field Services, Experimental Engineering, Procurement, Repair, Maintenance and Industrial War Plans. There were four major supply depots called Air Intermediate Depots, the one at Fairfield adjacent to Dayton and McCook, and others at San Diego, San Antonio and Middletown, Pennsylvania. The USAAC Materiel Division moved the San Diego depot to Sacramento (where it remains today) and established three overseas Departmental Depots in Hawaii, Panama and the Philippines.

In October 1939, with the onset of World War II in Europe, Materiel Division headquarters moved from Ohio to Washington, DC. In March 1941 its maintenance activities, still in Ohio, were consolidated into a 'provisional' Maintenance Command that became the Air Services Command in October. On 11 December 1941, three days after the United States went to war, the USAAF Air Services Command (ASC) became separate

Above: **As dawn breaks over Tularosa Basin, New Mexico, airmen of AFSC's Geophysics Laboratory prepare to release a helium-filled balloon.**

from the Materiel Division, which in turn became the USAAF Materiel Command in March 1942. On 1 April 1943 Materiel Command headquarters moved back to Wright Field, Ohio, adjacent to ASC headquarters at Patterson Field.

On 31 August 1944, the Materiel Command and the ASC (the two forerunners of AFLC and AFSC) joined as a single Command – the Air Technical Service Command (ATSC). The merger was effected under Lt General William Knudsen, who had been brought in from General Motors. Knudsen intended to run the Command in a businesslike manner, even to giving himself the title of Director rather than Commanding General. The new Command went on to preside over the development, production and delivery of the greatest aircraft fleet ever assembled. The end of the war brought a challenge almost as large. The American war machine had geared up for a maximum effort: now it was over. Engorged supply lines had to be cleared, vast quantities of materiel had to be recalled from far-flung battlefields and humming defense plants had to wind down without dislocating the American economy. The ATSC was faced with an enormous but apparently unproductive task. Contracts for $22 billion worth of work had to be cancelled and hundreds of government-owned factories disposed of. Ten billion dollars worth of USAAF supplies were suddenly surplus; vast numbers of aircraft and equipment had to be scrapped or mothballed. By early 1946 most of the materiel had been sold off or turned over to the War Assets Administration.

On 9 March 1946 ATSC was redesignated Air Materiel Command (AMC). Its tasks completed, personnel strength was gradually reduced. From a 1939 level of 6055 (5508 civilians and 547 military), the Command had reached a wartime peak of 486,267 (300,640 civilians and 185,627 military). By 1948 it was down to 93,606 (79,592 civilians and 14,014 military).

The onset of the Cold War, the Berlin Blockade and the advent of Russian nuclear weapons stimulated an Air Force-wide buildup and the need to enhance both logistics and R&D capabilities. Men like Dr Theodore von Karman, who had headed General Arnold's Scientific Advisory Group during the war, had lobbied hard for a separate research Command and found listeners when the new US Air Force was created in 1947. In 1950 Chief of Staff General Hoyt Vandenberg decided to remove R&D from the auspices of the AMC. An Air Research and Development Command (ARDC) was created under AMC in 1950; on 2 April 1951 it became an independent Command. Ten years later AMC became the present Air Force Logistic Command and ARDC the present Air Force Systems Command, which continued to complement one another. AFSC, now headquartered at Andrews AFB near Washington, DC, has responsibility for new systems in the conceptual and development stage. AFLC, still headquartered near Dayton at Wright-Patterson AFB, has the task of supporting the systems once they have been procured and made operational.

THE AIR FORCE SYSTEMS COMMAND

The Air Force Systems Command (AFSC) mission is still research and development. It develops and tests Air Force high-technology hardware in the form of systems ranging from aircraft and avionics to spacecraft and air-to-air missiles. The Command also conducts research, development and testing for other Defense Department agencies and NASA.

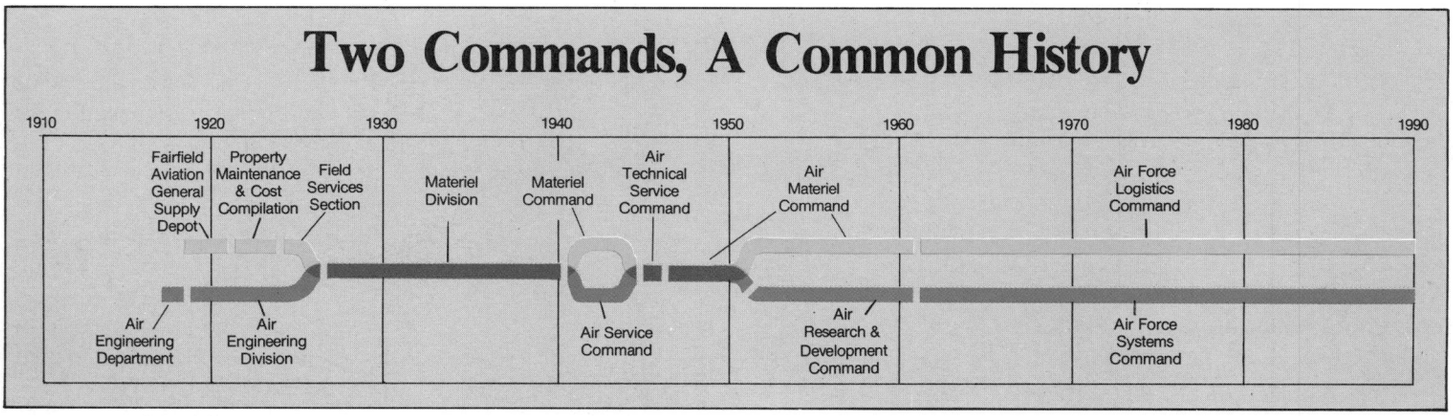

Experimental aircraft on the flight line at The Air Research and Development Command's Edwards AFB Flight Test Center, 1954.
Clockwise from bottom center: The needle-nosed Douglas X-3, a jet-powered aircraft designed for sustained flight at extremely high speeds; the Bell X-1A, a supersonic rocket-powered aircraft (successor to the X-1, first plane to exceed the speed of sound), which had reached speeds above 1600mph; the Navy's jet-powered Douglas D-558; the Convair XF-92 built to test the delta-wing configuration later used on the F-102 and F-106; the Bell X-5 variable-wing aircraft built to investigate the effects of changing the degree of wing sweepback during flight; the Navy's rocket-powered Douglas D-558, which had attained the highest altitude then recorded by a piloted aircraft; and the twin-jet Northrop X-4 built to explore the stability and flight characteristics of aircraft of the swept-back, all-wing configuration at transonic speeds. The nineteen fifties would see an unprecedented proliferation of experimental and research aircraft at the Edwards Test Center. These would range from the Ryan X-13 Vertijet, which took off straight up, to the North American X-15 rocket plane which had to be carried aloft, but which would fly higher and faster than any conventional aircraft.

AFSC's 50,000 personnel are equally divided between military and civilians, with two-thirds of the officers holding advanced degrees. AFSC has several divisions (responsible for specific types of systems) with activities conducted through a nationwide network of laboratories and centers.

The Aeronautical Systems Division (ASD), at Wright-Patterson AFB, accounts for over half of AFSC's budget and is responsible for development of aircraft, engines, aircraft systems, missiles and other airborne systems, as well as flight simulators. All new aircraft pass through ASD's hands in the experimental (X) phase. Under its direction are the Air Force Wright Aeronautical Laboratories (AFWAL) at Wright-Patterson AFB, including The Aero-Propulsion, Avionics and Flight Dynamics Laboratories.

The Space Division (SD) is headquartered at Los Angeles AFS in the heart of a major concentration of space-systems contractors and subcontractors. The Space Division has been closely linked with the Space Command (SPACECOM) since the latter's activation in 1983. The Commander of AFSC's Space Division is by designation SPACECOM'S Vice-Commander. The Space Division manages development of all Department of Defense (DoD) satellites, spacecraft and space systems, and is associated with the NASA Space Shuttle Transportation System. Systems within its jurisdiction include communications, meterological and technology development of satellites. Among the Space Division's units are the Air Force Satellite Control Facility (AFSCF) at Sunnyvalle AFS, California, which operates a global network of satellite-tracking stations; the Manned Space Flight Support Group at the Johnson Space Center near Houston; and the Space and Missile Test Organization (SAMTO) based at SAC's Vandenberg AFB. SAMTO manages testing for DoD ballistic-missile and space programs, conducting test launches at the two Space and Missile Test Centers that it operates. The Western Space and Missile Test Center (WSMC) is located at Vandenberg; its Western Test Range stretches across the Pacific into the Indian Ocean. WSMC conducts polar orbit space-launch operations, ballistic missile tests in conjunction with SAC, and effective 1985, Space Shuttle operations. The Eastern Space and Missile Center (ESMC) operates from Patrick AFB and Cape Canaveral AFS, the primary Space Shuttle launch site, with tracking and data-gathering stations on the islands of Grand Bahama, Grand Turk, Antigua and Ascension. The Eastern Test Range extends across the Atlantic into the Indian Ocean. In 1982 the Space Division got jurisdiction over the newly created Space Technology Center, which includes the Air Force Geo-

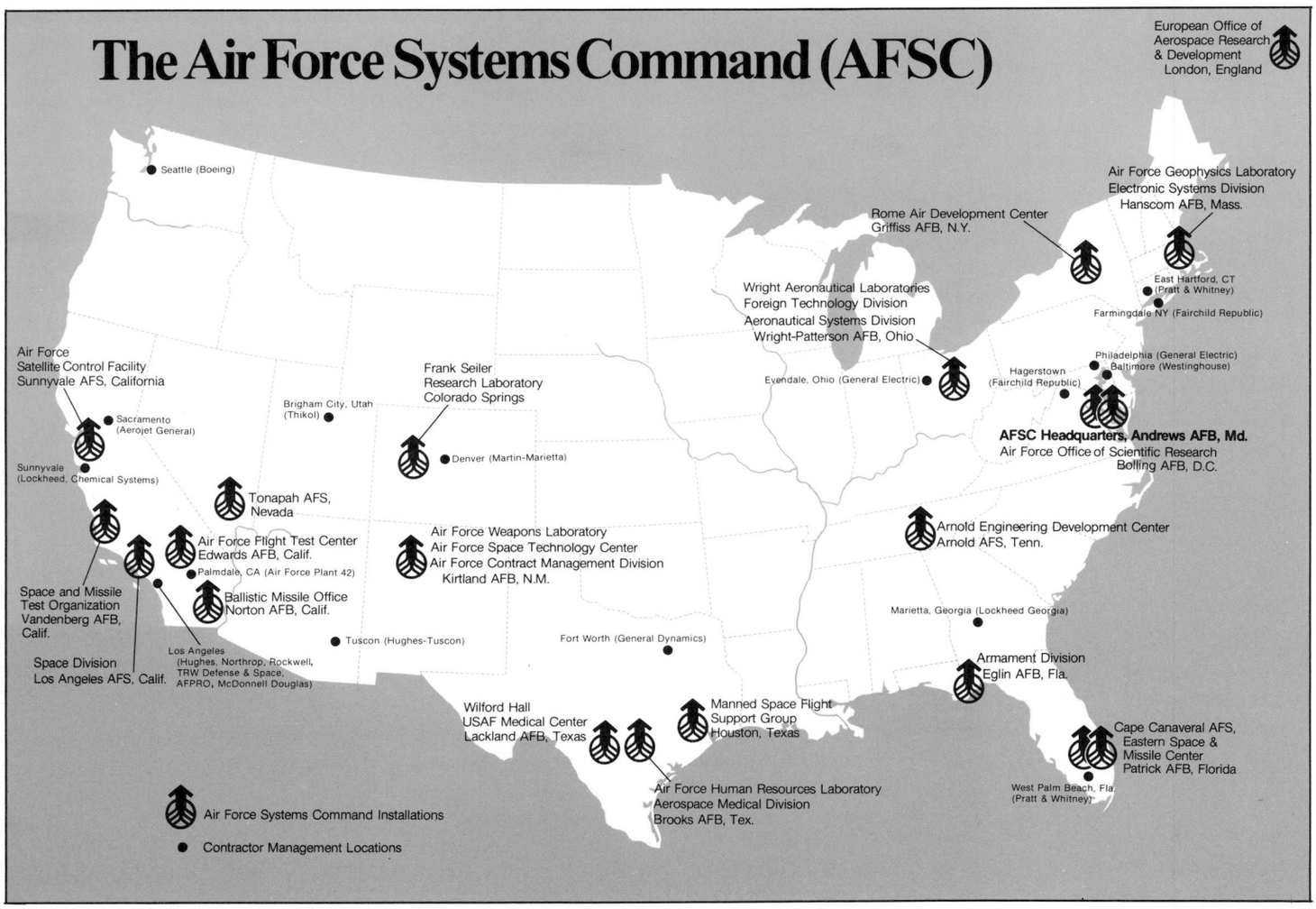

physics Laboratory (AFGL) at Hanscom AFB, The Air Force Weapons Laboratory (AFWL) at Kirtland AFB and the Air Force Rocket Propulsion Laboratory (AFRPL) at Edwards AFB.

The Ballistic Missile Office (BMO) is headquartered at MAC's Norton AFB and is responsible for planning, implementation and management of USAF ballistic-missile system and subsystem programs. It modernizes existing systems and develops future ICBMs. BMO is currently managing the MGM-118 Peacekeeper (formerly MX) ICBM and working on the next-generation ICBMs. Other weapons systems like aircraft have a prime contractor in the private sector who develops the system under contract with the Air Force and subcontractors. In the case of ICBMs, BMO acts as prime contractor, managing the project itself and co-ordinating private-sector subcontractors who supply components.

The Electronic Systems Division (ESD), headquartered at Hanscom AFB, is the primary USAF agency for development and acquisition of command-control, communications and intelligence (C^3I) systems: radar and optical detection systems used to locate and track aircraft, satellites and missiles. These range from SPACECOM's radar network to TAC's E-3A AWACS electronic reconnaissance aircraft. One of ESD's principal subsidiaries is Rome Air Development Center (RADC) at Griffiss AFB near Rome, New York. RADC's laboratory does C^3I research and development of systems and subsystems in reconnaissance, mapping and charting.

The Air Force Flight Test Center (AFFTC) at Edwards AFB is probably the best known of AFSC's bases and centers. It has served as the Air Force's primary flight test field for over 50 years. Located on California's Mojave Desert, it has one of the largest ground complexes in the world with 15,000 square miles of unrestricted airspace. The main runway measures 15,000 feet, and two dry lake beds provide a 40,000-foot runway for landing any type of research aircraft. Near-perfect flying weather and a semi-isolated location combine to provide a safe and secure environment for flight test operations. Edwards provided the ideal landing site for the early Space Shuttle flights. The Center plans, conducts and evaluates manned and unmanned aircraft and spacecraft for the Air Force, NASA and other agencies. Almost every aircraft that has become operational with the Air Force, and many research aircraft that never saw service, first went through their paces at Edwards.

The Arnold Engineering Development Center (AEDC) at Arnold AFS has the mission of ensuring that aerospace hardware – aircraft, spacecraft, missiles or propulsion systems – work right the first time they fly. Virtually every major American aerospace system has been supported by tests conducted at AEDC. Its clients include NASA, the other services and aerospace industry contractors. The Center operates the world's largest and most advanced complex of flight-simulation test facilities. Conditions can be simulated at altitudes from sea level to 1000 miles at speeds from subsonic to 20,000mph: test subjects range from small-scale wind tunnel models to full-scale vehicles.

The Armament Division (AD) of AFSC and its Air Force Armament Laboratory (AFATL), both at Eglin AFB, develop, test and procure all the Air Force's nonnuclear air weapons and related equipment: air-launched tactical and defense missiles, guided weapons, aircraft guns and ammunition, targets and related armament support equipment. AD activities are conducted in four phases: basic, exploratory, and advanced research and engineering development. AFATL's principal work is in free-fall

The Commanders of the Air Research and Development Command

Maj Gen David Schlatter	1 Feb 1950–24 June 1951
Lt Gen Earle Partridge	24 June 1951–20 June 1953
Lt Gen Donald Putt	30 June 1953–14 Apr 1954
Lt Gen Thomas Power	15 Apr 1954–30 June 1957
Maj Gen John Sessums, Jr	1 July 1957–31 July 1957
Lt Gen Samuel Anderson	1 Aug 1957–9 Mar 1959
Maj Gen John Sessums, Jr	10 Mar 1959–24 Apr 1959
Gen Bernard Schriever	25 Apr 1959–30 Mar 1961

The Commanders of the Air Force Systems Command

Gen Bernard Schriever	1 Apr 1961–31 Aug 1966
Gen James Ferguson	1 Sept 1966–30 Aug 1970
Gen George Brown	1 Sept 1970–31 July 1973
Gen Samuel Phillips	1 Aug 1973–31 Aug 1975
Gen William Evans	1 Sept 1975–31 July 1977
Gen Lew Allen, Jr	1 Aug 1977–13 Mar 1978
Gen Alton Slay	14 Mar 1978–1 Feb 1981
Gen Robert Marsh	1 Feb 1981–

and guided nonnuclear munitions and airborne targets and scorers. These include chemical and fuel-air explosives, energy sources and conversions, electronic and mechanical devices, bombs, dispensors, fuses and flares. AFATL also provides consulting services in the areas of nonnuclear munition safety and aircraft/munition compatability (as well as analysis and prediction of weapons effects). AD operates 720 square miles of land test ranges and has access to a 44,000-square-mile test area over the Gulf of Mexico.

The Aerospace Medical Division (AMD) of AFSC, based at Brooks AFB, conducts research and development in flight medicine, environmental health, biomedical education and epidemiology. AMD includes four major organizations for specialized biomedical activities. First, the USAF School of Aerospace Medicine (USAFSAM), also at Brooks AFB, conducts medical evaluation, education, consultation and aeromedical support services in clinical and laboratory settings. The USAF Occupational and Environmental Health Laboratory (OEHL) at Brooks provides consultation and laboratory services in USAF occupational, environmental and radiological health programs.The Air Force Aerospace Medical Research Laboratory (AFAMRL) at Wright-Patterson AFB specializes in theoretical and experimental biotechnology research and development in biodynamics, human engineering, combined aerospace stress and toxic-hazard effects. The Wilford Hall Medical Center (WHMC) at Lackland AFB is a 1000-bed hospital and one of the largest DoD medical centers, also engaged in clinical research in anesthesiology, dentistry, cancer, dermatology, drugs, internal medicine, pediatrics, and psychiatry.

The Foreign Technology Division (FTD), based at Wright Patterson AFB, collects, evaluates and analyzes information about foreign aerospace technology in conjunction with other AFSC divisions. The result is an assessment of the potential positive or negative effects of foreign developments on USAF operations. When Russian pilot Viktor Belenko defected to the West in a super-secret Soviet MiG-25 Foxbat in 1976, FTD was on hand to disassemble and study the plane before it was returned to the USSR.

The Air Force Contract Management Division (AFCMD), located at Kirtland AFB, administers DoD aerospace contracts for the Air Force as well as the other services and NASA. AFCMD operates from US and European offices called Contract Management Locations at the plants of major defense contractors. They maintain quality control and provide a liaison between the company that builds the hardware and the service or command that will acquire it.

Finally, there is **AFSC's Directorate of Laboratories**, which monitors a nationwide laboratory network at AFSC and other bases. The laboratories include the Frank J Seiler Research Laboratory (FJSRL) at the USAF Academy in Colorado, the Air Force Human Resources Laboratory (AFHRL) at Brooks AFB and the Air Force Engineering and Services Center Engineering and Services Laboratory (AFESC/RD) at Tyndall AFB. The Directorate of Laboratories also oversees the Air Force Office of Scientific Research (AFOSR) at Bolling AFB and the European Office of Aerospace Research & Development (EOARD) in London.

AIR FORCE SYSTEMS COMMAND BASES

Arnold AFS
Location: 7 miles SE of Manchester, Tennessee
Area: 40,118 acres
Altitude: 950 to 1150ft
Personnel: 145 Military
3816 Civilian (including 216 civil service)
Activated on 1 January 1950, the base is named for Henry H 'Hap' Arnold, Chief of Staff of the USAAF during World War II, and is the site of the Arnold Engineering and Development Center. The center manages the free world's largest complex of wind tunnels, jet and rocket-engine test cells and space-simulation chambers. Research and development activity here serves not only the Air Force, but other services and government agencies as well.

Brooks AFB
Location: 7 miles SE of San Antonio, Texas
Area: 1310 acres
Altitude: 600ft
Personnel: 1500 Military
1100 Civilian
Named for Sidney Brooks, a World War I flight cadet killed on his last solo flight before getting his wings, the base was activated on 8 December 1917. Today it is home to the School of Aerospace Medicine, the Air Force Occupational and Environmental Lab, the Air Force Human Resources Lab and the Air Force Medical Service Center.

Edwards AFB
Location: 20 miles east of Rosamond, California
Area: 301,000 acres
Altitude: 2302ft
Personnel: 3732 Military
4785 Civilian
The base was activated in 1933 and named Muroc Army Air Field after the vast salt flat known as Muroc Dry Lake that comprised a large part of the base. It was and is the location of the Air Force Flight Test Center. On 5 June 1948 Major Glen Edwards was killed here flight-testing the extraordinary YB-49 'Flying Wing' – it is for him that the base is now named. Primary landing site for the Space Shuttle evaluation flights, Edwards is also home to the USAF Test Pilot School, the USAF Rocket Propulsion Lab, the US Army Aviation Engineering Flight Activity and NASA's Dryden Flight Research Facility.

Above: An aerial view of the facilities at Arnold AFS.

Eglin AFB
Location: 7 miles NE of Fort Walton Beach, Florida
Area: 464,980 acres
Altitude: 85ft
Personnel: 11,024 Military
3904 Civilian
Activated in 1935, the base was later named after Lt Col Frederick Eglin, killed in a plane crash in January 1937. Eglin is home of the Air Force Armament Division and Laboratory, the Tactical Air Warfare Center, the 3246th Test Wing, the 39th and 55th Aerospace Rescue and Recovery Wings, the 33d Tactical Fighter Wing and the Air Force Reserve's 919th Special Operations Wing.

Hanscom AFB
Location: 17 miles NW of Boston, Massachusetts
Area: 846 acres
Altitude: 133ft
Personnel: 1848 Military
3189 Civilian
The base is named for Laurence Hanscom, killed in a plane crash in 1941, who was a long-time advocate of general aviation. Ironically, the base has no runway. Visiting aircraft must use a nearby state strip, also named for Hanscom. It is the Headquarters of AFSC's Electronic Systems Division, which oversees development and deployment of Command Control Communiations and Intelligence (C^3I) Systems. Also on the base, one finds the Air Force Geophysics Laboratory and its research into earth and space environments.

Los Angeles AFS
Location: In El Segundo, California, next to Los Angeles International Airport
Personnel: 1472 Military
1100 Civilian
Activated on 14 December 1960, the station is headquarters for AFSC's 1st Space Division, whose Commander is also Vice-Commander of Space Command. The 1st Space Division oversees development, deployment and orbital control of the Military Space Program.

Patrick AFB/Cape Canaveral AFS
Location: Two miles south of Cocoa Beach, Florida
Area; 2341 acres
Altitude: 9ft
Personnel: 3281 Military
6697 Civilian
Named for Maj Gen Mason Patrick, World War I AEF Air Service Commander (later Air Corps Commander), the base is operated by the Eastern Space and Missile Center. The center, in conjunction with Cape Canaveral AFS on the site of the nearby Kennedy Space Center, has provided support for over 2250 USAF, DoD and NASA missile launches since 1950.

THE AIR FORCE LOGISTICS COMMAND

The mission of the Air Force Logistics Command (AFLC) is 'to provide combat readiness to the US Air Force.' Its job is to buy, transport, supply and maintain virtually all the hardware required to keep the operational Commands combat-ready. AFSC develops the hardware and AFLC sees that it gets where it's needed and doesn't break down.

AFLC stocks and/or manages nearly 900,000 items and processes nearly 5,000,000 requisitions annually: not only missiles and aircraft, but nuts, bolts, kitchen sinks and electronic organs for the Chaplain's Office. AFLC's huge logistics operations make it the largest single-location employer in the seven states where it operates, except California. The combined floor space of AFLC's Logistics Centers is significantly larger than the State of Rhode Island. It operates six Logistics Centers dating back to the Air Corps Depots. One is at its Wright-Patterson AFB headquarters and the others at McClellan, Hill, Kelly, Tinker and Robins AFBs.

The International Logistics Center (ILC) at Wright-Patterson AFB manages Foreign Military Sales (FMS), the Grant Aid program and the International Military Education and Training program. ILC's Foreign Military Sales are valued at more than $14 billion annually, including both aircraft and support systems. ILC clients include more than 60 countries with over 8000 aircraft of 160 different types, ranging from C-47s to F-16s.

The Ogden Air Logistics Center at Hill AFB manages global logistics support for the Air Force's entire operational fleet of F-4s, RF-4s, F-16s and ICBMs (including the MX). Additional responsibilities include Maverick air-to-air missiles, GBU-15 guided bombs, nonnuclear explosives, solid propellants and ICBM rocket motors. Ogden ALC also provides global logistics support for aircraft landing gear wheels, brakes, struts, tires and tubes for all Air Force aircraft, as well as all photographic and reconnaissance equipment.

The Oklahoma City Air Logistics Center at Tinker AFB manages global logistics support for the Air Force fleet of A-7s, B-52s, E-3s, E-4s, and K/R/EC-135s; SRAM, ALCM, and GLCM missiles; and TF-30, TF-33, TF-41, F-101 and J-79 engines. The center is also the exclusive Air Force Technology Repair Center for air-driven accessories, automatic flight-control instruments, hydraulic/pneudraulic transmissions, oxygen components and engine instruments.

The Sacramento Air Logistics Center at McClellan AFB manages logistics support for F-111, FB-111 and A-10 aircraft; the Air Force Satellite Communications system (AFSATCOM); and the Space Shuttle. Sacramento ALC also manages such items as ground radar, ground communications and ground and airborne generators. It is responsible for maintenance and modification of F-4s and F-106s in its region.

The San Antonio Air Logistics Center at Kelly AFB provides worldwide support for aircraft from the huge lumbering C-5 to the small and agile F-5 and T-38. Its 600,000-square-foot maintenance hanger can hold six C-5s or 14 B-52s. Other systems managed by the Center include nuclear ordnance, 29,000 aircraft engines, 45,000 nonaircraft engines, all fuels and lubricants for the Air Force and NASA and the Air Force's small fleet of boats. The San Antonio ALC is also home to the DoD Dog Center, which procures and provides military working dogs for the Air Force, the Army and the US Customs Service.

Commanders of the Air Materiel Command

Gen Joseph McNarney	14 Oct 1947–31 Aug 1949
Lt Gen Benjamin Chidlaw	1 Sept 1949–20 Aug 1951
Gen Edwin Rawlins	21 Aug 1951–28 Feb 1959
Lt Gen William McKee	1 Mar 1959–14 Mar 1959
Gen Samuel Anderson	15 Mar 1959–31 Mar 1961

Commanders of the Air Force Logistics Command

Gen Samuel Anderson	1 Apr 1961–31 July 1961
Gen William McKee	1 Aug 1961–30 June 1962
Gen Mark Bradley, Jr	1 July 1962–31 July 1965
Gen Kenneth Hobson	1 Aug 1965–31 July 1967
Gen Thomas Gerrity	1 Aug 1967–24 Feb 1968
Lt Gen Lewis Mundell (acting)	24 Feb 1968–28 Mar 1968
Gen Jack Merrell	29 Mar 1968–11 Sept 1972
Gen Jack Catton	12 Sept 1972–31 Aug 1974
Gen William McBride	1 Sept 1974–31 Aug 1975
Gen F Michael Rogers	1 Sept 1975–27 Jan 1978
Gen Bryce Poe II	28 Jan 1978–31 July 1981
Gen James Mullins	1 Aug 1981–

The Warner Robins Air Logistics Center at Robins AFB Georgia manages the USAF F-15, C-130 and C-141 fleets and the remnants of the C-119 and C-123 fleet. It looks after the USAF helicopter fleet (UH-1, H-3 and H-53), and the AIM-7, AIM-9 and AGM-45 airborne tactical missiles. The Avionics Center meets maintenance needs for over 300 Air Force avionics systems. Other systems managed at Warner Robins ALC include vehicles, propellers, automatic data processing equipment, life support systems, hand guns and bearings.

AFLC also maintains several other unique and important facilities at or near Wright-Patterson – except for the **Military Aircraft Storage and Disposition Center (MASDC)** at Davis Monthan AFB. Located just outside Tucson, Arizona, in the dry air of the Sonoran Desert, MASDC is home to a vast fleet of 3200 mothballed aircraft stored here in the desert against future use. Known as 'the Boneyard,' the Center also stores aircraft from the other services, including the US Coast Guard. When an airplane arrives at MASDC for storage, it undergoes a preservation process to ensure that it will 'keep' indefinitely. Guns, explosives and classified material are removed. Engines and fuel lines are flushed and filled with a thin film of oil to protect them. Engine intakes and all openings on the top half of the aircraft are taped or covered and sprayed with a vinyl plastic compound called *Spraylat* that protects the interior from dust, rain and the high solar temperatures found in the desert. Openings are left in the lower parts of the aircraft to prevent condensation.

About half the aircraft in storage at MASDC have the *Spraylat* peeled off and their airframes restored to service either with the US or under a Foreign Military Sales contract. The other half of the planes parked under the Arizona sun at the Boneyard are cannibalized for spare parts. With many of the aircraft out of production, the Boneyard is the spare parts source of last resort. It is often vastly cheaper to strip used parts from MASDC planes than to have a contractor tool up to produce a dozen parts: the center pays its own way. For every dollar of operating expenses, MASDC returns $28 worth of hardware to the Defense Department in Foreign Military Sales.

The Air Force Contract Maintenance Center (AFCMC) was established in 1969 to administer AFLC's engine modification and regular scheduled maintenance contracts. Originally established to oversee domestic contracts, the center now has overseas operating locations in Germany (NATO AWACS), Greece (J-79 engine overhaul), Hong Kong (C-130 corrosion control), Israel, Korea (F-4 maintenance and modification and F-15 corrosion control), Saudi Arabia, Spain (F-4 maintenance and modification), and the United Kingdom (F-111 overhaul and the European Repair Facility).

The Aerospace Guidance and Meteorology Center (AGMC) is responsible for maintenance of the inertial guidance and navigation systems for all USAF missiles and aircraft. It runs the Air Force Meteorology and Calibration Program and the Air Force Measurement Standards Laboratories (to establish and maintain a single integrated measurement system and certify standards used in Precision Measurement Equipment Laboratories).

The Air Force Acquisition Logistics Division (AFALD) of AFLC co-ordinates AFLC/AFSC operations, establishing quality control and continuity between R&D activities and maintenance of the resulting systems. Two activities are managed jointly by AFALD and AFSC's Aeronautical Systems Division: The Productivity, Reliability, Availability and Maintainability (PRAM) Program and the Avionics Control Office.

The US Air Force Museum is AFLC's most visible division, the oldest and largest military aviation museum in the world. Located at Wright-Patterson AFB, the Museum displays over 2000 missiles and aircraft spanning the entire history of the USAAS, USAAC, USAAF and USAF. Its collections also include historical artifacts and memorabilia relating to Air Force history. Collection components also circulate among 20 Air Force Base Museums around the country and other displays and nongovernmental museums in the US and abroad. The Museum had its roots in an informal display of World War I planes at McCook Field and gradually grew to its present 200 acres on the Wright Field portion of the Wright-Patterson AFB complex. The main Museum building (large enough to contain a B-36) was completed in 1971 and a major addition in 1976.

AIR FORCE LOGISTICS COMMAND BASES

Wright-Patterson AFB (AFLC Headquarters)
Location: Ten miles ENE of Dayton, Ohio
Area: 8174 acres
Altitude: 824ft
Personnel: 8000 Military
16,000 Civilian

One of the most important Air Force installations since the Signal Corps established its Aeronautical Division, the base became Wright-Patterson AFB on 13 January 1948 through the merger of Wright Field and Patterson Field. The two fields are named for Orville and Wilbur Wright, who did much of their early flying here, and Lt Frank Patterson, killed 19 June 1918 when his DH-4 crashed. The Base has always been home to numerous AFLC and AFSC activities, as well as the AFRES 906th Tactical Fighter Group and 78 other Defense Department and other governmental activities.

Hill AFB
Location: Ten miles south of Ogden, Utah
Area: 7000 acres
Altitude: 4788ft
Personnel: 5280 Military
14,319 Civilian

Activated in November 1940, the base is named for Major Ployer Hill, killed test flying the first B-17 on 30 October 1935. Home of AFLC's Ogden Air Logistics Center, Hill is the largest employer in the state of Utah. The base houses TAC's 388th Tactical

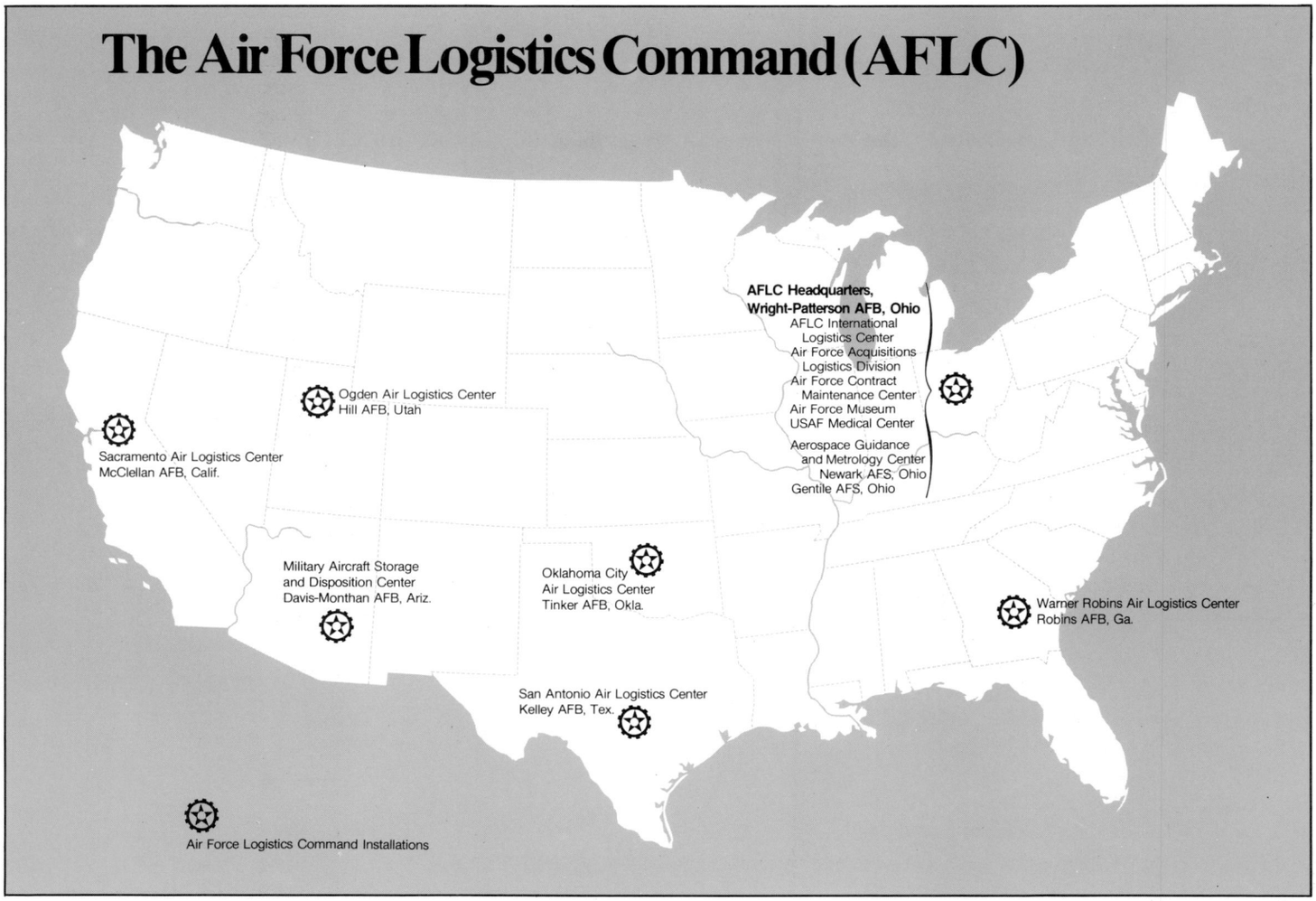

Fighter Wing, the AFRES 419th Tactical Fighter Group and AFSC's 6545th Test Group, which manages the Utah Test and Training Range; this area, with the Wendover Air Force Range, adds 961,896 acres to Hill's 7000 acres.

Kelly AFB
Location: Five miles SW of San Antonio, Texas
Area: 3992 acres
Altitude: 689ft
Personnel: 4837 Military
18,760 Civilian
Activated on 7 May 1917, the base is named for Lt George Kelly, who was the first Army pilot to die in a plane crash (10 May 1911). The site of AFLC's San Antonio Air Logistics Center, Kelly is also headquarters for the Electronic Security Command and the Centers of Electronic Warfare, Cryptologic Support and Joint Electronic Warfare. The base is also home to the AFRES 433d Tactical Airlift Wing and the Texas Air National Guard 149th Tactical Fighter Group. (*See photo, pages 4-5.*)

McClellan AFB
Location: Nine miles NE of Sacramento, California
Area: 2625 acres
Altitude: 76ft
Personnel: 3600 Military
14,400 Civilian
The base is named for Major Hezekiah McClellan, killed 25 May 1936, who pioneered many early Alaska Air routes during the 1930s. Activated in 1939, McClellan AFB is now home to the Sacramento Air Logistics Center, The Defense Logistics Agency, AFSC's 1155th Technical Operations Squadron, MAC's 41 Rescue and Weather Recon Wing, TAC's 431st Fighter Weapons Squadron, the Sacramento Coast Guard Station and the Headquarters of the AFRES Fourth Air Force.

Robins AFB
Location: 18 miles SSE of Macon, Georgia
Area: 8863 acres
Altitude: 294ft
Personnel: 3994 Military
15,332 Civilian
The base is named for Brig General Augustine Warner-Robins, an early Chief of the Air Corps Materiel Division who died 16 June 1940. It was activated in March 1942 and is the home of the Warner-Robins Air Logistics Center and headquarters for the Air Force Researve and SAC's 19th Bomb Wing.

Tinker AFB
Location: Eight miles SE of Oklahoma City
Area: 4277 acres
Altitude: 1291ft
Personnel: 6400 Military
17,600 Civilian
Activated in March 1941, the base was later renamed for Major General Clarence Tinker, a bomber pilot killed on 7 June 1942 in the Battle of Midway. The base is home to the Oklahoma City Air Logistics Center and is the largest single industrial employer in Oklahoma. The center provides logistics support for bombers and electronics aircraft like the E-3 Sentry AWACS. TAC's 552d Airborne Warning and Control squadron, sole operator of E-3 Sentry AWACS aircraft, operates here. The AFRES 507th Tactical Fighter Group is also based at Tinker.

COMMUNICATION AND ELECTRONIC WARFARE IN THE US AIR FORCE

C-CUBED

Flying Commands like TAC, PACAF, AAC, USAFE, SAC and MAC carry on the business of the US Air Force. They provide deterrence, intercept intruders, fight the battles and deliver the goods for the Army and Air Force. Commands like the AFSC, AFLC and ATC provide the men and machines that make it all possible. However, across the framework of the other commands stretch the two that tie them together: the Air Force Communications Command (AFCC) and the Electronic Security Command (ESC). This is done by Command Control and Communications (C^3 or C-Cubed), involving systems of unprecedented complexity and potential. Through satellite technology, it is now possible for units on opposite sides of the world to communicate as though they were a mile apart. By extrapolation it is possible for leaders to command and control widely separated forces anywhere in the world.

C^3 in the modern electronic Air Force has an even broader potential, involving both defensive and offensive possibilities: Intelligence (C^3 I), Electronic Countermeasures (C^3 CM) and Electronic Warfare (EW).

THE AIR FORCE COMMUNICATIONS COMMAND

The Air Force Communications Command (AFCC) provides all types of communications support services for the force. It resembles a seven-fingered communications glove, each finger covering the needs of a specific Major Command. AFCC's Strategic Communications Division covers the needs of SAC; the Tactical Communications Division covers TAC; the Airlift Communications Division covers MAC; the Space Communications Division covers SPACECOM; the European Communications Division covers USAFE; and the Pacific Communications Division covers PACAF. The seventh finger in the glove is the Continental Communications Division, which covers the other Major Commands and installations right up to USAF Headquarters at the Pentagon. AFCC is headquartered at Scott AFB and has permanent facilities at 130 bases; it also has a mobile force that can be deployed rapidly anywhere in the world.

AFCC's seven major Divisions each provide seven basic services: Base Communications (telephone and radio); Inter-Base Communications (radio, cable and satellite); Engineering and

Facing page: The official insignia of AFCC and ESC.

Left: An AFCC staff sergeant monitors a main radar unit and runs a system check for calibrating the unit, at Norton AFB in California.

Above: The Grumman EF-111 Raven electronic jamming systems aircraft is based on the General Dynamics F-111 (*see page 130*) but is a substantially different aircraft, specifically designed for electronic warfare. Two units are active with the Raven, one at Mountain Home AFB, and one at RAF Upper Heyford.

Below: The AFCC-managed radar antennae at AAC's Sparrevohn AFS on a windswept Alaska mountain top (*see page 120*).

Installation; Maintenance and Evaluation; Data Automation Systems (computer hardware and software); Air Traffic Control; and finally Combat Communications, which includes mobile C^3 and air-traffic control under emergency or wartime conditions.

Every time you land at an Air Force base or pick up one of their 650,000 telephones around the world, you are in the hands of the AFCC. The Interbase Communications systems include the Automatic Voice Network (AUTOVON), the Automatic Secure Voice Communications Network (AUTOSEVOCOM) and the Automatic Digital Network (AUTODIN). These are all part of the Defense Communications system, half of it leased from commercial firms and half (including the overseas part) USAF-owned and -operated.

AFCC's Air Traffic Control System is the largest military system outside the Soviet Union. AFCC controllers are in communication with their aircraft from AFB towers around the world 35,600 times a day, every day. When civilian air traffic controllers walked off their jobs in the summer of 1981, AFCC controllers were loaned to the Federal Aviation Administration (FAA) on an emergency basis and were on duty in commercial towers around the country in a matter of hours. The AFCC controllers fit in well at the 65 civilian airports to which they were assigned; despite the fact that AFBs are generally less busy than commericial airports, the traffic is not as strictly scheduled and the controllers have to be on their toes for all types of aircraft making all types of approaches. It is not uncommon at an Air Force Base for several aircraft to take off simultaneously from the same runway, a rare phenomenon at civilian airports. Air Force controllers also have the flexibility of experience on a number of different bases.

THE ELECTRONIC SECURITY COMMAND

The Electronic Security Command (ESC), headquartered at Kelly AFB near San Antonio, is the USAF's electronic warfare command. A Major Command in its present form since August 1979, ESC's forerunner was the US Air Force Security Service (USAFSS) formed in October 1948, which began with 11 officers and five enlisted men (compared to 12,000 personnel today). USAFSS worked in cryptology, a function performed for the USAAF by the Army Security Agency. It began with three former Army mobile radio squadrons: by the late 1950s it had 30% more personnel than today's ESC and a number of bases from Misawa in Japan to San Vito AS in Italy

The Commanders of the Air Force Communications Command
(Air Force Communications Service until 15 Nov 1979)

Maj Gen Harold Grant	1 July 1961–15 Feb 1962
Maj Gen Kenneth Bergquist	16 Feb 1962–30 June 1965
Maj Gen J Francis Taylor, Jr	1 July 1965–31 Oct 1965
Maj Gen Richard Klocko	1 Nov 1965–2 July 1967
Maj Gen Robert Paulson	15 July 1967–1 Aug 1969
Maj Gen Paul Stoney	1 Aug 1969–31 Oct 1973
Maj Gen Donald Werbeck	1 Nov 1973–24 Aug 1975
Maj Gen Rupert Burris	25 Aug 1975–31 Oct 1977
Maj Gen Robert Sadler	1 Nov 1977–1 July 1979
Maj Gen Robert Herres	1 July 1979–27 July 1981
Maj Gen Robert McCarthy	27 July 1981–

and Karamursel in Turkey. In October 1978, after 20 years with bases of its own, the last were turned over to the Theater Commands. The following year USAFSS was deactivated and ESC formed.

Today's ESC must develop an offensive capability in Electronic Countermeasures to jam, confuse or destroy the enemy's C^3 (C^3 Countermeasures or C^3CM), and prevent him from activating them. Like AFCC, ESC has divisions that operate with USAF combat Commands. Electronic Security, Strategic works with SAC; Electronic Security, Tactical works with TAC; Electronic Security, Alaska works with AAC; Electronic Security, Pacific works with PACAF and Electronic Security Europe works with USAFE. In addition to these divisions, the Air Force Electronic Warfare Center (AFEWC) and the Air Force Cryptologic Support Center (AFESC) at San Antonio, ESC Headquarters, report directly to ESC.

Since 1981 realistic Electronic Warfare (EW) training has been provided through the *Green Flag* exercises, sometimes held in conjunction with TAC's *Red Flag* exercises at Nellis AFB. Complex computer models test both the hardware and tactics of Electronic Warfare, whose origins lie in the Southeast Asian War when EB-66s were used to provide Electronic Countermeasures (ECM) support for *Rolling Thunder* bombing missions over North Vietnam. The Wild Weasel F-100s and F-105s used early antiradar missiles to attack enemy radar and SAM sites.

Today the primary Air Force EW/ECM tactical jamming aircraft is the Grumman EF-111A, based on the General Dynamics F-111 tactical fighter. The EF-111 is designed for both close-in and stand-off jamming operations and for escorting attack aircraft penetrating enemy airspace, as the EB-66 did over Vietnam. Its equipment includes the internally mounted ALQ-99 primary jammer, ALQ-137/ALR-62 self-protection systems and provision for carrying the new ALQ-131 externally. Augmenting the 42 EF-111s are the EC-130H *Compass Call* aircraft designed to perform stand-off jamming, disrupting enemy C^3 over large areas of the battlefront.

Compared to their Vietnam-era predecessors, today's Wild Weasels – F-4Gs – fly with more sophisticated electronics, and far more advanced weapons, including the AGM-88 High-speed Anti-Radiation Missile (HARM) and the AGM-122 Sidearm, a short-range anti-radiation Sidewinder. USAF combat aircraft are also equipped with external Electronic Countermeasures (ECM) pods that jam enemy radar used to locate aircraft and target them for attack, in effect turning any combat aircraft into a mini-EW. The old ALQ-101 pod is now giving way to the newer ALQ-119 (which can equip most aircraft) and the state-of-the-art Westinghouse ALQ-131. The ALQ-119 is the workhorse of

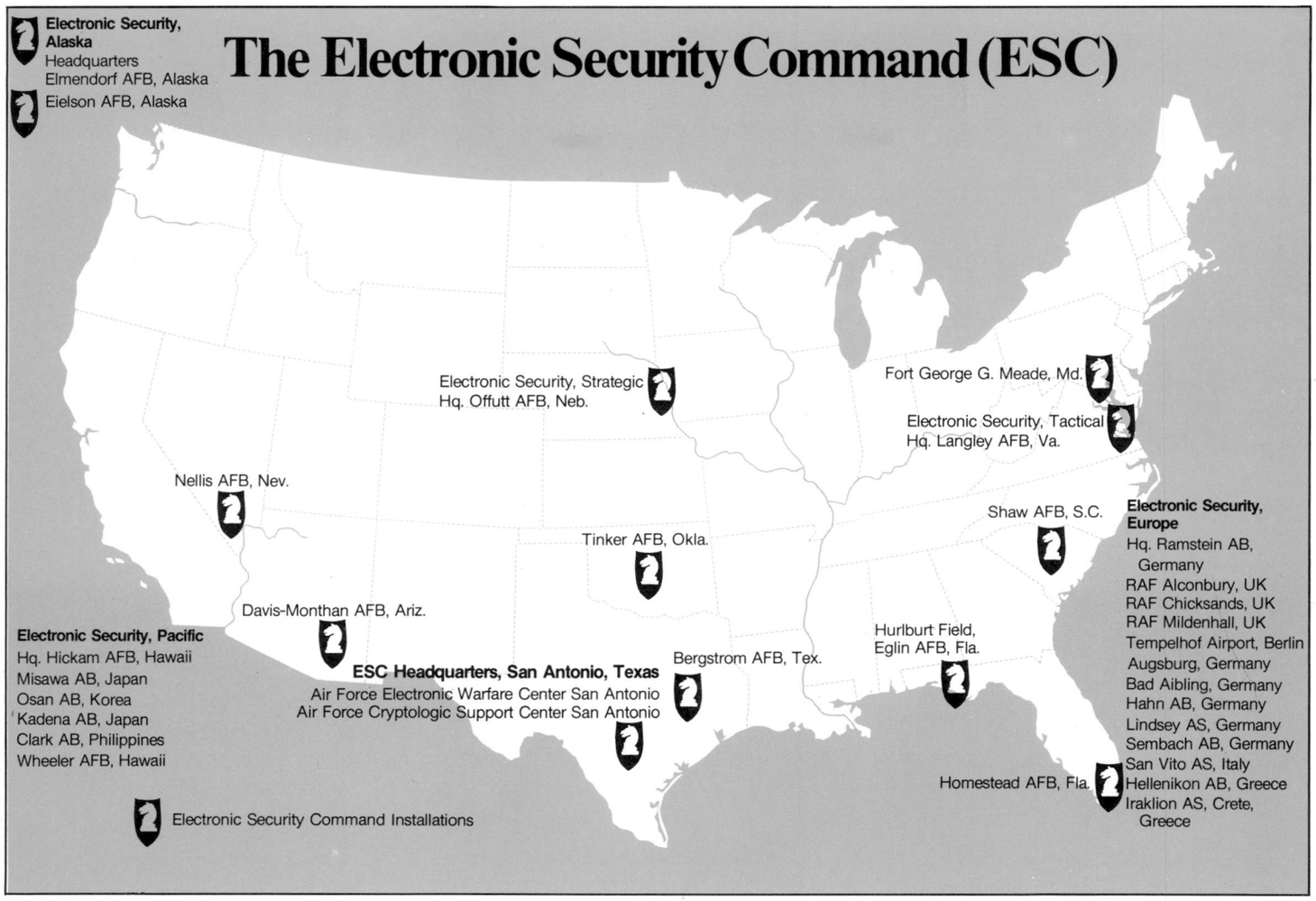

Air Force tactical jamming pods, equipping A-7s, A-10s, F-4s, F-111s and F-16s worldwide. Raytheon is currently under contract from the Warner Robins Air Logistics Center to upgrade the ALQ-119 pod under the program code-named *Seek Ice*. The ALQ-131 is a significant improvement over earlier EW jamming pods: it can be programmed on the flight line and contains on-board computer control of self-test and system control. It also provides for computer-aided maintenance and programming. Offensive jamming systems – Airborne Self-Protection jammers (ASPJ) like the ALQ-94/137 in the F-111 and FB-111, the ALQ-135 in the F-15 and the ALQ-165 in the F-16 – are being updated.

In addition to manned airborne systems, ESC also has both remotely piloted EW drone aircraft and ground-based systems. All these and others even more sophisticated are being developed because Electronic Warfare and C^3CM will be an integral part of any future war. Major General Doyle Larson, ESC's first commander, developed what he called the ten commandments or fundamental principles of C^3CM:

1. Modern military forces depend on electronic devices for command control and communications, C^3.
2. Electronic devices are susceptible to jamming, deception, destruction and exploitation.
3. The principles of surprise, mass and concentration of force apply to C^3CM.
4. A balance of lethal and disruptive options is required to conduct C^3CM effectively.
5. Execution of C^3CM is time-sensitive – seconds count. Sensor data for planning must be available in hours; sensor data for execution must be available in seconds.
6. Overall battle objectives dictate specific C^3CM targets and operations.
7. Communications between C^3CM elements must be jam-resistant and secure.
8. Good defensive C^3CM measures are essential for successful offensive C^3CM.
9. Intelligence analysts can provide essential quality control for deception activities.
10. Once channels of command and control are cut, military forces of modern warfare go into a state of disarray and confusion.

In General Larson's portrait of the battlefield of the future, events move with startling speed and destructive force is harnessed by an intricate web of C^3, which the opposing force will try to disrupt. In this scenario, disruption of the enemy's C^3 could spell his defeat.

The Commanders of the Electronic Security Command
(Air Force Security Service until 1 August 1979)

Col Roy Lynn	26 Oct 1948–5 July 1949
Col Travis Hetherington	6 July 1949–21 Feb 1951
Maj Gen Roy Lynn	22 Feb 1951–13 Feb 1953
Maj Gen Harold Bassett	14 Feb 1953–3 Jan 1957
Maj Gen Gordon Blake	4 Jan 1957–5 Aug 1959
Maj Gen John Ackerman	6 Aug 1959–20 Sept 1959
Maj Gen Millard Lewis	21 Sept 1959–31 Aug 1962
Maj Gen Richard Klocko	1 Sept 1962–15 Oct 1965
Maj Gen Louis Coira	16 Oct 1965–18 July 1969
Maj Gen Carl Stapleton	19 July 1969–23 Feb 1973
Maj Gen Walter Galligan	24 Feb 1973–16 May 1974
Maj Gen Howard Smith	17 May 1974–31 July 1975
Maj Gen K D Burns	1 Aug 1975–18 Jan 1979
Maj Gen Doyle Larson	19 Jan 1979–

THE US AIR FORCE IN SPACE

THE SPACE COMMAND

Space left the realm of science fiction and became mankind's final frontier when the first manmade object, Russia's *Sputnik I*, went into orbit in 1957. This resulted in the 'space race' that culminated twelve years later in the American achievement of a man on the moon. In those years the military potential of space took a back seat to scientific exploration. Since the early 1970s, space has lost much of its 'frontier' quality. Thousands of satellites have been placed into orbit, men have reached the moon and spacecraft have been to other planets. Space had become a 'place,' like air, land or sea. With this perception came the Soviet military space program and over 20 tests of Soviet antisatellite (ASAT) weapons between 1968 and 1982 – ammunition for US Air Force lobbyists who favoured a separate Major Command to control space activities. Many now saw space as a potential theater.

Against this background, the US Air Force Space Command (SPACECOM) came into being on 1 September 1982, taking as its headquarters Peterson AFB in Colorado, which had served in that role for the Aerospace Defense Command (ADC) until it became part of TAC in 1979. In the interim, SAC had taken over many ADC strategic assets, including Peterson AFB, Clear AFS in Alaska and Thule and Sondrestrom ABs in Greenland; these it passed on to SPACECOM. TAC Aerospace Defense Center Commander General James Hartinger was redesignated SPACECOM's first Commander.

Peterson AFB comprises 1176 acres at an altitude of 6200 feet in the Colorado Rockies, seven miles east of Colorado Springs. It was activated as a USAAF Field in 1942 and named for Lt Edward Peterson, killed in a crash here on 8 August 1942. The centerpiece of Peterson AFB is the Cheyenne Mountain Complex, the control center and headquarters of SPACECOM (and formerly ADC) as well as the North American Air Defense Command (NORAD). In the late 1950s the joint US-Canada NORAD Command agreed on the need for an impregnable underground command center that could be protected from enemy nuclear attack. Cheyenne Mountain was selected, and crews started drilling in 1961. Five years later ADC and NORAD moved into their new Center, buried 1700 feet within the solid granite of the mountain. Originally designed to track bombers, the Cheyenne Mountain Complex today still houses the Aerospace Defense Center, to which has been added SPACECOM's Space Defense Operations Center (SPADOC). SPADOC not only tracks satellites and spacecraft, but serves as a space-intelligence clearing house and space-operations command post as well. The new Consolidated Space Operations Center (CSOC) is located nine miles away, outside the mountain. From the CSOC, SPACECOM will control operational spacecraft and also plan, manage and control all Defense Department Space Shuttle flights.

Peterson AFB is not only the SPACECOM nerve center but headquarters for the 1st Space Wing, which controls SPACECOM's far-flung network of ground-based sensors and surveil-

Above: **The official SPACECOM insignia, adopted in 1982.**

Right: **The military applications Space Shuttle System will be an important part of SPACECOM operations in the years to come.**

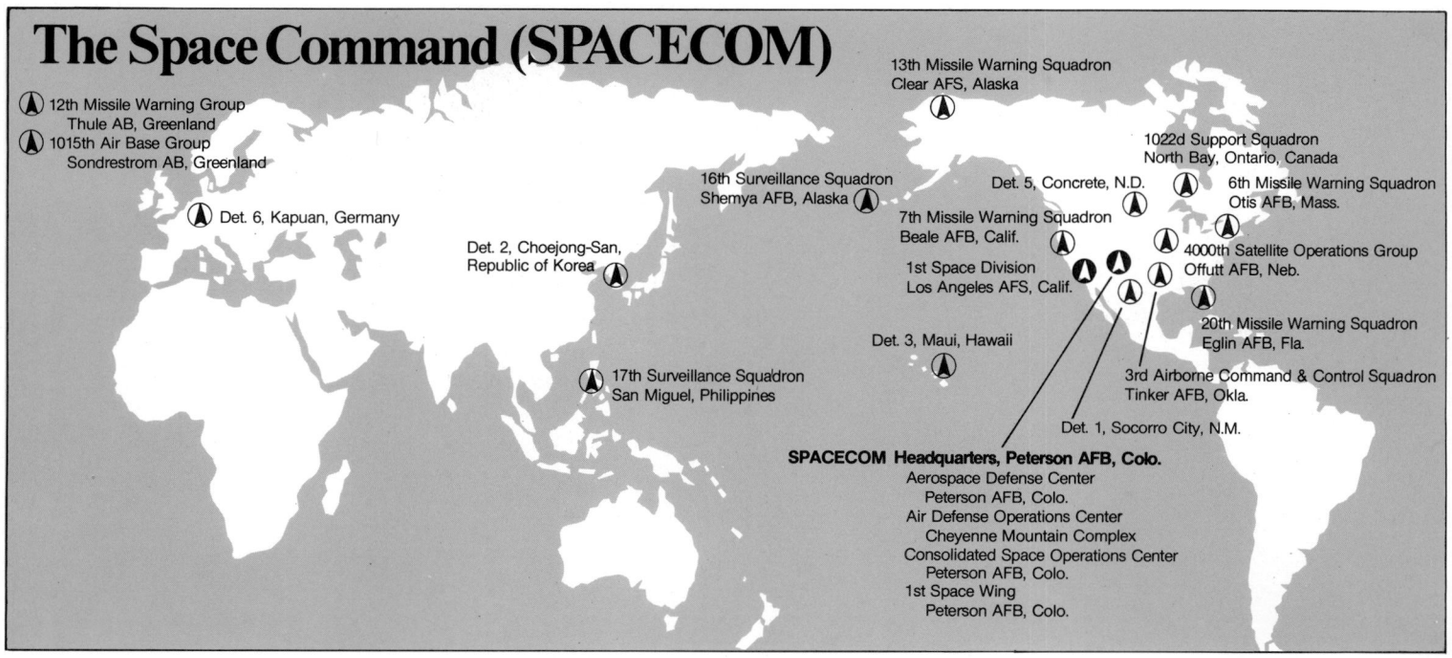

Above: **The global scope of the Space Command's operations.**

Left: **The entrance to Cheyenne Mountain, the vital NORAD/SPACECOM operations center.**

lance and tracking stations. These include Surveillance Squadrons at Shemya AFB and San Miguel in the Philippines; Missile Warning Squadrons at Beale AFB, Clear AFS, Eglin AFB and Otis AFB and Detachments in New Mexico, North Dakota and Germany. Other First Space Wing units are based at the SPACECOM bases in Greenland and at SAC headquarters. SPACECOM's new Ground-based *Electro-Optical* Deep Space Surveillance System (GEODSS) has sites in New Mexico, Korea and Hawaii plus two future sites, all of which will replace the older Baker-Nunn Deep Space *Camera* System still functioning at Edwards AFB, Mt John, New Zealand, and the USAFE's San Vito AS in Italy. SPACECOM also shares the First Space Division at Los Angeles AFS with AFSC; its Commander is SPACECOM's Vice-Commander. The First Space Division's role is development of space hardware for future SPACECOM use.

SPACECOM's evolution was inevitable, given the level of Soviet activity in space and the growing need to protect Air Force communications and reconnaissance satellites. Its mission will include:

1. Acting as a catalyst for the development of promising space technologies.
2. Developing space doctrine and strategy.
3. Managing the Military Space Shuttle Program.
4. Strengthening the weakest link in space systems development, 'the statement of operational needs.'
5. Promoting and overseeing space education, training and career development.
6. Acting as an advocate of the Air Force's Space Medicine Program.
7. Advocating a sound survivability program.
8. Providing comprehensive documentation of the Soviet space threat.
9. Incorporating space activities into USAF and joint military readiness exercises.

The mission of this newest command is far-reaching: its potential equals that of the one-time USAAF within the US Army. It is possible that SPACECOM will one day form the basis for a separate military service.

MAJOR USAF SATELLITE SYSTEMS

The Defense Satellite Communications System (DSCS, pronounced 'discus') had its origin in the late sixties as a voice, imagery, digital data and teletype communications system serving the entire Defense Department: 26 DSCS I satellites (with 18-month lifespans) were launched, and at least one was still functioning in the early 1980s. By that time, DSCS II was operational. Weighing half a ton, the six DSCS IIs are more than ten times the size of DSCS I. They offer orbit repositioning and allow concentration on small areas, permitting use of small portable ground stations.

Above: Inside the Cheyenne Mountain control room.

Above right: An artist's conception of one of the NAVSTAR Global Positioning System satellites.

The first of a dozen DSCS IIIs became operational the same year that SPACECOM was formed. DSCS III is a far more flexible system with a ten-year lifespan, Like DSCS II, it can communicate with small portable ground stations. DSCS III is resistant to Electro-Magnetic Pulse (EMP) and is designed to carry the nuclear 'go-code' to American nuclear forces.

The Air Force Satellite Communications System (AFSATCOM) is a complex array of communications systems 'piggy-backed' on systems like the Navy's five Fleet Satellite Communications System (FLTSATCOM) satellites designed by AFSC's Space Division. The FLTSATCOM satellites have a five-year lifespan and operate from 22,250-nautical-mile-high geosynchronous equatorial orbits. Each has 23 communications channels, 10 for Navy C^3, 12 for Air Force C^3 (AFSATCOM) and one reserved for the President in time of emergency. The AFSATCOM system also has its equipment aboard the Satellite Data System (SDS) satellites in polar orbit (two orbits every 24 hours).

The Air Force also operates a network of reconnaissance satellites, the best known of which are the 14-ton **Big Bird** satellites deployed since the early 1970s. With a lifespan of half a year, the *Big Bird* can remain on station six times longer than its Russian equivalents. *Big Bird* automatically photographs its targets and either returns television pictures or drops film packs for recovery and processing. More advanced reconnaissance satellites are the **KH-11 series**, first deployed in 1978, with a two-year lifespan and far more sensitive equipment. The KH-11s carry powerful cameras and infrared sensors and are equipped to return their information in digital form. The infrared system of the KH-11 reportedly allows it to 'photograph' events that have taken place in the recent past via extremely sensitive sensors that detect minute amounts of residual heat.

The NAVSTAR Global Positioning System (GPS) is an extremely accurate ground/satellite-based navigational system, providing positioning data in any weather to an accuracy of 52 feet in three dimensions (longitude, latitude, and altitude). This means that an F-15 pilot using NAVSTAR can find his position anywhere in the world with a margin of error less than the length of his own plane. NAVSTAR can also provide velocity data to a precision of within four inches per second. NAVSTAR satellites weigh about half a ton, with solar arrays spreading to a span of 17 feet 6 inches. The total system, which will be on-line by the end of the decade, will comprise a set of 18 satellites in subsynchronous orbits, 10,900 nautical miles above the earth and positioned to provide global navigational support to the air, land and sea forces of the US, 10 NATO nations, and selected 'properly equipped' civilian users. Master control for the GPS will be provided by SPACECOM's Consolidated Space Operations Center.

ANTISATELLITE WEAPONS

The first practical demonstration of antisatellite capability came in 1962 during a joint USAF/Atomic Energy Commission operation code-named *Starfish*. This was an experimental high-altitude nuclear explosion that accidentally knocked out a number of satellites, not by blast concussion, but by Electro-Magnetic Pulse (EMP), which can permanently effect all types of electronics and communications equipment. There had already been some apprehension about the possibility of the Soviets putting nuclear weapons into space, so in 1963 President Kennedy ordered that an antisatellite (ASAT) weapons system be developed using the EMP technology that had accidently been discovered. The US Army and Air Force began tests the following year. The Air Force set up an experimental ASAT facility on Johnson Island in the Pacific under ADC control, code-named *Squanto Terror*. In 1967 the Outer Space Treaty prohibiting space deployment of nuclear weapons was signed by the US and the Soviet Union: in 1968 the successful tests were cancelled.

Ironically, even as the *Squanto Terror* site was closing down, the Soviet Union began work on its own ASAT program, which became operational twelve years later (1980). This capability prompted the US to move toward development of an American ASAT.

Squanto Terror was a ground-based missile system, very accurate but limited to targets within range of Johnson Island.

Above: An artist's conception of one element of the Defense Satellite Communications System, Phase II (DSCS II) in earth orbit.

Right: The Boeing Space Operations Center (SOC) is one concept for an earth orbit space station that would give both SPACECOM and NASA a permanent manned presence in space by the end of the century.

Below: DSCS III, which is resistant to Electro-Magnetic Pulse, will provide secure first-line defense communications into the early 1990s.

JOHN OLSON 81

The Russian ASAT is a satellite itself, a 'killer satellite' launched by an SS-9 missile that can be placed into proximate orbit (about five miles) with an American satellite. Thereupon it would explode like a huge hand grenade, showering the American satellite with a hail of shrapnel and destroying its delicate systems. The limitations of this system are that it does not orbit above 1200 miles and has a narrow spectrum of inclination angles at which it can operate. This puts many important American satellite systems safely out of its range.

The new SPACECOM ASAT, on the other hand, is a much more versatile weapon. It is a two-stage Air-Launched Miniature Vehicle (ALMV) with a modified SRAM first stage, a Thiokol Altair III 6000-lb-thrust, solid-propellant second stage and a nonnuclear warhead. Produced by the Vought Corporation, the ALMV can be mounted under the fuselage of an F-15. The fighter carries the ALMV to high altitude and fires it into space, where infrared target trackers and a laser gyroscope help it locate its prey. The ALMV is more than a dozen times faster than a rifle bullet and more than 20% faster than the fastest satellite. The F-15 can get the ASAT into any position. Its speed then allows it to overtake and destroy any satellite, notably the Russian ocean reconnaissance satellites that keep tabs on the US Fleet, targeting them for possible attack. The first F-15 units to become operational with the ALMV are based at TAC/Air Defense Headquarters at Langley AFB and at McChord AFB in Washington State.

THE HIGH FRONTIER

On the night of 23 March 1983, President Ronald Reagan outlined a proposal to deal with the prevention of nuclear war. It came in the form of a challenge to those who form the backbone of American research and development – a challenge that, if met, would make the nation secure from nuclear attack.

'Let me share with you' said the President, 'a vision of the future that offers hope. It is that we embark on a program to counter the awesome Soviet missile threat with measures that are defensive. What if free people could live secure in the knowledge that their security did not rest upon the threat of instant US retaliation (the concept of Mutual Assured Destruction or MAD) to deter a Soviet attack, that we could intercept and destroy strategic ballistic missiles before they reached our own soil or that of our allies? I know that this is a formidable technical task, one that may not be accomplished before the end of this century. Yet current technology has attained a level of sophistication where it is reasonable for us to begin this effort.'

The technology of which the President spoke includes space-based particle-beam and laser weapons that could be used to destroy incoming Soviet ICBMs. The challenge that he issued was committed to AFSC (to develop the technology) and to SPACECOM (to deploy it).

Public reaction to the President's message, called the 'Star Wars' speech after the popular movie, was mixed. Those who had earlier promoted the technology of which he spoke, like General Daniel Graham of the Heritage Foundation's *High Frontier* Project, and those who feared a new cycle in the arms race, decried it. Hugh Sidey in *Time* Magazine compared Reagan to earlier Presidents with faith in an untried technology: Abraham Lincoln with the transcontinental railroads, Theodore Roosevelt with the Panama Canal, Franklin Roosevelt with conservation and later the atomic bomb, and John Kennedy with a manned lunar landing. Each had staunch opponents to 'prove' his vision was unworkable, yet each set in motion the events that would achieve it.

To develop an effective defense system using laser and particle-beam weapons is indeed a challenge, but the Soviet propensity to pursue the same technology made it essential to try. The Air Force had already experimented with airborne laser weapons in the form of the Kirtland AFB-based NKC-135 Airborne Laser Laboratory (ALL). Air Force ground-based lasers had been used to shoot down pilotless aircraft as early as 1973, and Congress had appropriated money in 1981 to the Defense Advanced Research Projects Agency (DARPA) to conduct space-laser research.

One of the overwhelming advantages of the use of either lasers or particle beams against ICBMs is their speed. An ICBM travels at many times the speed of sound, faster than rifle bullets or any aircraft. Lasers and particle beams can travel at the speed of light, 186,000 miles per second – over 1500 times the speed of an ICBM. Thus they can be fired at a missile thousands of miles away and hit it before it has gone more than a few feet.

As the President spoke, the only system approaching operational capability was the traditional **chemical laser**. These lasers (which, simply put, use chemical reactions to generate the laser beam) had been used in the earlier Air Force as well as DARPA/US Navy tests. The tests had been marginally successful, but the chemical laser system requires a large amount of fuel and an elaborate array of delicate optics that would be expensive and complicated to lift into space. While science has proven that these systems can be miniaturized, the technology seems to be moving away from chemical lasers toward the idea of a **nuclear-pumped X-ray laser** system that would be far more compact. The nuclear-pumped laser would also be more effective because it would focus a more concentrated beam on the target.

The latter is attractive: for a laser beam to destroy its target, it must strike it long enough to burn a hole in it. A more concentrated beam would require a shorter 'dwell time.' When the early tests were conducted, those that failed were often attributable to a phenomenon called 'jitter' whereby the beam did not focus for any length of time on any part of the target. To understand what went wrong, simply recall experiments that you might have conducted yourself on a sunny day with a magnifying glass and a piece of paper. By focusing the sunlight on the paper, you created a light beam (laser) that in turn focused a tiny bright spot of light and heat on the paper. If you kept the paper still, the concentrated light would start a fire and burn a hole in the paper. If you created a jitter motion, moving the paper about, the light and heat would not be focused on any spot long enough to burn.

Experiments with nuclear-pumped X-ray lasers at the Lawrence Livermore Laboratory east of San Francisco have shown considerable promise. The Lawrence Livermore system, known as *Excalibur*, could not be deployed operationally as soon as a chemical laser, but in the long run it would be more practical as a space-based system.

As a ground-based system, however, the chemical laser may have good potential because the support equipment would not have to be portable. Two such ground-based systems under study include an outgrowth of the Massachusetts Institute of Technology (MIT) *Fire Pond* program that would use a precision-aimed deuterium flouride laser, and another system of inexpensive halide excimer lasers. The ground-based systems would use a series of space-based mirrors to direct their beams to the target.

A third type of beam weapon that shows more far-reaching potential is the **neutral particle beam** system, which bombards its target with sub-atomic particles and does not need to heat the surface. The Los Alamos Scientific Laboratory is currently de-

Above: **The first test of SPACECOM's F-15-mounted Anti-Satellite Weapon (ASAT) took place over the Western Space and Missile Range near Vandenberg AFB in January 1984.**

veloping a particle-beam weapons system under the code name *White Horse*. Between 10 and 40 proposed *White Horse* battle stations would each weigh about as much as a fully loaded F-15 and would be based in low Earth orbit. The weapon would use a highly focused beam of hydrogen particles and could operate against ICBMs in both the 'boost' and 'mid-course' phases of their trajectories. The nature of the particle beam is such that it would not be affected by any kind of 'hardening' the Soviets might do to their ICBMs to protect them from the heat effects of laser beams.

To define the trajectory phases requires examination of the operational tactics of space weaponry. When antiballistic missile systems were first conceived in the 1960s, the idea was for incoming ICBMs to be intercepted by antimissile missiles in their re-entry phase as they hurtled toward the United States. When the 'Star Wars' defense was promulgated in early 1983, beam weapons were to be assigned to intercept ICBMs at various points along their trajectory including the 're-entry' phase. The final phase could also be called the 'almost-too-late' phase, so tactical thinking turned to the other end of the trajectory. To attack the ICBM in its 'boost' phase (the five to eight minutes of flight) is to catch it at its most vulnerable. To attack the missile at the beginning of the trajectory, which is possible with nuclear-pumped lasers and particle beams, also opens the possibility of hitting the ICBM again in 'mid-course' should the first attack fail. By attacking the ICBMs in the boost phase, before their MIRVs are deployed, these tactics negate the Soviet advantage in multiple-warhead missiles. While the boost-phase intercept is the most difficult, it must be perfected if the beam weapon defense system is to achieve anything approaching 99.9% accuracy.

In 1983 the Defensive Technologies Study Team, headed by former NASA administrator James Fletcher, reported on the levels of priority to be given various aspects of a space-based defense program. Their priorities were based on such factors as how advanced the systems were, how necessary they were to the overall program and their research-and-development cost effectiveness. The first priority included nuclear-driven X-ray lasers, large space optics, aiming and targeting systems and atmospheric compensation for ground-based lasers. The second priority included neutral particle-beam weapons, chemical infrared lasers, free-electron lasers and newer unspecified concepts. The third priority included space demonstrations of the specific technologies outlined in the earlier priorities and scaling them to operational size.

The Fletcher Report recommended a six-year development program that would provide some form of operational capability for space weapons systems in the early 1990s. Half their proposed $15-billion budget for the six-year program would be devoted to development of surveillance, target acquisition and tracking. Over 40% of the program budget would be devoted to the weapons systems themselves, nuclear-pumped X-ray lasers getting the biggest share, followed in order by chemical infrared lasers, excimer lasers, free-electron lasers and finally, particle-beam weapons. Of the final 10% of the budget, most will go to C^3, battle management, 'lethality' and systems concepts.

The first testing of America's prototype 'battlestar' is possible in the 1986-87 time frame utilizing the Space Shuttle as the basic transportation system. In the long run, when the orbiting beam weapon battle stations become operational with SPACECOM in the last decade of the twentieth century, they have the potential of providing a final deterrent by making nuclear weapons and war obsolete.

INDEX

Please note: Profiles (histories, commanders, bases and assigned aircraft) of the Major Commands are listed on page 5; Separate Operating Agencies and Direct Reporting Units (including the Air Force Academy) are profiled in alphabetical order in the first chapter beginning on page 6. Reserve and Air National Guard forces are profiled on pages 198-201. Lists of Commanders and Chiefs of Staff of the US Army Air Service; US Army Air Corps; US Army Air Forces; and US Air Force, as well as Secretaries and Chief Master Sergeants of the Air Force, appear on page 8.

A-1 Skyraider, *64, 67*, 67, *70*, 76
A-3 Skywarrior, 161
A-7 Corsair, *145*, 145
A-10 Thunderbolt, 42, *123*, 142, *144*, 144, *146*
AGM-45 Shrike, 149
AGM-65 Maverick, *144*, 149
AGM-69 SRAM, 169
AGM-86 ALCM, 168, *169*
AGM-109 Tomahawk, 149
AGM-HARM, 149
AIM-4 Super Falcon, *129*, 146
AIM-7 Sparrow, 148
AIM-9 Sidewinder, *141, 143*, 148
AIM-120 AMRAAM, 149
AIR-2 Genie, 148
Agent Orange, 62
Albrook AFB, CZ 104
Altus AFB, Okla, 184
Allen, James, 19, 20, *21*, 21
Allen, Gen Lew, Jr, 223
Anacostia Naval Air Station (NAS) D.C., 9
Andersen AFB Guam, *86, 87*, 100, 152, 153, 163
Anderson, Capt Ronald, 74
Andrews AFB Md, 9, 184
Armistead, Gen W K, 18
Arnold AFB Tenn, 205, 206, *207*
Arnold, Gen Henry H, 8, *28*, 30, 31, 38, *39*, 39, *40*, 41, *42*, 42, 43, 174, 175, 192, 203
Attack Aircraft (list), 130, 131

B-1, *164*, 165, 168
B-17 Flying Fortress, *31, 34*, 42
B-25 Mitchell, *29*
B-26 Marauder, *28, 53, 60*, 61, 63, 65
B-29 Superfortress, 31, 38, *39*, 42, *43*, 44, *48*, 48, 51, 117, 157
B-35 Flying Wing, 158
B-36 Peacemaker, 157, *157*, 158, 160
B-47 Stratojet, 42, *158, 159*, 159, 160
B-45 Tornado, *158*, 159, *159*
B-49 Flying Wing, *158*, 158, *159*
B-52 Stratofortress, *86, 87*, 101, *161*, 163, *166, 168*
B-57 Canberra, *65*, 68, *69*, 72, 160, *160*
B-58 Hustler, *161*, 161
B-66 Destroyer, *160*, 160, 161
Baily, Lt Col Griff, *97*
Band, Air Force *16*, 16, *17*, 17
Barksdale AFB La, 152, 153
Beale AFB Calif, *151*, 153, *166, 171*, 216
Belenko, Viktor, 119, 206
Berkstrom AFB Tex, 108
Berlin Airlift, 176-77, 181, 182
Blanchard, Jean Pierre, 18
Blue Book, 57
Blytheville AFB Ark, 154
Bolling AFB, DC, 9, *15*, 15, 16, 184, 206
Bolo, 84, 85, 96
Bombers (list), 162
Brereton, Maj Gen Lewis, 28
Brooks AFB Tex, 14, 193, 206, 207
Brown, Gen George Scratchley, 8, 57
Brown, Harold, 8, *81*
Brown, Lt Russell, 50
Burgess, H, 22
Bush, Vannevar, 44

C-5 Galaxy, 182, 186, *186*, 188, 189
C-9 Nightingale, 189, *190*
C-46 Commando, 176
C-47 Skytrain, *16*, 39, 61, 63, *90*, 92, 93, 176, 177, *178*
C-54, *175*, 177, *178, 179*
C-97 Stratofreighters, 55, 177, *179*
C-119 Flying Boxcar, *55, 178*, 181
C-123, *59, 60*, 62, 63, *67, 70*
C-124 Globemaster, 177, *178, 180*, 181
C-130 Hercules, *83*, 93, 130, 182, 186, *186, 188*, 188, *198*
C-141 Starlifter, *175*, 181, *182*, 182, *186*, 186, 188, *191*
Cannon AFB N Mex, 108
Carswell AFB Tex, 154, 161
Castle AFB Calif, 154, *161*
Chandler, Capt Charles, 22
Chanute AFB Ill, 196
Charleston AFB S C, 184, 190
Chennault, Brig Gen Claire, *28*, 28, 30
Clark AB Philippines, 26, 61, 63, 67, 69, 101, 109, 119, 182, 189
Clark, Capt Arthur, 74
Clay, Gen Lucius Jr, 104, 117
Columbus AFB Miss, 196
Cooney, Lt Col James, 98
Craig, Capt James, 88

Davis-Monthan AFB Ariz, *43*, 108, 161, 208
DeBellevue, Capt Chuck, *97*, 98, 99, 100
de Havilland DH-4, 23
DEW Line Stations, 121
Dixon, Gen Robert, 105
Doolittle, James, 25
Dover AFB Del, 185
Dyess AFB Tex, 154

E-3 Sentry, *145*, 145
EF-111 Raven, 210, *211*, 211
Eaves, Capt Stephen, 98
Edwards AFB Calif, 15, *133, 160, 164, 204*, 205, 206
Eglin AFB Fla, 15, 58, 205, 207, 216
Eielson AFB Alaska, 122, *123*, 193, *194*
Eisenhower, Gen Dwight D, 10, 12, 33, 36, 37, 61
Ellsworth AFB S Dak, 154
Elmendorf AFB Alaska, 120, *121*, 122, *124, 126*
England AFB La, 108

F-4 Phantom, 73, *74*, 75, 83, *84*, 85, 88, *96*, 96, *97, 98*, 99, *99*, 101, *137*, 137, *138*
F-5 Tiger, 92, 105, 106, 136, *137*, 140
F-8, 68
F-15 Eagle, 140, *141, 146*, 149
F-16 Fighting Falcon, *141*, 141, 142, *142, 143*
F-47 Thunderbolt, *44*
F-51, 44, *47*, 50, 51
F-80, 44, 46, *49, 50*, 50, 51, *53*, 55, 126
F-82 Twin Mustang, *50*, 51
F-84 Thunderstreak, *44*, 44, *51*, 51, 55, *126*, 126, 127, 160, *178, 200*
F-86 Sabre Jet, 44, *47, 50*, 50, 51, 52, *54*, 55, 126, *126*, 127, 128, 132, *148*, 159, *200*
F-89 Scorpion, *124, 126*, 126, 128, *129*, 129
F-94 Starfire, *50*, 128, *128*
F-100 Super Sabre, 68, 72, *79*, 101, 132, *132*, 133
F-101 Voodoo, *132*, 133
F-102 Delta Dagger, *62, 132, 134*, 134
F-104 Starfighter, *132, 133, 134*, 134, *135*
F-105 Thunderchief, 68, 72, *73, 77*, 85, *87*, 101, *132, 134*, 134
F-106 Delta Dart, 134, *135, 198*
F-110 Phantom, 124, *137*
F-111 Aardvark, *124*, 136, *137*, 137, *164*, 164
Fairchild AFB Wash, 155
Farm Gate, 61, 62, 63, 65, 79
Feinstein, Capt Jeffrey, *97*, 98, *98*, 100
Felt, Adm Harry, 62
Fighters (list), 130, 131
Fisher, Maj Bernard, 76
Fletcher, James, 221
Forrestal, James, 38, 39, 176
Foulois, Lt Benjamin, 8, *22*, 23, 25, 26
Frye, Lt Col Wayne, 98

GBU-15, 149
Gabreski, Col Francis, *54*
Gabriel, Col Arnald, *16*
Gabriel, Gen Charles A, 8, 22, 117, 223

Evolution of the US National Insignia

1906-1916

Used with and without white background circle. In use at the time of the Mexican Border Campaign.

1918-1920

The official American insignia during World War I. It began to be phased out in 1919.

1917, 1921-1941

Introduced prior to the American entry into World War I and officially readopted after the war.

1942-1943

The red center of the 1921-1941 insignia was removed unofficially in December 1941 and officially in May 1942 to avoid confusion with Japanese insignia.

1942-1943

Some aircraft in the European and Mediterranean theaters unofficially incorporated a yellow surround in the British style.

1943

Between 29 June and 14 August, the official national insignia incorporated white sidebars and an overall red surround.

1943-1947

The red surround of the official insignia was quickly changed to a *blue* surround. During its four years of use, this insignia appeared on more aircraft than all its predecessors combined.

1947-Present

With the reorganization of the Defense Department and the creation of the USAF, red bars were added to the official national insignia. A variation of this insignia appears officially without the blue surround on F-15 aircraft.

Low Visibility

Beginning in the late seventies low visibility markings have been introduced officially and unofficially on the aircraft of the USAF and other services. The grey insignia on the far left is the only insignia used on operational F-16s. It is followed by a more standard low visibility mark, used on A-10s and other aircraft. The stencil marks are becoming increasingly common on MAC, AFRES and Air National Guard aircraft.

George AFB Calif, 108
Gilmore, Maj Paul, 83
Goodfellow AFB Tex, 196
Grand Forks AFB N Dak, 155
Greely, Gen Adolphus, 21
Griffis AFB NY, 155, *168*, 205
Gunter AFS, Ala, 196
Hancock, AB NY, 109
Hanscom AFB Mass, 205, 207
Hangrove, Lt William, 99
Harkins, Gen Paul, 62, 67
Harris, Arthur (RAF), 36, 37
Harris, Gen Hunter, 73
Hartinger, Gen James, 104, 214
Hickam AFB Hawaii, 117, 118, *119, 179, 200*
Hill AFB Utah, *169*, 207, 208
Hodgdon, Lt Leigh, 95
Holcombe, Capt Ken, 74
Holloman AFB N Mex, *102, 106*, 109, 141
Hollomon, Col George, 109
Homestead AFB Fla, 109, 193
Howard AFB C Z, 104, *106*, 109, 189
Hurlburt Field, Eglin AFB Fla, 109, 189

Indian Springs AF Auxiliary Field Nev, 112
Ivy, William, 21

Johnson, Lyndon, 12, 63, 65, 68, 69, 78, 88
Jones, Gen David C, 8, 57, 117
Jones, Capt Ralph, *94*

KC-10 Extender, 166, *166*, 201
KC-135 Stratotanker, 166, *166*
KH-11 series, 217
Kadena AB Okinawa, 62, *119*, 119, 141, 163
Karman, Theodore von, 42, 203
Keesler AFB, Miss, 196
Kelly AFB Tex, 13, 207, 209, 211
Kenly, Gen William, 8, *22*, 24
Kenney, Gen George, *36*, 37, 117
King Salmon Airport Alaska, 120, 121
Kirtland AFB N Mex, 12, 15, 185, 205, 206
Kittinger, Lt Col Joseph, 96
Knerr, Gen Hugh, *32*
Kuster, Maj Ralph, *99*
Kuter, Gen Laurence, 39, *40*, 117, 176, 183

LGM-25 Titan, 169, 173
LGM-30 Minuteman, 169, 173
Lackland AFB Tex, 193, 194, 197, 206
Ladd AFB Alaska, 120, 122
Langley Field Va, 26, 104, 108, *108*, 141, 220
Langley, Samuel Pierpont, 21, 108
Larson, Maj Gen Doyle, 213
Lasers, 220-21
Laughlin AFB Tex, 197
Leigh-Mallory, Air Marshal, 36, 37
LeMay, Gen Curtis Emerson, 8, 56, 62, 67, 68, 69, 72, 117
Lindsey AS Germany, 10
Linebacker, 96, 100, 101, 150, 163
Little Rock AFB Ark, 185
Locher, Lt Roger, 95
Lodge, Maj Robert, 95, 96
Lockhart, Capt Hayden, 72
Los Angeles AFB Calif, 207
Lovett, Robert, 26
Lowe, Thaddeus S C, 19, *20*, 20, 21
Lowry AFB Colo, 12, 197
Luke AFB Ariz, 110
Luftwaffe, 26, 32, 114, 194, 195

MGM 118 Peacekeeper, 169, 173
MiGs, *47*, 48, 49, 50, 51, 52, *54*, 55, 63, 68, 73, 74, 75, 83, *84*, 85, *88*, 88, 95, 96, 99, 101, 106, 157
MiGCAP, 75, 85, 95, 99, 100
MacArthur, Gen Douglas, 37, 46, 48, 49, 117
McChord AFB Wash, 185
McClellan AFB Calif, 10, 207, 209
McConnell AFB Kans, 155
McConnell, Gen John Paul, 8, 57, *58*, 72, 81
MacDill AFB Fla, 73, 110, *141*, 152
McDowell, Gen Irvin, 19
McGuire AFB N J, 182, 185
McNamara, Robert, *65*, 65, 67, 69, 72, 78, 81, 89
Madden, Capt John, 99
Malmstrom AFB Mont, 155
Markle, Lt John, 98
Marshall, Gen George, 26, 33, 38, 49
Mather AFB Calif, 193, 195, 197
Maxfield, Lt Col Joseph, 21
Maxwell AFB Ala, 192, 193, 194, 195, 197
Miller, Maj Glenn, 16
Minot AFB N Dak, 155
Misawa AB Japan, 62, 211
Missiles, 42, 74, 95, *96*, 114, 121, 129, 134, 137, 141, 148-49, *151*, 152, 168, 169, *173*, 173, 204, 205, 207, 217, 220, 221
Mitchell, Billy, 24, 25, 37, *40*, 120
Monthan, Lt Oscar, 108
Moody AFB Ga, *111*, 111
Moore, Maj Gen J H, *58*, 67, *81*
Mountain Home AFB Idaho, 111
Myrtle Beach AFB Fla, 112

Nellis AFB Nev, 15, 105, 106, *112*, 112, *138, 146, 148*, 212
Neutral Particle beam, 220-21
Nixon, Richard M, 88, 90, 94, 96
Norstad, Maj Gen Lauris, 39, 117
Norton AFB Calif, 13, 185, *186*, 205, *211*
Nuclear weapons, 42, 44, 128, 150, 168, 217

Offutt AFB Neb, 152, 161
Olds, Col Robin, *84*, 85, 88, 96, 98
Oshkosh P-15 *14*

P-38 Lightning, *29*, 44
P-47 Thunderbolt, *29, 44*, 44, 51
P-51, 39, 44, 51
P-59 Airacomet, 51
Patrick AFB/Cape Canaveral AFS Fla, 10, 204, 207
Patrick, Gen Mason, 8, 22
Pease AFB N H, 155
Pershing, Gen John J, 22, 23
Peterson AFB Colo, 214
Plattsburgh AFb NY, 155
Poinsett, Joel, 18
Pope AFB N C, 185
Putt, Brig Gen Donald, 43

RB-29, 10, 44
RF-101, 62, 63, 69
RAF, 22, 28, 32, 33, 44
Ramstein AB Germany, 114, 181
Randolph AFB Tex, 14, 192, 193, 195
Red Flag, 105, 106, *112*, 112, 114, 119, *138*, 140, *188*, 193, 201, 212
Reese AFB Tex, 197
Rhein-Main AB Germany, 109, 114, 181, 189, *190*

GENERAL LEW ALLEN, JR
Tenth USAF Chief of Staff

Lew Allen, Jr was born in Gainesville, Texas, on 30 September 1925 and graduated from the US Military Academy at West Point in 1946. That November he was assigned to SAC's 7th Bomb Group at Carswell AFB, where he flew B-29s and B-36s. Between 1950 and 1952 he attended the University of Illinois Graduate School, earning a Master of Science degree in nuclear physics. He spent the next ten years in New Mexico, first assigned to the Los Alamos National Laboratory as a physicist in the Test Division, and later as Physics Division science advisor at the Air Force Special Weapons Center at Kirtland AFB. In December 1961 he was assigned to the Office of the Secretary of Defense, in the Space Technology Office of the Directorate of Research and Engineering in Washington, DC.

In 1965 he went to Los Angeles AFS as Director of Special Projects. After a stint in Washington as Director of Space Systems, he returned to his former position in Los Angeles. In 1973 he became a deputy to the Director of the CIA, and later Director of the National Security Agency. Between August 1977 and March 1978 General Allen served as Commander of the Air Force Systems Command, after which he became Vice-Chief of Staff of the Air Force. He served as Air Force Chief of Staff from 1 July 1978 to 30 June 1982, during which time the AGM-86 Cruise Missile and F-16 Fighting Falcon became operational, the B-1B bomber program began and the Space Command was created.

GENERAL CHARLES A GABRIEL
Eleventh USAF Chief of Staff

Charles A Gabriel was born on 21 January 1928 in Lincolnton, N C, and graduated from the US Military Academy in 1950. In Dec 1951 he completed advanced pilot training and went to Korea, where he flew 100 combat missions in F-51s and F-86s, shooting down a pair of MiG-15s. Between Dec 1952 and Nov 1955 Gabriel was assigned to the 86th FIW at Landstuhl AB in Germany. In 1955 he returned to the US, where he served at the US Air Force Academy and at Moody AFB. He was next assigned to the Directorate of Plans at USAF Headquarters.

In Aug 1967 Lt Col Gabriel returned to Europe as an executive officer to the Chief of Staff, Supreme Headquarters Allied Powers Europe. He returned to the States for combat crew training in July 1970 and was assigned to the 432nd TRW at Udorn RTAFB in Thailand. During his tour he flew 152 combat missions in F-4s, to become the second Chief of Staff to have flown combat missions in two wars.

In July 1972 he returned to the Air Staff, and on 1 Dec was promoted to Brigadier General. Between 1975 and August 1977 General Gabriel served as Deputy Chief of Staff for Operations at TAC. His next assignment was as Deputy Commander in Chief of US Forces in Korea. In August 1980 General Gabriel became Commander in Chief of USAFE and Commander of Allied Air Forces in Central Europe. On 1 July 1982 he was named USAF Chief of Staff.

Rickenbacker, Capt Eddie, *24*, 24
Richardson, Adm James, 38
Ridgway, Gen Matthew, 50
Ritchie, Capt Steve, *97*, 98, 99, 100
Roberts, Capt Thomas, 74
Robins AFB Ga, 207, 208, 209
Rockets, 128, 134, 148
Rolling Thunder, 72-75, *72*, 78-80, 83, 85, *88*, 88, 89, 90, 96, 100, 161, 212
Roosevelt, Franklin D, 26, 32, 33, 175
Royce, Gen Ralph, *32*
Rozier, Jean de, 18
Rusk, Dean, 67, 81
Ryan, Gen John Dale, 8, 57, 117, 121

SR-71 Blackbird, *151*, 168, *170*, 171
Samford, Maj Gen John, 44
Sarakon, Sgt Andy, *70*
Sawyer, K I, AFB Mich, 156
Schainer, George, 42
Schmisser, James, *93*
Scott AFB Ill, 182, 183, 192, *193*
Scott, Gen Winfield, 19, 20, 121
Scriven, Gen George, *22*
Sembach AB Germany, 114, *115, 144*, 181
Shaw AFB S C, 112
Seymore Johnson AFB, N C, 112
Shemya AFB Alaska, 122, 216
Sheppard AFB Tex, 193, 197
Sherburne, Joel, 18
Sherman, Vice-Adm Forrest, 39
Sims, Allen, *93*
Smith, Lt William, 83
Snyder, Ronald, *93*
Spaatz, Gen Carl Arthur, 8, *32*, 33, *36*, 36, 37, 38, 39, 40, 41, 43
SPADs, 23, *24*
Squier, Gen George, *22*
Stimson, Henry, 26
Stratemeyer, Gen George, 46, 49, 104, 117
Symington, Stuart, 8, 40, *43*, 44

T-6, *16*
T-28, *60*, 61, 63
T-33 *193, 194*
T-38, 192-195, *195*
TR-1, 168, *171*, 171
Talbott, Harold, 8, 12
Taylor, Gen Maxwell, 67
Tan Son Nhut AB South Vietnam, 62, 80, *81, 83, 100*, 182
Tedder, Air Marshal Arthur, 32, 33, 37
Tibbett, Capt Calvin, 99
Tinker AFB Okla, 207, 209
Torrejon AB Spain, 114, 126, 152
Travis AFB Calif, 182, 185, *186*
Truman, Harry S, 39, 44, 176
Tunner, Maj Gen William, 117, 176, 177, 181, 183
Twining, Gen Nathan Farragut, 8, 56
Tyndall AFB Fla, 13, 113, *198*, 206

U-2, 168, 171
U-10, *60, 63*

V-2 guided missile, 42
VC-137, 9
Vance AFB Okla, 197
Vandenberg AFB Calif, 152, 156, 204, *221*
Vandenberg, Gen Hoyt, 8, *29, 32*, 40, 43, 44, 45, *49*, 55, 203

Warren, Francis E, AFB Wyo, 155
Westmoreland, Gen William, 67
Westover AFB Mass, 152
Westphal, Lt Col Curtis, 100
Wheeler AFB Hawaii, 10, 119
White, Gen Thomas Dresser, 56
Whiteman AFB, 156
Williams AFB, 197
Wise, John, 19, 20
Wright-Patterson AFB Ohio, 13, 161, 204, 206, 207, 208
Wright, Wilbur and Orville, 21, 22, 192
Wurtsmith AFB Mich, 156

XF-91 Thunderceptor, *44*
XP-82 Twin Mustang, 51

Yokota AB Japan, 117, 119

AIRCRAFT DESIGNATION LETTERS

All US Air force aircraft are designated with a primary role designation letter and a sequence number. Thus, a B-47 is simply the Air Force's 47th bomber type. The primary role designation letter may be qualified by a secondary role designation *prefix* letter. The RB-47 is qualified as the reconnaissance version of the B-47, while the XB-47 is the experimental version, indicating that it is probably the first B-47 to be built. The XB-47 experimental version is followed by a service test vesion, YB-47, which is in turn followed by production aircraft which have *suffix* letters. The suffix letters are added to indicate the stage of the development of a production aircraft. The first would be B-47A, followed by B-47B and so on, with a new suffix letter added each time a major modification is incorporated. If one of these modifications results in an aircraft that is not destined for production, but rather as an experiment, that airplane may be assigned an X prefix as well as a suffix, such as with the XB-47D. If one version, or some of one version, are used for something other than the role designated by their primary role designation letter, the qualifying prefix is applied only to those aircraft affected. For example, RB-47Es existed alongside B-47Es. Additional suffixes are also assigned to identify manufacturers and manufacturing block numbers, although these are generally not used in referring to most aircraft. An aircraft with the designation B-47E-55-BW is thus identified as a B-47E in Block 55 of the B-47s manufactured by Boeing's Wichita factory.

There have been three systems of role designation and prefix letters with some letters added or deleted in the interim. The first system was adopted in 1924 after the need for it had been demonstrated in the First World War. The second system came into being during the overall reorganization of national defense that followed World War II and that also had resulted in the creation of the USAF and the Department of Defense. Throughout this time, the US Navy had a system of its own that was completely unrelated to the USAAS/USAAC/USAAF/USAF system. In 1962, however, it was decided that a single system should be adopted for all the services. The designation letters and prefixes are based on the earlier Army/Air Force system of but the numbering was started over at 1. This is the reason for aircraft types that have gone into service since 1962 having relatively low numbers. This is why the B-1 is chronologically later than the B-47 or B-52, and why there was another B-1 (the Keystone Super Cyclops) back at the beginning of the 1924 system.

Primary Role Designation Letters

Letter	1924 System	1948 System	1962 System	Letter	1924 System	1948 System	1962 System
A	Attack	Amphibian	Attack	R	Rotary Wing (1941-7)	Reconnaissance	Reconnaissance
B	Bomber	Bomber*	Bomber	S	Supersonic (1946-7)	Sailplane (1960)	Anti-submarine
C	Cargo (Transport)	Cargo (Transport)	Cargo (Transport)	T	Trainer	Trainer	Trainer
F	Photographic (1930-47)	Fighter*	Fighter	U	—	Utility	Utility
G	Gyroplane	Glider	—	V	—	VTOL/STOL	VTOL/STOL
H	—	Helicopter	Helicopter	X	—	Experimental	Experimental
L	Liaison (1942-7)	Liaison	—	Z	—	—	Airship
O	Observation	—	Observation	FB	—	—	Medium bomber
P	Pursuit (Fighter)	—	Patrol	TR	—	—	Tactical Reconnaissance
Q	Drone	Drone	Drone	SR	—	—	Strategic Reconnaissance

Secondary Role Designation Prefix Letters

Letter	1924 System	1948 System	1962 System	Letter	1924 System	1948 System	1962 System
A	Advanced. Assault.	Calibration	Attack				
B	Basic. Bomber. Bomb.	Bomber	—	O	Observation	—	Observation
C	Cargo (Transport)	Cargo (Transport)	Cargo (Transport)	P	Pursuit	Passenger	—
D	—	Drone Director	Drone Director	Q	—	Drone	Drone
E	—	Electronics**	Electronics	R	Restricted (1942-7)	Reconnaissance	Reconnaissance
F	Photographic (1944-7)	Fighter	Fighter	S	—	Search & Rescue	Anti-submarine
G	Glider. Glide. (1942-7)	Parasite Carrier	Grounded	T	Trainer (1943-7)	Trainer	Trainer
H	Heavy (1925-27)	—	Search & Rescue	U	Utility (1941-7)	Utility	Utility
J	Jet-propelled (1943-7)	Temporary Testing	Temporary Testing	V	—	VIP Transport	VIP Transport
K	Ferret (1944-7)	Tanker (Kerosene)	Tanker (Kerosene)	W	—	Weather	Weather
L	Light (1925-32)	Liaison	Cold-weather	X	Experimental (1928-47)	Experimental	Experimental
M	—	Medical Evacuation	Missile Carrier	Y	Service Test (1928-47)	Service Test	Service Test
N	—	Permanent Testing	Permanent Testing	Z	Obsolete (1928-47)	Obsolete	Project

*Fourteen B designation letters were given to strategic missiles and two F designation letters were given to interceptor missiles during the early years of 1948 system. These were later redesignated with missile designation letters.

**Prior to 1955 the E prefix was used to designate "exempt" and applied to most Air Research & Development Command aircraft to keep test programs alive if general orders were issued grounding certain aircraft types.

MISSILE DESIGNATION LETTERS

Missiles and rockets are designated by a series of letters describing them, with this series ending in M (missile) or R (rocket).

Initial Prefix Letter

A Air-launched
B Multiple
C Semi-Hardened Launcher
G Ground-launched
H Hardened Launcher
L Silo-launched
M Mobile Launcher
P Soft Launcher
R Ship-launched
S Submarine-launched

Second Prefix Letter

D Decoy
E Electronics
G Ground Attack
I Intercept
Q Drone
T Training
U Underwater Attack
W Weather

Some Examples of Typical Missile Designations

AIM Air Intercept Missile
MGM Land-Based Mobile Missile
AGM Air-to-Ground Missile
LGM Silo-Based Missile

(The Air-Launched Cruise Missile (ALCM) has a formal AGM designation)

The first missiles and rockets in USAF service were given fighter (F), and bomber (B) deignation letters. This gradually gave way to another (interim) system that survived until the present system, described above, was adopted in 1962.

Interim Misssile Designations

GAR Guided Air Rocket
GAM Guided Air Missile
IM Interceptor Missile
RM Research Missile
SM Strategic Missile
TM Tactical Missile
FFAR Folding Fin Aerial Rocket
HVAR High-velocity Aerial Rocket